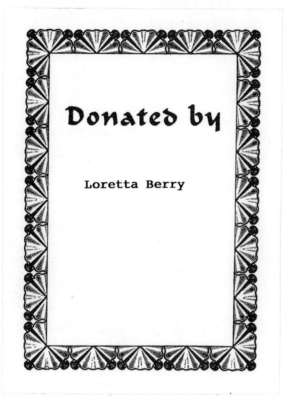

A History Of

ROWAN COUNTY,

North Carolina

Containing Sketches of
Prominent Families and Distinguished Men

By
Rev. Jethro Rumple

Bicentennial Edition

REPRINTED WITH A NEW INDEX
By Edith M. Clark

Baltimore
REGIONAL PUBLISHING COMPANY
1978

Originally Published
Salisbury, North Carolina
1881

Republished
Elizabeth Maxwell Steele Chapter, DAR
Salisbury, North Carolina
1916 and 1929

Reprinted with a New Index
Regional Publishing Company,
An *Affiliate* of Genealogical Publishing Co., Inc.
Baltimore, 1974, 1978

Library of Congress Catalogue Card Number 74-9870
International Standard Book Number 0-8063-7998-7

Made in the United States of America

FOREWORD

TO THE NEW INDEXED EDITION

Twice the Elizabeth Maxwell Steele Chapter, National Society Daughters of the American Revolution, reprinted Rumple's *History of Rowan County,* desirous of keeping alive for each generation the important record of this area central to North Carolina and the development of points south and west.

In the past few years there has been a resurgence of interest in history and genealogy as in this Age of Anxiety people look to the past for their roots and their place in history. Essential to this study is the history of Rowan County.

Rowan County was formed from Anson County in 1753, and most of the early records of Anson County were lost to fire. Anson had been formed in 1750 from Bladen County where many records were destroyed by fires in 1765 and 1893. In Rowan, where there has been no major loss of records, lie the earliest extant set of court records for the entire area.

Twenty-four counties in North Carolina and all of Tennessee have been formed from the area that was once Rowan, an area whose western boundary was the Pacific Ocean. For twenty-three years Salisbury, the county seat of Rowan, was the farthest west county seat in the colonies.

The importance of Dr. Jethro Rumple's *History of Rowan County* cannot be overestimated. Dr. Rumple came to Salisbury as pastor of the First Presbyterian Church in 1860 and remained here until the spring of 1904. Writing in the latter half of the nineteenth century, he had the opportunity to talk to men and women whose parents and grandparents were here when this section was the frontier and who formed the Committee of Safety and who fought in the Revolution. Dr. Rumple had access to family papers that no longer exist and an ear to the oral history of the period. While most of the history is accurate, it should be pointed out that there are known errors in the genealogies of the Michael Braun and Alexander Long families and that the primary source records will have to be searched by genealogists.

It is fitting that the Regional Publishing Company, affiliate of the Genealogical Publishing Company, should reprint Rumple's *History of Rowan County* as the Bicentennial approaches. No less fitting is it that Miss Edith Montcalm Clark, youngest daughter of Dr. Byron Currie Clark, also minister of the First Presbyterian Church in Salisbury, should have prepared a comprehensive index for the new edition.

The Elizabeth Maxwell Steele Chapter DAR congratulates the Regional Publishing Company on the reprint of this important History.

Jo White Linn (Mrs. Stahle Linn, Jr.)
Historian
Elizabeth Maxwell Steele Chapter DAR

A HISTORY OF

ROWAN COUNTY

NORTH CAROLINA

CONTAINING SKETCHES OF

PROMINENT FAMILIES

AND

DISTINGUISHED MEN

WITH AN

APPENDIX

BY REV. JETHRO RUMPLE

PUBLISHED BY J. J. BRUNER
SALISBURY, N. C.
1881

REPUBLISHED BY THE
ELIZABETH MAXWELL STEELE CHAPTER
DAUGHTERS OF THE AMERICAN REVOLUTION
SALISBURY, N. C.

ELIZABETH MAXWELL STEELE CHAPTER DAUGHTERS OF THE AMERICAN REVOLUTION

OFFICERS

1916

Mrs. Edwin C. Gregory .... *Regent*
Mrs. D. F. Cannon .... *Vice-Regent*
Mrs. Geo. A. Fisher .... *Recording Secretary*
Mrs. John McCanless .... *Corresponding Secretary*
Mrs. Wm. S. Nicolson .... *Treasurer*
Mrs. R. L. Mauney .... *Registrar*
Mrs. W. S. Blackmer .... *Historian*
Mrs. N. P. Murphy .... *Chaplain*

OFFICERS

1929

Mrs. John R. Deas .... *Regent*
Mrs. C. E. Stevenson .... *Vice-Regent*
Mrs. S. H. Wiley .... *Recording Secretary*
Mrs. H. L. Monk .... *Corresponding Secretary*
Mrs. W. S. Nicolson .... *Treasurer*
Mrs. M. N. Hoyle .... *Registrar*
Mrs. Jas. P. Moore .... *Historian*
Miss Sara E. Chunn .... *Chaplain*
Miss Mary Henderson .... *Parliamentarian*

MEMBERS

Adams, Maud Wheeler (Mrs. F. A.)
Beard, Mildred Patterson (Mrs. B. P.)
Bernhardt, Helen Crenshaw (Mrs. R. L.)
Blackmer, Clara A. (Mrs. W. S.)
Cannon, Ella Brown (Mrs. D. F.)
Chunn, Sara E. (Miss)
Cotton, Elizabeth Henderson (Mrs. L. A.)
Davidson, Clyde Cobb (Mrs. H. G.)
Daniel, Minnie (Miss)
Deas, Marian Heilig (Mrs. J. R.)
Eagan, Julia Goode (Mrs. H. E.)
Ellis, Lura Wood (Mrs. W. F.)
Fowler, Annie Osborne (Miss)
Fowler, Sara Wood (Miss)
Freeman, Martha Eaves (Mrs. W. S.)

Gorman, Emmie R. Gowan (Mrs. J. H.)
Gorman, Elizabeth (Miss)
Gregory, Mary H. Overman (Mrs. E. C.)
Grimes, Nancy Cordon (Mrs. J. P.)
Grimes, Sallie Hamlin (Miss)
Guille, Alice S. Cannon (Mrs. Gettys)
Harris, Agnes Rouche (Mrs. L. H.)
Heilig, Elsie Newman (Mrs. H. G.)
Henderson, Mary Ferrand (Miss)
Hines, Annie L. Ramsey (Mrs. T. M.)
Hobson, Johnsie (Miss)
Hobson, Rosalie Bernhardt (Mrs. W. H.)
Hoyle, Mary Belle L. (Mrs. M. N.)
Hurley, Jeanette Erwin (Mrs. J. F.)
Kluttz, Josephine (Miss)
Mauney, Annie Staples (Mrs. R. L.)
McCanless, Beatrice Hancock (Mrs. J. M.)
McCanless, Mary Rouche (Mrs. W. F.)
McCorkle, Lesora F. Thurman (Mrs. A. A.)
McKenzie, Mary DeNeal (Miss)
Miller, Hallie Viele (Mrs. T. H.)
Monk, Nannie Blackwell (Mrs. H. L.)
Moore, Beulah Stewart (Mrs. J. P.)
Neave, Ann Eliza Bernhardt (Mrs. J. W.)
Nicolson, L. Eva Dornin (Mrs. W. S.)
Overman, Jennie Williamson (Mrs. E. R.)
Preston, Annie S. Wiley (Mrs. J. F.)
Reynolds, Mary Bernhardt (Mrs. A. E.)
Roseboro, Margaret Foard (Mrs. C. H.)
Sasseen, Grace S. (Mrs. Phelps)
Scott, Callie Y. Foard (Mrs. Q. J.)
Sigmon, Marie Hardin (Mrs. Ross M.)
Smith, Mary Ledbetter (Miss)
Stevenson, Miriam Davis (Mrs. C. E.)
Sullivan, Jane C. (Miss)
Thomason, Edith Caroline (Miss)
Viele, Ada (Miss)
Waddell, Fannie V. Andrews (Mrs. Cameron, Jr.)
Wall, Elizabeth Nicolson (Mrs. H. C.)
Weant, Agnes Pugh (Mrs. W. W.)
Wiley, Beulah Bernhardt (Mrs. S. H.)
Woodson, Pauline Bernhardt (Mrs. W. H.)

A NEW PREFACE

In republishing the Rumple History of Rowan County, the Elizabeth Maxwell Steele Chapter, National Society of the Daughters of the American Revolution, has accomplished a twofold purpose, namely: "the encouragement of historical research, and the publication of its results." In fulfilling these primary objects of the Society, it has also furthered the ulterior aim of both editor and author, whose advocacy of these same objects—ten years prior to the organization of the National Society—made this little book possible.

By these recorded "facts of history, biography, and achievement," supplemented by priceless data gleaned from old documents, manuscripts, local tradition, and the personal recollections of many who have since been gathered to their fathers, the author has rendered an inestimable service—not only to the Rowan County of today, but the territory occupied by forty-five counties formed from this venerable mother, which when erected comprehended most of the western part of the State, and Tennessee.

Printed weekly from the galley proofs of the current newspaper article, on common material, and filed away to be later bound into book form, the first edition was of necessity limited, and was exhausted years ago. In presenting the second edition, the publishers hope to supply a long-felt want. The contents have not been built anew; in a few instances only, supplemental facts have been incorporated, and the past linked with the present through the medium of a limited number of photographs. In consideration of the ample domain formerly covered by Rowan County, its history is the common heritage of the people of Western North Carolina and a vast number of her sons and daughters who have made homes in other States—particularly those of the Middle West.

A copy of this little volume owned by the writer is thus autographed by its late beloved author: " 'History is Philosophy teaching by example.' So said one who deeply pondered the import of his words. If we would be wise and good, we should learn the best methods from the example of those who have gone before us." Primarily, the mission of this work was to rescue from oblivion the history of Rowan, and to preserve and perpetuate the honorable records of her citizens; and incidentally promote an intelligent interest in the early development of the County, and a more thorough knowledge of the first settlers—peaceable, industrious, and law-abiding men—"composed of almost all the nations of Europe," who came to make homes for themselves and children; "men and women who had suffered for conscience' sake, or fled from despotism to seek liberty and happiness unrestrained by the shackles of a wornout civilization." Intolerant of tyranny, yet characteristically conservative—when constrained to act, they were invincible! No people has a fairer and broader historic background, as yet almost unexplored. "Ill fares it with a State whose history is written by others than her own sons!"

Is it vain to hope that some *one,* among "the lineal descendants and present-day representatives of an illustrious dead"—kindled afresh by the holy fires of patriotism and pride of race—will arise phoenix-like from the ashes of our indifference, and write the noble annals of our State? "Earlier colonized in point of history, full of glorious examples of patriotism and chivalric daring, North Carolina has been neglected by her own sons and others." Too long have we felt the opprobrium of this neglect.

To those who have countenanced this effort, and to the friends who have rendered valuable assistance both by suggestion and contribution, many thanks are due. Should but one reader cease to be a "mute inglorious Milton," and sing inspiredly of the valor and glory of our forebears, then your support and this little book shall not have been in vain.

—Beulah Stewart Moore

PREFACE

This little book is an accident. While engaged in collecting material for another purpose, the writer was led to examine the early records preserved in the Courthouse in Salisbury, and in the course of his investigation happened upon a number of things that appeared to be of general interest. Mentioning this fact casually to the editor of the *Carolina Watchman,* the writer was asked to embody these items of interest in a few articles for that newspaper. This led to additional research, and to the accumulation of a pile of notes and references that gave promise of a dozen or more articles. These the editor thought should be printed in a pamphlet of fifty or a hundred small pages for preservation, and he began at once to print off a few hundred copies from the type used in the newspaper. As the work went on, other facts were gathered—from traditions, from family records, and from the pages of books written about North Carolina, such as the Histories and Sketches of Hawks, Caruthers, Foote, Bancroft, Wheeler, Lawson, Byrd, Jones, Wiley, Moore, Hunter, Bernheim, Gillett, and from miscellaneous diaries, periodicals, and manuscripts. These were intended to furnish a frame for the picture of Old Rowan, and sidelights that it might be seen to advantage. And thus the little pamphlet has swollen to its present proportions. It was written in installments from week to week, amid the incessant demands of regular professional duty, and without that care and revision that might have saved it from some infelicities of style or obscurities of expression. Both the writer and the publisher would have been glad to have expended more time and care upon the work, so as to render it more worthy of the noble County whose annals it is intended to recover and perpetuate. Still it is believed that very few serious errors have been made. Local traditions have been compared with general history, and have been found to coincide wherever they came in contact.

The writer has been indebted to a number of persons for the facts which he has recorded. Miss Christine Beard, a granddaughter of John Lewis Beard, and of John Dunn, Esq.—now eighty years of age, with a remarkably retentive memory—has furnished personal recollections of the Town of Salisbury, covering seventy years. She has also treasured up the stories heard in her youth from the lips of her ancestors, running back to the first settlement of the County. Messrs. J. M. Horah and H. N. Woodson, the Clerk and the Register, kindly gave access to the old records in the Courthouse, dating back to 1753. John S. Henderson, Esq., Rev. S. Rothrock, Rev. H. T. Hudson, D.D., Rev. J. J. Renn, Rev. J. B. Boone, Rev. J. Ingle, Rufus Barringer, Esq., Dr. D. B. Wood, M. L. McCorkle, Esq., Mrs. N. Boyden, and others, have either prepared papers in full, or furnished documents and manuscript statements that have been of special service. Mrs. P. B. Chambers furnished the diary of her grandfather, Waightstill Avery, Esq. Col. W. L. Saunders, Secretary of State, and Col. J. McLeod Turner, Keeper of the State Capitol, very kindly furnished, free of charge, a copy of the Roll of Honor of the Rowan County soldiers in the Confederate Army. The revision and completion of this Roll was superintended by Mr. C. R. Barker, who bestowed great care and much time upon this work. Many thanks are due to all these persons. In fact, it has been a labor of love, without hope of pecuniary reward, with the Author, and all those who have contributed to this performance. With these statements, the little book is sent forth, with the hope that it will be of some service to the citizens of North Carolina, and especially to the people of Rowan.

No attempt is made to point out typographical errors. They are generally of such nature as to be readily corrected by the intelligent reader. The following errors may be noted: On page 171, it is stated that no man knows where the grave of John Dunn, Esq., is. Further inquiry, however, revealed the fact that the spot is still known. The correction is given on page 228.

On page 285, Matthew Brandon is represented as having had two daughters. A fuller account reveals the fact that he had three other daughters—one who married a Mr. McCombs, of Charlotte; another who married Wm. Smith, of Charlotte; and still another who married George Miller, of Salisbury. A daughter of the last-named couple married Lemuel Bingham, Associate Editor of the *Western Carolinian,* in 1820-23. These were the parents of the Binghams now of Salisbury.

On page 288, John Phifer is represented as settling in Rowan, near China Grove. Further inquiry seems to show that John Phifer never lived in Rowan, but that his widow moved to that place after her marriage with George Savitz.

On page 394, it is stated that the Rev. W. D. Strobel and Rev. D. I. Dreher were ministers to the Salisbury Lutheran Church. This statement does not appear to be correct. It further appears that the Rev. S. Rothrock's first term of service in Salisbury was in 1833, and his second in 1836; and that the Rev. Mr. Rosenmuller came between Mr. Reck and Mr. Tabler.

The reader will observe in these sketches occasional reference to the Mecklenburg Declaration of May 20, 1775, and to its signers, with no expression of doubt as to its authenticity. This course has been pursued because the writer did not feel called upon to settle, or even discuss, that vexed question, and he did not feel authorized to set at defiance the conclusions that seem to be sustained by the bulk of the testimony, and to adopt instead the deductions of critics derived from real or supposed inconsistencies and contradictions in that testimony. With an array of documents before him, he prefers to allow Mecklenburg to settle that question for herself, while at the same time he is perfectly satisfied that the Mecklenburg patriots of 1775, either on the twentieth or thirty-first of May, or upon both occasions, acted in such a noble manner as to surround their names with the glory of patriotic devotion and heroic courage.

J. Rumple

SKETCH OF AUTHOR

REV. JETHRO RUMPLE, D.D.

Nearly a century ago, in an unpretentious farm-house in Cabarrus County, N. C., the subject of this sketch, Jethro Rumple, was born. Amid these humble surroundings, the life of the boy was developed, and so the first work of his hands must have been the homely chores of the farm, and the first regular journeyings of his boyish feet in the straight line of the furrow, as he followed the plough in the cornfield.

The first artificial illumination for his eyes was the light of the candle or smoky pineknot on the hearth, flickering on the leaves of the old "blue-backed speller," as he reclined at close of day in that first studious attitude of childhood, for the little Jethro must have been born with the love of books in his heart. He went to the little neighboring school, and between the jobs of the farm we can see the barefoot boy trudging the long way to the rough schoolhouse from which the first ambitions of his life must have come to him. Beyond the horizon of the wheatfield he early found the vision of better and higher things, viz.: classical education, and a place among the scholars of the land. Some years later, with this end in view, and after many struggles to raise or make arrangements for the necessary funds, we find him entering Davidson College, where he was graduated with distinction in 1850.

Teaching school and studying alternately, again, he spent the necessary three years of his theological education at the Seminary in Columbia, S. C.; and under the patronage of Concord Presbytery, of which he was for the remainder of his life a member, he was licensed in 1856 to preach the gospel. A little later he was ordained and installed as the pastor of Providence and Sharon Churches, in Mecklenburg County, N. C. After holding this pastorate for four years, he was called to the First Presbyterian Church of Salisbury, N. C., was installed as its pastor, November 24, 1860. There he found his life's work. Taking up the burden of this church with a membership of ninety, he continued to be their faithful and beloved pastor for the remaining years of his life on earth, and forty-five years later he laid it down with a living membership of four hundred thirty-four souls, a glorious harvest for the Master. Eight young men have entered the Gospel ministry, and two—Rev. Dr.

John W. Davis, of China, and Rev. Robert Coit, of Korea — the foreign missionary field.

Dr. Rumple developed, early in his work, a vigor and breadth of mind and heart that was felt by all denominations in his town, and abroad as well. Not content with working in his home field, he was one of the pioneers in the home missionary work in the mountains of North Carolina, giving his vacations often to that work. He organized the Presbyterian Church at Blowing Rock, N. C., and was largely instrumental in raising the funds for the first building. The second structure, a picturesque and unique gothic building of rough mountain stone, stands as a beautiful memorial to his labors and life.

In the department of literature, Dr. Rumple also made a place, for in addition to this History of Rowan County, first published in 1881, he wrote and published, in the pages of the *North Carolina Presbyterian* (the predecessor of the *Presbyterian Standard*), a History of Presbyterianism in North Carolina. This was intended to have been published later in book form, but the writer, amid the increasing duties of church at home and abroad, never found the time to completely finish and arrange it.

As a public speaker, Dr. Rumple was much in demand, and in 1887 he edited the "First Semi-Centenary Celebration of Davidson College, containing the addresses, historical and commemorative, of that occasion"; and in this publication he is the author of an excellent and well-written sketch of Davidson College.

While not professing to be an evangelist, in the present accepted meaning of that term, Dr. Rumple was often called to preach away from his home church, conducting the meetings of quarterly communion in the different churches; and he was quite successful in his work, the Spirit of God being manifest in these meetings, and giving him the blessing of many souls brought to Christ. He was a preacher of the old school, not disdaining the elaborate introduction to his sermons; and his style was clear, his diction elegant, and his moral always helpful and practical. Two generations of his hearers rise up and bless his memory, and we might have said three, for he lived to baptize the grandchildren in some instances of his early members, and having always kept up his interest in and attendance on the Sunday School he knew all the children of his congregation personally, and loved and was loved by them.

Quoting from the memorial sketch written by the Rev. H. G. Hill, and adopted by the Synod of North Carolina: "Dr. Rumple was a strong man in every part of his nature. His physical manhood was

FIRST PRESBYTERIAN CHURCH OF SALISBURY, N. C., WHERE DR. RUMPLE WAS PASTOR FOR FORTY-SIX YEARS

unusually vigorous and well developed. His intellectual powers were active, well-balanced, and capable of sustained exertion. His moral nature manifested excellence in all the varied relations of life. His spiritual attributes were plainly the graces wrought by the Holy Spirit. His gifts, his graces, and his rare capacity for work, caused him to be constantly employed, after entering the ministry, for about half a century. As pastor and preacher and presbyter, he was a zealous and faithful laborer. In the judicatories of the church, which he habitually attended, he was a wise counselor and an active member. As a trustee of Davidson College and of Union Theological Seminary for many years, he could always be depended on to perform efficiently any duty that devolved upon him. As the first president of Barium Springs Orphans' Home, he did more for founding and sustaining this institution than any member of our Synod. In his private and social relations, Dr. Rumple was a typical Christian gentleman, hospitable towards his brethren, considerate of the views and feelings of others, and genial in all his social intercourse. He had his personal and family sorrows, but they never led him to murmur at the orderings of Providence, nor to become morose in disposition, nor to cease active work for the Master. Down to the last months of his life, he held official positions, and amid growing infirmities discharged his duties with conscientious fidelity. He dropped the oar of toil only to receive the crown of life. 'The righteous shall be in everlasting remembrance, and the name of Jethro Rumple shall be honored among us as long as virtue is cherished and piety revered.' "

In October of 1857, Dr. Rumple was married to Miss Jane Elizabeth Wharton, daughter of Watson W. and Malinda Rankin Wharton, of Greensboro, N. C. She was a faithful and efficient home-maker, and a sympathetic helpmate in his work. Besides this, being possessed of musical ability and some training, she for years maintained a little musical school, thereby helping to furnish the means whereby the three children—Watson Wharton, James Walker, and Linda Lee—were educated. The first only reached eighteen years of age, dying in his senior year at Davidson College. The second, James W., became a lawyer of promise, but only lived to be twenty-nine, being drowned in the Shenandoah River in Virginia. He had, about two years previous to his death, been married to Jane Dickson Vardell, and one son, James Malcolmson, had blessed their union. The daughter, Linda Lee, in October, 1891, was married to Rev. C. G. Vardell, then pastor of the Presbyterian

Church in Newbern, N. C., but for the past eighteen years the president of the College for Women at Red Springs, N. C., known first as the Red Springs Seminary, and afterwards the Southern Presbyterian College and Conservatory of Music, and recently the name has been changed to "Flora MacDonald College." Mrs. Vardell has been the organizer and musical director of the Conservatory, one of the largest and highest grade conservatories in the South. It was at the home of his daughter, in Red Springs, N. C., after a decline of several months, that Dr. Rumple passed away from earth to the home above, on January 20, 1906.

"And I heard a voice from heaven saying unto me, Write, Blessed are the dead which die in the Lord. . . . and their works do follow them."—Revelation 14: 13.

—Mrs. Linda Rumple Vardell

J. J. BRUNER
Editor and Publisher

JOHN JOSEPH BRUNER, EDITOR

John Joseph Bruner was born in Rowan County, N. C., on the Yadkin River, about seven miles from Salisbury, on the twelfth of March, 1817. He was the son of Henry Bruner, and Edith his wife, who was the youngest daughter of Col. West Harris, of Montgomery County, N. C. Colonel Harris married Edith Ledbetter, of Anson County, and was a field officer in the Continental Army.

When the subject of this sketch was a little over two years old, his father died, and his mother returned with her two children, Selina and Joseph, to her father's house in Montgomery.

In the year 1825, he came to Salisbury, under the care of his uncle Hon. Charles Fisher, father of the late Col. Chas. F. Fisher, who fell at the battle of Bull Run. Mr. Bruner's first year in Salisbury was spent in attending the school taught by Henry Allemand. This was about all the schooling of a regular style that he ever received, excepting after he grew up. The remainder of his education was of a practical kind, and was received at the case and press of a printing office.

At the age of nine years, he entered the printing office of the *Western Carolinian,* then under the editorial control of the Hon. Philo White, late of Whitestown, N. Y. *The Carolinian* passed into the hands of the Hon. Burton Craige, in 1830, and then into the hands of Major John Beard, late of Florida, Mr. Bruner continuing in the office until 1836. In 1839, the late M. C. Pendleton, of Salisbury, and Mr. Bruner, purchased the *Watchman,* and edited it in partnership for about three years. The *Watchman* had been started in the year 1832, by Hamilton C. Jones, Esq., father of the late Col. H. C. Jones, of Charlotte. The *Watchman* was a Whig and anti-nullification paper, and was intended to support Gen. Andrew Jackson in his anti-nullification policy.

In 1843, Mr. Bruner retired from the *Watchman,* and traveled for a while in the Southwest, spending some time in a printing-office in Mobile, Ala. Returning home, he was united in marriage to Miss Mary Ann Kincaid, a daughter of Thomas Kincaid, Esq. The mother of Mrs. Bruner was Clarissa Harlowe, daughter of Col. James Brandon of Revolutionary fame, who married Esther Horah, an aunt of the late Wm. H. Horah, so long known as a leading bank officer in Salisbury. Col. James Brandon was the son of William Brandon, who settled in Thyatira as early as 1752, and whose wife was a Miss Cathey of that region. Having married, Mr. Bruner prepared for his life work by re-purchasing the *Watchman,* in partnership with the late Samuel W. James, in 1844. After six years, this partnership was dissolved, and Mr. Bruner became sole proprietor and editor of the *Watchman,* which he continued to publish until the office was captured by the Federal soldiers in the spring of 1865. After a few months, however, Mr. Bruner was permitted to re-occupy his dismantled office, and resume the publication of his paper. Three years later, Lewis Hanes, Esq., of Lexington, purchased an interest in the paper, and it was called the *Watchman and Old North State.* Retiring for a time from the paper, Mr. Bruner entered private life for a couple of years. But his mission was to conduct a paper, and so in 1871 he re-purchased it, and the *Watchman* made its regular appearance weekly until his death. At this date, the *Watchman* was the oldest newspaper, and Mr. Bruner the oldest editor in North Carolina. He was one of the few remaining links binding the antebellum journalist with those of the present day. The history of Mr. Bruner's editorial life is a history of the progress of the State. He was contemporary with the late Edward J. Hale, Ex-Governor Holden, Wm. J. Yates, and others of the older editors of the State. When he began to publish the *Watchman,* there was not a daily paper in North Carolina, and no railroads. In the forties and fifties, the *Watchman* was the leading paper in Western North Carolina, and had subscribers in fifty counties. None now living in Salisbury, and few elsewhere in the State, have had such extensive personal acquaintance and knowledge of men and things in the early years of this century. Names that have almost ceased to be spoken on our streets were familar to him. He knew such men as Hon. Chas. Fisher, Col. Chas. F. Fisher, Rowland Jones, Esq., Dr. Pleasant Henderson, Hamilton C. Jones, Esq., Hon. Burton Craige, the Browns, Longs, Cowans, Beards, Lockes, Hendersons, and hosts of others of a former generation. He sat under the preaching of every pastor of the Presbyterian Church since its organization—Dr. Freeman, Mr. Rankin, Mr. Espy, Dr. Sparrow, Mr. Frontis (by whom he was married), Mr. Baker, and Rev. Dr. Rumple, who was his pastor and friend for more than thirty years. He was a scholar in the Sunday School when Thos. L. Cowan was superintendent, and was afterwards a teacher and superintendent himself. Col. Philo White his early protector, was a high-toned Christian man, and he so impressed himself upon his youthful ward that he chose him for a model, emulated his example, and held his memory in cherished veneration to the end of his life. At the age of seventeen, Mr. Bruner was received into the communion of the Presbyterian Church of Salisbury, and in 1846 he was ordained a ruling elder in that Church, and continued to serve in that capacity through the remainder of his life. He was a sincere, earnest, and consistent Christian, and faithful in the discharge of all private and public duties of the Christian profession. The family altar was established in his household, and he brought up his children in the nurture and admonition of the Lord.

Mr. Bruner died, after a lingering illness, March 23, 1890. His end was peace. As he gently passed away—so gently that it was difficult to tell when life ended and immortality began—a brother elder by his bedside repeated the lines:

> "How blest the righteous when he dies!
> When sinks a weary soul to rest;
> How mildly beam the closing eyes;
> How gently heaves the expiring breast!"

In many things Mr. Bruner was an example worthy of imitation. His memory must ever shine as one of the purest, sweetest, best elements of the past. His character was singularly beautiful and upright. His life was an unwritten sermon, inestimably precious to those who will heed the lessons which it teaches, and to whom grace may be given to follow his good example.

He was emphatically a self-made man. His learning he acquired by his own unaided efforts; his property he earned by the sweat of his brow; and his reputation he achieved by prudence, wisdom, and faithfulness in all the duties of life. By his paper he helped multitudes of men to honorable and lucrative office, but he never helped himself. Politically, Mr. Bruner never faltered in his allegiance to those principles to which he believed every true Southern man should adhere. Up to the very last he was unflinching and unwavering in his love for the South, and in his adherence to the very best ideals and traditions of the land of his nativity. At no time during his life did he ever "crook the pregnant hinges of the knee, that thrift might follow fawning." In the very best sense of the word, he was a Southern gentleman of the old school. The old South and the new were all one to him—the same old land, the same old people, the same old traditions, the land of Washington, of Jefferson, of Calhoun and Jackson, of Pettigrew and Fisher, of Graham and Craige, of Stonewall Jackson, of Robert E. Lee and Jefferson Davis.

For more than a half-century Mr. Bruner was at the head of the *Watchman,* and through its columns, and in other walks of a well-spent life, impressed his high attributes of character upon the people—not only of his town and section, but throughout the State. A fluent, able, and conservative writer, with but one hope or purpose—to serve his State and people faithfully and honestly—he steered his journal from year to year, from decade to decade, from the morning of one century almost to the morning of another, until he made himself and his paper honored landmarks of this age and section. He was firm in his convictions, a bold and fearless advocate of the rights of the people, but at all times characterized by a degree of liberality and conservatism that won for him respect and friendship even from those who might differ with him in matters of Church or State. He recorded truthfully and without envy or prejudice the birth and downfall of political parties. He—inspired by a united effort to Americanize and weld together every section of this great Union—waxed eloquent in praise of wise and sagacious leaders, and he blotted with a tear the paper on which he wrote of sectional strife and discord. He chronicled with sober earnestness the birth of a new republic, and like other loyal sons of the South raised his arm and pen in its defense. He watched with unfeigned interest its short and stormy career, and then wrote dispassionately of the furling of its blood-stained banner. He was ever found fighting for what he believed to be the best interests of his people, and advocating such men and measures as seemed to him just and right. An old-line Whig before the war, he aspired not to political preferment or position, but only to an honored stand in the ranks of a loyal and beneficent citizenship. Joining in with the rank and file of the white men of the conquered South, he was content to lend all his talent and energy in aiding them in the upbuilding of an impoverished section.

Blameless and exemplary in all the relations of life, a Christian gentleman, he met all the requirements of the highest citizenship—and what higher eulogy can any hope to merit?

> "The great work laid upon his three-score years
> Is done, and well done. If we drop our tears,
> We mourn no blighted hope or broken plan
> With him whose life stands rounded and approved
> In the full growth and stature of a man."

—Mrs. Beulah Stewart Moore

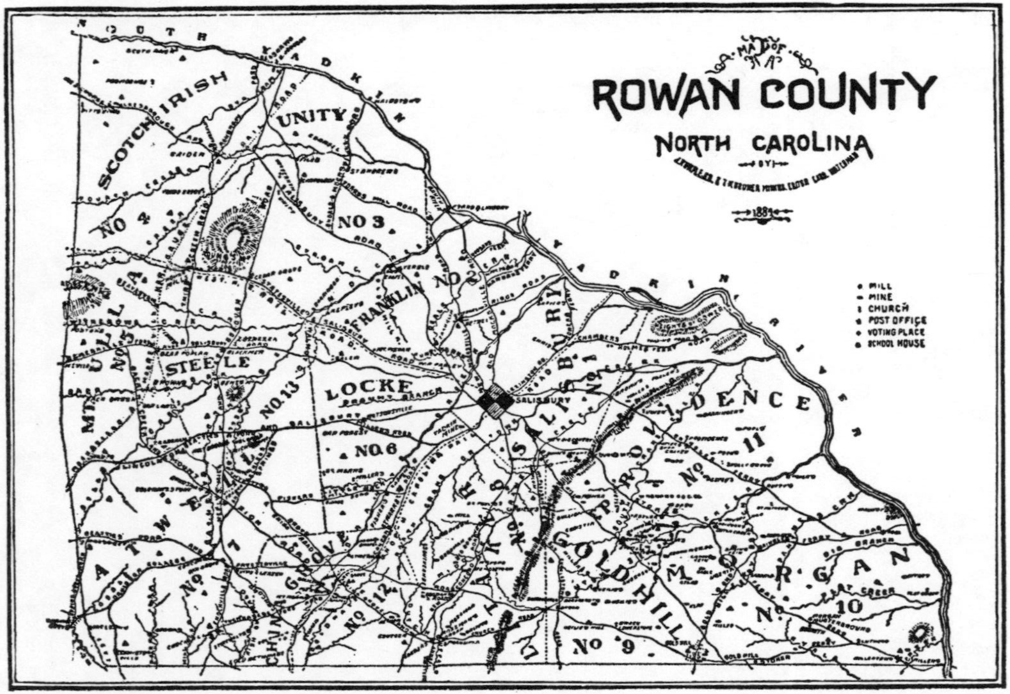

MAP OF
ROWAN COUNTY
NORTH CAROLINA
1884
SOUTH YADKIN
YADKIN RIVER
MILL
MINE
CHURCH
POST OFFICE
VOTING PLACE
SCHOOL HOUSE
SCOTCH IRISH
UNITY
NO 3
NO 4
FRANKLIN NO 2
MT. ULLA NO 5
STEELE
LOCKE
NO 13
NO 6
SALISBURY NO 1
SALISBURY
PROVIDENCE NO 11
ATWELL NO 7
CHINA GROVE NO 12
LITAKER NO 8
GOLD HILL NO 9
MORGAN NO 10

ROWAN COUNTY

CHAPTER I

GENERAL DESCRIPTION

It is but natural that the inhabitants of a country should desire to trace back its history as far as possible. No doubt many of the citizens of Rowan—the queenly mother of more than a score of counties—would love to know the early history of their native place, the appearance of the country when first seen by civilized men, and the character of the original inhabitants. Having had occasion to make some examination of early documents and histories, and to consult a few of the oldest citizens, whose memories are stored with the traditions of the past, the writer has conceived the opinion that many of his fellow-citizens would be glad to have access to some of these facts; and through the kindness of the Editor of the *Watchman,* a few sketches will be furnished for their entertainment.

We have a vague impression that the early white settlers found here a vast unbroken wilderness, covered with dense forests, with here and there a cluster of Indian wigwams, and varied with an occasional band of painted savages on the warpath, or a hunting party armed with tomahawks, bows and arrows. But beyond these vague impressions we have little definite knowledge. Nor is it possible at this late day to rescue from oblivion much valuable information that could have been gathered a generation or two ago. Still there are scattered facts lying at various places, that may be collected and woven into a broken narrative, that will be more satisfactory than the vague impressions now in our possession.

The earliest accounts of the hill-country of North Carolina, accessible to the writer, are those contained in Lawson's History of a Journey from Charleston to Pamlico Sound, in the year 1701. Starting from the former place in December, 1700, he passed around the mouth of Santee River in a boat, and thence up that stream for a distance in the same way. Then leaving the river he traveled up between the Santee and Pee Dee Rivers, until he crossed the Yadkin River at Trading Ford, within six miles of where Salisbury now stands. As there were no European settlers from the lower Santee to Pamlico, and as he often forgets to mention the scenes through which he passed, it is very difficult to trace his exact route. Still there are some waymarks by which we can identify a part of his course. Among the first of these is the High Hills of Santee, in Sumter County, S. C. Then the Waxsaws, Kadapaus (Catawba), and Sugarees, have left names behind them that indicate the spots he visited. The name "Sugaree" suggests the inquiry whether the ancient name of Sugar Creek, was not Sugaree, rather than "Sugaw," as found in old records.

From the Catawbas, Mr. Lawson traveled about one hundred miles, at a rough estimate, to Sapona Town, on the Sapona River. Taking into account the distance, in a route somewhat circuitous, the size of the river, and the description of the locality, there can remain little doubt on a reasonable mind that the place indicated as Sapona Town was the Indian settlement on the Yadkin River, near Trading Ford. This view is confirmed by the names and distances that are mentioned beyond the Sapona River, such as Heighwarrie (Uwharrie), Sissipahaw (Haw), Eno, the Occoneechees, the Neuse, which corresponds exactly with places and distances as now known. It is true that Lawson says that the Sapona is the "west branch of the Clarendon, or Cape Fair River"; from which some have supposed that he meant the Deep River. On the other hand, it is a noteworthy fact that Colonel Byrd, the author of the "History of the Dividing Line," a man of varied learning and close observation, says that Deep River is the "north branch of the Pee Dee." The error in both cases is excusable, from the fact that the places mentioned are several hundred miles in the interior, and far beyond the extreme verge of civilization in those days.

The region of country before reaching the Sapona—that is, the territory now occupied by Rowan County and those south of her—is described by Lawson as "pleasant savanna ground, high and dry, having very few trees upon it, and those standing at a great distance; free from grubs or underwood. A man near Sapona may more easily clear ten acres of ground than in some places he can one; there being much loose stone upon the land, lying very convenient for making of dry walls or any other sort of durable fence. The country abounds likewise with curious bold creeks, navigable for small craft, disgorging themselves into the main rivers that vent themselves into the ocean." (Lawson, History North Carolina, p. 80.)

Of the last day's journey before reaching Sapona, he says: "That day we passed over a delicious country—none that I ever saw exceeds it. We saw fine-bladed grass six feet high along the banks of the rivulets. Coming that day about thirty miles, we reached the fertile and pleasant banks of the Sapona River, whereon stands the Indian town and fort; nor could all Europe afford a pleasanter stream, were it inhabited by Christians and cultivated by ingenious hands. This most pleasant river may be something broader than the Thames at Kingston, keeping a continual warbling noise with its reverberating upon the bright marble rocks." [Marble, in its general signification, means any kind of mineral of compact texture, and susceptible of a good polish, whether limestone, serpentine, porphyry, or granite (See Webster). From his frequent mention of marble, as found in South Carolina and North Caorlina, we infer that Lawson used the word in this broad sense, as applicable to granite, sandstone, slate, etc.] "It is beautified by a numerous train of swans and other waterfowl, not common, though extraordinary pleasing to the eye. One side of the river is hemmed in with mountainy ground, the other side proving as rich a soil as any this western world can afford. * * * Taken with the pleasantness of the place, we walked along the river side, where we found a delightful island made by the river and a branch, there being several such plots of ground environed by this silver stream. Nor can anything be desired by a contented mind as to a pleasant situation but what may here be found, every step presenting some new object which still adds invitation to the traveler in these parts." (Lawson, pp. 81, 84, etc.)

The foregoing quotation presents several points of interest. The first is that the country was not then—one hundred and eighty years ago—clothed with dense forests as we are apt to imagine, but was either open prairie, or dotted here and there with trees, like the parks of the old country. Along the streams, as we gather from other pages of his narrative, there were trees of gigantic height, so high that they could not kill turkeys resting on the upper branches. This agrees with the recollection of the older citizens, and the traditions handed down from their fathers. A venerable citizen, now living in the southwestern part of this county, remembers when the region called Sandy Ridge was destitute of forests, and that his father told him that, when he settled there, about 1750, he had to haul the logs for his house more than a mile. Another honored citizen of Iredell, lately deceased, told the writer that he recollected the time when the highlands between Fourth Creek and Third Creek were open prairies, covered with grass and wild peavines, and that the wild deer would mingle with their herds of cattle as they grazed. A stock law in those days would have been very unpopular, however desirable in these days of thicker settlements and extended farms.

Another point is the exceeding beauty and fertility of the valley of the Sapona or Yadkin River. I suppose an intelligent man, who would read the description of Lawson, standing on the Indian Hill on the banks of the Yadkin a mile below Trading Ford, could hardly fail to recognize in the surrounding scenery every feature of the description. Beneath his feet would be the mound whereon stood the Sapona fort, surrounded by palisadoes. A hundred yards southeast roll the waters of the stream into which Lawson feared that the northwest storm of wind would blow him. Around him, on the mound and on the plain below, lie innumerable fragments of pottery, with rudely ornamented flint arrow heads, bones, shells, etc. Around him is a large level plateau of fertile land, perhaps one thousand acres in extent, a part of the famed "Jersey lands." Just above the ford is the beautiful island containing a hundred acres—the central part under culitvation, but its edges fringed with trees and clambering vines. In the center of the island he will find an Indian burying-ground, where numerous bones are turned over by the plow, and where Indian pottery and a huge Indian battle-ax have been found. Below the ford are several smaller islands, resting on the bosom of the smoothly flowing stream. The swans, beavers, deer, and buffaloes have fled before the march of civilization, but on the south side of the stream still stand the bold bluffs rising abruptly from the river bank. Some of these heights are now clothed with cedars and other forest trees, but one of them is crowned with an old family mansion, that was formerly known as "The Heights of Gowerie." At the foot of the hill is a spring of pure cold water, and nearby a mill, driven by water drawn from the river above by a long canal. A cedar grove waves its evergreen branches along the level stretch of ground opposite the island. Not many years ago a lady, with the hectic flush upon her cheeks, returned from a distant land to visit for the last time her native place—the old mansion on the hill. She was accompanied by a gentleman residing in the neighborhood, who after her departure penned the following lines, in which he has interwoven a description of the surrounding scenery, and which he courteously furnished at the request of the writer.

HEIGHTS OF GOWERIE

Pensive I stand on Gowerie's height,
All bathed in autumn's mellow light—
  My childhood's happy home;
Where Yadkin rolls its tide along
With many a wail and mournful song,
  As its waters dash and foam.

And memory's harp tunes all its strings,
When I catch the dirge the river sings,
  As it sweeps by Gowerie's side.
And viewless tongues oft speak to me,
Some in sorrow and some in glee,
  From the river's fitful tide.

On yon isle, just up the river,
Where sunbeams dance and leaflets quiver,
  Three fancied forms I see.
That blest—that sainted trio band,
Together walk adown the strand,
  And wave their hands at me.

A father 'tis, whom yet I mourn,
And sisters two, who long have gone—
  Gone to the other shore.
They beck me to the goodly land,
Where, with them, I'll walk hand in hand,
  Ne'er to be parted more.

When from the fount hard by the mill,
Just at the foot of Gowerie's hill,
  I drink the sparkling water;
Echoes from yon cedar grove,
From which the sighing zephyrs rove
  Say, "Come to me, my daughter."

CHAPTER II

THE ABORIGINES

The earliest inhabitants of this country known to the Europeans were the wild Indians of the Catawba, Woccon, and Sapona tribes, with the Keyauwees on the Uwharie River, and the Occoneechees on the Eno. These were stationary, or at least had their home here. But over the whole country, from the Great Lakes on the North to the rivers of Carolina, there roved hunting and war parties of Hurons, Iroquois, Sinnagers or Senecas—parts of the great Five Nations—who were the terror of the less warlike tribes of the South. On the upper waters of the Tar and Neuse Rivers dwelt the Tuscaroras, the most numerous and warlike of the North Carolina Indians, occupying fifteen towns, and having twelve hundred fighting men. The whole Indian population of North Carolina, in the year 1700, not counting the Catawbas on the southern borders, or the Cherokees beyond the mountains, is estimated at about five thousand.

Mr. Lawson speaks of the Indians of North Carolina, as a well-shaped, clean-made people, straight, inclined to be tall, of a tawny color, having black or hazel eyes, with white marbled red streaks. They were never bald, but had little or no beard, and they allowed their nails to grow long and untrimmed. In their gait, they were grave and majestic, never walking backward and forward in contemplation as the white people do. They were dexterous and steady with their hands and feet, never letting things fall from their hands, never stumbling, able to walk on the smallest pole across a stream, and could stand on the ridgepole of a house and look unconcernedly over the gable end. But with all their dexterity, the men had a supreme contempt for regular labor. Hunting, fishing and fighting were gentlemanly accomplishments, and in these enterprises the men would undergo any amount of fatigue, but the hoeing, digging, and all arduous labor were left exclusively to the women.

Like the inhabitants of the Mauritius, as mentioned in Bernardin St. Pierre's "Paul and Virginia," they named their months by some outward characteristic, as the month of strawberries, the month of mulberries, the month of dogwood blossoms, the month of herrings, or the month when the turkey gobbles. They had few religious rites, yet they offered firstfruits, and the more serious of them threw the first bit or spoonful of each meal into the ashes; which they considered equivalent to the Englishman's pulling off his hat and talking when he sat down to meat.

The best view of the theological and religious opinions of the Sapona Indians, who dwelt on the banks of the Yadkin, is that given by "Bearskin," the Sapona Indian hunter, who accompanied the Commissioners of Virginia in running the dividing line between Virginia and North Carolina, in 1728. (See History Dividing Line, pp. 50, 51.) In substance, he stated that they believed in one supreme God, who made the world a long time ago, and superintended the sun, moon, and stars; that he had made many worlds before. That God is good, and loves good people, making them rich and healthy, and safe from their enemies, but punishing those who cheat and tell lies with hunger and sickness, and allowing them to be knocked in the head and scalped by their enemies. He also supposed there were subordinate gods, or evil spirits. He believed in a future state, and that after death the good and the bad started off on the same road, until a flash of lightning separated them, where this road forks into two paths. The right hand path led to a charming country of perpetual spring, where the people are ever young, and the women as bright as stars, and never scold. In this land there is abundance of deer, turkeys, elks, and buffaloes, ever fat and gentle, and trees forever laden with fruit. Near the entrance of this fair land a venerable man examines the character of all, and if they have behaved well, he opens to them the crystal gate, and allows them to enter.

They who are driven to the left hand find a rugged path that leads to a barren country of perpetual winter, where the ground is covered with eternal snow, and the trees bear nothing but icicles. The inhabitants are always hungry, yet have nothing to eat except a bitter potato, that gives them the gripes and fills the body with painful ulcers. The women there are old, ugly, shrill-voiced, and armed with claws like panthers, with which they scratch the men who fail to be enamored with them. At the end of this path sits a dreadful old woman, on a monstrous toadstool, with her head covered with rattlesnakes instead of hair, striking terror into the beholder as she pronounces sentence upon every wretch that stands at her bar. After this they are delivered to huge turkey buzzards that carry them off to their dreadful home. After a number of years in this purgatory they are driven back into the world, and another trial given to them.

Gross and sensual as this religion is, it embraces the cardinal points of belief in a God, the distinction between right and wrong, and the future state of rewards and punishments. But these children of nature had very few acts expressive of religious feeling, and those of the rudest kind. Lawson in his travels (History of North Carolina, p. 65) was permitted to witness among the Waxsaws a feast "held in commemoration of the plentiful harvest of corn they had reaped the summer before, with an united supplication for the like plentiful produce the year ensuing." This ceremony does not seem to have been accompanied by any spoken prayers or addresses, but consisted of a feast of "loblolly," i. e., mush of Indian meal, stewed peaches, and bear venison; and a dance. Their music was made on a drum constructed of an earthen porridge pot, covered with a dressed deerskin, and with gourds having corn in them. It was a masquerade, and their visors were made of gourds, and their heads were plentifully adorned with feathers. Some of the dancers had great horse bells tied to their legs, and small hawk bells about their necks. Modern civilization has not yet adopted the bells and gourd masks of the Waxsaws, but there is no telling what "progress" may accomplish in that direction. In these dances the men figured first alone, and after they were done capering, the women and girls held the ground for about six successive hours. Though the dancing was not "promiscuous," after the modern style, it was nevertheless accompanied by acts so unbecoming and impure as to render it highly immoral and corrupting.

In addition to this worship of dancing, Mr. Lawson says that the Indians were much addicted to the practice of sacrificing chicken cocks to the God who hurts them, that is the devil (History of North Carolina, pp. 97, 98). But the only visible objects of reverence among the Indians were the bones of their ancestors, especially of their chiefs, which they kept rolled up in dressed deerskins, and carried with them wherever they went. Among some of the tribes they had a building called a "Quiogozon," in which they kept the bones of their dead kings, and as Mr. Lawson says (p. 324) their "idols," where the King, the conjurer, and a few old men were wont to spend several days at a time in practicing secret and mysterious religious rites.

Our country abounds in scattered relics of this departed race, in the shape of the blue flint arrow heads, fragments of pottery, and especially mounds of earth in various places. A gentleman of our county of antiquarian tastes and accomplishments reports that there are several mounds in Davie County supposed to contain relics of the Indians. There is also another artificial mound near Mount Pleasant, beside a small stream, some sixty feet in diameter and six or eight feet high, but not containing any relics. Several mounds abounding with relics are known to exist in Caldwell County. One or more have been found in Montgomery County, near Little River, and it has been reported that large vases, or sarcophagi, have been recently discovered in one of them. In that same region beautifully dressed quartz mortars, supposed to have been used for grinding and mixing paints, have been found. These savages were in the habit of painting their faces and bodies before going into battle, that by their hideous appearance they might terrify and demoralize their enemies. And it can scarcely be doubted that this painting was used as a disguise, that it might not be known by the enemy who was the slayer of their fallen warriors; for the law of "blood revenge" prevailed among them, not much unlike that of the ancient Israelites. Hence it might prove inconvenient to be known as the slayer, as it was a fatal thing for Abner to be known as the slayer of the light-footed Asahel.

In addition to these mounds, Mr. Baldwin, in his "Ancient America" (p. 24), mentions "Harrison Mound" in South Carolina, four hundred and eighty feet in circumference, and fifteen feet high. This mound is attributed to the "Mound Builders," or ancient Toltecs. A still larger "Mound" has recently been brought to public notice through the columns of the Salisbury *Watchman,* situated in Old Rowan County—now Davidson—about eight miles from Salisbury. In many respects this is a work of considerable interest, both as to its situation and character. It stands within one hundred yards of the Yadkin River, at the point where Lawson seems to locate "Sapona Town," on "Sapona River," near the celebrated "Trading Ford." As this lies in the ancient territory of Rowan, it will require a more particular notice. The "Trading Ford" is so named because it was on the ancient "Trading Path," leading from Virginia to the Catawba and other Southern Indians. Colonel Byrd, in his History of the Dividing Line (1728), describes this "Path" as crossing the Roanoke at Moni-seep Ford, thence over Tar River, Flat River, Little River, Eno, through the Haw Old Fields, over the Haw, the Aramanchy (Alamance), and Deep River. The next point was Yadkin River, where he says, "The soil was exceedingly fertile on both sides, abounding in rank grass and prodigiously large trees, and for plenty of fish, fowl, and venison is inferior to no part of the Northern continent. There the traders commonly lie still for some days to recruit their horses' flesh, as well as to recover their own spirits. Six miles further is Crane Creek, so named from its being the rendezvous of great armies of cranes, which wage a more cruel war at this day with the frogs and fish than they used to do in the days of Homer. About three-score miles more bring you to the first town of the Catawbas, called Nauvasa, situated on the banks of the Santee (Catawba) River. Besides this town there are five others belonging to the same Nation, lying on the same stream, within the distance of 20 miles. These Indians were all called formerly by the general name of Usherees, and were a very numerous and powerful people * * * but are now (1728) reduced to little more than four hundred fighting men, besides women and children" (History Dividing Line, p. 85). Speaking of the Sapponies, or Saponas, Colonel Byrd remarks that they formerly lived upon the "Yadkin River," not far below the mountains; thus placing them exactly where Lawson puts them, though he calls the river by another name, i. e., "Yadkin," instead of "Sapona." When these Indians had become reduced in numbers, and no longer able to resist the incursions of the Northern Indians—Iroquois or Senecas—they resolved to form a combination, or fusion of the Saponas, Toteros, Keyauwees, and Occoneechees, for mutual defense and protection. Two or three years after Lawson passed here, that is, about 1703, these consolidated tribes removed from Carolina into Virginia, and settled at Christiana, ten miles north of the Roanoke (Lawson, p. 83); (Dividing Line, p. 89). After remaining there twenty-five or thirty years, they returned to Carolina and dwelt with the Catawbas (Dividing Line, p. 89). Colonel Byrd describes these Saponas as having "something great and remarkable in their countenances," and as being "the honestest as well as the bravest Indians" he was "ever acquainted with." Colonel Spotswood—the Governor of Virginia—placed a schoolmaster among them to instruct their children, though from the shortness of time they were under his tuition, he taught them little else than the much needed grace of cleanliness.

It was these Saponas that occupied the important post near "Trading Ford," when the trading caravans, with their goods packed on a hundred horses, stopped to recruit for five or six days, and doubtless to trade with the Saponas and their confederates. Of the transactions at that deserted metropolis, we have no records. Tradition says that at "Swearing Creek," a few miles beyond Sapona, the traders were in the habit of taking a solemn oath never to reveal any unlawful proceedings that might occur during their sojourn among the Indians.

The "Indian Hill," as it is now called, standing in sight of the North Carolina Railroad, about a half-mile in front of Dr. Meares' residence, was evidently once the fort of the Indian Town of Sapona. Besides the pottery and arrow heads and chips of flint lying on its sides and base, the older citizens remember that in their boyhood they were accustomed to find lead there, in the shape of shot, bullets, etc. This lead was either dropped by the traders or the Indians, in their early days, or the fort was the scene of some unrecorded conflict between the Saponas and Iroquois after the introduction of firearms. Or it may be that Indian Hill was the scene of some old-time shooting match between the sturdy marksmen of the "Jerseys," in the forgotten days of a past generation.

The origin of this mound is surrounded with more doubt than its use by the wild Indians. It contains ten or fifteen thousand cubic yards of earth, some of it carried from pits a hundred yards or more distant. This would require, with their rude implements and dilatory habits, a hundred workers for a half-year. Now there is nothing better known than the improvidence, lack of foresight, and especially detestation of drudgery, that characterized the "gentleman savage." If done by the Indians, it was the work of the women alone; and this fact suggests the existence of a large and powerful tribe, somewhat more civilized than the wild Indians. And though it is not commonly held that the Toltecs, or Mound-builders, penetrated so far east as the Atlantic slope, still it is possible that in the distant ages when this civilized race dwelt in the valley of the Mississippi and the Ohio, there may have been some solitary out-stations, or colonies, between the valley of the Mississippi and the Atlantic Ocean. When the "Ishmaelitish" wild Indians succeeded in overpowering their more civilized rivals, these mounds, on which wooden or adobe temples once stood, would lie in ruins like the mounds marking the site of Babylon and Nineveh. In process of time, the wild Indians would utilize them as sites for forts, or refuges from the floods.

In closing, I may be allowed to mention that about a half-mile this side of Trading Ford, the old Trading Path turns off from the present road towards the south, and that it crosses Crane Creek somewhere in the neighborhood of "Spring Hill," running perhaps a mile southeast of Salisbury and so on to the southward between Salisbury and Dunn's Mountain. Along this path, before civilized men dwelt here, caravans passed to and fro, visiting the Redmen in their towns, and selling them guns, powder, shot, hatchets, or tomahawks, kettles, plates, blankets, cutlery, brass rings and other trinkets. Parallel to this path the great North Carolina Railroad now rushes on, bearing the commerce of the nation. And it was along this same path that emigrants from Pennsylvania and Virginia began to pour into Old Rowan in the first half of the last century. Of these we will speak in our next chapter.

CHAPTER III

THE FIRST EUROPEAN SETTLERS

The earliest settlements in North Carolina were made on the coast, along Albemarle and Pamlico Sounds, and near the mouth of the Cape Fear River. In a map of the inhabited parts of North Carolina, made by John Lawson, the surveyor-general, in 1709, we see the outlines of the settlements. The line commences at the mouth of Currituck Inlet, and sweeps around in a semi-circle, crossing the Roanoke at Aconeche Island, passing by the head of Pamlico Sound, crossing the Neuse near the mouth of Contentnea Creek, and so on east of where Fayetteville now stands, to the Atlantic, thirty miles south of the mouth of the Cape Fear. The population was then less than seven thousand (Hawks, Vol. I, p. 89). In twenty years more, about three thousand had been added to the population, and there were five small towns: Bath, Newbern, Edenton, Beaufort, and Brunswick. Of these, Edenton was called the metropolis.

In the year 1729, the King of Great Britain, according to act of Parliament, purchased seven-eights of the territory of the Carolinas from the Lords Proprietors, for twenty-five hundred pounds (£2,500) for each eighth part. But John, Earl of Granville, the son and heir of Sir George Carteret, refused to part with his portion, and his lands were laid off to him, extending from latitude thirty-five degrees, thirty-four minutes to the Virginia line, and westward to the South Sea, or Pacific Ocean. It is within the limits of Earl Granville's lands and on the western portion of them that Rowan County was situated.

The Royal Governors of North Carolina were as follows: George Burrington, 1731-34; Nathaniel Rice, 1734—a few months; Gabriel Johnston, 1734-52; Nathaniel Rice, 1752-53; Matthew Rowan, 1753-54. During the terms of these Governors the population rolled upwards and westward, county after county being set off as the land was occupied. Bladen was set off from New Hanover in 1734, Anson from Bladen in 1749, Rowan from Anson in 1753, and Mecklenburg from Anson in 1762. Of course, population was in advance of county organizations, and there was a sufficient number of settlers in the territory of Rowan, previous to 1753, to demand a separate county government. But it becomes a difficult task to ascertain when and from whence came the first white settlers.

In his Sketches of North Carolina, Colonel Wheeler says: "Rowan was early settled (about 1720), by the Protestants from Moravia, fleeing from the persecutions of Ferdinand II; and by the Scotch, who, after the unsuccessful attempts of Charles Edward, grandson of James II, to ascend the English throne, and whose fortunes were destroyed on the fatal field of Culloden (sixteenth of April, 1746), had fled to this country; and by the Irish, who after the rebellion of the Earls of Tyrone and Tyrconnel, in the time of James I, were forced to leave the country. These, or their ancestors, previously had come from Scotland, and hence the term Scotch-Irish" (Wheeler, Art. Rowan County). It would be difficult to crowd more mistakes into one short paragraph than are found in this brief account of the settlement of Rowan. First of all, Ferdinand II, Emperor of Germany, reigned from 1618 to 1648, more than one hundred years before the time required, and the Moravians, or United Brethren, did not appear in Moravia until 1722, in England in 1728, in New York and Georgia in 1736, and in North Carolina not until 1753. Again, very few of the Scotch came to Rowan directly, but to the Cape Fear section, and not there in numbers until some time after 1746. It was not the native Irish, after the rebellion of Tyrone and Tyrconnel, but the descendants of the Scotch whom James I had placed on their escheated lands, who came to Rowan. They remained in Ireland for more than one hundred years, enduring many trials and disabilities during that period, and then in the early part of the eighteenth century immigrated to New Jersey and Pennsylvania, and thence to North Carolina.

The earliest settlements in Rowan of which we have any accurate knowledge were made about 1737. Dr. Foote, in his Sketches of North Carolina, states that the Scotch-Irish began their settlements in Shenandoah Valley in Virginia in 1737, and in North Carolina soon afterwards. Some scattered families followed the Trading Path and settled in chosen spots from the Roanoke to the Catawba. As the Indians were friendly, and the caravans of the traders frequent, it would be but natural that immigrants would be attracted by their glowing descriptions of the fertile prairies that lay between the Yadkin and the Catawba—a land abounding in game, and whose streams were stocked with fish, and its flowery meadows affording pasturage for their cattle. (See Foote, p. 188.)

Fortunately for the settlement of this point, the Clark family, who have resided on the Cape Fear since about 1745, have preserved memoranda showing that, as early as the year 1746, a family or a company of emigrants went west of the Yadkin to join some other families that were living sequestered in that fertile region (Foote, p. 189). Thus it appears that there were settlers, families, residing here previous to 1746. They would scarcely think it necessary to enter lands in a region where all was open to them, and if they did, their deeds would be recorded in the Court of Bladen or New Hanover, of which Rowan then constituted a part. It is worthy of notice that there was once a settlement and a church of the Scotch in South Rowan, called Crystal Springs, and in the old minutes of the Presbyterian Church, Crystal Springs and Salisbury are represented as asking for ministerial supplies. This church was about ten miles nearly south of Salisbury, near the residence of Dr. Paul Sifford, and in its old graveyard lie the remains of the McPhersons, the Mahans, the Longs, and others. Since 1812, this church has not been in existence, as it is said that at that time the members were transferred to Old Bethphage, about eight or ten miles west of Crystal Springs.

But the Scotch-Irish were probably the most numerous and the leading people of the settlement. The old records of the Court here show the names of many of these old families, some of them now extinct, such as the Nesbits, Allisons, Brandons, Luckeys, Lockes, McCullochs, Grahams, Cowans, McKenzies, Barrs, Andrews, Osbornes, Sharpes, Boones, McLauchlins, Halls, with many others whose names are as familiar as household words.

But along with these Scotch-Irish immigants, and settling side by side with them, there came settlers of another nationality to whom Rowan is no less indebted for her material wealth and prosperity. These were the Germans, or as they were familiarly called the "Pennsylvania Dutch." They were of course not of Dutch or Holland extraction, but Germans from the Palatinate, and from Hesse Cassel, Hesse Homburg, Darmstadt, and the general region of the upper and middle Rhine. Prominent among these for its history and the number of its emigrants is the Palatinate, or "Pfalz" as it is called in the maps of Germany. This country lies on the western banks of the Rhine, below Strasburg, and along the eastern boundaries of France. This beautiful land is watered by numerous small streams, the tributaries of the Rhine, and is divided by a range of mountains, the Haardts, running from north to south. Manheim and Speyer (Spires) are the two principal cities, situated on the Rhine, while Neustadt, Anweiler, Zweibrucken, Leiningen, are among its towns. This Province was the theater of many bloody and atrocious deeds during the reign of Louis XIV, of France, a time when such great generals as the Prince of Conde, Marshal Turenne, Prince Eugene, the Duke of Marlborough, and William, Prince of Orange, won glory or infamy on the bloody field of battle. It was in the Palatinate that Turenne sullied his glory by an act of the most savage barbarity in laying waste the country with fire and sword, reducing two cities and twenty-five villages to ashes, and leaving the innocent inhabitants to perish of cold and hunger, while the unfortunate Elector looked helplessly on from the walls of his palace at Manheim. And a few years after, Louis again invaded the Palatinate, and laid the cities of Mentz, Philipsburg, Spires, and forty others, with numerous villages, in ashes. Thus this little principality, whose inhabitants by their industry and peaceable habits had made it the most thriving and happy state in Germany, was literally turned into a desert. Ravaged by fire and sword, and trodden down under the iron heel of despotism, the wretched inhabitants were forced at last to leave their beautiful country and seek a home among strangers. Their first place of refuge was the Netherlands, where a liberal and Protestant government afforded them a safe asylum.

From the Netherlands many of them found their way into England, where Queen Anne gave them a safe refuge from their enemies. But England was itself a populous country, and the English government determined to induce as many of the Palatines as possible to cross the Atlantic and become settlers in the American Colonies. In that broad land they could find comfortable homes, and by their industry they might make its deserts blossom as the rose. Some of them came over with De Graffenried and Mitchell and found homes on the lower waters of the Neuse, where a New "Berne" would remind the Swiss portion of the colonists of the old Berne they had left behind them among the Alps. Others found homes in the State of New York, and others still in Charleston, S. C., and along the banks of the Congaree and Saluda Rivers. Many others from this general section of Germany settled in Lehigh, Northampton, Berks, and Lancaster Counties in Pennsylvania. Finding this country thickly settled and good land to be secured only at high prices, in a few years they turned their attention southward. Here Earl Granville's lands—lately set off to him—were offered at a cheap rate, and the climate was much more mild than in the homes they had chosen in Pennsylvania. The first arrival of Germans in Western North Carolina, in the bounds of Old Rowan, is believed to have taken place about 1745, though it was five years later that the great body of them came. The stream thus started continued to flow on for years, many of them arriving after the Revolutionary war. They traveled with their household goods and the women and children in wagons, the men and boys walking and driving their cattle and hogs before them. They came side by side with their Scotch-Irish neighbors, sometimes settling in the same community with them, and at other times occupying alternate belts or sections of country. Thus we can trace a German stream through Guilford, Davidson, Rowan, and Cabarrus Counties, and just by its side a stream of Scotch-Irish. But as years passed away these streams, like the currents of the Missouri and Mississippi Rivers, have mingled into one, resulting in a mixed race of German-Scotch-Irish, perpetuating the virtues and perhaps also the weaknesses of all the races. Dr. Bernheim, in his interesting work on German settlements in North and South Carolina, has given a list of names, found in common use in Pennsylvania and in North Carolina, such as Propst, Bostian, Kline (Cline), Trexler, Schlough, Seitz (Sides), Rheinhardt, Biber (Beaver), Kohlman (Coleman), Derr (Dry), Berger (Barrier), Behringer (Barringer). To this list may be added other names familiar in Rowan County, such as Bernhardt, Heilig, Meisenheimer, Beard, Mull, Rintelman (Rendleman), Layrle (Lyerly), Kuhn (Coon), Friese, Eisenhauser, Yost, Overcash, Boger, Suther, Winecoff, Cress, Walcher, Harkey, Savitz, Henkel, Moser, Braun (Brown) and many others familiar to all our people. The German settlers have generally been remarkable for industry, economy, and the habit of living within their means and not getting into debt.

During their sojourn here, a century and a quarter, they have passed through the ordeal of changing their language. As the laws were written and expounded in English, and all public affairs conducted in that language, the Germans were incapable of taking part, in most cases, in public affairs. Hence, letting public affairs alone, and attending to their home interests, they surrounded themselves with well-tilled farms, and adorned their premises with capacious barns and threshing floors. Who has not seen the immense double barns, with wide double doors, to admit a four-horse wagon with its towering load of hay or straw or wheat; and the threshing floor, where the horses tramped out the wheat, and the "windmill" blew the chaff into the chaffhouse? And who has forgotten the long stables where the cows were yoked to the troughs, each one knowing her place, while the calves were tied to a trough at the other wall?

But the "Pennsylvania Dutch" has almost ceased to be heard on our streets where once its quaint tones of mingled German, French, and English were so familiar. The dialect is gone, but the accent and the idiom still linger on many tongues, and the traditions and folklore of the old world still flow in a deep undercurrent in many families.

Not long after the Scotch-Irish and Pennsylvania Germans came into the territory of Old Rowan, came another people that have added much to the wealth of the State. I mean the Moravians, or United Brethren. These people purchased a tract of 98,985 acres, called the "Wachovia Tract," in what is now Forsyth County, but originally Rowan. This was in 1751, but the deed for the tract was signed in 1753, and in the autumn of this year twelve single brethren came from Bethlehem, Pa., and began the settlement of Bethabara. Bethany was founded in 1759, and Salem in 1766; Friedburg and Friedland, in 1769 and 1770. In 1804 the well-known Salem Female Academy was founded, at which many of the fair daughters of the South have been educated.

Along with these settlers from Ireland and Germany came, from time to time, others of English, Welsh, and Scotch descent, who have mingled with the former in working out the destiny of Old Rowan—the mother of counties.

Although Rowan was not settled by Cavaliers or Huguenots, or by the aristocracy of old-world society, she has good reason to be proud of the early pioneers who laid here the foundations of their homes. They were men and women who had suffered for conscience' sake, or fled from despotism to seek liberty and happiness unrestrained by the shackles of a wornout civilization.

CHAPTER IV

ORGANIZATION, BOUNDARY, ETC.

The early settlers of Rowan were peaceable, industrious, and law-abiding men, who had come to this land to make their homes for themselves and their children. When therefore their numbers had increased sufficiently to justify the measure, steps were taken for the formation of a county government, and the appointment of county officers and courts of justice. Accordingly, at the sessions of the General Assembly of the Province of North Carolina begun and held at Newbern, March 27, 1753, an Act was passed establishing the County of Rowan. Gov. Gabriel Johnston, after a long and prosperous term of office, had died in August, 1752, and the duties of the office devolved upon Nathaniel Rice, first Counselor of the King's Commission. But President Rice lived only until January, 1753, and at his death the Hon. Matthew Rowan, the next Counselor in order, qualified as President, in Wilmington, on the first of February, 1753. As he was now President of the Council, and acting governor, the new county formed during his administration was called after his name. The Act of the Assembly establishing the county is, in part, as follows: "That Anson County be divided by a line, to begin where (the) Anson line was to cross Earl Granville's (line), and from thence in a direct line north to the Virginia line, and that the said county be bounded on the north by the Virginia line, and to the south by the southernmost line of Earl Granville's: And that the upper part of said county so divided be erected into a County and Parish by the name of Rowan County and St. Luke's Parish, and that all the inhabitants to the westward of said line, and included within the before-mentioned boundaries shall belong and appertain to Rowan County" (Iredell's Laws of North Carolina, Ed. 1791, p. 154.) To get an idea of these extensive boundaries, we have only to remember that, in 1749, Anson was cut off from Bladen by a line starting where the westernmost branch of Little Pee Dee enters South Carolina, thence up to the headwaters of Drowning Creek, and so on by a line equi-distant from Great Pee Dee and Saxapahaw. All west of this somewhat indeterminate line was Anson County. The design in 1753 was to include in Rowan all that part of Anson which was comprised in Earl Granville's lands, that is, all north of latitude thirty-five degrees, thirty-four minutes as far as to the Virginia line. The "point" where Anson line was to cut Earl Granville's line, as well as can be determined by the writer, must have been somewhere near the southeastern corner of the present County of Randolph, not far from the point where Deep River passes from Randolph into Moore County. The eastern line of Rowan, if this be correct, would run due north from that point, along the eastern boundaries of the present Randolph, Guilford, and Rockingham Counties. The southern boundary, beginning at the southeast corner of Randolph, ran due west along Earl Granville's south line, on the south side of Randolph, Davidson, Rowan, and Iredell, as they now lie (latitude thirty-five degrees, thirty-four minutes), to the Catawba River, a short distance above Beattie's Ford; thence due west, cutting into Lincoln County, and running a few miles north of Lincolnton, through Cleveland and Rutherford, through Hickory Nut Gap, and on through Buncombe, Haywood, Jackson, Macon, and Cherokee, and on to the westward indefinitely. Old Rowan included in its ample domain the territory occupied today by thirty counties and parts of counties in North Carolina, besides the indefinite and unexplored regions of the west, as far as the South Seas, embracing the western section of Granville's vast inheritance. It is true, indeed, that the region beyond the mountains in the early days was unknown, and in the farther West was the French territory of Louisiana, that practically cut down these gigantic proportions. But theoretically, and according to the Charter, such was its vast territory.

It may not be amiss to recall to the mind of the student of North Carolina history that Charles II, of England, in the fifteenth year of his reign, granted to the Earl of Clarendon, the Duke of Albemarle, the Earl of Craven, Lord Berkeley, Lord Ashley, Sir George Carteret, and Sir John Colleton, the whole territory of America lying between latitude thirty-one degrees, thirty-six minutes and thirty-six degrees, thirty-one minutes north, and extending from the Atlantic Ocean to the South Sea, or Pacific Ocean. After making the experiment of a Proprietary government for more than a half-century, under the famous constitution of Locke and Shaftesbury, and otherwise, seven of these Lords Proprietors surrendered their interest in the Carolinas to the Crown, in the third year of George II (1729), for the sum of twenty-five hundred pounds (£2500) each, as stated in a previous chapter. But John, Earl of Granville, Lord Carteret, and Baron of Hawnes, as he is styled, the son and heir of Sir George Carteret, declined to surrender his eighth part of the land, preferring to dispose of it to the settlers by means of special agents. In 1743, his eighth part was set off to him, and was situated between latitude thirty-five degrees, thirty-four minutes and the Virginia line. His southern line began on the Atlantic Ocean near Cape Hatteras, crossed Pamlico Sound, passed on west not far from Washington, across the Counties of Beaufort, Pitt, Greene, Wayne, and Johnston, on the north side of Moore, and so on westward along the line indicated as the south line of Rowan County. Granville does not appear to have exercised any authority over the people in his lands, nor any control in the enactment or execution of the laws. He was simply a mighty landowner, with a vast body of desirable land to sell to the best advantage. After 1743 all grants and sales of lands were made in his name. The curious inquirer may look into the office of our Register of Deeds, in the Courthouse in Salisbury, and see volumes upon volumes of old land deeds, reciting over and over again the titles and dignities of Earl Granville, conveying lands to the Allisons, Andrews, Brandons, Grahams, Lockes, Nesbits, etc., and signed by his Lordship's attorneys and agents, Francis Corbin and James Innes, or by sub-agents William Churton and Richard Vigers.

It appears that the General Assembly of North Carolina, at this early day, began to exercise more power than was entirely agreeable to the royal government in England, and by the multiplication of counties the assembly was increased in numbers too rapidly. Hence the policy of repression was early adopted. In 1754, the year after the erection of Rowan County, King George II, in privy council, revoked the acts of 1753, establishing Rowan, Cumberland, and Orange Counties. But upon a more thorough understanding of the subject, he was pleased the next year to allow the said counties to be re-established, and the Assembly at its sessions in 1756 did re-establish these counties, and validated all deeds and conveyances that had been made during the period of the royal revocation. It appears that the disapprobation of the King made no break in the Courts of Rowan County, for the record shows that they went on precisely as they would have gone on had the King fully approved. So far away were they from the Court of England, and so full of the spirit of independence, that they were ready to practice, if not assert, the inherent right of self-government.

The county having been established in March, 1753, in June of the same year the Court of Pleas and Quarter Sessions met somewhere in the county and proceeded to their work. But where the first Court was held, the writer has not been able to determine. There are several vague traditions and recollections that point to different times and places; and with the hope that someone will be able to probe this matter to the bottom, these traditions are given.

1. There is a vague impression floating in certain legal circles here, that an old "Docket" has been seen in our courthouse, dating back a number of years before the establishment of the county. If this be so, there must have been some kind of itinerant or circuit Court held at occasional times on the frontiers. But of this I have seen no historical or documentary proof whatsoever.

2. There is a tradition that the first Courts were held in the Jersey Settlement, not far from Trading Ford, on a place once owned by Thales McDonald, now the property of Mr. Hayden; and the venerable oaks that shaded the premises were pointed out some twenty-five years ago, and may be still standing. This is rendered somewhat probable from the fact that the Jersey lands were early occupied, and were probably more thickly settled at that period than the region between the Yadkin and the Catawba. In connection with this location there is another tradition that preliminary steps were once taken to lay out a town in the vicinity of Trading Ford. With such a beautiful stream, easily capable of being made navigable from the Narrows far up into the mountains, the wonder is that a town has not long since sprung up in that delightful region.

Another tradition, that has been constant in one family, is that the first Courts of Rowan were held in a building that stood on the premises now owned by Miss McLaughlin, about thirteen miles west of Salisbury. This place is midway between Thyatira and Back Creek churches, and not far from Sill's Creek. An old door is still preserved there, which the family say has always been known to have belonged to the building in which the Court was held.

It is possible that there is substantial truth in all these traditions. In those early days the General Assembly of the Province was migratory, being held at Edenton, Newbern, Wilmington, and Hillsboro, and it is not impossible that one or two of the first Courts of Pleas and Quarter Sessions of Rowan were held outside of Salisbury, before a courthouse was erected. The early records contain no mention of the place where the Courts were held, and the first leaf is missing.

Daniel Boone

CHAPTER V

THE FIRST COURT

As stated on a former page, it is not certainly known where the first Court was held. But from the records in the office of the Superior Court Clerk, in Salisbury, it appears probable that it was held in June, 1753, only a few months after the county was established. The names of the justices who presided at the Courts the first year were Walter Carruth, Thomas Lovelatty, James Carter, John Brandon, Alexander Cathey, Squire Boone, Thomas Cook, Thomas Potts, George Smith, Andrew Allison, John Hanby, Alexander Osborne, James Tate, and John Brevard. We know, or have some reasons for conjecturing, the neighborhoods from which several of these magistrates came. Walter Carruth owned lands, and probably resided, on the east side of Coddle Creek, adjoining the McKnights, in the Prospect neighborhood. James Carter owned the lands in the southeast quarter of Salisbury, on both sides of Water Street, and on towards Crane Creek, now called Town Creek, and probably lived in the present corporate limits of the town. John Brandon lived six miles south of Salisbury, near the Concord Road, on the plantation now owned by Charles H. McKenzie, Esq. Alexander Cathey lived on Cathey's Creek, near Thyatira Church, and was the ancestor of the late Alexander Long, M.D., of Salisbury. Squire Boone lived on the Yadkin, at Alleman's or Boone's Ford, and was the father of the great hunter and pioneer, Daniel Boone, of Kentucky. At this place young Daniel spent the days of his boyhood, and no doubt often hunted over the hills and through the thickets of the Yadkin. Thomas Potts probably lived in the Jersey Settlement, where Potts' Creek, running into the Yadkin River just below the site of the Indian Town of Sapona, perpetuates his name. George Smith was probably from the same neighborhood, where a prominent family of that name still resides. Andrew Allison owned large tracts of land on Fourth Creek, a few miles from Statesville, where a large and influential family of that name may still be found. Alexander Osborne lived on the headwaters of Rocky River, about two miles north of Davidson College. He was a leading man in the community, a colonel, the father of Adlai Osborne, and the ancestor of the late eloquent and popular Judge James W. Osborne, of Mecklenburg. John Brevard was probably from the same neighborhood, a little farther west, and not far from Beattie's Ford, on the Catawba. At least this was the neighborhood of the Brevards, one of whom, Dr. Ephraim Brevard, is reputed to be the composer of the celebrated Mecklenburg Declaration of Independence. Of Lovelatty, Cook, Hanby, and Tate the writer has no knowledge, though doubtless some of their descendants may be still residing among us. There is a Ford on the Catawba, and a postoffice in Caldwell County called "Lovelady," perhaps a remembrance of Justice Lovelatty, of the Rowan County Court.

A good part of the time of the first Court was taken up in registering the marks and brands which the citizens had invented to distinguish their cattle and other livestock; and the changes are rung on "crops," "half-crops," "slits," and "swallow-forks," in the "off" and "near" ear, and other quaint devices for marking. The cattle that were to be identified by the marks and brands registered in the Rowan Court, ranged over the meadows and prairies of the Yadkin, the Catawba, the Deep, the Saxapahaw, and the Dan Rivers. Constables were also appointed whose beats lay as much as a hundred miles from the seat of justice. These old "records" of the Rowan Court of Pleas and Quarter Sessions, for 1753-54-55-56, are full of interest to anyone who will take the trouble to decipher them. For instance, here is a list of constables and their beats for 1753. Preston Goforth for the South Fork of the Catawba. (This was for the region from Hickory to Lincoln.) John McGuire, south side of the Yadkin. John Attaway (?) for Dan River. John Robinson for south side of Yadkin, "from the mouth of Grant's Creek to the ford of the same; thence across to the Trading Path; thence along said Path as far as Coldwater; thence with his Lordship's line." This shows that the Trading Path ran to the point where Coldwater Creek runs from Rowan into Cabarrus. "John Nesbit had his beat from James Cathey's Creek to the Western Path, as far as the fork of said Path. James Howard from Cathey's Creek to Third Creek, and as far as the Division Ridge between the two settlements. Benjamin Winslow, as far as the Catawba River, and along the King's line and Lamb's Mill, and down as far as William McKnight's. John Doller on Abbott's Creek, as far as the Western Path. David Stewart on the north side of Yadkin, from Muddy Creek and upward. William Fisher for the district included in the Forks of Yadkin. James Watkins from the Orange line as far as Beaver Island Creek, on Dan River. James Hampton from Beaver Island Creek and upwards" (i. e., higher up the Dan). These names of men and local-

BOONE MEMORIAL CABIN

Erected on the site of the Original Boone Cabin on the Banks of the Yadkin River in Davidson County, North Carolina

ities show the extent of the jurisdiction of the Rowan Court, stretching from the Orange line and Dan River to the King's line, and as far west as the south fork of the Catawba, northwest of Lincolnton. The following were the officers of the county, viz.:

Richard Hilliar, Deputy Attorney-General; John Dunn, Court Clerk; James Carter, Esq., County Register; John Whitsett, County Treasurer; Francis Corbin, Esq., Colonel of Rowan Regiment of Foot; Scotton Davis, Captain in Corbin's Regiment.

The following persons are named as composing the Grand and Petit Juries of the first Court, viz.: Henry Hughey, John McCulloch, James Hill, John Burnett, Samuel Bryant, John McDowell, James Lambath, Henry Dowland, Morgan Bryan, William Sherrill, William Morrison, William Linvil.

Samuel Baker asked this Court (1753) to declare his mill on Davidson's Creek (near Center Church) a public mill, and his request was granted. John Baker proved before this Court that his ear had been bitten off in an affray (not cropped off for larceny), and obtained a Court certificate to that effect.

In those days innkeepers were not allowed to charge at their own discretion for the drinks and other entertainments which they furnished to their patrons, but the Court took the matter in hand and made a schedule of prices. In 1755, after fixing the prices for wine, whiskey, beer, etc., they decided that the keepers of ordinaries, inns, or taverns, should charge as follows:

For dinner of roast or boiled flesh, one shilling.

For supper and breakfast, each, six pence.

For lodging over night, good bed, two pence.

For stabling (24 hours), with good hay or fodder, six pence.

For pasturage, first twenty-four hours, four pence, every twenty-four hours after, two pence.

For Indian corn or other grain, per quart, two pence.

This was to be paid in Proclamation money, which was about on a par with Confederate the second or third year of the late war.

Salisbury was well supplied with licensed ordinaries, or inns, in those days. The licensed houses were as follows: In 1755, John Ryle's ordinary was licensed. In 1756, John Lewis Beard, Peter Arrand, Jacob Franck, Archibald Craige, James Bower, and Thomas Bashford and Robert Gillespie received licenses. Jacob Franck occupied the lot where the late Dr. Alexander Long resided, and Bashford and Gillespie occupied the corner next to the present court-house, i. e., corner Corbin and Council Streets. Robert Gillespie was the first husband of the celebrated Mrs. Elizabeth Steele, of Salisbury, and the father of the wife of the Rev. Saumel E. McCorkle, D.D. A few years after this, Paul Barringer, Esq., of Mecklenburg (Cabarrus), bought the lot on the east corner of Corbin and Innes Streets, ninety-nine feet down Corbin and one hundred and ninety-eight feet down Innes, from a man who is described as an "ordinary keeper." From this it appears probable that the corner now occupied by Kluttz' drugstore was occupied as an ordinary at an early day, as we know that it was at a later day, when William Temple Coles kept an inn there, where John Dunn, Esq., died in the winter of 1782-83.

We may remark in passing that John Dunn and William Monat were appointed attorneys by Governor Dobbs, and presented their Commissions to the Rowan Court in 1755. Of William Monat little or nothing appears in the records of Rowan County; but for thirty years John Dunn occupied a prominent place in the public affairs of Rowan County, both before and after the War of the Revolution. He deserved well of his country, and his name is embalmed in the hearts of a large circle of honored descendants, and his memory is perpetuated in the name of Dunn's Mountain, in sight of the Public Square of Salisbury, at the foot of which his remains lie interred. This name will often recur in the course of these sketches.

At the June term of 1753, the Court proceeded to select a place for the erection of a courthouse, pillory, stocks, and gaol. The action of the Court is substantially as follows: "The courthouse, gaol, and stocks shall be located where the 'Irish Settlement' forks, one fork leading to John Brandon's, Esq., and the other fork along the old wagon road over Grant's Creek, called Sill's Path, and near the most convenient spring." John Brandon, as stated before, lived six miles south of Salisbury, on the Concord Road, and "Sill's Path" was probably the Beattie's Ford Road, crossing Sill's Creek about seventeen miles west of Salisbury. The most "convenient spring" is thought to be a spring in the garden of the late Dr. Alexander Long, where Jacob Franck's ordinary and still-house were afterwards established, the lot afterwards owned by Matthew Troy, the father-in-law of the late Maxweil Chambers. The exact site of the courthouse was the center of our present Public Square, at the intersection of Corbin and Innes Streets, where the great town well now is. Tradition says that this spot—originally considerably higher than it now is—was a famous "deer-stand," where the rifleman stood, and with unerring aim brought down the fleet-footed doe or antlered stag, as he fled before the music-making pack of hounds.

The Court directed that the courthouse should be of frame work, weather-boarded, thirty feet long and twenty feet wide, a story and a half high, with two floors, the lower one raised two feet above the ground. It was to be provided with an oval bar, and a bench raised three feet above the floor, with a table and seat for the Clerk, and "cases" for the attorneys. There was to be a good window behind the bench, with glass in it, and a window near the middle of each side, and a door in the end opposite the bench. This simple structure of wood, with one door and three windows, appears to us, after the lapse of a century and a quarter, to have been an insignificant affair. But doubtless it compared favorably with the finest structures to be found in the wilderness, only about ten years after the first settlers arrived, and it accorded well with the temper and the habits of those earnest and honest Justices who sat upon the "bench," and arraigned evildoers at their bar. No complicated suits, involving nice points of law, often came before them for adjudication, but rather affrays, trespass, and larcenies, with now and then a homicide, would make up the docket. Suits would not be apt to linger long. They did not erect a very large or very strong jail, for the culprit was apt to find himself speedily in the pillory or stocks, or at the whipping-post. I presume that few offenders escaped upon legal technicalities, or on the plea of insanity, for the administrators of the law were more likely to consult the dictates of primitive justice than the niceties of any written code or precedent.

CHAPTER VI

THE COURTHOUSE BUILT

The contract for building the courthouse was taken by John Whitsett, the County Treasurer, but for reasons not explained it was not finished until 1756, at which time the Court met in the building for the first time. Before this time the Court probably met in private houses, or in the public room of some convenient ordinary. At the second term of the Court, October, 1753, the Justices adjourned once to the house of James Alexander, and at another time afterwards to Peter Arrand's (Earnhardt?) ordinary. James Alexander seems to have been a resident of Salisbury, where he died in 1754. We conclude from this fact that the second term of the Court was held in Salisbury. And since the common gaol, pillory, and stocks were already up and in use in 1754, we have conclusive evidence that the Courts from and after that date were held near these public buildings. Tradition states that the old gaol building was located at or near the site of the present old gaol building, now standing at the northwest corner of Corbin and Liberty Streets. Arrangements were early made to secure suitable lands for the

Township of Salisbury

At the Court in 1753, Edward Hughes, Esq., was appointed trustee for Rowan County, and directed to "enter" forty acres of land, at the place selected for the "County Seat," and to see that a title was secured from Earl Granville's agents. At the same time, John Dunn, Esq., and John Whitsett, the Treasurer, were directed to see that the land was laid off in a manner suitable for the purpose intended. It appears that Mr. Hughes did not succeed in securing immediately the forty acres required by the Court, though some of the public buildings were at once erected. The deed for the Township lands is dated February 11, 1755. At that date William Churton and Richard Vigers, agents for Earl Granville, having received a grant from Francis Corbin, Granville's attorney—conveyed by deed *six hundred and thirty-five* (635) *acres* of land for "Salisbury Township," to James Carter, Esq., and Hugh Foster, farmer, trustees—including the land upon which the public buildings had been erected. The deed for the land calls for the following distances, *viz.*:

"BEGINNING at a point near the 'Public Square'—James Carter's corner, and running due east with James Carter's line, 66 chains; thence north 37¼ chains; thence west 103½ chains; thence east 37½ chains, crossing Crane Creek three times; thence north, 66 chains, crossing Crane Creek, to the beginning." The Township lands, the streets, and the streams are pretty fairly represented in the following diagram.

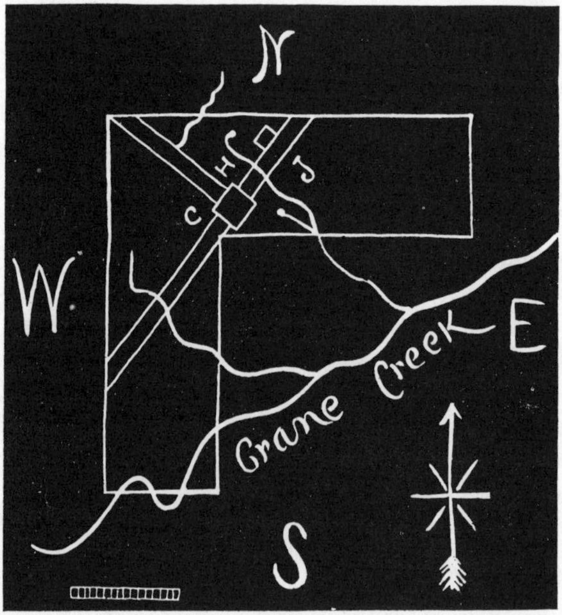

"The point near the public square, James Carter's Corner," appears from an old map of the town, drawn about fifty years ago, and now in the possession of Miss C. Beard, to have been in the middle of Corbin or Main Street, in front of the present store of R. J. Holmes.

It will be seen from the above diagram that several small streams took their rise in the Township lands, no doubt each of them much more bold than now, and flowing with pure and sweet water. As the Indians had for several years given place to the white settlers, and the practice of burning off the country employed by the Indians for the purpose of securing open hunting grounds having been suspended, the ground began to be covered by a beautiful young forest growth. Under the shelter of these young trees, and with the ground

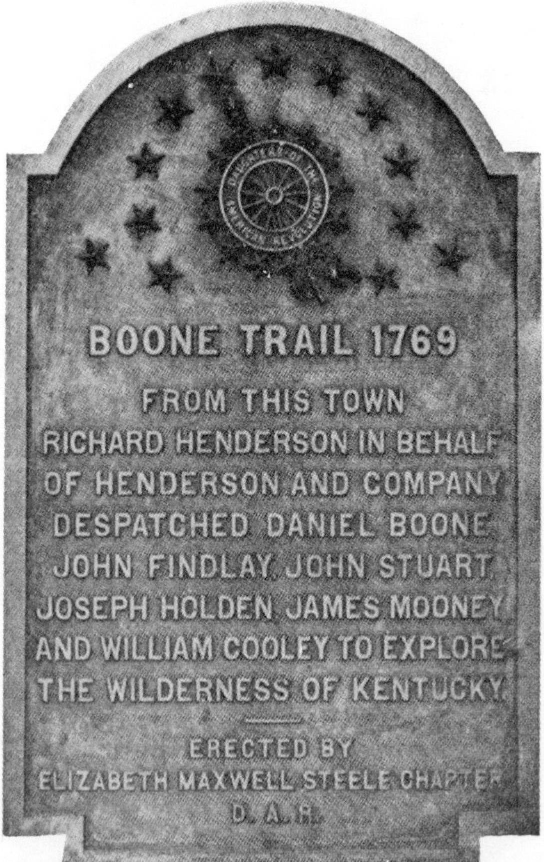
BOONE TRAIL 1769
FROM THIS TOWN
RICHARD HENDERSON IN BEHALF
OF HENDERSON AND COMPANY
DESPATCHED DANIEL BOONE
JOHN FINDLAY, JOHN STUART,
JOSEPH HOLDEN, JAMES MOONEY
AND WILLIAM COOLEY TO EXPLORE
THE WILDERNESS OF KENTUCKY.
ERECTED BY
ELIZABETH MAXWELL STEELE CHAPTER
D. A. R.

covered with luxuriant herbage, the streams were fuller and purer than in modern days. There is reported to have been a fine spring of water rising near the eastern corner of the Episcopal Church yard, with a stream flowing between the site of the present courthouse and jail. The tokens of former culverts are still to be seen near the courthouse. After crossing Corbin Street the stream was joined by another flowing from Franck's Spring. Here Jacob Franck, in 1756, obtained license to keep a village inn, and on this lot he afterwards run a distillery, for the benefit of those whose thirst could not be adequately quenched by the purer and wholesomer waters of his spring. No doubt many of the affrays and murders that claimed the attention of the Court took their origin in the firewater that was brewed in the boiling caldrons and flowed trickling down through the coiling worm of Jacob Franck's distillery, licensed and perhaps patronized by themselves. We notice that on several occasions the Court imposed fines upon jurymen who were not able to serve because of drunkenness. The distiller and vender reaped the profits, the Court had the trouble, and the citizens of the county had to bear the burden of the expense.

It is to be regretted that there is a propensity to change the names of places as time moves on. This is often a real inconvenience and a positive loss; for it not infrequently happens that lines and boundaries cannot be identified because of this change. The popular modern name for the stream that flows southeast of Salisbury is "Town Creek," but in the deed conveying the Township lands it is rightly called "Crane Creek," and the lines cross it four times. It is so called in Colonel Byrd's History of the Dividing Line. There are other deeds for lands higher up the stream that call it by that name. The next stream flowing on this side of Dunn's Mountain was anciently called "Middle Crane Creek."

Then again we always speak of "Main Street," forgetful or ignorant of the fact that the old deeds always speak of it as Corbin Street. It was named after Francis Corbin, Granville's attorney. It is not surprising, perhaps, that the older citizens should dislike to call the street after this grasping attorney who extorted illegal and exorbitant fees from the people, and who was once mobbed at Edenton for his extortion. Our modern town authorities have also taken the liberty of altering the spelling of James Innes' name, and we now see every day staring down upon the passerby, "Inniss Street." The signature of James Innes may now be seen in the Register's office to hundreds of deeds, and it is invariably written "Innes."

There were probably few private residences in Salisbury, and probably no inn, until 1755. In the fall of 1755, the Rev. Hugh McAden, a Presbyterian minister, on a missionary expedition, passed from the "Jersey Settlement" and over "Trading Ford" to James Allison's owning land, about four or five miles south of Salisbury on Crane Creek, but he made no call at Salisbury. Perhaps he followed the Trading Path, and so traveled up between the two branches of Crane Creek. Perhaps Mr. Sloan, from whose house in the "Jerseys" he came, knew of no Presbyterian family in the little village, and could not encourage him with the hope of congenial entertainment. At all events, duty or inclination led him to pass on to James Allison's, and from Mr. Allison's to John Brandon's, living on the west side of the plantation now owned by C. H. McKenzie, Esq. Thence he journeyed to Thyatira, to Coddle Creek, to Center, to Rocky River, to Sugar Creek, and on to the western part of South Carolina.

CHAPTER VII

EARLY SETTLERS IN SALISBURY

We have already mentioned James Alexander, who died here in 1754, as one of the first settlers in Salisbury. We have also mentioned the names of those who were licensed to keep ordinaries or taverns, in 1755-56, as John Ryle, John Louis Beard, Peter Arrand, Jacob Franck, Archibald Craige, James Bower, Thomas Bashford, and Robert Gillespie. Bashford and Gillespie seem to have been in copartnership, and bought up a number of lots in the town, evidently with the view of holding them until the growth of the town should enhance their value. In 1757 they purchased lots Nos. 3, 11, and 12 in the great "East Square," from Carter and Foster, trustees of the Township. These lots contained one hundred and forty-four square poles each, and on one of them they established a village inn.

Before leaving these early settlers, the reader must have a special introduction to a few of them who played a more conspicuous part in public affairs. The first of these is a sturdy German, by way of Pennsylvania, not yet naturalized. His name is

John Louis Beard

While he lingered in Pennsylvania, Mr. Beard was married to Miss Christina Snapp, of that Province. Coming to Salisbury, he was naturalized in 1755. While many of the German settlers, unacquainted with the English language, and therefore incapable of taking part in public affairs, were content to remain several years as aliens, and whose names therefore seldom appear on the public records, Mr. Beard, with a vigor that characterized his after life, immediately assumed his place as an active and energetic citizen. He did not at first settle within the corporate limits of the town, but opened up a farm on Crane Creek, near the Bringle's Ferry Road. He afterwards owned the lot on which the courthouse now stands, and erected a large dwelling-house thereon. In 1768, Mr. Beard was bereaved of a beloved daughter, and having laid her in a grave on a lot of his own, he made, the same year, a title to said lot of one hundred and forty square poles to certain trustees of the Evangelical Lutheran Church of Salisbury. These trustees were "to erect and build thereon a church, for the only proper use and behoof of the said German Lutheran congregation forever." He also granted in the deed the use of the church to the "High Church of England, and to the Reformed Calvin ministers, at such times as the said Lutheran minister doth not want to perform divine service in it." The "Reformed Calvin ministers" were probably the "German Reformed," who were intimately associated with the Lutherans, often using the same building. This lot given by Mr. Beard is the one known as the "Lutheran graveyard," on which formerly stood the Lutheran church. It is now sometimes called the "Salisbury Cemetery," and has been recently enclosed with a substantial brick wall by the united contributions of citizens of all denominations. Within its spacious enclosure and beneath its somber-hued cedars, sleeps the honored dust of multitudes of the once active and earnest citizens of Salisbury. Mr. Beard left a large family of sons and daughters, whose descendants are still among us.

Another early settler here, appearing at the session of the first Court, in June, 1753, was

John Dunn, Esq.

This gentleman was a native of Ireland, born at Waterford, and on his mother's side connected with the Erskine family. He was a younger brother, and was early sent to Oxford University, that he might prepare himself to carve out his own fortune. When he was about twenty years of age he left Oxford, and emigrated to America, landing in Charleston, S. C. After a brief residence there he came to Salisbury, where he spent the remainder of his life. He became in 1753 Clerk of the Court of Pleas and Quarter Sessions, which office he held until he became a licensed lawyer in 1755. His residence in Salisbury was on the corner of Innes and Church Streets, on the lot now occupied by Mr. P. B. Meroney. After the style of those days, the house was built as close to the street as possible. Here the writer saw a freedman, a few days ago, throw up old pieces of old bricks, as he was digging out a place in which to plant a sycamore tree—doubtless the debris of John Dunn's family residence, or perhaps the foundation of his law office. There is also a deed on record, from Earl Granville to John Dunn, dated June 10, 1758, for four hundred and seventy acres of land on the south branch of Middle Crane Creek, adjoining the lands of John Brandon. He purchased lot No. 5, in the East Square, of Carter and Foster, in 1755. He was also the owner of a large tract of land, including Dunn's Mountain, where he made his home after the Revolutionary war.

William Temple Coles

was another of the early settlers in Salisbury. He was a native of Dublin, Ireland, and was related to the Temple family. In Salisbury he was the proprietor or keeper of a tavern, situated on the corner of Corbin and Innes Streets, where Kluttz's drug store now stands—the same property that Paul Barringer purchased from Magoune in 1768. He was a Freemason, as he records himself. His Will, still on file in the Register's office, is something of a curiosity. He bequeaths to his wife, Sarah, four lots in the town of Salisbury—her choice from all his Salisbury lots. He leaves to his son, William Temple Coles, Jr., "the whole town of Salisbury," as conveyed to him by Foster, a former trustee. His furniture he left to his daughter, Henrietta Coles. He bequeathed a half-acre of ground in the South Square of Salisbury for a burying-ground, one-half of it to the Freemasons, and one-half to the citizens. This lot lay where the North Carolina Railroad track now is, where the Bank Street bridge crosses the said road. It is remembered that when the "cut" for the road was made many human bones were exposed. By what means the right of the citizens and of the Freemasons to said lot passed away we know not. Neither do we know exactly what claims Mr. Coles had to the "whole town of Salisbury." And what became of William Temple Coles, Jr., or Henrietta Coles, or where the elder Coles was buried, are questions more easily asked than answered.

Though not permanent residents of the County of Rowan, the names of James Innes and Francis Corbin were very familiar in the days of the early settlement of Salisbury. These were Earl Granville's land agents, and had in their hands the whole disposal of the lands in the Earl's vast estate. Mosely and Holten were the first agents, and after them Childs and Corbin. Hillsboro was first called Childsburg, after one of these agents. Upon the removal of Childs, the agents were Corbin and Innes. These gentlemen had an office on the corner of Innes and Church Streets, where the fountain in Mr. R. J. Holmes' yard now is, in close proximity to John Dunn's law office. Francis Corbin was a citizen of Chowan, and resided a few miles from Edenton. He is represented as an extortioner, charging exorbitant fees for his official acts. At one time ten or fifteen men of Halifax County arrested him and compelled him to give a bond that he would produce his books and return all money received by him above his proper fees. Instead of doing this he commenced a suit against the rioters, and some of them were lodged in the Enfield gaol. But on the next day the prison doors were broken down, and the prisoners liberated. Corbin then thought fit to discontinue the suit and pay costs.

James Innes was a citizen of Wilmington and a baron of the Court of Exchequer there. He was associated with Corbin in the Salisbury land office, and one of the principal streets was named after him. But even more prominent among our people were two brothers, who probably came to this county along with Francis Corbin from Halifax or Edenton. Their names were

John and Thomas Frohock

The name of John Frohock, in beautiful round hand, appears as "Court Clerk" on the records as early as 1756; and for a number of years after the large volumes of land titles of various kinds are recorded in the same beautiful hand, and authenticated over his signature. Step by step he grew very wealthy, chiefly, it would appear, by entering and selling public lands. The books are largely filled by conveyances either to him or from him. In his Will, dated 1768, and proved in 1772, there are named thousands of acres of land in Rowan County, in the forks of the Yadkin, near Salisbury, on Saxapahaw, on Tar River, and in Virginia, bequeathed by him to his two brothers, Thomas and William Frohock, besides thirty or forty slaves, one of which he liberated at death. He was once the owner of the lot on which the *Watchman* office and Crawford's hardware store now stands, and in a transfer of said lot between John Frohock and William Temple Coles, the street now called "Fisher Street" is called "Temple Street." He mentions neither wife nor child in his Will, and it is presumed that he was not married. Besides the kindness shown in the education and liberation of his body servant, Absalom, he expressly enjoins that his debtors should not be oppressed or sued, but ample time given to them to pay their debts to his executors. His brother William does not appear to have resided here, but had his home in Halifax, though one of his daughters married and settled in the vicinity of Salisbury.

Thomas Frohock

resided on what has been known as the McCay place, and inherited the mill and the lands adjoining from his brother, John Frohock, who was probably the builder of the mill—certainly the owner of it, and of all the lands lying between the town and Grant's Creek.

Dr. Caruthers designates Thomas Frohock as a "bachelor," but the evidence of his Will is to the contrary. His Will, in 1794, leaves his property to his son, Alexander Frohock, and to his daughter, Elizabeth, who was married to Charles Hunt, a merchant of Salisbury. There are two or three items of his history of peculiar interest. The first is that he gave to the town that lot now known as the "English Graveyard," or "Oak Grove Cemetery," and the schoolhouse lot immediately in front. The oldest stone in this yard is that of Capt. Daniel Little, who died in 1775, and was laid peacefully to rest just as the stormy days of the Revolutionary war were coming on. In this place, it is said that some of Gates' soldiers, after the battle of Camden, wounded there, or worn out in their flight, were buried. And here were interred some of the British soldiers, who died in 1781 during the time that Cornwallis occupied Salisbury. The graveyard lay unenclosed until about fifty years ago, when William Gay, the father of the late Mrs. Mary Brown, left a legacy for the purpose of enclosing it. With the proceeds, a wooden paling or plank fence was put around it, and renewed from time to time until, in 1855, the present substantial granite wall was erected by the voluntary contributions of the citizens of this town.

Another matter mentioned by Caruthers, in his Life of Caldwell (page 114), is that "Thomas Frohock in Salisbury, and Edmund Fanning in Hillsboro, were Clerks of the Superior Courts in their respective counties, and had become exceedingly obnoxious to the people by their extortions." * * * "It is said that Frohock charged fifteen dollars for a marriage license; and the consequence was that some of the inhabitants on the headwaters of the Yadkin took a short cut. They took each other for better or for worse; and considered themselves as married without any further ceremony." In his last Will, Thomas Frohock enjoins upon his executors to pay all his just debts of under three years' standing, but to plead the "statute of limitation" upon all claims older than that, whenever they could.

A constant tradition represents that Thomas Frohock lies buried in an unmarked grave on the hillside, within two hundred yards of McCays—once Frohock's—mill.

It is now one hundred years since these old citizens, Dunn, Beard, Coles, Corbin, Innes, John and Thomas Frohock, lived and acted their part in the ancient Township of Salisbury. Now their names are never heard except as the antiquarian rummages among the dusty records of a bygone generation, or questions some old citizen whose memory is stored with the traditions of the past. The places that knew them once will know them no more forever.

CHAPTER VIII

CHARTER REGULATIONS

In modern days towns and cities rise like mushrooms along the lines of railways, or in the regions of the great West. But the growth of towns at the early settlement of this country was a much more gradual thing. The people did not originally come to this section with the view of making fortunes by trade, nor by the possession of lucrative offices, but to earn a living by the simpler process of cultivating the soil or by mechanical pursuits. They were not therefore disposed to congregate in towns, but to scatter far and wide, where the most fertile lands were to be found, where game was most abundant, or where they supposed they would enjoy the best health. For many years therefore the towns were composed of the public buildings, the residences of some of the county officials, a store or two, a hatter shop, a blacksmith shop, a tailor shop, and a few inns or ordinaries furnishing "entertainment for man or beast." "Hotel" was an unknown word among those people, who had not yet learned to disguise an English article under a French name. It required a half-century for the population to increase to five hundred; for it was about 1803 that Salisbury is represented as containing one hundred houses, and the custom is to estimate five inhabitants to each house. And yet the little village at once became a point of importance as the place where the Courts of Oyer and Terminer and General Gaol Delivery, for the counties of Anson, Mecklenburg, and Rowan, were held.

The Court system of North Carolina adopted in 1746 (See Swan's Revisal, pp. 224-25) provided that the "Court of Chancery, and the Supreme or General Court," should be held in Newbern, where the Chancery and other offices were to be located. Besides this Court, the Chief Justice was required, twice every year, to hold a "Court of Assize, Oyer and Terminer and General Gaol Delivery," in the towns of Edenton and Wilmington, and the courthouse in Edgecombe.

After the erection of Anson, Rowan, and Orange Counties, it appears that Salisbury was added as a fourth place for holding such Courts. At least the earliest records (dated 1755) in Rowan courthouse show that such a Court was held here. And as about twenty leaves or more are torn off from the first part of the record, it is probable that there were earlier Courts. In 1756, the Hon. Peter Henly presided at such a Court here, for Rowan, Anson, and Orange, with Charles Elliott, Esq., as Attorney-General. In 1758, the Hon. James Hasell, Chief Justice, presided. At the next Court, Marmaduke Jones, Esq., Associate Justice, presided, with Edmund Fanning, Esq., Attorney for the King, and John Frohock, Esq., Clerk. At this Court, Abner Nash, Esq., produced his license from Governor Dobbs to practice as a lawyer in the Province.

In 1762 "a Superior Court was held here, presided over by the Hon. Stephen Dewey, a Justice of the Superior Courts of Pleas and Grand Sessions." In 1763, Maurice Moore, Esq., Associate Judge, with Edmund Fanning, Esq., Attorney-General, and John Frohock, Clerk, officiated at a Court in Salisbury. These extracts and references reveal the fact that, soon after the organization of Rowan County, Salisbury became a center in the Court system of Western Carolina, and to this, among other causes, is to be attributed the fact that she was the most prominent and populous town in the West. This prominence continued until the modern railroad system superseded the Court system in influence, and fixing the centers of trade elsewhere built up other thriving and populous towns, which have outstripped Salisbury in the rapidity of their growth.

The Superior Courts were established by Act of the General Assembly at Newbern, in the year 1766, during the administration of Governor Tryon. The State was divided into six districts, viz.: Wilmington, Newbern, Edenton, Halifax, Hillsboro, and Salisbury districts, the latter embracing the counties above named. These Courts were presided over by a Chief Justice and two Associate Justices, appointed by the Governor. The Clerks of these Courts were appointed by the Chief Justice. The Chief Justice, by act of 1770, was to receive a salary of six hundred pounds (£600), and also the sum of fifty pounds (£50) for each Court he attended, while the Associate Justices, by act of 1766, received forty-one pounds (£41) for each Court attended; that is, about one hundred dollars, specie, for each Court; or, for the twelve Courts, twelve hundred dollars per annum. The salary of the Chief Justice would be about equal to thirty-three hundred dollars, in specie.

At its first establishment the little village of Salisbury was not provided with a Charter or municipal government, nor for twelve or fifteen years afterwards. But in 1770 an Act was passed by the Assembly for "Regulating the Town of Salisbury." The preamble states that Salisbury is a "healthy, pleasant situation, well watered, and convenient for inland trade." Even at that early day Frohock's—afterwards called McCay's—millpond was in existence, and no doubt the deadly miasma rose from its broad surface of nearly a square mile in area, for we learn that Mr. Frohock's residence on a hill on the southeast side of the pond, in later years called "The Castle," was regarded as an unhealthful place, and many of his slaves died annually of the fever. But the pond was separated from Salisbury by a forest growth, whose leafy branches absorbed or dissipated the noxious exhalations, so that for many years, even up to the present century, the town was resorted to for health by people from the lower portions of the State. And it is a happy circumstance that, after standing for over a hundred years, its present owners generously consented to cut the huge embankment and drain off the festering waters. Thus for the last half-dozen years the city is restored to its ancient condition of healthfulness, and the people from a warmer climate again begin to resort here, even in the summer time, without fear, especially those who desire to secure the benefit of the skill of our most excellent physicians.

The Common

It was customary for the towns in England to have a "Common" or open tract of public land in their immediate vicinity, where the cattle might graze at will, where the children might play, and the gatherings of the citizens be held on extraordinary occasions. In accordance with this custom, the Act of the Assembly specifies a "Common" in connection with the town of Salisbury. Its precise locality has been difficult to determine, but the Act appears to describe it as lying "on each side of the Western Great Road leading through the frontiers of this Province." If this "Western Great Road" was Beattie's Ford Road of modern days, crossing Grant's Creek at the bridge near the head of McCay's pond, the said road ran through the westward of town, leaving Corbin Street with "Temple" or Fisher Street, running diagonally through the square occupied by the late Dr. Jos. W. Hall, and back of the residence of the late Judge Caldwell—now the residence of M. L. Holmes. The "Common" on each side of this road would include the square now occupied by the grounds of the Presbyterian manse, and the spring that was anciently on it, as well as the spring at the head of the stream starting behind Paul Heilig's residence, and running through the grounds of the "National Cemetery." Persons still living remember when these grounds were unoccupied and covered with small oaks and chinquapin bushes. In a plan of the town made about sixty years ago, now lying before the writer, these lots are marked as belonging to Troy, Chambers, Caldwell, Thomas Dixon, H. C. Jones, Dr. Polk, John Beard, Louis Beard, Lauman, Brown, Woodson, etc. These lots, originally constituting the Common, had probably been recently sold, perhaps as a financial enterprise to relieve the town of some unfortunate debt, or to carry out some promising scheme of internal improvement that was destined never to see light. It is a matter of profound astonishment that town corporations will part with grounds that would make desirable parks or breathing places, for a mere trifle, and condemn the citizens to live in a long, unbroken line of houses, unrelieved by shade, when they might so easily retain a Common or Park, where the inhabitants might resort at will in summer weather, and refresh themselves by breathing the pure air that comes whispering through the rustling leaves of the trees. It is really more difficult, in some of our larger towns, to escape from the dust and glare of the streets and painted houses into a pleasant and shady retreat, than it is in the great cities where the land is worth hundreds of dollars per square yard.

The Act provides that all inhabitants of Salisbury shall have free access to all natural springs and fountains, whether on private lots or on the Common, and that it was lawful for anyone to "cut and fell," and appropriate to his own use, any tree or trees standing on the Town Common." That was before the exquisite poem, beginning "Woodman, Spare That Tree," was composed, and the early inhabitants were more anxious to enjoy their liberties, and to have an open grazing place for their cattle, than to have a shady park for public resort.

It is worthy of notice that a strict "hog law" prevailed in the sylvan shades of the ancient borough of Salisbury. Cows were indeed a privileged class, and might roam at will over the streets and Common, but it was enacted that "no inhabitants of said town shall, on any pretense whatsoever, keep any hog or hogs, shoat or pigs, running at large within the corporate limits of said town, under a penalty of twenty shillings," while anyone had the right to "shoot, kill, or destroy" the offending pig at sight. As a protection against fire, every householder was required to keep a ladder, and two good leather buckets. Fast riding and fast driving incurred a penalty of five shillings for each offense. It further appears that the pioneer settlers were provided with a market-house for the mutual benefit of the buyer and seller.

Taking them all in all, the municipal regulations of 1770 were good and wholesome, and in some particulars might still stand as models.

The gentlemen who were authorized, as Town Commissioners, to put these regulations into execution were prominent citizens, selected for their standing and their fitness for the high trust, and were generally the owners of a large real estate in the town. The list is as follows: William Steel, John Dunn, Maxwell Chambers, John Louis Beard, Thomas Frohock, Wm. Temple Coles, Matthew Troy, Peter Rep, James Kerr, Alexander Martin, and Daniel Little. These Commissioners were appointed by the General Assembly, and in case of a vacancy, the place was to be supplied by appointment of the Justices of the Rowan Inferior Court. Holding their offices for a term of years, or during life, these Commissioners would be able to mature and carry out extended schemes of improvement, without having before their eyes the constant fear of being left out the next year if they should chance to offend any of the people by the conscientious and faithful discharge of unpopular duties. This was the conservatism of monarchy, and doubtless it had its evils as well as the fickleness and instability of popular democracy. Perhaps the best results would be secured by a policy lying between these two extremes.

CHAPTER IX

RELIGION AND CHURCHES, WITH A RESUMÉ OF THE PARISH LAWS

The early settlers of Rowan County were religious people. The Presbyterians, of Scotch-Irish extraction, were probably the most numerous in the section now comprising Guilford County, in the Jersey Settlement, in Western Rowan and Iredell counties. The Lutherans and German Reformed (the latter sometimes called Calvin congregations, and Presbyterians), prevailed in parts of Guilford, Davidson, East and South Rowan, and Catawba Counties. I name the regions as they are now known, but they were all then in Rowan. In Davidson and Randolph there were Baptist churches. In Salisbury, in the "Jerseys," and elsewhere, there were some members of the Church of England. It is probable that William Temple Coles and his family, John Dunn, perhaps Corbin and Innes and the Frohocks were attached to that communion. We infer this simply from their nativity and their connection with Earl Granville and Governor Dobbs, as agents or officers of the crown. In regard to Dunn we have a more certain tradition, as we shall hereafter mention. It will be remembered that

St. Luke's Parish

was established contemporaneously with the county, as a part of the great system of government here wrought out, or attempted; as nearly conformed to the system of the mother country as practicable. During the administration of Governor Dobbs—in 1754, according to Wheeler—ten years later according to other authorities (See Wheeler, p. 357; Caruthers' Caldwell, p. 175), steps were taken to provide for the ministry of the word according to the rubric of the Church of England. A petition, signed by thirty-four persons in the County of Rowan, and addressed to Governor Dobbs, represents: "That His Majesty's most dutiful and loyal subjects in this county, who adhere to the liturgy and profess the doctrines of the Church of England, as by law established, have not the privileges and advantages which the rubric and canons of the Church allow and enjoin on all its members. That the Acts of the Assembly calculated for forming a regular vestry in all the counties have never, in this county, produced their happy fruits. That the County of Rowan, above all counties in the Province, lies under great disadvantages, as her inhabitants are composed almost of all nations of Europe, and instead of a uniformity in doctrine and worship, they have a medley of most of the religious tenets that have lately appeared in the world; who from dread of submitting to the national Church, should a lawful vestry be established, elect such of their own community as evade the Acts of the Assembly and refuse the oath, whence we can never expect the regular enlivening beams of the holy Gospel to shine upon us."

From the fact that there were only thirty-four signers to this petition from the vast territory of Rowan, we may naturally infer that the population in those days was hopelessly plunged into "Dissent." And yet it was the purpose of the far-away rulers of England, and of the North Carolina Assembly, to have the Province conform as far as possible to the ecclesiastical system at home. And so the parish system of England, as far as practicable, was incorporated in the system of North Carolina law. What that system was, can be gathered from a voluminous Act, of thirty-three sections, passed by the General Assembly at Wilmington in 1764. Other Acts and regulations of the same general tenor had been adopted on various occasions before, but the Act of 1764—with a supplementary one in 1765—is the most full, and gives an impartial view of the system as perfected, just before the final downfall of the whole scheme at the Declaration of Independence in 1776. I will endeavor to give an impartial resumé of the parish system.

According to this "Act" the Freeholders of each county, on Easter Monday of every third year, were required to elect twelve vestrymen to hold said office for the term of three years. A "Freeholder" according to existing laws was a person who owned at least fifty acres of land, or a lot in some town. These Freeholders were required to vote for vestrymen under a penalty of twenty shillings—equal to two dollars and fifty cents in specie—and the vestrymen so elected were required to subscribe an oath that "they will not oppose the doctrine, discipline, and liturgy of the Church of England, as by law established"; and in case of refusal to qualify, any vestryman-elect was to be declared incapable of acting in that capacity. Out of the twelve vestrymen two church wardens were to be chosen, who were required to hold office at least one year, under a penalty of forty shillings, equal to five dollars in specie or sterling money, and they were to forfeit five pounds (£5) if they did not set up their accounts for public inspection in the courthouse. These vestries might appoint one or more clerks, or readers, to perform divine service at such places as they might designate.

The vestry were also empowered to lay a tax of ten shillings, proclamation money, on each "taxable" in the county, for the purpose of building churches or chapels, paying ministers' salaries, purchasing a glebe, erecting "mansions or parsonages," etc.

"Taxables," as we gather from another Act, were all white male persons over sixteen years of age, all negroes, mulattoes, and mustees, both male and female, over twelve years of age, and all white persons male and female over twelve years of age who intermarried with negroes or persons of mixed blood. Such a tax, faithfully collected, would have yielded an immense revenue for the support of religion. Being a poll tax, and not a property tax, it fell heavily upon the poor, and lightly on the rich. The tax thus levied was to be collected by the sheriff, as the other taxes, and paid over to the vestry; and in case of refusal, the sheriff was required to "distrain" the goods of the delinquent and sell them at public auction, after publishing the sale by posting it on the courthouse door, the church door, and by public announcement to the people immediately after divine service. (See Davis' Revisal of North Carolina Laws, Edition 1773, pp. 304, 309.)

By an "Act" passed in 1765, during the administration of William Tryon as Lieutenant-Governor, and called an "Act for establishing an orthodox clergy," it was provided that every minister of a parish was to receive a stated salary of £133, 6s., 8d., and for each marriage solemnized in the parish, whether he performed the ceremony or not, provided he did not refuse, twenty shillings; for preaching each funeral, forty shillings. In addition to this he was to have the free use of a "mansion house" and "glebe," or "tract of good land" of at least two hundred acres, or twenty pounds (£20) additional until such time as the "mansion house" and "glebe" were provided. The "mansion house was required to be thirty-eight feet in length, and eighteen feet in width, and to be accompanied with a kitchen, barn, stable, dairy, and meathouse, with such other conveniences as they may think necessary." (See Davis' Revisal, 1773, pp. 338-39.) From this it will appear that the Assembly of North Carolina made a fair and liberal provision for the support of her parish ministers, and with the exception of the glebe, which he need not cultivate himself, rendered him "free from worldly cares and avocations." But the difficulty lay in putting these regulations into effect. In Governor Dobb's letter to the "Society for the Propagation of the Gospel in Foreign Parts," he informs the Society, in 1764, that in North Carolina "there were then but six clergymen, though there were twenty-nine parishes, and each parish contained a whole county." (Rev. R. J. Miller's letter to Dr. Hawks, 1830.) The fact was that a large part of the population were "Dissenters," and they resisted every effort to settle a parish minister over them, and thus refused to subject themselves to additional taxation. In Unity Parish, in Guilford County, the people elected non-Episcopalians for vestrymen, and it became necessary for the Assembly to dissolve the vestry and declare their actions null and void. (See Caruthers' "Caldwell.")

But let Parson Miller, in the letter above referred to, tell how matters were conducted in Rowan County, and in Salisbury especially. He says: "Subsequently to the year 1768, the Rev. Mr. (Theodore Drane) Draig came to Salisbury, in Rowan County, which was then St. Luke's Parish, and so far succeeded as to be able to have a small chapel erected in what is called the Jersey Settlement, about nine or ten miles east of Salisbury. But the opposition made to his settlement as rector of that parish, by the Presbyterians, was so very rancorous as to raise great animosity in their minds against all his endeavors to that end—they being far the most numerous body, having several large congregations well organized in the adjacent counties, and one of them in the vicinity of Salisbury. I well remember an anecdote told me by Dr. Newman [and] John Cowan, Sr., in their lifetime, and indeed by several others in the vicinity of Salisbury, some of whom may yet be living: 'That on Easter Monday, when an election according to the then law of the Province was to be held for the purpose of electing vestrymen, the Presbyterians set up candidates of their own persuasion and elected them, not with any design either to serve or act as vestrymen, but merely to prevent the Episcopalians from electing such as would have done so.' This caused much bitter animosity to spring up between the parties, and so, much discouraged the reverend gentleman. Perhaps the approach of the Revolutionary War had its influence also; but be that as it may, after a four years' fruitless effort to organize an Episcopal congregation in this section, he left it as he found it, without any" (Rev. Mr. Miller's letter in *Church Messenger,* October 15, 1879). A full sketch of each of the churches of Salisbury will be furnished in the future chapters, but so much was deemed necessary here, to give a glimpse of the early days before the Revolution. To the stirring times immediately preceding the great struggle for American liberty we must now direct our attention, for Rowan County was rather before than behind her neighbors in that struggle, as the record will show.

CHAPTER X

THE INDIAN WARS; SCHOOLS; SOCIAL LIFE

Though the Indians had retreated from the lands occupied by the whites, yet they still continued upon the frontiers, and both in peace and war were often seen in the "settlements." On the records of the Rowan County Court, about 1756, there is an account of a visit from a party of Indians, one a Sapona Indian, another a Susquehanna Indian, who were passing through Salisbury on their way to the Catawbas. Their object was to conclude a treaty of peace with the latter, and they asked that a "pass" be granted to them, and as a token of their good will they left a "belt," or "string" of "wampum," in the hands of the Clerk of the Court. But their visits were not all of such a peaceful character. The terrible war-whoop sometimes rang out in the dead hours of the night, and families of settlers were mercilessly slaughtered, or carried off to a hopeless captivity beyond the mountains, west of the Blue Ridge.

Where the shadows of the giant mountain-peaks lingered longest in the morning, lived the powerful and warlike Cherokees. Bancroft, in language that beautifully describes the scenery of that region, thus pictures the land of the Cherokees. "Their homes were encircled by blue hills rising beyond hills, of which the lofty peaks would kindle with the early light, and the overshadowing ridges envelop the valleys like a mass of clouds. There the rocky cliffs, rising in naked grandeur, defy the lightning, and mock the loudest peals of the thunderstorm; there the gentler slopes are covered with magnolias and flowering forest trees, decorated with roving climbers, and ring with the perpetual note of the whippoorwill; there the wholesome water gushes profusely from the earth in transparent springs; snow-white cascades glitter on the hillsides; and the rivers, shallow, but pleasant to the eye, rush through the narrow vales, which the abundant strawberry crimsons, and coppices of rhododendron and flaming azalea adorn. At the fall of the leaf, the fruit of the hickory and the chestnut is thickly strewn on the ground. The fertile soil teems with luxuriant herbage on which the roe-buck fattens; the vivifying breeze is laden with fragrance; and daybreak is welcomed by the shrill cries of the social nighthawk and the liquid carols of the mocking-bird. Through this lovely region were scattered the little villages of the Cherokees, nearly fifty in number, each consisting of but a few cabins, erected where the bend in the mountain stream affords at once a defense and a strip of alluvial soil for culture." (History United States, Volume 3, pp. 246-47).

In 1759 the whole frontier of the Southern Provinces was threatened by the savages, and the Indian scalping knife had already begun its bloody work upon the unsuspecting borderers. After the reduction of the French forts of Frontenac and Duquesne by the American forces, the Cherokees, who were allies of the Americans, on their return home, appropriated some horses to their own use from the pastures of the Virginia settlers. Upon this the Virginians rose against them and slew twelve or fourteen of their warriors. This ill-advised severity aroused the whole nation, and the young warriors flew to arms, and began an indiscriminate slaughter of the white settlers. Governor Littleton of South Carolina promptly called out the troops of the State, and in this campaign young Francis Marion first fleshed his maiden sword. Col. Hugh Waddell, of Belmont, Bladen County, N. C., was sent to the West to aid in holding the Indians in check. His headquarters were in Salisbury, while his troops ranged through the foothills of the Blue Ridge. Under his direction Fort Dobbs, on the headwaters of the South Yadkin, near Statesville, was erected, and Fort Tellico appears to have been another outpost in the same region of country. Colonel Waddell, though not a citizen of Rowan County, spent a considerable portion of his time in the neighborhood of Salisbury, and was the owner of a large amount of lands in the county, including a town lot, over six hundred acres on the south side of Fourth Creek, and about seven hundred acres adjoining the south line of the Salisbury Township lands, on both sides of Crane Creek. His Fourth Creek lands he sold in 1767 to Walter Lindsay, Esq., and his lands near Salisbury were sold in 1793 to Conrad Brem and Louis Beard.

At the defeat of General Braddock, in 1755, Major Hugh Waddell appears as the commander of two Companies of North Carolina troops, and in the expedition against Fort Duquesne, in 1758, Major Waddell with some North Carolina troops served under General Washington. It was a North Carolina soldier, named John Rodgers, a sergeant-major in Waddell's troops, that captured the Indian whose information led to the attack on and subsequent abandonment of that celebrated fort at the junction of the Monongahela and Allegheny Rivers, where Pittsburgh now stands. Rodgers obtained a reward from the Assembly of North Carolina for his meritorious services.

In 1759, Col. Hugh Waddell, with all the provincials and all the militia of Orange, Anson, and Rowan Counties, joined with the troops of South Carolina in an expedition against the Cherokees. Fort Prince George, on the banks of the Isundaga River, within gunshot of the Indian town of Keowee, was the place of rendezvous for the North Carolina forces. The Chief of the Cherokees, Atta Calla Culla, alarmed at the approach of so numerous an army, sued for peace, and a treaty was concluded. Colonel Waddell returned home, where with five hundred militia kept in constant service he protected the frontier from the incursions of the Cherokees, whose hostility still manifested itself on every suitable occasion, notwithstanding the treaty of peace.

Society and Schools

Such was the condition of the inhabitants of Western North Carolina from its first settlement, about 1745, up to the period of the Revolution. Moore, in his History of North Carolina, describing this period of time, with great truth and force says: "Life in the eastern counties was full of pleasure and profit. The Indians, save those of King Blunt on the Roanoke, were all gone toward the setting sun. The rude cabins of the first settlers had been replaced by brick or framed houses. Hospitality was unbounded, and the weddings and other social gatherings were largely attended. West India rum and the negro fiddlers added charms to the midnight revel. The strict morals of the Puritans and Quakers did not prevail in the Albemarle region. The curled and powdered gentlemen, and the ladies with their big hoops, were never so well pleased as when walking a minuet or betting at a rubber of whist. Horse races and the pursuit of the fox were also in high favor as pastimes. Very different were the men of Rowan, Orange, and Cumberland. Swarms of Cherokee warriors were just beyond the Blue Ridge Mountains, and death by the tomahawk was possible at any moment. Long persecution had stimulated the zeal and enthusiasm of the Scotch-Irish, until religious devotion became the absorbing habit of whole communities. The log churches were to them almost what Solomon's temple had been to the Jews. The ministers in charge and the ruling elders were followed implicitly, both in matters of church and State" (School History, p. 37). Those were the days from 1758 until 1766, when the Rev. Alexander Craighead resided in Mecklenburg County, but extended his labors to the settlements of Rowan, and laid the foundation of Thyatira, Fourth Creek, and Center

Churches. The inhabitants, being of that respectable middle class of society, equally removed from the cultivated vices of the rich and from the ignorant meannesses of the abject poor, generally possessed the rudiments of an English education, and could "read and write, and cipher as far as the Single Rule of Three' with considerable accuracy. The German settlers brought their Luther's translation of the Bible along with them, and their "Gemainschaftliches Gesangbuch," or Union Hymn Book, adapted to the wants of both Lutherans and German Reformed. In those days the "old-field schools" were established, and taught by some citizen whose knowledge of letters was something above the average. They obtained the name of "old-field" schools because they were frequently built on or near an old field or other open piece of ground. The open ground furnished a fine place for the games of the boys, such as "town-ball," "bull-pen," "cat," or "prisoner's base," while on its edge the rosy-cheeked lasses enjoyed themselves with the less laborious games of "blind-man's-buff," "drop-the-handkerchief," "fox-and-geese," "barley-bright," and "chichama-chichama-craney-crow." The passing traveler could easily identify the log schoolhouse, by the bell-like tones of mingled voices of the boys and girls as they studied their spelling and reading lessons aloud—sometimes rendering the schoolroom a very babel of confused sounds. As the weather grew warmer—if the school did not close up for the summer—the children would devote themselves to the gentler games of marbles, mumble-peg, or housekeeping in leafy arbors, with moss carpets, beneath the spreading branches of the trees.

Academies

But the people were not content with the common "old-field school." About 1760 a classical school was established at Bellemont, near Col. Alex. Osborne's residence, called the "Crowfield Academy." The location is about two miles north of Davidson College, on the headwaters of Rocky River, and in the bounds of Center congregation. Here a number of distinguished men, who acted well their part in their day, received their education, or were prepared for college. Among these were Col. Adlai Osborne, who was for a long time Clerk of Rowan Superior Court, and a leading man in the Rowan Committee of Safety at the opening of the Revolution. Dr. Samuel Eusebius McCorkle, the pastor of Thyatira and preacher in Salisbury, and who for a long time conducted the "Zion-Parnassus Academy," near Thyatira, also began his classical studies at

"Crowfield." Dr. James Hall, the soldier-preacher of the Revolution, the founder and conductor of "Clio's Nursery School," on the headwaters of South Yadkin, began his literary course at this same institution. The same is true in regard to Dr. Ephraim Brevard, who is said to be the author of the Mecklenburg Declaration of May 20, 1775. The Rev. David Caldwell, about 1766, is said to have taught in the Crowfield Academy for a short season. But he soon removed to northeastern Rowan—now Guilford—where after a short time he established a school on the headwaters of North Buffalo, about three miles from where Greensboro now stands. This school was in operation ten years before the Declaration of Independence, and also a number of years after, and it is computed that there were about fifty ministers, besides a large number who entered the other liberal professions, who were educated at this "Log College" of North Carolina. The old-field schools and a few classical academies comprised the educational facilities of Western North Carolina at this time. But those whose means would allow it were sent to complete their education at Princeton, or "Nassau Hall," as it was then called. There, under the instructions of President Witherspoon—the clerical signer of the National Declaration of Independence—they imbibed not only a knowledge of the liberal arts and sciences, but also the principles of liberty and independence, which brought forth such rich fruit a few years afterwards.

CHAPTER XI

"THE REGULATION"

The echoes of the Indian war-whoop had not died away before the mutterings of another storm was heard over the hills and valleys of Orange and Rowan Counties. This is what is known in the history of North Carolina as the war of "THE REGULATION." It can scarcely be called a war, and yet it rises above the dignity of a riot. It was rather the first blind, unorganized rising of the spirit of liberty against a long train of oppressive acts, for which there was no remedy and of which there appeared to be no end. As the men of Rowan were to some extent connected with this struggle, some on each side, it will not be amiss to give a brief sketch of its rise and sad termination—though a detailed account would exceed the limits proposed in these papers.

As the first factor in this problem we have a liberty-loving population, who came to the wilds of North Carolina for the express purpose of escaping from political and ecclesiastical oppression. Such were the early refugees from Virginia, who settled on the Albemarle Sound; such the hardy Scotch who came from the Highlands to the banks of the Cape Fear; such the Swiss and Palatines on the Neuse and Trent; and in a peculiar sense were the Scotch-Irish and Germans of ancient Rowan, Orange, and Mecklenburg. These, or their fathers, had once felt the weight of the oppressor's iron hand, crushing out their liberties—almost their manhood; and having once suffered they were jealous of the approaches of tyranny in their new homes.

As the next factor we have the most wretched system of misgovernment of modern times. This misgovernment began with the cumbrous and Utopian Constitution prepared by Locke and Shaftesbury, having in it the germs of a provincial nobility—landgraves and caciques—totally uncongenial to the wild and free spirit of the people. And such governors as Seth Sothel, George Burrington, and Richard Everard were a reproach to humanity and a stench in the nostrils of decency. The testy and prosy Irishman, Governor Dobbs, the warlike and ambitious Tryon, and the incapable Josiah Martin, who enacted the last scenes in the drama of the royal government, were peculiarly calculated to irritate and annoy the people, to aggravate and sting to rebellion a population far less independent and intelligent than the inhabitants of North Carolina. Nor could the prudence of such governors as Drummond, Archdale, and Johnstone counteract the deep-seated opposition of the people to the oppressive and tyrannical legislation dictated by the royal cabinet of England, and enacted by an obsequious Colonial Legislature.

The struggle between the Province of North Carolina and its foreign rulers began one hundred years before the yoke was thrown off—in 1669, when the "Grand Model" was forced upon an unwilling people, and when the obnoxious *Navigation Act* crippled and strangled the commerce of the infant colony. The struggle became more serious, when the "Parish Laws" were enacted, disallowing all marriages to be celebrated by dissenting ministers, and taxing the country for the support of a religious system which was distasteful to an overwhelming majority of the people. The obstinancy and nepotism of Governor Dobbs added fuel to the flame. Governor Tryon was not a bigot, but his tastes and his expenses were princely. Aided by the blandishment of his elegant wife and her bewitching sister, Miss Esther Wake, Tryon secured from the cringing General Assembly an appropriation of fifteen thousand pounds (£15,000), equal to nearly seventy-five thousand dollars, for the erection of a palace at Newbern more suitable for a prince of the blood royal than for the governor of an infant provincial colony. This palace was said to exceed in magnificence any structure of that day found upon the American continent, and its erection rendered a large increase of the taxes necessary. But Tryon never did things by halves. He must needs make a military expedition to the land of the Cherokees, in order to run a dividing line of a few miles in length, and returned with the significant title, bestowed by the Indians, of "THE GREAT WOLF OF NORTH CAROLINA." All this was very expensive, and to supply the means, not only were the direct taxes increased, but the governor required a share of the fees allowed to the various crown officials for their services. The crown officers, in their turn, taking the cue from the Governor, doubled or tripled their charges for every act done for the people. The lawyers also refused to serve their clients for the established fees, and thus closed up all the avenues to the temple of justice. In this emergency there arose the two persons necessary to bring on a collision. These two persons were a poet or ballad-monger, and a popular leader. The rhymester was named Rednap Howell, a native of New Jersey, who occupied the position of old-field schoolmaster somewhere on Deep River. He was the author of about forty songs or ballads, in which he mercilessly lampooned the extortioners and crown officers of the day.

Prominent among these were Edmund Fanning, Esq., of Hillsboro, the Court Clerk, and son-in-law of Governor Tryon, and John Frohock, Clerk and Register in Salisbury. The following effusion of Howell's upon these two officers affords a fair specimen of his political rhymes.

Says Frohock to Fanning, "To tell the plain truth,
When I came to this country I was but a youth.
My father sent for me: I wa'nt worth a cross,
And then my first study was to steal for a horse.
I quickly got credit, and then ran away,
And haven't paid for him to this very day."

Says Fanning to Frohock, " 'Tis folly to lie,
I rode an old mare that was blind of an eye:
Five shillings in money I had in my purse;
My coat, it was patched, but not much the worse;
But now we've got rich, and it's very well known,
That we'll do very well if they'll let us alone."

By such rhymes as these, sung and repeated from plantation to plantation, from the Eno to the Yadkin; called for at every house-raising, log-rolling, and corn-shucking, at every Court and vendue, at every wedding and funeral, the minds of the people were wrought up to a high pitch of excitement and indignation against the crown officers and the lawyers.

When this leaven had worked sufficiently, a popular leader arose in the person of Herman Husbands, from Sandy Creek, near the line between Guilford and Rowan—now in Randolph County. Husbands was by birth a Pennsylvania Quaker, and said to have been a relative of Benjamin Franklin. He possessed great shrewdness of character, a naturally vigorous mind, and by boldly protesting against extortion upon all occasions he won the regard of the multitude. By the influence, and under the guidance of this man, many of the people of Orange were induced to associate themselves together in bands, sometimes called "the mob," sometimes the "Sons of Liberty," and at last the "Regulators." The first general or public meeting of Regulators was held at Maddock's Mill, in Orange County, October 10, 1766. They proposed to consult concerning their grievances and the proper mode of securing redress. Fanning and other crown officers were invited to be present, but refused to come, on some pretext or other. From this time sympathy with the "Sons of Liberty" spread far and wide, and many people, not only in Orange and Guilford, but in Rowan, Mecklenburg, and Anson Counties, were ready to venture into the same perilous path. They first stated their grievances to the Governor, and appealed to him for relief. He promised what they asked, and ordered a schedule of fees to be made out and posted up for public inspection. But the officers laughed in their sleeves at the gullibility of the people, and went on demanding the same or larger fees. At last a true bill was found against Edmund Fanning, for extortion in no less than six instances. When the trial came on at Hillsboro, in 1768, Fanning pleaded guilty in each count, and was fined—*six pence and costs.* Such a mockery of justice, under the very eye of Tryon—for he was present—and in the case of his son-in-law, plainly demonstrated that no relief was to be expected from the Courts of Justice. The very foundation of justice was corrupt, and poured forth streams of bribery and oppression. The Regulators were maddened, and committed several acts of violence and lawlessness upon the person of Fanning, and threatened to control the Court by violence, and at their suggestion many refused to pay any taxes. But Governor Tryon was also alive to his own interest, and began to put into operation measures to allay the irritation of the public mind, and overawe the disaffected. One of these measures was a journey, or progress to the western counties, with a body of troops escorting him. In July, 1768, he marched to the Yadkin River, and crossing that stream reached Salisbury on the eighteenth of August. After a brief stay he visited Captain Phifer in Mecklenburg (now Cabarrus), and from thence went to Captain Polk's, returning to Salisbury by the twenty-fifth, in order to review the troops or militia of the county. Here Col. Alexander Osborne called upon His Excellency for instructions concerning the parade, and read to him a letter from the Rev. Messrs. David Caldwell, Hugh McAden, Henry Patillo, and James Creswell, Presbyterians, touching the conduct of the Regulators. These ministers labored in Guilford, Orange, and Granville Counties, and as Colonel Osborne and the four ministers were of the same church it is presumed that the tenor of the letter would be such as not to irritate the Governor against them. In fact, while these ministers sympathized with the people in their oppression, they appear to have done all in their power to prevent violence, and secure the restoration of peace and harmony.

Eleven companies appeared in Salisbury in this review—all except Captain Knox's Company, whose sympathies appear to have been decidedly in favor of the Regulators. Colonel Wheeler states that this Captain Knox was the maternal grandfather of James K. Polk, the President in after years of the United States. President Polk was born in Mecklenburg County, ten miles south of Charlotte, and his maternal grandfather, James Knox, resided also in Mecklenburg, in the Hopewell region, and it does not appear probable that he was the Captain Knox of the Rowan militia Company that failed to appear at the Salisbury review; still it may have been the same. Some of the Polk family, relatives of the President, were in after years citizens of Salisbury, and their dust lies under marble slabs in Oakgrove Cemetery, in that city.

From the Salisbury review Governor Tryon went to see the spot where in 1746 the commissioners left off running the dividing line between the King's lands and Earl Granville's lands. He found the place about five or six hundred yards east of Coldwater Creek—on the present dividing line between Rowan and Cabarrus. He then paid a visit to Capt. John Paul Barringer, in Mecklenburg (now Cabarrus), drank freely of the Captain's rich wine, and tried his hand at mowing, with a Dutch scythe doubtless, the green meadows of Dutch Buffalo. The Governor then visited Col. Moses Alexander's, on Rocky River, and returning to Salisbury spent eight days in the town and surrounding country. A gentleman, a soldier, a genial companion, his visit no doubt was one reason why Rowan County did not enter more fully into the Regulation struggle.

But while the policy of the Governor stayed for a season the rushing of the torrent of rebellion, it did not avert the final catastrophe. Matters grew worse and worse, and in the Spring of 1771 the Governor left Newbern a second time with a body of troops to enforce the laws and disperse the Regulators. At Tryon's approach the Regulators were massed near the Great Alamance River, and here the long delayed collision took place, on the sixteenth of May. It is not necessary in sketches of Rowan to enter into the details of this battle—if it can be called a battle; for the Regulators were not organized as a military force, and had no officers beyond the rank of a captain. Many of them were unarmed and seemed to be rather spectators than soldiers, and the rest were armed with their hunting pieces, with enough ammunition for a day's sport in the woods. So perfectly unprepared were they to engage with the troops of the Governor that the Rev. David Caldwell, who was present, after passing backward and forward several times, vainly trying to prevent bloodshed, at last advised the Regulators to submit to any conditions they could obtain, or disperse, rather than engage in the hopeless contest.

It is said that Colonel Fanning, better acquainted with the logomachy of the courtroom than with the dangerous contests of the battlefield, withdrew his Company at the beginning of the firing. Husbands, the leader of the Regulators, is reported to have followed his example, and saved himself by flight. Thus the two men who did more than any others to excite to conflict left their adherents to fight it out without their presence.

Some time previous to the conflict Governor Tryon sent General Hugh Waddell to Salisbury with a division of troops from Bladen, Cumberland, and the western counties. These troops were to remain at Salisbury until a supply of powder, flints, blankets, etc., from Charleston should reach them. But the "Cabarrus Blackboys," as they have been called, intercepted the convoy at Phifer's mill, three miles west of Concord, unloaded the wagons, stove in the kegs of powder, tore up the blankets, and forming a huge pile blew up the whole. The military stores failing to reach him, General Waddell, with two hundred and fifty men, left Salisbury and attempted to join Tryon in Orange or Guilford County. But when he reached Potts' Creek, about two miles east of the Yadkin, he was confronted by a large force of Rowan Regulators, who threatened to cut his troops to pieces if he offered to join the army under Tryon. Calling a council of officers, he discovered that the Regulators outnumbered him by far, and that his men had no desire to engage in battle with their brethren. He wisely resolved to fall back across the river to Salisbury. This was on the tenth of May, 1771, six days before the battle of Great Alamance.

A few days after the battle, Tryon marched to the east side of the Yadkin, where he effected a junction with General Waddell, and extricated him from his painful position.

I must not omit to mention that, on the seventh of March, 1771, a public meeting was held in Salisbury, probably just before General Waddell arrived here, at which a large and influential committee was appointed to meet the clerk, sheriff, and other crown officers, and require them to disgorge their unlawful fees. These officers agreed to the demand of the committee, and signed a paper to that effect. Matthew Locke and Herman Husbands, with others, were appointed on the committee to receive and distribute the unlawful fees, but it is doubtful whether any were ever returned. After the affair at Alamance, the ruling party acquired additional power, and no doubt for a season longer had everything their own way.

At this day, as in that, it is difficult to make a proper estimate of the character of the Regulation. In Rowan, Anson, and Mecklenburg, public opinion was divided. On the Governor's side, either actively or in sympathy, were such men as Colonel Waddell, Samuel Spencer, Richard Caswell, Waightstill Avery, Griffith Rutherford,

Wm. Lindsay, Adlai Osborne, John Ashe, and others of the noblest men of the State, who afterwards proved their devotion to the cause of liberty. While no doubt they were opposed to the exactions of the officials, they still adhered to the regular administration of the law in the hands of the constituted authorities. The struggle can neither be properly characterized as the noble uprising of an oppressed people in behalf of liberty, nor condemned as a mob or insurrection. It would seem rather to have been a good cause, prematurely, rashly, and violently conducted, and led on by men incapable of allaying or controlling the storm they had evoked, and the effect was disastrous, for Governor Tryon so entangled the consciences of many of them with oaths of allegiance, that when the real struggle came, six years later, a great number of the Regulators felt constrained to cast in their lot with the Tories.

CHAPTER XII

CAUSES OF THE REVOLUTION

It has been truthfully said that the "Revolution" took place before the Declaration of Independence, and that the document proclaimed in Philadelphia on the Fourth of July, 1776, was simply a public recognition of a state already existing. The skirmishes at Lexington and Concord took place April, 1775; the battle of Bunker Hill in May of the same year; while Boston was evacuated by the British in 1776. In North Carolina the battle of Moore's Creek Bridge, between the Patriots and the Tories, was fought in February, 1776, and in consequence Lord Cornwallis, who was hovering around the mouth of the Cape Fear, took his departure, carrying away with him Josiah Martin, the last royal Governor of this Province. In fact the Revolution was no sudden occurrence, but the result of a long continued series of events, culminating in the independence of the State and country. It may be useful to take a glance at the events that led up to this wondrous consummation, especially to dispel the illusion of those who have been told and who believe that nothing worth the expenditure of the blood and treasure required was achieved by the War of the Revolution.

The grievance of the Americans, though appearing in different forms, consisted in the despotic principle that a people may be taxed without being represented in the lawmaking assembles. While every borough and shire in England, Wales, and Scotland was represented in the English House of Commons, not a single representative, delegate, or commissioner could appear in that body from the thirteen colonies of America. And yet the Parliament took complete and sovereign control of many of the most vital interests of the colonies. By the odious "Navigation Act" of the British Parliament, no production of Europe, Asia, or Africa could be brought into the colonies except in British ships, commanded by British captains, and manned by British crews, nor could the exports of the colonies be removed in any other way. The design of this law was to "protect" the British marine merchant service, and the design was effectual, since no other nation could underbid their own vessels. But it left the colonies at the mercy of the grasping ship-owners.

But even this indirect taxation was not enough. England had expended large sums in her recent wars, and especially in the French and Indian wars waged in behalf of the colonies. In return, the mother country, perhaps not unreasonably, expected the colonies to bear their portion of the burden. And no doubt, if the matter had been presented in a proper form, the colonies would have consented to tax themselves to meet the expenses incurred for their protection. But when England proposed to lay this burden on them without so much as consulting them upon the subject, the universal opinion of the Americans was that it was a tyrannical invasion of the rights of free men, and that if England could take any part of their property without their consent, she could take the whole upon the same grounds; and that if they submitted to such taxation, the Americans virtually became the slaves of the people from whom they descended.

On the twenty-second of March, 1765, the Parliament of Great Britain adopted what was called the "Stamp Act," requiring all contracts, notes, bonds, deeds, writs, and other public documents, to be written on governemnt paper, which had a "stamp" on it, and which was to be sold at a high price by government agents, and from the sale of which a large revenue was expected to flow into the English treasury. The passage of this "Act" produced great excitement in all the colonies, and in none more than in North Carolina. The General Assembly of North Carolina was in session when the intelligence of the passage of this Act arrived, and no doubt would have taken some decided action upon the matter had not Governor Tryon prudently prorogued that body after a session of fifteen days. John Ashe, the Speaker of the House, plainly informed the Governor that the Act would be resisted "unto blood and death." And when, early in the year 1766, the British sloop of war "Diligence," with the odious "stamps" on board, arrived in the Cape Fear, Cols. John Ashe and Hugh Waddell, with their respective militia regiments under arms, informed the commander of the ship that the landing of the "stamps" would be resisted. In the meantime, a boat of the "Diligence" was captured and borne through the streets of Wilmington at the head of a procession. Colonel Ashe also demanded of Governor Tryon, the stamp-master—one James Houston, who was lodged in the Governor's house, and upon refusal to deliver him up threatened to fire the house. Upon this the stamp-master was produced, and compelled to take a solemn oath that he would not attempt to dispose of the obnoxious stamps. This ended the matter of the stamps, for the Act was repealed by Parliament, in March, 1766.

The "Stamp Act" was the cause of the first General Congress of the American Colonies, which was held in the City of New York, June 6, 1765. This convention or congress was held by the agreement of a number of the colonies, at the suggestion of their respective Assemblies; but the Provinces of New Hampshire, Virginia, North Carolina, and Georgia were not represented in it, for the reason that their respective Legislatures were not in session in time to take the necessary steps for the appointment of delegates.

Although the English Parliament repealed the "Stamp Act," they did not abandon their claim to tax the colonies, but directly asserted it. And so in 1767 another Act, not less an invasion of colonial liberty, was adopted. This was the famous "Bill" imposing a tax on glass, paper, painters' colors, and tea, imported into the colonies. This Act being resisted was followed by other Acts of unfriendly legislation, such as the suspension of the Legislative Assembly of New York, and closing the port of Boston. In consequence of this, the "General Court" of Massachusetts sent a circular to the other colonies, asking their co-operation in devising some method of obtaining a redress of grievances. This circular was laid before the General Assembly of North Carolina, in November, 1768, by Col. John Harvey, the Speaker of the House, but no decisive steps appear to have been taken. In fact, the Governor kept his watchful eye upon the Assembly and stood ready to prorogue its sessions at the first indication of the spirit of union and independence. Thus it happened that North Carolina was not represented in the first Provincial Congress of the Colonies, nor indeed until the General Congress assembled in Philadelphia, in September, 1774. The way the "Provincial Congress" of North Carolina came into existence at the last was as follows: In 1773, the House of Burgesses of Virginia resolved upon establishing committees of correspondence between the several colonies, and sent forth circulars to the various Provincial Legislatures. The Virginia "Circular," as well as letters from some of the other Provinces, was laid before the North Carolina Assembly by Speaker Harvey in this same year, and the Assembly seized the opportunity to appoint a committee to watch the proceedings of the English Parliament and to concert with the other Provinces measures for the general defense. The committee appointed consisted of Speaker Harvey, Richard Caswell, Samuel Johnston, Hewes, Vail, Harnett, Hooper, John Ashe, and Howe. When the Virginia House of Burgesses proposed the holding of another General Congress, after the closing of the port of Boston, Governor Martin intimated that he would repeat Governor Tryon's old trick of proroguing the North Carolina Assembly, and thus prevent the Province from being represented in that Congress. But the brave and fearless John Harvey, though fast sinking into the grave by incurable disease, resolved if necessary to sacrifice his few remaining days by a counterstroke of policy. He therefore issued a proclamation over his own signature, calling upon the people to elect members to a Provincial Congress that would not be subject to the Governor's orders, but responsible only to the people. Our children have been taught to admire the courage of John Hancock, who signed the Declaration in letters so large that all the world might read it, and of Charles Carroll, who added "of Carrollton" to his name, to prevent the possibility of being confounded with another Charles Carroll. But who has paused a moment to tell them of the heroic Col. John Harvey, of Perquimans County, N. C., who dared, in defiance of Governor Martin and the royal authorities, to issue a proclamation, inviting the people to assume their rights as free men, and join with the other Provinces in concerted action? The act was performed, not under the pressure of enthusiasm, or in the midst of a patriotic crowd of sympathizers, but in the seclusion of a quiet home, under the united pressure of the infirmities of age and enfeebling disease! He did not live to see the final results of the impending struggle, but sank into the grave just as the storm of the Revolution burst upon the country. His name and his service deserve a grateful remembrance.

In pursuance of the "proclamation" of Harvey, the Assembly of 1774 was supplemented by another body called a "Congress." Both bodies were composed, generally, of the same members, and Colonel Harvey was chosen "Speaker" of the Assembly, as usual, and "Moderator" of the Congress. The Congress met in Newbern on the twenty-fifth of August, 1774, and was composed of brave and judicious men, quite a number of whom are distinguished in the annals of the State. On the list we find the names of Samuel Spencer of Anson, Robert Howe of Brunswick, Samuel Johnston of Chowan, Richard Caswell of Dobbs, Thomas Person of Granville, Willie Jones of Halifax, John Ashe and William Hooper of New Hanover, John Harvey of Perquimans, and Abner Nash of Newbern. Rowan County was represented in this Congress by William Kennon, Moses Winslow, and Samuel Young.

On the third day of their session, August 27, 1774, the Congress adopted twenty-five resolutions, that embody the principles of independence and resistance to tyranny. These resolutions prudently affirmed a loyal regard for the British constitution, and devotion to the House of Hanover, but at the same time declared that allegiance should secure protection; that no person should be taxed without his own consent, either personal or by representation; that the tax on tea was illegal and oppressive; that the closing of the port of Boston, and sending persons to England to be tried for acts committed in the colonies, were unconstitutional; and that it was the duty of our people to cease all trade with the mother country, or any Province that refused to co-operate in measures for the general welfare. They also approved the movement for a General Congress in Philadelphia, in September following, and appointed William Hooper, Joseph Hewes, and Richard Caswell to represent this Province in said General Congress. After authorizing Moderator Harvey, or in case of his death Samuel Johnstone, to call the Congress together, if occasion should require it, the body adjourned. In the Spring of the year 1775, the Provincial Congress met again in Newbern, and Rowan sent as deputies Griffith Rutherford, William Sharpe, and William Kennon. At subsequent meetings of this Congress, at Hillsboro and Halifax, Rowan was represented by Matthew Locke, James Smith, and John Brevard.

J G Ramsay

CHAPTER XIII

MEMBERS OF THE PROVINCIAL CONGRESS

In the last chapter it was mentioned that Rowan County was represented in the Provincial Congress by Griffith Rutherford, James Smith, Matthew Locke, Moses Winslow, William Kennon, William Sharpe, Samuel Young, and John Brevard. These were doubtless the most influential and prominent men in the county, chosen not from party prejudice, but because they possessed the confidence of their fellow-citizens. It will doubtless be interesting, after the lapse of a hundred years, to gather up, and reflect upon, the history and the character of the men who exercised such an influence upon public affairs.

It will be observed, as we progress, that they were chosen from different sections of the county, and different settlements. In those early days the country was not filled up with farms and families, as now, but the people gathered in settlements, where lands were most fertile, and society was considered most desirable. Prominent among these settlements was the Grant's Creek region, stretching from near the Mecklenburg (now Cabarrus) line, along the west side of Salisbury, to the Yadkin River, about two miles above Trading Ford. This region was filled up with the Lockes, Brandons, Grahams, Nesbits, Allisons, Rutherfords, Lynns, Gibsons, Frohocks, and others, whose descendants still remain in the county.

From this region, in 1775, was chosen, to represent Rowan County in the Provincial Congress at Newbern.

Gen. Griffith Rutherford

The Rutherfords are Scotch-Irish, and one of the families in the "Land of Bruce." The family is mentioned in the early annals of Scotland as friends of King Ruther, from whom they received the name, and large tracts of land. For centuries they have been classed among the most ancient and powerful families in Teviotdale, on the borders of England. They have intermarried with the royal families, and from inherited honors and from honors conferred have been prominent among the nobility. The mother of Sir Walter Scott was a Rutherford.

The Rev. Samuel Rutherford, the author of the Rutherford Letters, was one of the ablest leaders of Presbyterianism. He was sent as a delegate from Scotland to Westminster to defend that faith. This, together with his political opinions freely expressed, caused some of the family to be banished from Scotland, and to take refuge in Ireland, where John Rutherford was married to Miss Griffith, an exile from Wales. Their son Griffith came to America with his son—also called Griffith—and settled near Salisbury, Rowan County, N. C. This son—the subject of this sketch—married Elizabeth Graham, a sister of James Graham, who was also descended from a long line of noble Scotch ancestors. Both families lived in what was then called the Locke or Thyatira settlement. They had five sons and daughters. Their eldest son, Major James Rutherford, was killed in the battle of Eutaw. In 1770, the subject of this sketch was a captain of militia under Governor Tryon, but joined James Graham and others and formed the Regulators against Tryon the following year. He was appointed a member of the Committee of Safety, and was a juryman in the trial of Tories in 1775. He was a member of the Provincial Congress which met at Halifax, April 4, 1776. He and Matthew Locke represented Rowan County. He was also a member of the Provincial Congress of 1775. In April of 1776, he was appointed brigadier-general, and in the same month was a member of the Constitutional Convention. In September, he marched at the head of twenty-four hundred men into the Cherokee country, and killed a number of Indians, destroyed their crops, burned their habitations; and finally forced them to sue for peace and surrender a part of their lands. In this campaign, his loss was only three men killed. He returned to Salisbury, and disbanded his army at that place. He commanded a brigade at the battle of Sanders Creek, near Camden, where he was wounded and taken prisoner. He was first sent to Charleston, S. C., and later taken to St. Augustine, Fla., where he remained until exchanged, June 22, 1781. He again took the field, and was in command at Wilmington when the town was evacuated by the British at the close of the war.

During the continuance of the war, he was a State Senator from 1777 to 1780, and from 1782 to 1786. In the year 1786, he removed to Tennessee, and settled in Sumner County. In 1794, George Washington, our first President, appointed General Rutherford a member of the Territorial Legislature which met at Knoxville, Tenn. The *Knoxville Gazette,* of date 1794, contains account as follows, viz.: "On Monday last, the General Assembly of the Territory commenced their first session in this town. Gen. Griffith Rutherford, for distinguished services in the Legislature of North Carolina, is appointed president of the Legislative Council."

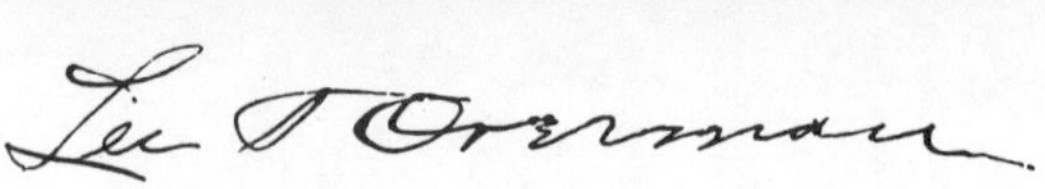

United States Senator from North Carolina and
descendant of Major James Smith

Rutherford County, N. C., was formed in 1779, and Rutherford County, Tenn., in 1803; both were named in honor of this distinguished Revolutionary soldier and statesman, Griffith Rutherford, who died in Sumner County, Tenn., in 1800, in old age and full of honors.

The following sketch of another distinguished member of the Provincial Congress, and soldier of the Revolution, was prepared for this article by one of his descendants, Lee S. Overman, Esq.

Major James Smith

Of the many and brave men associated with our American Revolution, very few figured more prominently, or did more for the cause of liberty in this section of our State than the subject of this sketch.

The son of James Smith, who emigrated from Holland to New Jersey, he, with a colony of young married men, came to North Carolina some time before the Revolution and settled on the left bank of the Yadkin River, and made what is known as the Jersey Settlement in Davidson County, then Rowan.

In stature he was over six feet tall, straight as an arrow and of a commanding appearance. He was by occupation a planter, and was possessed of means in addition to the land he owned, which he obtained by grant from McCullough. He had slaves, by whom he was much loved, for, though they were carried off south by the Tories, they in time made their escape and returned to their old home.

James Smith served as Ensign, in 1776, under King George III. (See report of Commandant of Court of Public Claims, held at Newbern, N. C., on the sixth day of November, 1756), to wit: "James Smith, an Ensign in Rowan County, was allowed his claim of twelve pounds and nineteen shillings (£12/19), for ranging on the frontier as per account filed" (State Records, Vol. XXII, page 842).

At a council held at Newbern, November 10, 1769, "a commission of Peace and Dedimus of Rowan County" was issued to James Smith (Vol. 8 of Colonial Records, page 149).

In the Court of Pleas and Quarter Session of Rowan County, in 1772 (on minute docket of Rowan County, 1768-72), is the following: "Wednesday, fourth of November, 1772, Griffith Rutherford, Colonel, and James Smith, Captain, produced their commission in open Court, qualified, and signed the test agreeable to law."

James Smith served as Justice presiding over the "Court of Pleas and Quarter Session for Rowan County," under King George III, during the years 1770-71-72-73-74-75, at Salisbury, N. C.

In 1775, he took a prominent and active part in every movement tending to throw off the yoke of tyranny and looking to the Declaration of Independence by the country at large. He was a member of the Committee of Safety for Rowan County, and so far as we are able to find out was present at every meeting thereof. During this same year he was appointed to address the citizens of his county upon the subject of American freedom, was chairman of the Committee to examine certain citizens as to their political sentiment, and also was one of the Committee of "Secrecy, Intelligence, and Observation." Also, he was chosen by the friends of liberty in his county to represent them in the Convention of Patriots Adverse to the Oppression of Great Britain, which met at Hillsboro, on the twenty-first of August of the same year.

At the Halifax Congress, April 22, 1776, he was appointed Major of the Salisbury District, of which Francis Locke was Colonel, and Griffith Rutherford, Brigadier-General. He was a member of the Provincial Congress which met at Halifax on the twelfth day of November, 1776, and which framed our first civil Constitution. In 1777 he was a member of the House of Commons, with Matthew Locke as his associate and Griffith Rutherford in the Senate.

Not only did he thus appear in the public assemblies of our country, in behalf of the people's rights, but no one was more active than he in repelling the Tories. He buckled on his sword at every call, and was always at the front, fighting for freedom and his native land. He made several campaigns with his regiment against the British, and engaged in several hard-contested battles, until he was severely wounded, when he was furloughed home. He had not been long returned before the Tories heard of his whereabouts, and being eager for their prize they sought him immediately. Mr. Sloan, who lived in the neighborhood, had heard of their designs, and sent his servant, Ben, to inform the Major of his danger. Poor Ben, who lived until 1860 to tell the tale, was destined never to deliver his message, for before he had proceeded far, Captain Wood and forty men overtook him, shot him through and left him for dead. They then went to the Major's residence and demanded his surrender. His wife, Clara, met them at the door, as tradition has it, with one of the long-handled frying-pans which were used in those days, and defied them. She was soon overpowered, however, and her husband was seized, and with John Paul Barringer, of Mecklenburg, and others, carried to Camden, S. C., and imprisoned. Soon he was attacked with smallpox, and died. His good and brave wife followed him and nursed him in his last moments. She saw his remains deposited in the grave, and returned to comfort her three children she had left behind. Of these children, James, who was only twelve years old at the time of his father's capture, was for a long time Sheriff of Rowan, and of Davidson after the division. Sheriff Smith's daughter, Alice, married Fielding Slater, who for many years was also Sheriff of Rowan County, which office he filled with great acceptability to the people. Also two of his sons now live in the county of Davidson, fit representatives of their honored ancestor. In both counties there are many descendants of this brave and noble man, all of whom are noted for their good character and moral worth as public-spirited citizens.

Intimately associated with General Rutherford and Major Smith, in the Provincial Congress of North Carolina, and in the public affairs of Rowan County during and after the War of the Revolution, was

Hon. William Sharpe

While Rutherford represented the Central Rowan, or Grant's Creek, section, and Smith came from the "Jerseys" or Eastern Rowan section, Sharpe was from the West, and represented that region now included in Iredell County.

William Sharpe was the eldest son of Thomas Sharpe, of Cecil County, Md., and was born in that State, December 13, 1742. In the year 1763 he immigrated to North Carolina, and settled in Mecklenburg County, where he married the daughter of David Reese. Mr. Reese was from Pennsylvania—the brother of the Rev. Thomas Reese, a prominent minister in Mecklenburg, and afterwards in South Carolina. David Reese was a leading citizen in his day, and his name is honored with a place among the signers of the Mecklenburg Declaration of Independence.

Mr. Sharpe, soon after his marriage, moved to Rowan County, and in the Revolution took an early and decided part in all public affairs, and was a staunch advocate for independence. At the formation of the Committee of Safety for Rowan County in 1774, William Sharpe was selected as a member, and his name is attached to the minutes of the Committee as secretary. At the adjournment of the Committee, in 1776, the minutes appear to have been left in his hands, and were preserved in his family, until they were brought to light by the researches of Prof. E. F. Rockwell, and published in 1851, in Wheeler's Sketches of North Carolina.

In 1775 he represented Rowan in the Provincial Congress at Newbern and Hillsboro, and he was also a member of the convention that formed the first constitution of the State, at Halifax, in 1776. The same year he acted as aide to General Rutherford in his campaign against the Cherokee Indians.

In 1779 he was the representative of the Salisbury District in the Continental Congress of Philadelphia. At the battle of Ramsour's Mill, June, 1780, two of Captain Sharpe's sons, William and Thomas, served under the command of Col. Francis Locke. William was in command of a Company and conducted himself with distinguished gallantry. It was a shot directed by him that struck down one of the Tory captains, near the close of the action, and thus contributed to the speedy termination of the battle in favor of the patriots.

Mr. Sharpe, during the Revolutionary War, was a magistrate of Rowan County and his name appears frequently on the records as one of the presiding Justices in the County Court. On the seventh of February, 1785, he presented a lawyer's license, and took the customary oath of an attorney. After this period he appears as a lawyer in many cases in Court, and enjoyed, as Dr. Hunter says, an extensive practice.

Mr. Sharpe died in 1818, in the seventy-seventh year of his age, leaving a widow and twelve children. These children, with his own reputation for distinguished services, constitute his legacy to his country.

In concluding this sketch I will mention that, besides his sons, by whom the name of Sharpe is perpetuated, there were two daughters, who became mothers of extensive and influential families. The eldest of these was named Matilda, and was united in marriage to William W. Erwin, of Burke County. Their union was blessed with a family of fifteen children, many of whom have held prominent and honorable positions in the State, and their descendants are still found as honored and useful citizens in the Piedmont regions of North Carolina.

Ruth, the second daughter of the Hon. William Sharpe, was married to Col. Andrew Caldwell, of Iredell County. Colonel Caldwell represented Iredell County in the House of Commons in 1806-07-08, and in the Senate in 1812-13.

His two sons, Judge David F. Caldwell, so long a prominent citizen of Salisbury, and the Hon. Joseph P. Caldwell, who represented his district in the National Congress, sustained the reputation of their distinguished ancestor by their public services.

John Brevard

Another name on the list of members of the Provincial Congress of North Carolina was John Brevard. The family is of French extraction, and its history is associated with the stirring events that accompanied the Reformation of the sixteenth century, in France. The Calvinistic subjects of the French King were persecuted and harassed through long years, until driven to madness they allied themselves with the Prince of Condé, and attempted resistance. But their plans were discovered and frustrated, and they were subjected to still greater persecutions. At length, however, Henry IV, by the famous Edict of Nantes, in 1598, granted equal rights to his Protestant and Catholic subjects. For about three quarters of a century the Huguenots, or French Calvinists, enjoyed comparative safety, during which time they multiplied and prospered. At length, however, Louis XIV, instigated by Madame de Maintenon, began to renew the cruel work of persecuting his Protestant subjects, by imposing disabilities and fines upon them. In 1685 he revoked the Edict of Nantes, and endeavored to suppress all forms of worship except the Romish. By this cruel and short-sighted policy he drove from his dominions more than a half-million of his most useful and industrious subjects—farmers, artisans, laborers, producers of all kinds. They crossed into Switzerland, Germany, Holland, England, wherever the frontiers were more easily passed. Among these Huguenot emigrants was a young man of the name of Brevard, who found his way to the north of Ireland. Here he made the acquaintance of a family by the name of McKnitt, of Scotch extraction. He determined to cast in his lot with this family in their projected emigration to the New Yorld. It happened that there was in the McKnitt family a fair young lass, for whom the ardent Huguenot conceived a tender passion, and responsive affection was awakened in the bosom of the maiden. The result was a marriage, and the young couple upon reaching America settled in a home on Elk River, in Maryland. There were born unto them five sons and a daughter. The eldest of these was John Brevard, the Rowan County farmer and member of the Provincial Congress.

Before his removal to North Carolina he was united in marriage to a sister of the Rev. Alex. McWhorter, D.D., a distinguished Presbyterian minister, who was for a short time president of "Queens Museum" College, in Charlotte.

John Brevard settled in Rowan County, about three miles from Center church, some time between 1740 and 1750, coming on with the first immigrants to that section. There he led a quiet and useful life, rearing a large family, consisting of eight sons and four daughters, whom he trained to be useful citizens. When the troublous times of the Revolution came, Brevard was an old man, but not too old to represent Rowan County in the Provincial Congress. And though too old to take the field, his sons gallantly obeyed the call to arms, and entered into the military service. On that dark morning of the first of February, 1781, when Gen. William Davidson fell at Cowan's Ford, while resisting the passage of the British troops, Mr. Brevard's house was burned down by order of some of the British officers. A part of the invading army crossed at Beattie's Ford, and so passed directly by Brevard's house. The old gentleman was absent from home, and his daughters had been sent across a swamp, out of harm's way, leaving none but the venerable wife and mother at home. A British officer, riding up and taking a paper out of his pocket, declared that the house must be burned, alleging as a reason that Brevard had eight sons in the rebel army. Though the venerable matron tried to save some of her property, it was snatched from her hands, and cast into the flames. Gen. William Davidson, who was killed that morning, was the son-in-law of John Brevard, having married Mary, his eldest daughter. Their son, William Lee Davidson, Esq., was an early friend and patron of Davidson College, and made a donation of the land upon which the College now stands. Dr. Ephraim Brevard, the secretary of the Mecklenburg Convention, was the eldest son of John Brevard. Dr. Foote says of him: "He thought clearly; felt deeply; wrote well; resisted bravely, and died a martyr to that liberty none loved better and few understood so well."

Hon. Matthew Locke

From the first volume of records in the office of the Register of Deeds in Salisbury, we learn that, from 1752 to 1754, there were three men by the name of Locke—probably brothers—who acquired titles to land in Rowan County. One of these was Francis Locke, who purchased over a thousand acres from John Brandon, called the "Poplar Lands," on both sides of the wagon road leading from the Yadkin River to the "Irish Settlement." In 1752 there was a grant from Earl Granville to George Locke of a tract in the neighborhood of "Poplar Spring," adjoining the lands of John Thompson. These tracts are said to be on the south side of the Yadkin, but whether near that stream or not is not mentioned. In 1752 there was a grant of six hundred acres from Earl Granville to Matthew Locke. From these three persons sprang the numerous families of

Lockes that resided in Rowan County in the closing years of the last and the opening years of the present century.

But it is with special reference to the last-mentioned of the three, the Hon. Matthew Locke, that this article is penned.

He was the owner of a fertile tract of land, on the east side of Grant's Creek, about five miles south of Salisbury, adjoining the plantations of John Brandon, James Allison, and John Nesbit. The family mansion stood on the Concord Road, at or near the place where Dr. Scott's residence was, now the home of Mr. Philip Owens.

Mr. Locke was born in 1730, and was probably a grown young man when he came to the county, and contributed his part in laying the foundations of society; and when the Regulation troubles arose he was in the prime of life, having already established a reputation for capacity in business and integrity in the most delicate of trusts. In 1771, when the people of Rowan were groaning under the pressure of exorbitant taxation, and a committee of the people had met the clerk of court, sheriff, and other officers of the crown, and exacted from them a promise to return all moneys received by them over and above their lawful fees, Matthew Locke was among those selected as proper persons to receive and return to the people these unlawful fees. As General Waddell soon appeared in Salisbury with the Governor's troops, and the whole scheme of the Regulation was crushed out in the battle of Alamance only two months after this appointment, it is probable that no indemnity for the past was secured; but the appointment of Locke for the discharge of such a delicate duty shows the confidence reposed in him by his fellow-citizens.

He was chosen to represent Rowan in the Provincial Congress, which met in Hillsboro, August 20, 1775, along with James Smith, Moses Winslow, Samuel Young, William Kennon, and William Sharpe. Mr. Locke was chosen by this Congress, along with Maurice Moore, Richard Caswell, Rev. Henry Patillo, and others, to confer with such persons as entertained religious or political scruples with respect to associating in the common cause of America, to remove those scruples, and to persuade them to coöperate with the friends of liberty.

Mr. Locke also served on the committee, along with Caswell, Hooper, Johnson, Hewes, Spencer, and others, which prepared the plan for the regulation of the internal peace of the Province in the absence (!) of Governor Martin. He also served on Committees of Public Finance, Ways and Means, for arrangement of minute men, commissaries, and other important matters. At a meeting of the Provincial Council, held at Johnston Courthouse, October 18,

1775, Matthew Locke, Esq., was appointed paymaster of the troops stationed in the District of Salisbury, and also of the minute men in said District, and Richard Caswell, the "Southern Treasurer," was directed to pay into his hands five thousand two hundred and fifty pounds (£5,250) for that purpose.

At the meeting of the Provincial Congress, at Halifax, April 4, 1776, Mr. Locke, with General Rutherford, represented Rowan County, and was made chairman of the Committee on Claims, to settle and allow military and naval accounts. He was also on the Committee of "Secrecy, Intelligence, and Observation," was appointed to receive, produce, and purchase firearms for the soldiers of Rowan County. In view of these facts, gathered from the minutes of the North Carolina Provincial Congress, as found in Peter Force's "American Archives," it appears that Mr. Locke was a working man in public affairs, and that he was entrusted with much of the important business of the Congress, especially such as related to the public finances.

After the formation of the State Constitution, Matthew Locke was chosen to represent Rowan County four successive years: 1777-78 in the House of Commons, and the two succeeding years, 1781-82, he was a member of the Senate. After this he served six years again in the House of Commons—making in all twelve years in the Legislature.

From 1793 to 1799 he was a member of the Congress of the United States. His public services lasted almost as long as his life, for in 1801, the seventy-first year of his age, he departed this life.

He was married to a daughter of Richard Brandon, an early patriot of Rowan County, and had at one time four sons in the Revolutionary War. One of these sons, Lieut. George Locke, was killed by the British at Kennedy's Farm, between Charlotte and Sugar Creek Church, in a skirmish, when Lord Cornwallis captured Charlotte, on the twenty-sixth of September, 1780. His remains were interred at his father's residence, near Salisbury.

Col. Francis Locke, who was appointed Colonel of the First Rowan Regiment by the Provincial Congress, in April, 1776, with Alexander Dobbins as Lieutenant-Colonel, James Brandon First Major, and James Smith Second Major, was a nephew of the Hon. Matthew Locke. Colonel Locke was in the command of General Ashe in the beginning of 1779, when that officer was sent to Georgia, unprepared, with two thousand North Carolina militia. Against the remonstrances of General Ashe, General Lincoln pushed these troops forward at Brier Creek, where they were surprised and defeated by General Prevost. Colonel Locke was one of the court-martial to examine into that disastrous affair. The unfortunate General Ashe, being broken in spirt by the result of this transaction, retired from the army and was no more in active service. The reader will remember that it was Col. Francis Locke who, with four hundred men from Rowan and Mecklenburg, attacked and defeated the Tories at Ramsour's Mill, on the twentieth of June, 1780, in a hard-fought battle, against a superior force entrenched on ground of their own choosing. In this battle seven Whig captains, namely: Falls, Knox, Dobson, Smith, Bowman, Sloan, and Armstrong, were killed, and the bodies of six of them sleep under a brick monumental structure, on the southern brow of the rising battleground, about fifty or sixty yards from the present public road. The remains of Captain Falls were carried to his home in Rowan, near Sherrill's Ford, on the Catawba, and there interred. His sword was in the possession of the late Robert Falls Simonton, his grandson, at the time of his death four years ago.

In Thyatira graveyard stands a monument to the memory of the Hon. Francis Locke, which states that he was born on the thirty-first of October, 1766, elected Judge of the Superior Court in 1803, elected Senator of the United States in 1814, and died in January, 1823. He never married.

The Hon. Matthew Locke, as before stated, married a daughter of Richard Brandon, and left eight sons as follows: George, killed near Charlotte; William, died young; John, died young; Francis, moved West; Richard, Matthew, James, and Robert.

Gen. Francis Locke, nephew of the above, and probably a son of Francis or George, mentioned in the beginning of this article, also married a Brandon, and left four sons, viz.: Francis, John, William, and Matthew. This genealogical notice was obtained by Gen. R. Barringer from Mrs. David Parks, of Charlotte, *née* Locke.

A generation or two ago the Locke family in Rowan County was numerous, and held a prominent place in public affairs. But by removals and deaths it has come to pass that few of that name remain. Still, in the female line, there are prominent citizens in Rowan and adjoining counties who worthily represent the blood of the statesmen, counselors, and warriors who once proudly bore the name of Locke. And it is well that one of our principal townships has been deputed to carry down that honorable name to posterity.

Our people cannot afford to lose the patriotic influence that is exerted by the names of the sages and heroes of past generations.

Samuel Young

The traveler who leaves Salisbury on the Western North Carolina Railroad, after passing over Grant's Creek and Second Creek, will begin to see, on his right, a wooded range of hills or small mountains looming up near by. It is only a few hundred feet in height, yet high enough to be seen for twenty or thirty miles around. Here the Indian's watchfire, or signal fire beacon, would have flashed its light to different mountain peaks—to Dunn's Mountain, to the Pilot, and to King's Mountain, sixty miles away to the southward. This eminence is called *Young's Mountain,* and is named after Samuel Young, the subject of this sketch.

Somewhere about 1750 an Irishman came over the waters, and joined in the stream of emigration that was flowing through Western Carolina. With a skill that marked him out as a man of foresight, he selected, entered, or purchased a body of land containing not less than four thousand acres, the richest in Rowan County. It lay up and down Third Creek from the church to Neely's old mill, a distance of three or four miles, and included the mountain mentioned before. He chose for his residence a spot about two hundred yards from Third Creek, on land now belonging to Mrs. John Graham, not far from the site of the church. The first grant of his is dated March 25, 1752, and is for three hundred and forty acres, from Earl Granville. This was before the County of Rowan was formed, and the land is described as lying on "Third Creek, County of Anson." In 1756, Michael Dickson, weaver, sold to Samuel Young, planter, five hundred and twenty-five acres on the north side of Third Creek.

Mr. Young appears as one of the magistrates of Rowan County, at an early day, and he was a prominent actor in public affairs for many years. Supposing him to have been twenty-five or thirty years old upon his arrival here, he would be a man of mature years, between fifty and sixty, at the opening of the Revolutionary War. At that time of trial our people needed the wisest counselors and the most prudent leaders. Among these, Rowan County selected Samuel Young. When the patriotic and courageous John Harvey, as speaker of the Assembly, and chairman of the Permanent Committee of Correspondence for North Carolina, issued his proclamation, in 1774, calling upon the people to elect members to a Provincial Congress, to be held in Newbern, Rowan County chose Moses Winslow and Samuel Young, and the Borough of Salisbury chose William Kennon, Esq., as their Representatives. This Congress was opened August 25, 1774. The reader who wishes to know the opinions of that Congress upon the subject of human rights will find a series of resolutions adopted by them, on pages 734-37 of Vol. I, Fourth Series, of Peter Force's American Archives. These resolutions struck the keynote of American liberty, though they did not hint at independence. We have at hand no means of deciding as to the authorship of those resolutions, since the Congress very wisely and prudently kept their minutes anonymously. But as to the source of their inspiration there can be little doubt. On pages 360-61 of the second volume of Colonel Wheeler's History, we find a series of resolutions by the Committee of Safety of Rowan, adopted August 8, 1774, *just seventeen days before the Provincial Congress met.* Samuel Young of Third Creek, and William Kennon of Salisbury, were members both of the Rowan Committee and the Provincial Congress, and went directly from the former to the latter. They doubtless carried a copy of the Rowan resolutions to Newbern. A careful inspection of the two papers will show that the paper of the Congress is an amplification and modification of the Rowan paper, employing the same general course of thought, and sometimes toning down the warmer and more independent expressions of the Rowan paper. The author of the Rowan Resolutions is not named, but there was on the Committee a number of persons capable of composing it, such as William Kennon, the chairman; Samuel Young, John Brevard, Matthew Locke and others. This paper, while it affirms loyalty to the House of Hanover, and is no premature Declaration of Independence, nevertheless bodily affirms the rights of freemen, the right to be free from all taxation except such as is imposed by their representatives. It proposes a general association of the American Colonies to oppose all infringements of their rights and privileges; discourage trade with Great Britain; declares that homespun clothing ought to be considered a badge of distinction, respect and true patriotism. This is the first extended declaration of principles and purposes I remember to have seen. There were meetings in other counties, where true patriots expressed their sympathy and offered help to the Boston sufferers, but they usually contented themselves with approving the assembling of a Provincial and Continental Congress, without declaring their principles in detail.

After the adjournment of the Provincial Congress of 1774, Mr. Young was appointed by the Rowan committee to correspond with said Congress, and to see that its resolutions, as well as those of the Continental Congress, were carried out.

On the first of June, 1775, Samuel Young appears as chairman of the Rowan Committee of Safety, and was directed to draw up an address to the several militia companies of the county, and was made military treasurer of the county. At the same time an address was prepared to be sent to the Mecklenburg Committee. This address to Mecklenburg expresses the desire that greater unity may be secured in supporting the common cause, and "that we may have one constitution as contained in Magna Charta, the Charter of the Forest, the Habeas Corpus Act, and the Charter we brought over with us, handed down to posterity; and that under God, the present House of Hanover, in legal succession, may be the defenders of it." That was Wednesday, June 1, 1775, the week of Court in Salisbury, when Captain Jack brought the Charlotte Declaration to Salisbury, handed it to Colonel Kennon, who caused it to be read in open Court, according to Captain Jack's certificate.

In August, 1775, Samuel Young was again sent as a member of the Provincial Congress at Hillsboro, along with Matthew Locke, William Sharpe, Moses Winslow, William Kennon, and James Smith. This Congress appointed as field officers of the Rowan "Minute Men," Thomas Wade of Anson, Colonel; Adlai Osborne of Rowan, Lieutenant-Colonel, and Joseph Harben of Rowan, Major.

In the years 1781 and 1782 Samuel Young served as a member of the Legislature of North Carolina. After this period we have no record of his life and actions. He lived, however, long enough to see the cloud of war roll away, and the bright sun of peace and independence shine upon his adopted country, to see the constitution of the United States adopted, and George Washington inaugurated as the first President of the Republic.

From his last Will and Testament, dated August 24, 1793, and proved in Court November 9, 1793, we gather that he closed his earthly career some time between these dates—the fall of 1793. From this document it appears that he left seven children to inherit his estate, viz.: William, Janet, Samuel, James, Margaret, John, and Joseph. William, the eldest, was married and had a son named Samuel, to whom his grandfather left a small legacy by his Will. Of this William Young there are many traditional stories told, especially with regard to his presence of mind in danger, and his remarkable activity. Upon a certain occasion, as he was about to cross Third Creek on a footlog, at the head of Neely's Pond, he saw a panther in the act of springing upon him from the opposite bank.

It was the work of a moment to level his gun and pull the trigger. The shot met the panther as he sprang, and striking it in the head the ferocious beast fell dead in the middle of the stream. In 1781, while Lord Cornwallis was moving up the Yadkin, in pursuit of General Greene, his encampment was at a Mrs. Campbell's, near Rencher's Ford—his line of tents extending from where Mr. William Watson now lives to the farm of Mr. Robert Johnston. Tradition says that William Young, then a young man, moved with curiosity, strayed unexpectedly into the British camp, and suddenly found himself hemmed in and ordered to surrender. But instead of surrendering, he trusted to his fleetness and agility, and actually leaped over three covered wagons in succession, and so escaped. Following the British as they were about to cross South Fork at Rencher's Ford, he was unexpectedly approached by some cavalrymen. Starting off up the hill at full speed, he soon distanced the troopers and again escaped. Another story is that he won a wager from a British officer by beating the most active soldier that could be produced in feats of agility.

The second son, Samuel, received by his father's Will a plantation near Cathey's Meeting-house, (Thyatira). The oldest daughter, Janet, was married to a man named Webb, and their oldest child, Samuel Webb, received a small legacy from his grandfather. James' portion was alloted to him on Coddle Creek, near the Wilmington Road. Margaret married John Irvin, and three of her sons are named Christopher, Joseph, and John—the last still living near Third Creek Church, at the ripe age of seventy years. John had his portion of land on Third Creek, and Joseph, the youngest according to Scotch-Irish customs, received the home place as his patrimony. From these are descended many families, such as the Irvins, Foards, Kilpatricks, Matthews, Woods, and others. Mr. Young evinced his Presbyterianism in his Will by providing a sum to purchase for each of his children a Bible and a Westminster Confession of Faith. But his library seems to have been his special delight, composed as it was of about one hundred volumes of standard works. He left this library to be divided into lots and kept by his five sons—the lots to be exchanged as they might desire. But no book of any lot was to be loaned, hired, or otherwise disposed of, under the penalty of forfeiture of all claim to the library; and in the event the sons should jointly agree to a loan, exchange, or sale, then the whole library was to be sold, and the proceeds paid over to the two daughters. Books of this library are still to be found in Third Creek. As it may be interesting to the curious to know what kind of books were found in an intelligent planter's library one hundred years ago, I give the list that accompanies the Will: "Henry's Commentary, Burket on New Testament, Theory of the Earth, Derham on Isaiah, Beatty on Truth, Lee's Law Commonplaced, Muller's Fortification, Derham's Astrotheology, Life of David, Puffendorff's History of Europe, Salmon's Gazette, Law of Evidence, Salmon's Geography, Blackstone's Commentaries, Mair's Bookkeeping, Brown's Dictionary of the Bible, Hobbs on Human Nature, Nature of the Passions and Affections, Athenian Sport, Virgil, Owen on Sin, Man of Pleasure, Various Subjects, Nature Displayed, Moor's Dialogues, The Soul of Astrology, Locke's Essays, Dryden on Poesy, Cruikshank's History of the Church, Cunn's Euclid, Gulliver's Travels, Baxter on Religion, Addison's Spectator, Watson's Body of Divinity, Book of Gauging, Young's Night Thoughts, Salmon's Chronology, Junius' Letters, Matho, Stackhouse (6 vols.), Flavel's Works (8 vols.), Cole's Dictionary, Oziel's Logic, Abridgement of Irish Statutes, Religion of Nature, Young Man's Companion, Atkinson's Effectum, Tisset, Seller's Navigation, Theory of Fortification, The Independent Whig, Parker's Justice."

Scripture, theology, literature, history, military tactics, navigation, poetry—a good library of the best books, graced the shelves of the Third Creek patriot and planter. His library shows that he was a man of no ordinary taste and judgment. Drinking in knowledge from so many and such healthful fountains, we can well understand why he was put forth by his fellow-citizens in times of trial and danger.

The facts and traditions above written were gathered from Wheeler's History, American Archives, a note from Dr. B. D. Wood—a greatgrandson of Samuel Young, Mr. Franklin Johnston, and others.

Moses Winslow and Alexander Osborne

The southwestern corner of Old Rowan County was occupied by a noble and patriotic race of people one hundred years ago. There you will find the original home of families known by the names of Davidson, Reese, Hughes, Ramsay, Brevard, Osborne, Winslow, Kerr, Rankin, Templeton, Dickey, Braley, Moore, Emerson, Torrence, Houston. There the Rev. John Thompson closed his labors, and lies sleeping in Baker's graveyard. His daughter, the widow Baker, afterwards married Dr. Charles Harris of Cabarrus, the ancestor of the late William Shakespeare Harris, Esq. Prominent among these families were the Osbornes and Winslows.

Alexander Osborne

was born in New Jersey in 1709, and came to Rowan County about 1755. He settled on the headwaters of Rocky River, and called his place "Belmont." A neighbor of his selected for residence the name of "Mount Mourne," after a mountain in Ireland. Another, not to be outdone in names called his place "Purgatory." These names are still familiar to the people of that section. Osborne was a colonel in the Colonial Government, and a man of influence in his day. He married Agnes McWhorter, the sister of the Rev. Dr. McWhorter, for some time president of Queens Museum, in Charlotte. Their place was the home of the early traveling missionaries to the South. Here the Rev. Hugh McAden stopped, in 1755, and preached at the "New Meeting House" nearby (Center). Here about the same time was established the "Crowfield Academy," where David Caldwell taught a few years later. In Center Church yard is a double headstone, telling the inquirer that Alexander Osborne died on the eleventh day of July, 1776, and his wife, Agnes, two days later. He probably never heard of the Declaration of Independence, made seven days before his death. He had gone to a brighter world, where the alarms of war never come. These parents left two children—Adlai Osborne and Jean Osborne. Adlai was graduated at Princeton College in 1768. His name appears as Clerk of the Rowan County Court under the Royal Government, and he held that post in the New Government until 1809. He died in 1815. Among his children were two sons whose names are distinguished. The one was Spruce Macay Osborne, who was graduated at the University of North Carolina in 1806, became a surgeon in the army and was killed in the War of 1812, at the massacre of Fort Mimms. The other son, Edwin Jay Osborne, the father of the late Hon. James W. Osborne, of Charlotte, was himself an eminent lawyer, distinguished for his learning and eloquence. Intimately connected with the Osborne family, was the family of

Moses Winslow

Benjamin Winslow or Winsley, as it was first written, obtained a grant of eight hundred and twenty-five acres of land, "on both sides of the South Fork of Davises Creek—waters of Catawba River," under date of May 11, 1757. A still earlier grant to Benjamin Winslow, under date of March 25, 1752, is for five hundred and eighty-seven acres, in the same neighborhood, adjoining the lands of John McConnell. This is described as lying in Anson

County, Parish of ——. This was before Rowan was erected into a county. In 1758, Benjamin Winslow, Sr., made a deed of gift to his son, Benjamin Winslow, Jr., of five hundred and thirty-five acres, adjoining the lands of Hugh Lawson, Patrick Hamilton, Mrs. Baker, and Moses White. From these records we get a glimpse of families residing in the neighborhood. The first Moses White emigrated from Ireland about 1742, and married the daughter of Hugh Lawson, named above. James White, son of the above couple, and the eldest of six brothers, was a soldier of the Revolution, but moved to East Tennessee in 1786, and was one of the original founders of the now flourishing city of Knoxville. He was distinguished for his bravery, energy, and talents, and was a brigadier-general in the Creek War. His illustrious son, Hugh Lawson White, was a Judge of the Supreme Court of Tennessee, a Senator of the United States, president of the Senate, and in 1836 a candidate for President of the United States. His remains sleep peacefully under the vines and grass of the churchyard of the First Presbyterian Church of Knoxville.

From these deeds, and other sources, we learn that Benjamin Winslow had three children—Benjamin, Moses, and Mary. Of these we propose to record a few facts.

Alexander Osborne and Benjamin Winslow were near neighbors, living only two or three miles apart. As a matter of course their boys, Moses and Adlai, were early companions and associates. Adlai Osborne had a fair young sister—pretty Jean Osborne, the rose of Belmont. It was the same old story, told under the leafy oaks of Rowan, and pretty Jean Osborne became the bride of young Moses Winslow. This was in 1760. They settled upon some of the Winslow lands, according to the custom of the day; for the original settlers, tinctured with European notions, rarely gave land to their daughters, but divided the inheritance among the sons. The home of this couple was not far from Center Church—the property owned by the late Sidney Houston, Esq. For sixteen years their home was without children. But in the eventful year of 1776 came the first child, a daughter whom they named Dovey. She grew up to be a famous beauty and belle of that region. Her heart was at length won by Dr. Joseph McKnitt Alexander, son of John McKnitt Alexander. Her life was not a long one, but she left one son, Moses Winslow Alexander, who lived about ten miles north of Charlotte on the Statesville Road. Some of his children are still living.

On the first day of February, 1771, Cornwallis' troops crossed the Catawba River and marched towards Salisbury. In their march several houses were burned down. When they reached the house of Moses Winslow, knowing that he was a prominent man, a member of the Provincial Congress, and on the Rowan Committee of Safety, the soldiers applied the torch to his residence. At the same time some ruffian soldiers were endeavoring to cut from Mrs. Winslow the capacious outside pockets, so fashionable in that day, in which she had deposited some of her household valuables. While she was helplessly submitting to the indignity Lord Cornwallis himself rode up, and in obedience to the instincts of an English gentleman ordered them to desist, and to extinguish the fire kindled against the house.

Moses Winslow lived to be eighty-three years of age. He and his wife sleep in the graveyard of Center Church, where her father and mother are resting side by side.

Besides their beautiful daughter, Dovey, they had two other daughters, named Cynthia and Roscinda. The reader may have remarked that while these venerable pioneers were apt to name their sons after one of the patriarchs, prophets, or twelve apostles, with now and then a selection from the kings of England, they gave poetical or fanciful names to their daughters—Cynthia, Roscinda, Lillis, or Juliette. Cynthia Winslow was married to Samuel King, and was the mother of the well-known and talented Junius and Albert King. Roscinda Winslow married her cousin, William J. Wilson, and their daughter, Mary Wilson, became the wife of Ezekiel Polk—the grandfather of the President, James Knox Polk. Our illustrious North Carolina statesman, the late Hon. William A. Graham, was also a descendant of Mary, the sister of Moses Winslow. So likewise was Col. Isaac Hayne, of Charleston, with numerous other prominent and influential citizens. The old homesteads have fallen to ruins, and the plowshare of strangers, who never heard the names of these noble old families, runs smoothly over the ground where their altar fires once burned brightly. Emigration has borne them away, and in the new States the old names are found. But North Carolina should treasure up their history as an incentive to noble deeds in the days of trial yet to come.

Before closing these sketches, I must put on record all that is known here of the history of one who left his name on the records of our Courts and Committees.

William Kennon

appears prominent among the actors in public affairs at the opening and during the first years of the war. He was a lawyer, and it is supposed that he came to Salisbury from Wilmington, or from some other portion of Eastern Carolina. On the twenty-fifth of August, 1775, he represented the town of Salisbury in the Provincial Congress at Newbern. As early as the eighth of August, 1774, he was chosen as a member of the Rowan Committee of Safety, and on the twenty-seventh of September of the same year, he appears as chairman of this Committee, with Adlai Osborne as Clerk. Colonel Kennon was a very zealous patriot, and his name appears among the signers of the Mecklenburg Declaration of May 20, 1775. The appearance of his name on that paper can be accounted for only on the theory that the Mecklenburg patriots had no very rigorous committee on credentials on that occasion. Colonel Kennon seems to have been the prime mover in the abduction of John Dunn and Benjamin Boothe Boote, Esqs. Whether the young lawyer, so popular among the people, was jealous of the old lawyers, who got the most of the legal business of Salisbury, or whether the old lawyers, always the most conservative, and constitutional sticklers for precedent, moved too slowly for the ardent patriotism of the young lawyer, it is impossible at this late date to determine. But this much appears to be true—that somewhere about August, 1774, John Dunn, B. B. Boote, Wallace Lindsay, and one other man, signed a paper containing a general declaration of fidelity, allegiance, obedience, and submission to the British Acts of Parliament. This paper seems to have been a kind of private protest against rebellion, kept by Mr. Boote for future emergencies. The parties signing it do not appear to have taken any public steps against the movement then in progress, but as crown officers contented themselves with the quiet discharge of duty. The paper, however, or a copy of it, got out among the people, and aroused suspicion. At the instance of Colonel Kennon, Dunn and Boote were hurried off in the night to Charlotte, thence to Camden, and ultimately to Charleston. The conduct of Colonel Kennon was deemed arbitrary and malicious by some of the citizens of Salisbury, and Dr. Anthony Newman, and others, men of unimpeachable patriotism, presented a petition to the Committee embodying the idea that the affair was arbitrary and malicious. Be that as it may, Dunn and Boote never got a hearing, though they prayed to be heard, and were kept in confinement for many weary months in Charleston.

Just at this point it becomes necessary to correct an error which Colonel Wheeler published, and which has been repeated by other writers since. It is that John Dunn and B. B. Boote never returned to North Carolina, but after the war was over settled in Florida. This leaves the two gentlemen in the attitude of permanent disaffection to the cause of American liberty; but there is abundance of proof in the records of Rowan Court to prove that both returned and conducted themselves as good and patriotic citizens, at an early period of the War of Independence. In March, 1777, B. B. Boote bought a tract of land in Salisbury, and proved a deed in open Court. On the eighth day of August, 1777, Mr. Boote took the oath of expurgation for disaffected or suspected persons.

On the same day, August 8, 1777, John Dunn, Esq., took the required oath of an attorney in the State of North Carolina, and shortly after this date he became State's Attorney for Rowan County. Certainly at this period there remained not the least lingering doubt of his sympathy with the cause of American freedom. Still further, on the eighth of August, 1781, five months after the battle of Guilford Courthouse, John Dunn and Matthew Troy, Esqs., were appointed Commissioners by the County Court, Adlai Osborne being chairman, to repair the courthouse in Salisbury. From this it would appear that all suspicion or unfriendliness, if any ever existed, had vanished from the mind of the high-toned Osborne. Mr. Dunn died in Salisbury in the early part of 1783. Letters of administration on the estate of John Dunn were granted to Francis Dunn and Spruce Macay on the twenty-fifth of March, 1783. The traditions of his family relate that he was taken sick while pleading a case in the old courthouse, where the Public Square in Salisbury is, and that he was carried down to a hotel belonging to William Temple Coles, where Kluttz's drug store now stands. After lingering awhile he passed away. His body was interred on his own lands near Dunn's Mountain. No man knows where his grave is, but the mountain he owned, with its granite cliffs, standing in full view of the Public Square of Salisbury, is his monument. There it stands, a solitary sentinel, overlooking not only the broad lands he once owned and his unknown grave, but the very spot where for a quarter-century he won laurels as the leading lawyer of Salisbury bar.

The events at the opening of the war are to be accounted for, first on the principle that old men, especially lawyers, are slow and cautious in exchanging their allegiance. None knows so well as they what are the results that follow in the wake of revolution. They are in the habit of looking at results and consequences. A second cause is found in the characteristic violence and intolerance of such times of excitement and struggle. Reports fly rapidly and gain ready credence. That Committee of Safety actually resolved that good old Maxwell Chambers, their Treasurer, be publicly advertised *as an enemy to the common cause of liberty,* for raising the price of his goods above that of the year past. Furthermore Dunn and Boote were men of great influence, and the easiest way to dispose of them was to send them away without a hearing. No doubt, if granted a hearing, they would have cleared themselves of all acts or purposes of hostility to American liberty. But this the Committee did not know. Colonel Kennon, being the leader in this affair, seems to have removed from Salisbury to Georgia, at or about the time that Dunn and Boote returned. So far as known to the writer he lived an honored and useful life in the State of his adoption. One of his descendants was in Salisbury a few years ago, but he knew little of his ancestor.

Authorities: *Mrs. H. M. I., in Southern Home; Hunter's Western North Carolina; Wheeler, Records of Rowan Court; Miss C. B.*

CHAPTER XIV

ROWAN COUNTY COMMITTEE OF SAFETY

Who sounded the first note of liberty in North Carolina? There are claimants for this honor, but their claims are not fully established. In the unsettled state of affairs immediately preceding the Revolution of 1776, public opinion was drifting insensibly for a number of years in the direction of a higher form of civil liberty.

Besides this, many have confounded liberty with independence. The desire to preserve their liberties was universal before the thought of independence gained any hold upon the public mind. Colonel Moore, in his History of North Carolina, affirms that as late as the meeting of the Continental Congress, in September, 1774, there were but three men in America who contemplated actual independence of the crown of England. These were Patrick Henry of Virginia, William Hooper of North Carolina, and Samuel Adams of Massachusetts. These three had given utterance to sentiments of independence, but the Congress avowed its loyalty to the King, and protested its devotion to the British constitution. The Congress of North Carolina, in August, 1774, protested the same loyalty; but at the same time there were opinions on the subject of human rights, and plans and purposes on the subject of trade and taxation, and resolves on the matter of a union of the colonies, whose inevitable consequence was the ultimate independence of the colonies, unless the British Parliament should recede from the position they had deliberately chosen. It matters little who first called for independence, provided we know who first avowed the principles that inevitably led to that result.

Without claiming that these principles were first conceived in Rowan County, or even that they were first avowed here, from the documentary evidence before the public for thirty years it may be affirmed that the first recorded adoption of these principles occurred in Salisbury. Nearly a year before the patriotic citizens of Mecklenburg adopted their famous "Resolves" of the thirty-first of May, which so irritated Governor Martin, and provoked his angry letter from the lower Cape Fear; and nearly two years before the National Declaration of Independence, the citizens of Rowan adopted a paper that contains the germs of independence. This was on the eighth of August, 1774. The evidence of this is found in the Journal of the Committee of Safety of Rowan County, found recorded on pp. 360-62 of Colonel Wheeler's Sketches of North Carolina, Vol. II. This document was discovered in Iredell County, among the papers of the Sharpe family, by the Rev. E. F. Rockwell, and published by Colonel Wheeler in 1851. William Sharpe was the last secretary of the Committee, and preserved the Minutes that were found in the hands of his descendants. Colonel Wheeler vouches for the genuineness of the document.

This Committee of Safety began its sessions, according to these Minutes, on the eighth of August, 1774, seventeen days before the assembling of the first North Carolina Provincial Congress. This committee was probably chosen at the time appointed for electing members to the General Assembly of the Province, or it may have come into existence before that time in obedience to the wishes of the people. The members of the committee were chosen from all parts of this grand old county, and numbred twenty-five. The following is a list of their names: James McCay, Andrew Neal, George Cathey, Alexander Dobbins, Francis McCorkle, Matthew Locke, Maxwell Chambers, Henry Harmon, Abraham Denton, William Davidson, Samuel Young, John Brevard, William Kennon, George Henry Barringer, Robert Bell, John Bickerstaff, John Cowden, John Lewis Beard, John Nesbit, Charles McDowell, Robert Blackburn, Christopher Beekman, William Sharpe, John Johnson, and Morgan Bryan.

At their first recorded meeting, August 8, 1774, this committee adopted seventeen resolutions upon public affairs, showing that they were in the very forefront of liberal and patriotic opinions.

As this paper is not generally known, we give it entire.

"At a meeting of the committee, August 8, 1774, the following resolves were unanimously agreed to:

Resolved, That we will at all times whenever we are called upon for that purpose, maintain and defend, at the expense of our lives and fortunes, His Majesty's right and title to the crown of Great Britain and his dominions in America, to whose royal person and government we profess all due obedience and fidelity.

Resolved, That the right to impose taxes or duties, to be paid by the inhabitants within this Province, for any purpose whatsoever, is peculiar and essential to the General Assembly, in whom the legislative authority of the colony is vested.

Resolved, That every attempt to impose such taxes or duties by any other authority is an arbitrary exertion of power, and an infringement of the constitutional rights and liberties of the colony.

Resolved, That to impose a tax or duty on tea by the British Parliament, in which the North American Colonies can have no representation, to be paid upon importation by the inhabitants of the said colonies, is an act of power without right. It is subversive to the liberties of the said colonies, deprives them of their property without their own consent, and thereby reduces them to a state of slavery.

Resolved, That the late cruel and sanguinary acts of Parliament, to be executed by military force and ships of war upon our sister colony of Massachusetts Bay and town of Boston, is a strong evidence of the corrupt influence obtained by the British Ministry in Parliament, and a convincing proof of their fixed intention to deprive the colonies of their constitutional rights and liberties.

Resolved, That the cause of the town of Boston is the common cause of the American Colonies.

Resolved, That it is the duty and interest of all the American Colonies firmly to unite in an indissoluble union and association, to oppose by every just and proper means the infringement of their common rights and privileges.

Resolved, That a general association between all the American Colonies not to import from Great Britain any commodity whatsoever (except such things as shall be hereafter excepted by the General Congress of this Province), ought to be entered into, and not dissolved till the just rights of the colonies are restored to them, and the cruel acts of the British Parliament against the Massachusetts Bay and town of Boston are repealed.

Resolved, That no friend to the rights and liberties of America ought to purchase any commodity whatsoever, except such as shall be excepted, which shall be imported from Great Britain after the General Association shall be agreed upon.

Resolved, That every kind of luxury, dissipation, and extravagance ought to be banished from among us.

Resolved, That manufacturers ought to be encouraged by opening subscriptions for that purpose, or by any other proper means.

Resolved, That the African slave trade is injurious to this colony, obstructs the population of it by free men, prevents manufacturers and other useful immigrants from Europe from settling among us, and occasions an annual increase of the balance of trade against the colonies.

Resolved, That the raising of sheep, hemp, and flax ought to be encouraged.

Resolved, That to be clothed in manufactures fabricated in the colonies ought to be considered as a badge of distinction, of respect, and true patriotism.

Resolved, That Messrs. Samuel Young and Moses Winslow, for the County of Rowan, and for the town of Salisbury, William Kennon, Esq., be, and they are hereby, nominated and appointed Deputies upon the part of the inhabitants and freeholders of this county, and town of Salisbury, to meet such Deputies as shall be appointed by the other counties and corporations within this colony, at Johnston Courthouse, the twentieth of this instant.

Resolved, That, at this important and alarming crisis, it be earnestly recommended to the said Deputies at their General Convention, that they nominate and appoint one proper person out of each district of this Province, to meet such Deputies in a General Congress, as shall be appointed upon the part of the other Continental Colonies in America, to consult and agree upon a firm and indissoluble union and association, for preserving, by the best and most proper means, their common rights and liberties.

Resolved, That this colony ought not to trade with any colony which shall refuse to join in any union and association that shall be agreed upon by the greater part of the other colonies on this continent, for preserving their common rights and liberties."

An analysis of these resolves shows that these early patriots comprehended all the great doctrines of civil liberty. They began with the profession of loyalty to their king. An examination of a large number of similar papers adopted about the same time, in Virginia and in the more northern colonies, reveals the same acknowledgment of loyalty to the House of Hanover. To have omitted it would have been evidence of treasonable designs. Men educated under monarchical rule sometimes affirm their loyalty in amusing ways. The Parliament of England, in the days of Charles I, levied war against the king in the name of the king himself, for his own good. In the case of the Revolutionary patriots, there is little reason to doubt the genuineness of their profession in the early days of the struggle. They entertained hopes of securing their liberties by the repeal of the odious laws, as they had done in the matter of the stamp duties several years before.

In the next place they firmly declared that no person had a right to levy taxes upon them except their own representatives in Assembly. This was the pivot on which the whole matter turned. And to prevent the arbitrary imposition of taxes, they proposed an indissoluble union and association of all the American Colonies, and do all in their power towards securing this union, by appointing Deputies to a Provincial Congress and recommending those Deputies to secure the appointment of representatives to a Continental Congress. The other resolutions concerning luxury, home manufacture, the slave trade, and sympathy with Boston, are subordinate to the others.

Having affirmed their political creed, the Committee adjourned until the twenty-second of September, 1774. At the next meeting, William Kennon appears as chairman and Adlai Osborne as clerk. Their first business was to read and approve the resolves of the Provincial Congress that had met in the interval, and take steps towards carrying them out. Maxwell Chambers was appointed treasurer of the committee, and an order issued that each militia company in the county pay twenty pounds (£20), proclamation money, into his hands. As there were nine companies of militia in the county, this would aggregate the sum of one hundred and eighty pounds (£180), or between four and five hundred dollars. This money was to be used by the committee at discretion, for the purchase of powder, flints, and other military munitions. This conduct, as early as September, 1774, showed that the idea of resistance was growing up rapidly in the minds of the patriots of Rowan. This committee fixed the price of powder, and examined carefully into the political sentiments of the people. If they were not satisfied with a man's conduct, they did not hesitate to declare him an enemy to liberty, and to put him under suitable restraint. They also, in after days, took control of Court matters, allowing some to enter suits against others, and forbidding some. No doubt many of their acts were arbitrary in a high degree, and sometimes an infrigement of the liberty they proposed to protect. But when the storm of war was about to break upon the country, the committee acted vigorously, awaking zeal, suppressing disaffection, embodying militia companies, providing ammunition, and doing all they could to support the cause of freedom. Nor did they confine themselves to deliberation, but they took the field. General Rutherford, Colonel Locke, Gen. William Davidson, and others, won for themselves honorable names in many a march and skirmish, and many a hard-fought battle.

CHAPTER XV

MILITARY AFFAIRS

The Provincial Congress of North Carolina held its fourth meeting at Halifax, beginning on the fourth of April, 1776. Rowan was represented by Griffith Rutherford and Matthew Locke. This Congress was fully aware that the General Congress at Philadelphia was continuously moving towards a general declaration of independence, and was in full sympathy with it. The North Carolina statesmen were well aware that independence could not be achieved except by a fearful struggle against the military power of Britain. In order to be ready for this emergency, the judicial districts were made into military districts, and a Brigadier-General appointed for each. Griffith Rutherford was appointed General for the Salisbury district. In Rowan County there were two regiments and two sets of field officers. Of the first regiment, Francis Locke was Colonel; Alexander Dobbins, Lieutenant-Colonel; and James Brandon and James Smith, Majors. Of the second regiment (up the Catawba River), Christopher Beekman was Colonel; Charles McDowell, Lieutenant-Colonel; and Hugh Brevard and George Wilfong, Majors. Among the Company officers, we notice Captains Robert Smith, William Temple Coles, Thomas Haines, and Jesse Saunders, with Lieutenants William Brownfield, James Carr, William Caldwell, David Craige, Thomas Pickett, William Clover, John Madaris, and Pleasant Henderson. Among the officers of Light Horse Companies, we notice Martin Phifer, Captain; James Sumner, Lieutenant; and Valentine Beard, Cornet. These were all, or nearly all, from Rowan County. This military organization was intended for active service, whenever emergencies should rise. And the emergency for calling out the soldiers of the Salisbury district soon arose. Early in July of the same year, General Rutherford led nineteen hundred men across the mountains to scourge and hold in check the Cherokees. This was more of an excursion than a war, for there was no open enemy to face, nothing but hills and mountains and rivers to be overcome, and a secret enemy waylaying their march and firing upon them from the wilderness, or from inaccessible crags along their way. But the object was accomplished, and the Cherokees were compelled to sue for peace.

In the organization and drill of these military companies strange scenes were sometimes enacted. Mingled among the patriots there were often men disaffected to the cause of freedom. Some of these men had been Regulators a few years before, and at the conclusion of that contest, terrible oaths had been imposed upon them, which now entangled their consciences. When the Declaration of Independence had been made, and it was understood that they might soon be called to fight against the troops of England, the disaffected began to draw back, while the Whigs were for moving forward. In the Company from the forks of the Yadkin one of these strange scenes was once enacted. Captain Bryan of that Company was disaffected, while the lieutenant, Richmond Pearson, was a Whig. On the muster, a dispute arose upon political matters between these two officers, and the Company decided that this great national question should be decided by a fair fist-fight between the captain and the lieutenant, and that the Company should go with the victor. The fight came off in due time and manner, and Lieutenant Pearson succeeded in giving Captain Bryan a sound thrashing. The Forks Company after that became zealous Whigs, while the crowd from Dutchman's Creek followed Captain Bryan and became Tories. Captain Pearson with his Company took the field against Lord Cornwallis as he passed through North Carolina. They were present at Cowan's Ford on the first of February, 1781, when General Davidson fell. Captain Pearson was the grandfather of the Hon. Richmond M. Pearson, the distinguished Chief Justice of North Carolina for so many years.

Captain Bryan became a confirmed loyalist, and was the notorious Colonel Bryan, who according to Dr. Caruthers, on the spur of the moment collected eight hundred Tories in the Forks of the Yadkin, and marched them off to Anson Courthouse to the British. While Colonel Fanning headed the Loyalists in the region of Deep River and the upper Cape Fear, and Colonels McNeil, Ray, Graham, and McDougal did the same for the region of the lower Caper Fear and Pee Dee, and Col. Johnson Moore, with Major Welch, and Captains Whitson and Murray, sustained the Loyalists' cause in Lincoln, Burke, and Rutherford Counties, Colonels Bryan and Hampton, and Major Elrod were the Tory leaders of Rowan County. The chief field of their operations was the region called the Forks of the Yadkin. This was an extensive tract, lying between the main Yadkin and the South Fork, beginning at the junction of these two streams about five miles from Salisbury, called "The Point," and extending from "The Point" northward and westward for a distance of forty or fifty miles. There Colonel Bryan ranged over plains and hills, through the Brushy Mountains, to the foothills of the Blue

Ridge. He was connected with Colonel Fanning's troop only in a general way, and does not seem to have been, like him, a cruel and bloodthirsty man. In 1781, Colonel Bryan headed his troop of Loyalists in the partisan warfare in South Carolina. He was under Major Carden, at the military post established by Lord Rawdon, at Hanging Rock, in South Carolina, in 1781. Major William R. Davie, of North Carolina, with his cavalry troop and some Mecklenburg militia, under Colonel Higgins, hastened to attack this post at Hanging Rock. As he was approaching he learned that three Companies of Bryan's Loyalists were encamped at a farmhouse, on their return from a foraging expedition. He immediately went in search of them, and soon made a vigorous attack upon them in front and rear, completely routing them, and killing or wounding all of them but a few. The spoils of this victory were sixty horses and one hundred muskets. Major Davie, though an Englishman by birth, was a law student in Salisbury during the first years of the war. In 1779 he was elected Lieutenant in a troop of Horse raised in Mecklenburg and the Waxhaws, and was attached to Pulaski's legion. He soon rose to the rank of Major; but being wounded in the battle of Stono, below Charleston, he returned to Salisbury and resumed his studies. In the winter of 1780 he again raised a troop of cavalry, and in the absence of any statement to the contrary we would naturally infer that his Company was raised in Rowan County, especially since Lieut. George Locke, of Rowan, was in it. It was with these troops, and the Mecklenburg militia, that he cut to pieces Colonel Bryan's Companies at Hanging Rock. It was thus that our people were arrayed against each other in this terrible struggle for liberty.

Colonel Bryan was afterwards tried by the Courts of North Carolina for disloyalty to his country, but no act of inhumanity was proved against him, and no charge was made out except that of being in arms against his country.

From the time that Lord Cornwallis left the lower Cape Fear, in the early part of 1775, until 1780, there were few if any British troops in North Carolina. But during all these four years the flower of the North Carolina soldiery were far from their homes—in the north under General Washington, or in the South under General Lincoln, Gates, or other National Commanders. Thus we read in history that the North Carolina Continentals and a brigade of militia under Gen. John Ashe were present at Charleston, June 8, 1776, when Sir Peter Parker was beaten off from Fort Moultrie on Sullivan's Island. At the same time General Rutherford of

Rowan, with Colonels Polk of Mecklenburg, and Martin of Guilford, marched nineteen hundred men against the Indians in what is now Tennessee. Early in 1777 the North Carolina Continentals went to the support of General Washington in the North. The whole of the North Carolina Continentals were with General Washington at the battle of Brandywine, September 11, 1777. North Carolinians were also at the battle of Princeton. At Germantown also North Carolina troops made for themselves a glorious record, and on that fatal field was poured out some of the best blood of the State. There Gen. Francis Nash, of Orange County, brother of Gov. Abner Nash, commanded a brigade under General Washington, and fell in battle. There too fell Col. Edward Buncombe and Colonel Irwin, besides a large number of subalterns and privates. In 1778 the North Carolina Continentals were found engaged in the battle of Monmouth. Shortly after this time all the North Carolina battalions, except the third and fifth, were transferred under General Lincoln to Charleston, S. C. In 1779, we find two thousand North Carolina militia, under General Ashe, at the battle of Brier Creek, in Georgia. In consequence of the precipitation of General Lincoln in rushing untrained militia upon dangerous ground, this affair of Brier Creek was a sad defeat. But immediately after this disaster, the North Carolina Assembly ordered the enrollment of eight thousand new levies. These were placed under the command of Gen. Richard Caswell. In the year 1779, General Lincoln's forces at Charleston consisted chiefly of six North Carolina batallions. These, by years of service, had become veterans. General Lincoln placed these battalions in the center, while Major William R. Davie with his mounted troops led on the right, at the bloody battle of Stono. And when, on the twelfth of May, 1780, General Lincoln surrendered Charleston to Sir Henry Clinton, all the North Carolina Continentals and a thousand of her militia became prisoners of war. This was a terrible blow to North Carolina, at this particular juncture. Lord Cornwallis at once assumed charge of the British forces and marched towards North Carolina, at the very time when her entire forces of trained soldiers were consigned to an enforced military inactivity. But to make matters worse, General Caswell, with a considerable portion of the North Carolina militia, became connected with General Gates' army, and on the fifteenth and sixteenth of August of the same year, sustained the disastrous defeat near Camden, S. C. General Rutherford with Colonels Lockhart and Geddy were among the captives. Major Davie with his small band of troopers still hovered around the Waxhaws, while Gens. Jethro

Sumner and William Davidson still kept the field with a few North Carolina militia on the borders of the State. But even these were pressed back as far as Charlotte by the British forces. With one hundred and fifty cavalry, and fourteen volunteers under Major Graham, Colonel Davie gave Tarleton's legion a warm reception at Charlotte Courthouse. But they could not hold their ground against overwhelming numbers. Retreating on the Salisbury Road, a skirmish occurred between Charlotte and Sugar Creek Church, at which Lieut. George Locke was slain. Lord Cornwallis did not remain long at Charlotte. So hostile were the people, and so much did bodies of armed men harrass his troops on their foraging excursions, that Cornwallis bestowed upon that section the name of the "Hornets' Nest," a name that every patriotic son of Mecklenburg cherishes as fondly as an Englishman does the titles of knighthood, or the decorations of the Star and Garter. Colonel Tarleton says: "It was evident, and had been frequently mentioned to the King's officers, that the Counties of Mecklenburg and Rohan (Rowan) were more hostile to England than any others in America. The vigilance and animosity of these surrounding districts checked the exertions of the well affected, and totally destroyed all communications between the King's troops and Loyalists in other parts of the Province. No British commander could obtain any information in that position which would facilitate his designs, or guide his future conduct." Steadman says that the only way they could secure their foraging parties from destruction was for Lord Rawdon to take one-half of the army one day, and Colonel Webster the other half the next day, to protect them from the inhabitants.

Owing to these causes, and further to the destruction of Ferguson at King's Mountain, on the seventh of October, Lord Cornwallis determined to return to South Carolina.

Such was the condition of matters in North Carolina at the time when Lord Cornwallis reëntered the State, the twentieth of January, 1781.

During this time the able-bodied men were either in the troops of Colonels Davie, Locke, or Gen. William Davidson, or were prisoners of war, or on parole, and therefore prevented from taking up arms. As a consequence the women of that day were left at home, often entirely unprotected, or with only the old men and the boys, the former too old, the latter too young, for military duty. But these ladies were the mothers, wives, daughters, sisters, and sweethearts of heroes on the tented field, and their hearts burned with patriotic feelings. Those whom they loved were exposed to hardship and danger and in behalf of their homes and families, and thus the love of the patriots' cause was not with them an abstraction, or a sentiment, but an undying passion. As an illustration of this, we quote from Lossing's "Pictorial Field Book (Vol. II, p. 626. note 2): "On one occasion, the young ladies of Mecklenburg and Rowan entered into a pledge not to receive the attentions of young men who would not volunteer in defense of the country, they being of the opinion that such persons as stay loitering at home, when the importunate calls of the country demanded their military services abroad, must certainly be destitute of that nobleness of sentiment, that brave and manly spirit, which would qualify them to be the defenders and guardians of the fair sex." (From *South Carolina Gazette,* February, 1780.) As early as May 8, 1776, the young ladies of Rowan had taken important action upon this subject. At a meeting of the Committee of Safety of that date, we have the following entry upon the Minutes, viz.: "A letter from a number of young ladies in the county, directed to the chairman, requesting the approbation of the committee to a number of resolutions enclosed, entered into, and signed by the same young ladies, being read:

"Resolved, That this Committee present their cordial thanks to the said young ladies for so spirited a performance, look upon their resolutions to be sensible and polite; that they merit the honor, and are worthy the imitation of every young lady in America."

What a pity that we have not a copy of these spirited resolutions, and the names of the fair signers! They were probably similar to those entered into by the Mecklenburg and Rowan ladies four years later, including perhaps a resolution in behalf of simplicity in dress, abstinence from luxuries, and sympathy with the cause of independence, not yet declared at Philadelphia. And then the names! Who were they? Daughters of the Brandons, Lockes, Youngs, Chamberses, Gillespies, Osbornes, Davidsons, Winslows, Simontons, Brevards, Sharpes, no doubt; but the dainty signatures to the "spirited performance" are lost, and the fair signers that signed them have moldered away. For is it not one hundred and four years since all this was done? A further illustration of matronly zeal and self-denial in behalf of the cause of liberty will be recited in its proper place.

CHAPTER XVI

GENERAL GREENE AND LORD CORNWALLIS IN ROWAN COUNTY

Lossing in his "Field Book," says that "the village of Salisbury is the capital of Rowan County, a portion of the 'Hornets' Nest' of the Revolution. It is a place of considerable historic note. On account of its geographical position it was often the place for the rendezvous of the militia preparing for the battlefields of various regular corps, American and British, during the last years of the war, and especially as the brief resting-place of both armies during Greene's memorable retreat" (Vol. II, p. 615). The writer is not aware that the British troops were ever in Salisbury, except once, when Lord Cornwallis was in pursuit of General Greene. Mr. Lossing seems to have been peculiarly unfortunate in his visit to Salisbury. He seems to have seen nothing there that had any historic interest, although the house occupied by Cornwallis, as his headquarters, was still standing there (January, 1849), besides other buildings where the British officers congregated, as we shall see. He seems however to have heard of the famous Rowan "Natural Wall," which he locates in Salisbury, and supposes to be "a part of the circumvallation of a city of the Mound Builders!" The fact is that about three miles from Salisbury, and again about nine miles from Salisbury, in the direction of Mocksville, there are "trap dikes," or natural walls of trap rock, beneath the surface of the ground, from twelve to fourteen feet deep, and twenty-two inches thick, as Lossing says, that have the appearance of being laid in cement. But this cement is nothing but a fine decomposition of the trap rock itself, or an infiltration of fine material from without. Mr. Lossing does however give us in his book a beautiful little moonlight sketch of Trading Ford, showing the point of the island, and the row of stakes that then stood there to guard the stranger from the deep water below. There General Greene, with General Morgan and his light troops, crossed the Yadkin, February 2, 1781.

After the unfortunate battle of Camden, August 16, 1780, General Gates was superseded by General Greene, who immediately proceeded to his field of labor. Passing through Delaware, Maryland, and Virginia, and ascertaining what supplies he was likely to obtain from these States, he hastened on to Charlotte, the headquarters of the Southern Army, where he took formal command, December 3, 1780. Cornwallis had fallen back to Winnsboro. Greene divided his little army, sending the larger portion to the Pee Dee, near Cheraw, about seventy miles to the right of Lord Cornwallis. The other portion, consisting of about one thousand troops, he sent under General Morgan about fifty miles to the left of Cornwallis, to the junction of Broad and Pacolet Rivers, in Union District, S. C. General Morgan with his little force gained the memorable battle of the Cowpens over Colonel Tarleton, January 17, 1781. Colonel Tarleton, with the remnant of his troops, retreated precipitately to the main army of Cornwallis, while General Morgan with his prisoners hastily crossed the Broad River, and pressed towards the Catawba, to effect a junction with General Greene. This brought on the famous retreat of Greene, a military maneuver that will not compare unfavorably with Xenophon's famous "Retreat of the Ten Thousand." Mortified at the disaster that had befallen his favorite officer, Tarleton, and hoping to recover the prisoners carried away by General Morgan, Cornwallis began his pursuit on the twenty-fifth of January. At Ramsour's Mill—Lincolnton—he destroyed all his superfluous baggage, and hastened towards the Catawba River, hoping to overtake Morgan, encumbered as he was with prisoners, before he could effect a junction with General Greene's main army, supposed to be now hastening up from Cheraw. But we will probably get a clearer idea of this affair by following each party in succession, one at a time.

On the same day that Cornwallis began his pursuit—January 25, 1781—General Greene was apprised of Morgan's victory at Cowpens, and ordered General Stevens, with his body of Virginia militia, whose term of service was almost expiring, to hasten to Charlotte, relieve Morgan of his prisoners, and convey them to Charlottesville, Va., while he himself left the camp on Pee Dee under Generals Huger and Williams, and hastened, with one aide and two or three mounted militia, to meet Morgan on the Catawba. On the route he was informed of the pursuit of Cornwallis, and immediately sent orders to General Huger to break up the camp on the Pee Dee and meet Morgan in Salisbury or Charlotte. General Greene reached Sherrill's Ford on the Catawba, ten or fifteen miles above Beattie's Ford on the thirty-first of January, meeting General Morgan there, and taking charge of the future movements of his detachment. General Greene immediately placed the prisoners in the hands of Morgan's militia, to be carried to Virginia by a more northern route, while Morgan, with his five hundred regulars, was left unencumbered, and ordered to guard the Fords of the Catawba. On the same day General Greene issued a stirring appeal to Colonel Locke of Rowan, urging him to embody the militia and hasten to his assistance. But so many of the soldiers of Rowan were prisoners of war at this time, and the Fords of the Catawba were so numerous, and the enemy so near, that very little could be done to stay their progress. Gen. William Davidson succeeded in collecting three hundred militia, and was posted at Cowan's Ford, a few miles below Beattie's Ford, while Morgan with his regulars was higher up the river. In order to create the impression that the British would cross at Beattie's Ford, Cornwallis sent Colonel Webster with his brigade to that point, while he with the main body of his army decamped at midnight, and hastened to Cowan's Ford, which he reached a little before dawn, February 1, 1781. Plunging into the stream, nearly five hundred yards wide, and waist deep, the British soon reached the Mecklenburg shore, where they were received by General Davidson and his three hundred militia with a galling fire. The guide having deserted the British at the first shot of the sentinel, they missed the ford, and came out a considerable distance above the place where General Davidson was stationed. Davidson at once led his men to that part of the bank which faced the British. But by the time of his arrival, the light infantry had reached the shore, and quickly forming, they soon dispersed the handful of patriots. General Davidson was the last to leave the ground, and as he was mounting his horse to make his escape, he received a mortal wound. Dr. Caruthers states that General Davidson was killed by a shot fired by Frederick Hager, a German Tory, who piloted the British across the river, but this statement does not agree with the generally accredited story, that the pilot deserted at the sentinel's first fire. He was killed in Dr. Samuel E. McCorkle's great coat, which he had borrowed the day before. The Rev. Thomas H. McCaule, another Presbyterian minister, with Col. William Polk accompanied General Davidson to the river that morning. And when Cornwallis, after tarrying about three hours for the purpose of burying his dead, had proceeded in the direction of Salisbury, David Wilson and Richard Barry, both of whom were at the skirmish that morning, returned, and secured the body of General Davidson, and buried it in Hopewell churchyard that same night by torchlight. The Congress on the following September ordered a monument, costing not more than five hundred dollars, to be erected to his memory, but the resolution was never carried out. But it is a pleasing fact that a half-century later there was established near that place an institution of learning that was named Davidson College, after the brave and patriotic General. His son, William Lee Davidson, Esq., who was an early friend and patron of the College, gave the lands upon which it is situated to the trustees, and when leaving this State placed his father's trusty sword in the College. There it hangs today in the College Museum.

From Cowan's Ford, the British pressed on and soon met Colonel Webster's division, which had crossed at Beattie's Ford, at Torrence's Tavern; which Lord Cornwallis in his general orders styles "Crossroads to Salisbury," and Tarleton in his map designates as "Tarrant's." This place is about two miles above Davidson College, and within a quarter-mile from where "Center Depot," on the Atlantic Tennessee, and Ohio Railroad, now stands. They burned the house of Mr. Torrence, of John Brevard, General Davidson's father-in-law, and set fire to Moses Winslow's house; but the fire was extinguished by order of Lord Cornwallis. At Torrence's Tavern, Colonel Tarleton with his light horse found about three hundred American militia, with a motley company of refugees in their wagons, from South Carolina and elsewhere, fleeing for safety. Tarleton made an onslaught upon these, killed a few of the militia, less than ten, and scattered the refugees. He sustained a loss of seven men and twenty horses in this action. This was about two o'clock in the afternoon. From Cornwallis' order book we learn that the British army encamped at Torrence's that night, and began its march in pursuit of Greene at half-past five o'clock on the morning of the second of February. From Tarleton's map we learn that the route of the army was almost directly eastward for some fifteen or twenty miles, to a point which is called "Grimes," southeast of Salisbury. This was probably Graham's plantation, on the west side of Grant's Creek, near "Wiseman's Mill." This was in the immediate neighborhood of General Rutherford's residence, among the Lockes, Grahams, Brandons, Nesbits, and Allisons. Lord Cornwallis designates his headquarters for that day "Canthard's Plantation." As the Registry of Deeds shows no such name as "Canthard," this is probably a mistake for some other name. And since the "Order Book," as well as Tarleton's map, is full of errors in the spelling of names, arising from the fact that their information as to localities was frequently derived from ignorant persons, the better class keeping out of the way—it is easy to see how a stranger in hot pursuit of an enemy would confound familiar names. Or perhaps the printer might easily misread a manuscript written in haste by a busy secretary. It is probable therefore that instead of "Canthards" we should read "Rutherford's Plantation." From "Wiseman's Mill," there may be seen at many places the deep-cup bed of an old road, crossing the County westward, and passing a little southward of Villa Franca, the residence of the late Dr. F. N. Lucky. This road probably led on past "Atwell's" old place, past General Kerr's, now Mr. Hedrick's residence, and so on past Spring Grove, Cross Keys, and on to Torrence's. This was once called the "Old Wilmington Road." Having left Torrence's at half-past five that morning, February 2, a march of fifteen or eighteen miles would bring them to "Rutherford's Plantation." Anyone acquainted with these roads in midwinter, after a hard day's rain, will consider this a good half-day's march.

General Morgan was ahead of them, and the Yadkin was about fifteen miles from this post. There was therefore but a short rest, and they were on the march again. In a few miles they fell into the old "Trading Path," five or six miles south of Salisbury. And as darkness gathered around them, we conceive that they would be passing along that old "Pathway," then the Great South Road, somewhere about the western slopes of Dunn's Mountain, in haste to reach Trading Ford before Morgan should cross. Lord Cornwallis appears to have halted at a place which he styles "Camp Cassington," a fanciful name perhaps. This place may have been at a point about four miles east of Salisbury, between the residence of Dr. I. W. Jones and the railroad. We are led to this conjecture from the fact that there are quite a number of graves in the forest at that point, and none can account for their being there except on some such hypothesis. But while Cornwallis halted, he sent forward General O'Hara, Colonel Tarleton, and the Hessian Regiment of Bose, to the Trading Ford, hoping to find Morgan on the western bank. But the hope was a vain one. Morgan had crossed early in the evening, securing all the boats and flats on the eastern side. When therefore O'Hara and Tarleton reached the Ford at midnight, they found only a small detachment of American riflemen, left there to guard some wagons and stores belonging to the frightened country people, who were fleeing from the British army. A slight skirmish ensued, but the Americans escaped in the darkness. It was those who were killed at this skirmish, as well as some wounded ones that were brought from Cowan's Ford and Torrence's, that we suppose to have been buried at "Camp Cassington."

During the night, the river, already swollen by recent rains, and always pretty deep in winter, arose to an inmpassable height, and cut off all hope of pursuing the American troops on that route. It was now the third of February, and the British troops, after cannonading across the river from the "Heights of Gowerie," at the rear of the Americans, turned to retrace their steps, and either wait till the river fell or seek another route.

The following extract from the minutes of the Inferior Court of Rowan fixes these dates beyond dispute:

"Be it remembered that the British army marched into Salisbury on Saturday, preceding the February term, 1781, and continued in town until Monday night or Tuesday morning following; therefore the Court was not called according to last adjournment.

The minutes of this term were transcribed from Mr. Gifford's rough minutes."

(Signed) "ADLAI OSBORNE, C. C. C."

A calculation, carefully made from the court records, shows that the "Saturday preceding the February term of 1781 fell on the third day of February, and coincides with the foregoing account of the march, as well as the 'Order Book' of Lord Cornwallis. There has been some confusion of dates upon this point by various writers—Dr. Hunter, in his Sketches, bringing the British to Salisbury on the night of the first of February, and Lossing on the night of the second. The truth appears to be that the main army of the British passed near Salisbury on the evening of the second, and returned and occupied the town on Saturday, the third. It is however probable that a squadron of dragoons passed through the town on the second, where Tarleton says 'some emissaries informed him that Morgan was at the Trading Ford, but had not crossed the river.' "

CHAPTER XVII

GENERAL GREEN IN SALISBURY

Having followed the track of the British army from the Catawba River to Salisbury, thus giving a continuous narrative of their march, let us now return and trace the course of Generals Greene and Morgan over nearly the same ground. Unfortunately we have not in this case the benefit of journals, maps, and "order book," as before, but still we shall be able to ascertain some facts concerning this day's march.

General Morgan crossed the Catawba River at the Island Ford, on the northern border of Lincoln County, on the twenty-eighth of January, 1781, only two hours ahead of the British vanguard, under Brigadier-General O'Hara. It was just at the hour of sunset when the British came to the banks of the broad stream, sweeping onward with its wintry current from the foot of the Blue Ridge. In the darkness there was danger in crossing the stream, especially with the courageous Morgan and his army on the other side to receive them. But with a trained army of two thousand, unencumbered with baggage or prisoners, the British commander could confidently calculate upon overtaking the Americans, numbering only about one thousand in all, half of whom were militia, and embarrassed with the five hundred prisoners lately captured at Cowpens. The passage of the Catawba was therefore postponed until the next morning. That delay was the salvation of Morgan and his little army. During the night the rain fell in torrents, and by morning light the river was brimful and unfordable, in which condition it remained for forty-eight hours. For two days the British were compelled to linger on the western banks, while Morgan and Greene were on the other side planning the details of the retreat. Sending the five hundred prisoners off under the care of the five hundred militia, by a route higher up the country towards Virginia, General Morgan with his regulars seems to have remained on the east bank of the Catawba, watching the British, and prepared to dispute their passage. But when it was ascertained that they had crossed below him, at Cowan's Ford, on the first of February, General Morgan began his retreat towards the Yadkin. As he was higher up the river, we conjecture that his route was along one of the upper roads, either the Beattie's Ford or Sherrill's Ford Road to Salisbury. His forces appear to have reached Salisbury late the same afternoon, and were not concerned in the skirmish at Cowan's Ford, or at Torrence's Tavern. There is a tradition in Salisbury that, as Morgan's troops filed past George Murr's house, at the east corner of Main and Franklin Streets, where Charles Gordon now lives, some of the men mischievously punched out some panes of glass with their bayonets. This must have been late in the afternoon, for Morgan's troops encamped that night about a half-mile east of Salisbury, on the Yadkin Road. No doubt the prospect of a good night's rest, and a bountiful repast, developed in the bosoms of those veterans the exuberance of spirit that suggested the mischief. The encampment must have been in the grove where the residence of John S. Henderson, Esq., now is. There they would have the advantage of two or three excellent springs of water, abundance of fuel, while at the same time they would be near enough to the town for convenience of supplies, and directly on the line of march for an early start in the morning.

It appears that Dr. Read, the surgeon of Morgan's army, with the hospital stores, and some wounded and disabled British officers, who were prisoners, had reached Salisbury some time in advance of the troops. He was stopping at the tavern of Mrs. Elizabeth Steele. This tavern was on the northwest side of Main Street, between the old courthouse and the corner where the present courthouse now stands, probably at the corner of Main and Liberty Streets, adjacent to the present courthouse corner. Dr. Read was sitting in the apartment overlooking Main Street, engaged in writing paroles for such British officers as were unable from sickness or debility to proceed further, when he saw riding up to the door General Greene, unaccompanied by his aides or by any person whatsoever, and looking quite forlorn.

"How do you find yourself, my good General?" eagerly inquired Dr. Read.

"Wretched beyond measure—without a friend—without money—and destitute even of a companion," replied Greene, as he slowly dismounted from his jaded horse. The General had dispatched his aides to different parts of his retreating army and had ridden through the rain and mud of Rowan winter roads, over thirty miles in a direct line, not allowing for excursions to the right and left, during this exciting day. Besides this, he had for themes of sad meditation the two disastrous skirmishes of the day, and apprehensions of the near approach of Colonel Tarleton and his light dragoons. This condition was truly a discouraging one. But help was nearer than he imagined. Mrs. Steele, the patriotic and kind-hearted hostess, had

THIS TABLET IS ERECTED
TO THE MEMORY OF
ELIZABETH
MAXWELL STEELE
PATRIOT
BY THE
ELIZABETH MAXWELL STEELE
CHAPTER
DAUGHTERS OF THE
AMERICAN REVOLUTION
1781–1911

overheard his desponding remarks upon alighting, and determined that he should obtain such relief as she was able to afford.

In due time a bountiful repast was spread before her distinguished guest, while a cheerful fire crackled on the hearth and shed its genial warmth throughout the room. While General Greene was sitting at the table, and the discouragement engendered by hunger, fatigue, and cold was disappearing before the comforting influences of his environment, Mrs. Steele approached him, and reminding him of the desponding words he had uttered upon his arrival, assured him of her sympathy and friendship. Then drawing two small bags of specie from under her apron she presented them to him, saying gracefully: "Take these, for you will want them, and I can do without them." Mrs. Steele was not poor, as the remarks of some writers upon this subject would lead us to infer, and perhaps could have filled his pockets with "proclamation money," worth less than Confederate notes were in the beginning of 1865. But silver and gold were scarce in those days, and no American officer or gentlemen would have complained of the burden of carrying it along with him. The General accepted this timely gift with gratitude, and doubtless it was all the more welcome because accompanied by graceful words of kindness and encouragement. The hero's heart was lightened by this opportune kindness, and after a few hours of rest he went forth to superintend and direct the retreat of his little army, and provide for their transportation across the Yadkin.

Just before the departure from Salisbury, General Greene left a memorial of his visit of a peculiar kind. His eye caught sight of a portrait of George III, hanging on the walls of the room. This portrait had been presented to a connection of Mrs. Steele by a friend in the Court of England, some years before. The sight of this picture recalled to the mind of the General the sufferings which at that moment his countrymen were enduring, and the blood that had been shed in the struggle to throw off the shackles of slavery which the English king and Parliament were trying to fasten upon the American people. In a moment he took down the picture, and with a piece of chalk wrote on the back of it; "O George! hide thy face and mourne." He then replaced it, with the face to the wall, and mounting his horse rode away. The picture, with the writing still visible, is the property of the family of the late Archibald Henderson, Esq., of Salisbury, a descendant of Mrs. Steele; but it has not been in possession of the family for many years. When Dr. Foote wrote his Sketches of North Carolina, in 1846, it was in the postoffice at Charlotte. When Colonel Wheeler published his History of North Carolina, in 1851, it was in the possession of Governor Swain, the president of the University, at Chapel Hill. It is thought to be now in the hands of the widow of Governor Swain, in Raleigh.

Mrs. Steele's first husband was Robert Gillespie, who in partnership with Thomas Bashford purchased a large number of lots in Salisbury, about 1757, and among them the lot on which they carried on a village inn, the same that was afterwards owned and occupied by Mrs. Steele. Mr. and Mrs. Gillespie had two children. One of these was a daughter, named Margaret, who became the wife of the Rev. Samuel Eusebius McCorkle, D.D., so long the pastor of Thyatira Church, and principal of the "Zion Parnassus Academy," where he educated so many men during the closing years of the last century. The other child was a son, named Richard Gillespie, who was a captain in the Revolutionary War, and died unmarried. He was of a peculiarly bold and defiant spirit, and when the British entered Salisbury he rode in sight of them, waving his sword towards them in a menacing manner. As he had but one companion, "Blind Daniel," so called from having lost one eye, a kind of hanger-on in Salisbury, of course he did not remain to carry out his menaces. After the death of Mr. Gillespie, his widow married Mr. William Steele of Salisbury, by whom she had an only son, the distinguished General John Steele, who was an ornament to his native town, and to his whole country. His services were rendered at a later day.

During the day of the second of February, Generals Greene and Morgan proceeded to the river, at Trading Ford, and succeeded in crossing that stream, and securing all the flats and boats that had been used in carrying over the baggage and infantry on the other side. About midnight, as before related, General O'Hara, with the vanguard of the British army, reached the river, and had a slight skirmish with the detachment left behind to guard some refugees with their wagons and household stuff. But Morgan's cavalry had forded the stream long before, and his infantry had passed over in a bateau. Another copious rain in the mountains had swollen the Yadkin to a mighty river, and the British commander, like a lion robbed of its prey, stood chafing on the western bank of the stream. From the Heights of Gowerie—generally known as the "Torrence Place"—the British, with their field glasses, could sweep their vision far over the famed "Jersey Settlement," with its rich lands and substantial farmhouses. The Torrences, the Macnamaras, the Smiths, the Potters, and other prominent families dwelt in that region. General Greene himself seemed in no hurry to leave that region. From this height the British opened a furious cannonade across the river. Dr. Read, the American surgeon, before mentioned, has left this record of the scene, as given in Colonel Wheeler's History. "At a little distance from the river was a small cabin in which General Greene had taken up his quarters. At this the enemy directed their fire, and the balls rebounded from the rocks in the rear of it. But little of the roof was visible to the enemy. The General was preparing his orders for the army and his dispatches to the Congress. In a short time the balls began to strike the roof, and the clapboards were flying in all directions. But the General's pen never stopped, only when a new visitor arrived, or some officer for orders; and then the answer was given with calmness and precision, and Greene resumed his pen." This cabin stood about two hundred yards east of Holtsburg depot, and a rod or two to the north of the county road, at the foot of the hill.

The reader will recollect that it was a part of Greene's original plan that the larger part of his army, which he had stationed at Cheraw, should hasten to join Morgan's division at Charlotte or Salisbury. But the rapidity of their movements effectually prevented the accomplishment of this purpose. Instead of meeting Morgan's division, General Huger marched up on the eastern side of the Pee Dee, past the Grassy Islands, through Richmond, Montgomery, and Randolph Counties, to meet General Greene at Martinville, or Guilford Courthouse, where he arrived on the evening of the seventh of February.

From Trading Ford, General Greene moved on to Abbott's Creek meeting-house, still in Old Rowan, and halted for two or three days to rest his troops and await further developments. During his stay there he made his headquarters at the house of Colonel Spurgen, a Tory, who of course was not at home to receive him. But his wife, Mary Spurgen, was as true a Whig as her husband was a Tory, and like Mrs. Steele in Salisbury she showed him all the kindness in her power. While staying there he was naturally anxious to know whether the British were still in Salisbury, or whether they were moving up the river. In this state of perplexity, he inquired of Mrs. Spurgen whether she knew anyone whom he could trust to send back to the river for information. Mrs. Spurgen promptly recommended her son John, a mere youth, as perfectly trustworthy. After convincing himself that this was the best he could do, he mounted John on his own horse, directing him to go to Trading Ford, and if he could not hear of the British to go up the river until he could gain information. John went, and hearing nothing at the Ford went several miles up the river. Still hearing nothing he returned home and reported. Greene started him off again, and told him, that he must go as far up as Shallow Ford, if he could hear nothing before that time. John took the road again, and actually went as far as Shallow Ford, some thirty miles from home, where he saw the British crossing the river. Hastening home with all speed he reported his discovery to the General. Instantly Greene ordered his horse and was off for Martinville, where he met General Huger and the eastern division of his army, as mentioned above, on the evening of the seventh of February.

CHAPTER XVIII

REVOLUTIONARY INCIDENTS

General Greene having escaped across the Yadkin, Lord Cornwallis with the main body of his troops returned to Salisbury and remained at that place two days. They reached the town on Saturday and continued there until Monday night or Tuesday morning. Monday was the time for opening the sessions of the Quarterly Inferior Court, but as may well be supposed, the magistrates who presided, being ardent Whigs had no disposition to place themselves in the hands of the British. Adlai Osborne, the clerk, was absent in the Patriot army, and had been for some time, Mr. Gifford acting as deputy clerk, and taking notes of proceedings which were afterwards written up by Mr. Osborne.

There still remain among our people several traditions of the period of British occupation, which though trivial in themselves, are yet of interest to the citizens of Salisbury and vicinity. Let it then be understood that the greater part of this chapter is founded upon local tradition; but so direct and constant is that tradition, that it is thought to be entirely trustworthy in its main features.

Upon entering the town Lord Cornwallis took up his headquarters at the house of Maxwell Chambers, a prominent and wealthy Whig, a merchant of Salisbury, a former member of the Rowan Committee of Safety, and its treasurer. After the war, Maxwell Chambers moved to Spring Hill, about three miles east of Salisbury. His eldest son was named Edward Chambers, who was the next owner of "Spring Hill." The late William Chambers, whose monument stands near the wall in the Lutheran graveyard, was the son and heir of Edward Chambers. During the Revolution, Maxwell Chambers lived on the west corner of Church and Bank Streets—the corner now occupied by the stately and substantial mansion of S. H. Wiley, Esq. The house of Mr. Chambers used by the British Commander remained standing until about ten years ago, and its old-fashioned and quaint appearance is familiar to everyone whose recollection can run back ten or twelve years. It is surprising that none was found to show Mr. Lossing, in 1749, this relic of the Revolution. During these two days of occupation the British buried some soldiers on the spot known as the "English-Graveyard," and from this circumstance it is said to have derived its name. But it was a burying-place before that time. Near the center of it, leaning against a tree, there is an ancient headstone of some dark material, that says that Capt. Daniel Little, who died in 1775, lies buried there. It is more probable that it was called the "English" in distinction from the "Lutheran" or "German" graveyard, on the eastern side of town. Colonel Tarleton stopped at John Louis Beard's, in the eastern part of town, the north corner of Main and Franklin Streets. Mr. Beard, being a well-known Whig, was absent in the army at the time, and so the entertaining devolved upon Mrs. Beard. But Colonel Tarleton, it seems, was perfectly able to take care of himself, and made himself quite at home. When he wanted milk he ordered old Dick—the negro servant—to fetch the cows and milk them. Mrs. Beard had a cross child at the time, whose crying was a great annoyance to the dashing colonel. Upon one occasion his anger overleaped the bounds of gentlemanly courtesy, and he ordered the child to be choked to stop its crying. Mrs. Beard was very much afraid of him, and we may well suppose that she did all she could to please him.

It is said that Lord Rawdon put up at the residence of Thomas Frohock, at his place called "The Castle," about two miles northwest of Salisbury, on the hill just east of Frohock's (afterwards Macy's) pond; and that he had charge of Frohock's mill upon that occasion. The writer has looked in vain, in the history of the campaign, for the name of Lord Rawdon. He was present in Charlotte the previous summer, and fell back with Cornwallis to Winnsboro in the fall. But neither the histories, nor the "General Order Book," mention his name in this pursuit of Greene. Still the grandmother of Miss Christine Beard, one of our oldest citizens, whose memory is stored with these ancient traditions, and is never at fault, was often heard to state that Rawdon was at Frohock's. Mrs. Eleanor Faust, the lady in question, was the daughter of John Dunn, Esq., and her memory was excellent. The same statement was also made by Mrs. Giles, the sister of Mrs. Faust, who was a temporary inmate of Frohock's family at the time. On the other hand, we learn from Lossing and other historians that Lord Rawdon was left in command of the Southern Division of the Royal army, with headquarters at Camden, when Cornwallis marched into North Carolina. And there General Greene found him when he marched into South Carolina after the battle of Guilford Courthouse, and engaged in the unfortunate battle of Hobkirk's Hill, on the twenty-fifth of April, 1781. The only solution of the apparent contradiction between tradition and history is that Lord Rawdon may have proceeded with Lord Cornwallis as far as Salisbury, and then returned to his field of operations in the South after Greene had been extricated from their grasp by the rise of the Yadkin River.

Another distinguished personage was along with Lord Cornwallis in Salisbury, though we hear little of him. This was no less a personage than Josiah Martin, the last Royal Governor of North Carolina. The day after the British crossed at Cowan's Ford, an elegant beaver hat, made after the fashion of the day, and marked in the inside, "The property of Josiah Martin, Governor," was found floating on the Catawba River about ten miles below Cowan's Ford. In his dispatches after the battle of Guilford Courthouse, Cornwallis reports that Governor Martin had accompanied him in his campaign through North Carolina, cheerfully bearing all the hardships of camp life, hoping by his presence to aid in the work of restoring the Royal authority in the State. Though he was along with the troops, he does not appear conspicuous. "Inter arma leges silent" is an old maxim, and the powerless governor was completely overshadowed by the plumed and epauletted chiefs of the march and of the battlefield. Had he not lost his hat in the Catawba, and had not Cornwallis kindly mentioned his name in his dispatches, we would have been entirely ignorant of his last visit to Salisbury. We do not know where he "put up" while in town. At the northeast corner of Innes and Church Streets, now the property of Mr. Philip P. Meroney, stood the law office of John Dunn, Esq., and in the same yard, a little back of it, was the residence of his daughter, Mrs. Eleanor Faust. These premises were occupied as the headquarters of the British commissary department. The encampment of the army was two or three hundred yards to the north of the courthouse, somewhere in the neighborhood of the English graveyard, perhaps on the line of Fulton Street, not far from the present residence of Dr. Whitehead and that of the Hon. F. E. Shober. The commissary headquarters would thus be between the camp and center of town. It is related that Mrs. Faust owned a favorite calf that grazed in the yard, which the commissary took a fancy to, and tried to purchase for Lord Cornwallis' own table. But Mrs. Faust refused to sell upon any terms. The commissary thereupon proceeded to "impress" the calf, and after killing it he laid down a piece of gold before Mrs. Faust as pay. Irritated and indignant, she pushed away the money, and left his presence.

During the stay of the British, Mrs. Faust lost a child, that died of smallpox. As all things were in confusion, and none could be hired to perform such services, her father, John Dunn, took the coffin upon his horse, and interred the body at the family burying-ground, three miles south of Salisbury.

Dr. Anthony Newnan, familiarly called Dr. Anthony, was then a citizen of Salisbury. He lived in the house that still stands on the southeast side of Main Street, next to "Cowan's brick row." The building is now occupied as a harness and boot and shoe shop, and is very old and dilapidated. It has undergone many changes, but is still substantially the same. Parts of the old heavy molding and the wainscot and paneling are still to be seen, as well as the hard oaken cornerposts and studding, and the weatherboarding fastened with home-wrought iron nails. It is reported that the builder of this house got drunk, and rolled from the roof of the piazza into the street and was thereby killed. At all events Dr. Newnan, a good Whig, lived in this house, and entertained some of the British officers. One day while Colonel Tarleton and some other British officers were enjoying the hospitality of Dr. Newnan, the Doctor's two little boys were engaged in playing a game with white and red grains of corn, perhaps after the style of "Fox and Geese," or "Cross the Crown." Having heard much talk in the past five days of the battle of Cowpens, the British, Colonel Tarleton, and Colonel Washington, it occurred to the boys to name their white and red grains of corn Americans and British, with Washington and Tarleton as leaders, and "play" the battle of Cowpens. All at once, and forgetful of Tarleton's presence, one of the boys shouted out "Hurrah for Washington! Tarleton is running! Hurrah for Washington!" The fiery Tarleton looked on awhile in silence, but his temper was too hot to restrain him from uttering a curse against the rebel boys.

Dr. Newnan married a daughter of Hugh Montgomery, a wealthy citizen, who owned much property in lands and cattle in Wilkes County. Montgomery lived in the old "Yarboro House," then standing upon the site of Meroney's Hall, but now rolled back and standing in the rear of it, and occupied as a hotel for colored people. Montgomery was the ancestor of the Stokeses and Welborns of Wilkes County. Dr. John Newnan was the son of Dr. Anthony Newnan, and lived on the lot now occupied as the residence of Dr. Julius A. Caldwell. The burying-ground of the Newnans may still be seen on the lot in the rear of Mr. Alexander Parker's residence, not far from the railroad depot. Quite a number of old and prominent citizens of Salisbury lie buried just behind Meroney's Hall, under and around the colored hotel.

Incidents at the Stone House

About three miles southeast of Salisbury, and near the supposed line of the old "Training Path," stands a remarkable relic of the early settlement of Rowan. It is known far and wide as the "Old Stone House." A smooth stone tablet over the front door tells the visitor that Michael Braun (Brown), erected this house in 1766. It is built of native, unhewn, but rather well-shaped blocks of granite, laid in cement so durable that it still stands in ridges between the stones. The lower story was pretty well finished with plaster, and contained five rooms. At one end of the house there is a double chimney, with fireplaces in corners of two rooms. At the other end there is a huge chimney facing outwards, and around which is built a wooden kitchen. This kitchen chimney is eight feet in the clear, and four feet deep. Michael Braun not only provided a solid house to live in, but he had enlarged ideas of cooking facilities, and no doubt many a big dinner was cooked there in the olden time. But the most curious part of the arrangements was a wonderful firebox or stove in the east room, that was fed through an opening in the back of the kitchen chimney. The plates of this ancient firebox or stove, are still lying there, massive and highly ornamented with curious figures, circular, oval, and diamond shaped, with flower vases filled with lilies and lanceolate leaves. On one plate is this inscription:

COM-BAN-NI
1766

Another plate contains the following:

GEORGE ROSS-ANN
MARY ANN
FURNACE

It appears that George Ross and Mary Ann's "Combanni" (Company), wherever it was located, had some original methods of spelling, and "Mary Ann" had practical ideas about woman's rights, and has succeeded in transmitting her own name along with George's to posterity.

The north side of the building, it is said, is covered with the original cypress shingles put there in 1766. They are decayed in some places, but generally covered with lichen and moss, and have turned the rains and upheld the snows of one hundred and fourteen summers and winters.

It is conjectured that the main body of the British army passed by this stone house on the evening of the second of February, 1781, on their march to the Trading Ford. It has been constantly reported that on that occasion, an American officer, who was probably on a reconnoitering expedition, was nearly overtaken by British dragoons near this house. He turned and fled for life. As the party came thundering down the hill the American rode full tilt into the front door of this house, leaped his horse from the back door, and so escaped down the branch bottom and through the thickets, towards Salisbury.

Another local tradition tells of a furious hand-to-hand encounter between an American and a British soldier in the front door of the stone house. The deep gashes of the swords are still shown in the old walnut doorposts. There can be little doubt that some such conflict took place there. It is true that the cuts and gashes might have been made with any other kind of instrument. But the descendants of Michael Braun still live there, and they, as well as the neighbors, still tell the tale as they heard it from their forefathers, substantially as above written.

In the little graveyard, walled in with stones, a few hundred yards from the stone house, lie the remains of Michael Braun, and his wife, with quite a number of his descendants. The following is the inscription of a plain old-fashioned headstone, dedicated to the memory of the wife and mother.

1771
GESTORBEN JULIUS 20
HIER LIEGHT DER LIEB
MRCREDA BRAUN DES
ML. BRAUN'S EHE WIEB
HAT 9 KINDER, 6 SON
3 D. ALT 37 JAHR 2 MO.

The above inscription is in the dialect known in North Carolina as "Pennsylvania Dutch." The following is perhaps a good translation of the epitaph:

1771, DIED JULY 20

Here lies the body of Margaret Braun, Michael Braun's wedded wife. She had nine children, six sons and three daughters. Aged thirty-seven years and two months.

As Michael Braun had an extensive family, and his descendants in this and adjoining counties are numerous, the reader may not object to see an account of this family as far as known.

Michael Brown was married several times, and the following is a list of his children so far as known. In the absence of complete records we depend to a large extent upon the memory of one who knew personally most of the individuals named. It is not positively certain that the sons of Michael Braun are mentioned in the order of seniority. They were named John, Peter, Moses, James, and Jeremiah.

1. John, the eldest, for some reason or other, was called "Continental John," probably because he served in the Continental army during the Revolution. He was the father of the late Mrs. Jacob Myers of Salisbury.

2. Peter married Miss Susanna Bruner, a daughter of Mr. George Bruner, who lived at the place which is the present residence of Dr. Albert Powe, now known as the "Powe Place," formerly called the "Bruner Place." This couple were blessed with a number of children. Their daughter Elizabeth married Thos. L. Cowan of Salisbury, and was the mother of the late Mrs. Charlotte Jenkins and Mrs. Mary Hall. Mary, another daughter, married Barny Bowers. Susan married a Mr. Thompson, of Randolph. Margaret married Joseph Chambers, of Iredell County, and was the mother of Major P. B. Chambers, now of Statesville. Sally married Dr. Satterwhite.

Besides these daughters, Peter and Susanna Brown had two sons, the late Michael and George Brown, of Salisbury. These two sons married daughters of Alexander Long, of Yadkin Ferry, and sisters of the late Dr. Alexander Long, of Salisbury.

Peter Brown first settled about two miles east of Salisbury, but soon moved into town. He purchased the building on the west corner of Main and Innes Streets, where he carried on a store for many years. The place was occupied by his son, Michael Brown, after him, until about 1860. The place is commonly known as McNeely's corner, and is now occupied by the firm of Ross & Greenfield.

3. Moses, the third son in the above list, was born February 24, 1773, and married Catherine Swink. The oldest son of Moses and Catherine Brown was named Michael S., and was born December 28, 1797. He lived near his birthplace, and left a large family. He died November 28, 1849.

A second son was the late Moses (L.) Brown of Salisbury, who lived where Martin Richwine now lives, and his daughters, Mrs. Richwine and Mrs. Johnston are residents of Salisbury.

A third son of Moses (son of Michael Braun) was the late Peter (M.) Brown, of Charlotte. Peter (M.) Brown was first married to Elizabeth Pool, of Salisbury, by whom he had two children, John L. Brown, Esq., of Charlotte, and Margaret C. Brown, who was married to Dr. John R. Dillard, of Virginia. John L. Brown, of Charlotte, married Miss Nancy I., daughter of the late Jennings B. Kerr, of Charlotte, and has represented his County—Mecklenburg—three sessions in the Legislature; each time being elected almost unanimously. Moses Brown (son of Michael) had also another son, Alfred Brown, who settled in Concord; and two daughters, Sophia and Sally.

4. The fourth son of Michael Braun, of the "Stone House," was named James. He continued to live in the old neighborhood, and his descendants are found scattered around the place of their nativity.

5. Another, the youngest son of Michael Braun, of the "Stone House," was Jeremiah. He married the widow of Tobias Furr. Mrs. Furr was the mother of three children by her first marriage—Mary Furr, who married John Murphy; Elizabeth Furr, who married Samuel Lemly; and Louisa Furr, who married William H. Horah, all of Salisbury. By her marriage with Jeremiah Brown she had also three children—Margaret, who married Thomas Dickson; Delia, who married John Coughenour; and the late Col. Jeremiah M. Brown, whose widow and children still live in Salisbury.

6. The last wife of Michael Braun of the "Stone House" was Mrs. Eleanora Reeves. Mrs. Reeves was a Maryland lady, named Wakefield, and was first married to William Reeves, when quite young, by whom she had four children—Thomas, Samuel, Sally, and Nancy, Samuel was the late Samuel Reeves, the father of Dr. Samuel Reeves and of Mrs. Sarah Johnston. Nancy Reeves married a Mr. Kiestler, and was the mother of Mrs. Jane Price, and the grandmother of Robert Wakefield Price and others, now of Salisbury.

By her marriage with Michael Braun, Mrs. Reeves had one child, Clementine, who was married to Charles Verble. Their daughter Eleanora is the wife of Mr. Thomas E. Brown, and mother of Lewis V. Brown of Texas, and Frank Brown of Salisbury. Of the daughters of Michael Braun the writer has no knowledge, nor has it been thought fit to extend the notice of other descendants to a later period. It is perhaps necessary to remark in closing this notice that the German word "Braun" signifies dark or brown, and that it was pronounced in German exactly as our English word, "brown." Old Michael's descendants therefore discharged the German spelling and signed themselves "Brown."

Dunn's Graves

On the north side of the Stone House farm, and adjoining it, were John Dunn's country farm and residence. The house was built of wood and has long since disappeared, but a depression in the ground still marks the spot where the old lawyer's cellars once existed. Not far from this spot there is a small cluster of graves, known in the neighborhood as "Dunn's Graves." The plow of the farmer has gone over the spot, the wheat and the corn have grown rankly over it, and the eye of the stranger would never detect the place. But aged citizens, who may not linger long to hand down the tradition, are still able to point out with precision the spot where their fathers said John Dunn is sleeping his last sleep, side by side with some of his own race and kindred. As a general guide to the locality, it may be stated that the spot is a short distance—say a half-mile—from Mr. Asa Ribelin's house, in the direction of Salisbury. It is a pity that so many of these country burial-grounds are allowed to fall into decay, to pass into the hands of strangers, leaving no trace of the spot where the pioneers of this land are laid in their last resting-place.

Capt. Alexander Shannon

was an officer in General Greene's army, who lost his life in Salisbury in 1781. He was engaged in some unrecorded skirmish or reconnoitering expedition, somewhere on the slope of the hill now covered by the South Ward of Salisbury, where he was slain by the British. Twenty years ago some of the older citizens could remember, in one of our cemeteries, a headstone, marked with his name. But it has either fallen down, been removed, or sunk beneath the turf. Captain Shannon was from Guilford County, a brave soldier and a true patriot. He was the grand-uncle of our fellow-townsman, S. H. Wiley, Esq.

Joseph Hughes and Col. David Fanning

Colonel Fanning, the notorious Tory marauder, who kept Randolph, Orange, and Moore Counties in terror for several years, is said to have paid Salisbury at least one visit during the war. The reader of North Carolina annals will remember his atrocious murder of Col. Andrew Balfour, of Randolph County, on the ninth of March, 1782. About the time, an Englishman by the name of Joseph Hughes was keeping a village inn, at the place afterwards known as "Slaughter's Hotel," in Salisbury. This place was afterwards known as the "Robard's Hotel," and the place is now occupied as a residence by Mr. Theo. F. Kluttz. Having heard that Fanning was crossing the Yadkin, somewhere about the Island Ford, and having lost an arm, and being thereby disabled from fighting, Hughes determined to save himself and family by a stratagem. Accordingly he rolled some barrels of whiskey into the street in front of his inn, knocked the heads out, and placed a number of tin cups conveniently around. The bait took, and Fanning's myrmidons got beastly drunk, and so were disabled from doing the mischief they intended to do. Hughes seized the opportunity to escape through the thickets and brushwood in the rear of his house. It is not known that these desperadoes did any serious mischief in the town. Joseph Hughes left one son, Hudson Hughes, who married the daughter of Col. Andrew Balfour. The daughter of this couple, Mary, became the wife of Samuel Reeves, Esq., and the mother of the late Dr. Samuel Reeves, and of Mrs. Sarah Johnston, now of Cincinnati.

The Oldest Tree

Before quitting this ramble among the antiquities of Salisbury and vicinity, it may not be uninteresting to call attention to the "oldest inhabitant" of Salisbury, in the shape of a venerable sassafras tree—the "Big Sassafras" of John Beard. It stands very near the embankment of the Western North Carolina Railroad, just after leaving the Company's workshops, on the town side of the embankment, on the same square on which Mr. Charles Gordon's house is located. A recent measurement of the tree, two feet from the ground, makes it fourteen feet two inches in circumference—nearly five feet in diameter. It was standing there in 1806, and seemed then almost as large in the body, and much larger in the crown than at present. At that day John Beard had extensive orchards all around in the neighborhood, and he chose the sassafras as the fulcrum of a cider press. It was on the hillslope of a beautiful meadow, and just above a crystal spring. Here on the green grass lay heaps of blushing apples, which were crushed and pressed beneath the powerful lever until the golden-colored cider gushed out in great streams. The children from the whole settlement—for Salisbury was then a mere village, and most of its families connected with each other—gathered in the grassy valley, and drank to their heart's content of the beverage, so sweet to their simple tastes. That was three-fourths of a century ago. Nearly all the children that played there then have passed away, while the old tree still stands, with trunk decaying, but leaves glossy and aromatic as in early days.

How old is it? Everyone who knows the slow growth of that species of tree, will think that it would require more than a hundred years to attain such a size. It is probably two hundred years old, or more, and began its growth long before the first white settler pitched his tent or built his cabin between the Yadkin and the Catawba. Long may it stand!

"Woodman! spare *that* tree,
 Touch not a single bough;
In youth it sheltered me,
 And I'll protect it now."

Lord Cornwallis Departs

But it is time to return from these sketches, that have little or no connection with the occupation of the British army, to the departure of Lord Cornwallis. Having remained in Salisbury part of three days, he took his departure early on Tuesday morning, the sixth of February. His march was up the Wilkesboro Road, crossing Grant's Creek, Second Creek, Third and Fourth Creeks. A march of about fifteen or eighteen miles brought them to their first encampment, on the west side of the South Fork of the Yadkin, not far from Rencher's (or Renshaw's) Ford. A little stream, called Beaver Dam, would furnish them water, and the well-to-do farmers of South River and Fourth Creek—the Johnstons, Luckeys, Grahams, Gillespies, and Knoxes—had capacious and well-filled barns, cribs, and granaries. It was at this encampment that William Young, mentioned in a previous chapter, had his adventures with the British soldiers. On the seventh, the British crossed the Shallow Ford of the main Yadkin, where little John Spurgen caught sight of them, and hastened with the news to General Greene. They there passed out of Rowan County. The general histories of the State will inform the reader of Greene's retreat across the Dan, Lord Cornwallis' march to Hillsboro, the return of both armies to Guilford, where the battle of Guilford Courthouse was fought on the fifteenth of March following; of Lord Cornwallis' march to Wilmington, and Greene's hasty march to Camden, and his battle with Lord Rawdon at Hobkirk's Hill on the twenty-fifth of April. But these movements do not fall within the scope of these papers. The great armies had swept on, and Rowan County was left to herself. But it was an uneasy and unsettled time, for many were the Tories that hung around her borders, and depredations were frequently committed upon the peaceful families of the Whigs. The men who were able for war were absent, and the feeble noncombatants were unable to resist the violence of Tory raiders. But brighter days were near at hand. Cornwallis surrendered at Yorktown, October 19, 1781. On the fourth of March, 1782, the British House of Commons passed a resolution in favor of peace, and active hostilities ceased. This day has been chosen as the day for the inauguration of the Presidents of the United States.

CHAPTER XIX

THE FIRST YEARS OF PEACE

On the nineteenth of October, 1781, Lord Cornwallis surrendered to General Washington, at Yorktown, in Virginia. It was in the middle of the night, a day or two after, that the news of this closing scene in the mighty drama reached Philadelphia. A watchman in the street called out. "Twelve o'clock, and a cloudy morning—*Cornwallis taken.*" In a short time the whole city was aroused, and the wildest manifestations of joy were displayed. The same news ran rapidly over all the States, and the people in every village and hamlet were filled with gladness. In England, all hope of subjugating the States was abandoned, and Lord North retired from the Ministry and the Whigs took charge of the government. Negotiations for peace were entered into, and five commissioners from the United States met a like number from England in Paris, and a provisional treaty of peace was signed September 3, 1782. A final treaty was signed at the same place, on the third of September, 1783, and each of the original Thirteen Colonies was acknowledged by Great Britain to be an Independent and Sovereign State.

But though peace with England was declared, there were many bitter heartburnings in the breasts of the people among themselves. The army was unpaid, and efforts were made to array it against Congress, and thus turn over the public civil government into a military despotism. Nothing but the courage and patriotism of General Washington averted that sad calamity.

Besides this there were many Loyalists in every part of the country, some of whom had taken up arms in behalf of Great Britain, and many others had remained neutral in the struggle. When peace came the Whigs could scarcely feel that their Tory neighbors ought to enjoy equal rights and privileges with themselves, and no doubt were easily provoked to taunt them with insulting epithets. These were days of violence, and he who had the brawniest arm, or was most active of limb, came out conqueror. Many of the Loyalists voluntarily removed to distant parts of the country, while others received legal notice to depart. Besides this, suits were brought against many for the confiscation of their property for disloyalty, according to Act of the Assembly of North Carolina. This Act was adopted at the first meeting of the General Assembly under the Constitution, at Newbern, April 8, 1777, and declared it to be treason and punishable with death and confiscation of goods, to take commission in the army of Great Britain in North Carolina, or to aid or assist in any way the enemies of the State. The law was terribly severe, and was never fully executed. Still, in 1782, twenty-two persons were summoned to appear before the Rowan Inferior Court charged with disloyalty. Some were found guilty and some were acquitted. But the sale of the property of those found guilty was postponed. At the Inferior Court of Rowan for February, 1783, no less than one hundred and sixty persons were cited to appear and show cause why their estates should not be confiscated. Though the citation was signed with the names of Griffith Rutherford, James Macay, William Sharpe, and Robert Mackie, magistrates, holding the Court, it is recorded that the entire lot made default, and thereby ignored or defied the Court. The curious reader will find a list of their names on Minute Docket of Rowan Inferior Court for February, 1783, volume 1778-86. It has been supposed that a considerable part of the German population of Rowan were neutral or averse to the war. But if such was the case not many of them committed any overt act bringing them within purview of the law providing against disloyalty. Out of one hundred and eighty-two names but a small part—about one-fifth—are German names; the rest are common English names. The revolution of one hundred years have softened the asperities and rounded off the sharp prejudices engendered by the great conflict, and we are now able to see that it could be possible for a man to be conscientiously convinced that it was his duty to maintain his loyalty to the king to whom he had given his oath of allegiance. But it was more than could be reasonably expected of the suffering patriots of that day to see it in that light. Still—slowly, imperceptibly—better days came on, and the husbandman could again devote his whole time to the improvement of his farm, and the good housewives to their domestic affairs. In those days the farmer's life was far more independent and self-sustaining than at present. With the exception of a few articles, such as iron, salt, a little sugar and coffee or chocolate, pepper and spice, the farm, the flocks and herds yielded all that was consumed at the homes of our people. The table was loaded with home productions.

The operations of the farm were carried on with rude and simple implements and in a primitive way. The market for grain and flour was several hundred miles distant, and the expense of transportation was too great to justify the raising of more than was needed on the farm. The rich new grounds and bottom lands with their virgin soil brought forth a bountiful crop with little labor, and left a large margin of time for fishing and hunting. There was always a "slack season" between the "laying by" of crops and fodder-pulling time. That was the time to hunt squirrels, and the crack of the rifle might be heard around the cornfields on all sides. And then fishing expeditions, were organized to some favorite pond or stretch of the river, where with long circling seine the jumping trout and the blushing redhorse were captured. The farmers' boys knew where the sweetest wild grapes or the most tempting muscadines grew, or where the thinnest-shelled scalybarks, or fattest hickory nuts, or the plumpest and juciest black haws were to be found, and visited them accordingly. Those same farmers' boys also knew the haw trees, persimmon trees, and grapevines in all the country around that were likely to be frequented by the fat opossums in the later fall, and they had their 'possum dogs in good training by the time the first hard frost ripened the persimmons and the opossum himself, and made his flesh fit for eating. But before that time came around, even the "slack season" had some work to be done. No circulating threshing machine or separator was then to be found, to clean up the wheat and oats of a farm in a single day. Instead of that the farmer built his double log-barn with a threshing or tramping floor between the stables. The wheat and oats were hauled from the harvest fields and packed on the stable lofts, and on the loft over the barn floor. This floor was usually twenty-five or thirty feet square, and was shut in on both sides with huge folding doors. When the tramping time came a floor of wheat was thrown down, bundles untied and laid in a circle around the center of the floor. The folding doors were thrown open, and several spans of horses were put in to walk around and around upon the wheat until it was separated from the straw and chaff—the attendants in the meantime turning over the straw as required. At first the wheat was winnowed with a sheet, or coverlet tied up by two corners, and briskly swung by two men, while one slowly poured down the mixed wheat and chaff. But wheat fans were soon introduced, and their clatter could be heard at a great distance, doing up the work neatly and rapidly.

The oats, being more easily crushed by the hard hoofs, and the straw being used to make "cut feed" for the horses, were usually threshed out with flails, the bundles being kept entire. No matter if the grain was not entirely taken out—the horses would get it in their feed.

Later in the fall was the time for pulling and shocking the corn. A huge long heap, or straight or crescent-shaped, containing thirty, fifty, or a hundred loads of corn in the shucks, was piled up in the barnyard. On a given day a boy was sent out to ask hands to come in to the shucking on a night appointed. Fifty hands perhaps, might come just at dark. A rail would be placed in the middle, and the hands divided by two captains who threw up "cross and pile" for first choice of hands. Then came the race, the shouting, the hurrahing, and the singing of corn songs if any negroes were present. And generally a bottle of brandy was circulated several times and was sampled by most of those present. Quite a number would sometimes get excited by the liquor, but it was considered disgraceful to get drunk. Sometimes a fight would occur, especially if the race was a close one. The winning side would try to carry their captain around the pile in triumph, but a well-directed ear of corn, sent by some spiteful hand on the beaten side, would strike a member of the triumphal procession, and thereby bad blood would be excited, and a promiscuous fight occur. But these were rare accidents. After the corn was shucked, and the shucks put into a pen, came the shucking supper—loaf, biscuits, ham, pork, chicken pie, pumpkin custard, sweet cakes, apple pie, grape pie, coffee, sweet milk, buttermilk, preserves, in short a rich feast of everything yielded by the farm. It required a good digestion to manage such a feast at ten or eleven o'clock at night, but the hardy sons of toil had a good digestion. Or if anything were wanting, a tramp of four or five miles, on an opossum or coon hunt, lasting till one or two o'clock in the morning, would be sufficient to settle the heartiest shucking supper that ever was spread on the farmers' tables in bountiful Old Rowan County.

The tanner and the shoemaker, the hatter, the blacksmith, and the weaver plied their vocations all over the county. The wandering tinker came around at intervals, with his crucible and his molds for spoons, plates and dishes, and melted and transformed into bright new articles the old broken pewter fragments that were carefully preserved. How the youngsters would stare at him as he stirred the molten pewter with his bare finger! And how diligently the boys hunted the rabbit, mink, muskrat, otter, and raccoon, and preserved their skins, to be taken to the hatter at Jumping Run or Cross Keys or Dutch Second Creek, to be made into a sleek and shining beaver, to be worn as the first "fur hat," instead of the old heavy, hard "wool hat," that was now to be used only as an everyday hat. Every house had its pairs of cards for wool and cotton, its large and small spinning wheel, revolving rapidly under the pressure of deft fingers or strong and elastic foot, while the thread of yarn, by the "cut" and "hank," hung on pegs on the wall. As the visitor approached the house, as soon as the morning chores were "done up," he would hear the deep bass rumbling of the large wheel, or the buzzing of the little flax wheel, with its hooked "flyers" whirling the thread around until sufficiently twisted, and then letting the thread skillfully in on the spool. Or perhaps he would hear the creaking of the reel, with its sharp click, as it told when a "cut" was reeled from the spool. Or perhaps he would see a pair of huge "warping bars," or "winding blades" slowly revolving, as they measured off the "chain" or "filling" of the next six hundred "slaie" of plain white shirting or copperas cloth, or it may be of "linsey" or perhaps "jeans." And then what efforts were put forth to secure the most brilliant dyes, and the fastest colors! The garden contained a bed of "madder," whose roots gave the brown or red dye. A patch of indigo furnished the blue. Walnut roots and bark, or maple bark, with a little copperas, supplied the tints of black and purple, or a little logwood gave a lustrous black. No "aniline dyes" were known, but roots, barks, and leaves lent their essential colors to the fabrics spun and woven by fair maidens and hearty matrons. The Fourth of July in those days was the grand holiday of the year. An orator was procured and the Declaration was impressively read, and the daring deeds of the illustrious statesmen of 1776 were commemorated. It would be varied with now and then a military parade, with screaming fife and rattling drum, and now and then a barbecue. Early in the spring the good wives began to get up the Fourth of July suits for their husbands, each priding herself on having the most nicely dressed husband on that gala day. Old silks were cut up into shreds, picked to pieces, and carded with cotton to make a "silk mixed" coat. Vests with "turkey red" stripes, cut bias, and pointing like chevrons to the buttons, were in the height of fashion. Knee breeches, with long stockings tied with garters, and shoes with huge silver buckles had not gone out of style in those days. The material of the breeches was not infrequently a soft, pliant, yellow buckskin, very "stretchy" of a rainy day. The wife of a distinguished citizen of Salisbury in those days is said to have excelled all the rest by rigging her husband out on a certain Fourth of July in a full suit of "nankeen cotton," carded, spun, woven, and made in her own house. Another textile fabric of those days was flax. The flax patch, with its delicate blue blossoms, was a pleasing spectacle. And the flax was skillfully pulled, the seed threshed out, and in due time laid out to "rot." When the inner stem was sufficiently "rotted," the ponderous strokes of the huge "flax brake" could be heard, and the swish of the scutcher as he cleaned the fiber with his sharp-edged paddle. And lastly, the heckling process separated the tow from the perfect linen. The flax-wheel with its "rock" wound with flax required the highest skill, and the product when bleached furnished the beautiful linen whose snowy whiteness was the pride of the most ambitious and thrifty housekeepers of Rowan. Her own attire was also made by her own fingers, and she was an adept in stripes and checks, knew how to insert gores and gussets, and if tall, how to eke out the cloth to the proper length. But finer articles were often needed for female attire than these home-made fabrics. Ribbons and laces, with satin and brocade, were also in demand from the looms of France and Italy. A leghorn or dunstable, or perhaps a silk gig bonnet, prunella or morocco shoes, bound on with ribbons crossing coquettishly over the foot and around the ankle, and peeping shyly beneath the short dress, completed her attire. And then, mounted on a spirited horse of her own, or maybe on a pillion behind, she was ready to accompany her escort for a ten or twenty mile ride to church, to a wedding, a party, or a quilting frolic. Those were active, healthful, buoyant, blithesome times, those early days of American Independence, and it is probable that the sum total of social and domestic happiness was greater than in these advanced days. The more people help themselves, as a general rule, the happier they are. There is gladness in the successful ingenuity required to supply the real and artificial wants of domestic and social life. Someone has recently said that the American is the only man that has ever had enough to eat. And now that he has got to the West, and can go no further without going to the East, he is turned back upon himself to grow and to prove what can be made of a man in a land of plenty. And those were days of plenty. The virgin soil brought forth bountifully. Herds of cattle and droves of swine fed at large, unrestrained by any stock law. Bears, deer, turkeys, wild geese, and ducks abounded. The Yadkin and the Catawba were filled with shad, trout, redhorse, pike, bream, perch, catfish, and eels, and the fisherman seldom returned without a heavy string of fish.

Besides this, the early Rowan man was a man of faith. He may have been a little rough and free in his manners, but he had his religious beliefs, and his religious observances. On the western side of the county the Presbyterians had their churches—Thyatira, Third Creek, and Bethphage, where Dr. McCorkle, Rev. Joseph D. Kilpatrick, and Rev. John Carrigan preached and taught the people the strong Calvinism of their creed. In the eastern division, at the

Organ Church, the Lower Stone, and elsewhere, the devout Lutheran and German Reformed churches and ministers led the people in the way of life. Salisbury could boast of but one church, the Lutheran; standing where the Lutheran graveyard now is. It did not always have a pastor, but it was open to all evangelical ministers. Salisbury Presbyterians were a branch of Thyatira, and here Dr. McCorkle often officiated, and married his wife in this place. Schools were kept up and eminent teachers were employed to give instruction to the young. In this way matters moved on with nothing more exciting than a popular election or a general muster, for several years after the close of the war.

CHAPTER XX

GENERAL WASHINGTON'S VISIT TO SALISBURY

The most distinguished visitor that Salisbury has ever welcomed was Gen. George Washington—the President of the United States. Wishing to see for himself the whole country, and no doubt hoping to grasp by the hand many of the war-worn veterans who had followed his standard in a hundred marches and battles, he planned and accomplished a southern tour in the spring of 1791. Irving, in his Life of Washington, states that the whole tour was accurately planned, the places to be visited, and the times he would reach and leave each place, before he left Mount Vernon, and that he carried out his plan with the utmost precision, not failing a single time. He traveled in his family carriage, perhaps the one that was on exhibition at the Centennial in Philadelphia. He passed down from Virginia through North Carolina, South Carolina, and Georgia, near the coast, as far as Savannah, and returned through Augusta, Columbia, Camden, Charlotte, Salisbury, Salem, and so on to his home. Several incidents of this trip are worth recording. Upon his arrival at Charleston, it is related that someone unrolled a bolt of carpeting on the ground for him to walk upon. His severe republican simplicity revolted at such homage paid to a man. He rebuked them for their adulation, informing them that such tokens of honor were due from man to his Creator alone. He, of course, refused to walk upon it. Many years after Washington's visit to Camden, the Marquis de LaFayette, "the Nation's Guest," paid a visit to the same town. The committee of arrangements were anxious to have every article of the finest quality for the distinguished Frenchman. A certain lady offered a quilt, somewhat faded, as a covering for his bed. The committee rejected it as quite unfit for so important an occasion. Gathering up her quilt in her arms, the lady began to retire, but repeating with indignant tones these words, "a greater and better man than LaFayette slept under this quilt. If it was good enough for Washington, it was good enough for General LaFayette." The astonished committee would fain have recalled their hasty decision, but the indignant lady, wth her precious quilt in her arms, had disappeared.

As General Washington approached the borders of North Carolina, Capt. John Beard, of Salisbury, with the Rowan "Light Horse Company," set out for Charlotte to meet and escort him to Salisbury. As the cavalcade was approaching Salisbury a little incident occurred of pleasing character. Richard Brandon, Esq., then lived six miles southwest of Salisbury, at the place known by our older citizens as the Stockton place, now owned by C. H. McKenzie, Esq. The old building stood, till a few years ago, on the west side of the road, near a little meadow, about halfway between St. Mary's Church and Mr. McKenzie's present residence. As the party neared this place early in the day, the President being then sixty years old, and wearied with his journey, and knowing too that a long and fatiguing reception awaited him in Salisbury, bethought him that a little refreshment would strengthen him for the day's work. So he drove up to the farmer's door, and called. A neat and tidy lass of some twelve or fourteen summers—a daughter of Squire Brandon, answered the call. The President immediately asked whether she could give him a breakfast. She replied that she did not know—that all the grown people were gone to Salisbury to see General Washington. The President kindly assured her that if she would get him some breakfast, she should see General Washington before any of her people, adding pleasantly, "I am General Washington." The breakfast—for the President alone—was prepared with great alacrity, and the blushing maiden had the pleasure, not only of seeing, but of conversing with General Washington, as she dispensed to him her bountiful hospitality.

This little girl's name was Betsy Brandon, the daughter of Richard Brandon. Her mother's maiden name was Margaret Locke, the sister of Gen. Matthew Locke, and the aunt of Judge Francis Locke. A few years after this, Betsy Brandon was married to Francis McCorkle, Esq., of Rowan, and some of their descendants still reside in Rowan, Iredell, and Catawba Counties. James M. McCorkle, Esq., of Salisbury, and Matthew Locke McCorkle, Esq., of Newton, are grandsons of Francis and Betsy McCorkle. The Brandons came originally from England, and the Lockes from the North of Ireland.

As General Washington approached Salisbury, on the Concord Road, some half-mile from town, and at a point near where Mr. Samuel Harrison now lives, he was met by a company of boys of Salisbury. Each of these boys had a bucktail in his hat—a symbol of independence, and their appearance was quite neat and attractive. The President expressed himself much pleased by the boys' turnout, saying that it was "the nicest thing he had seen."

The illustrious visitor was of course the guest of the town, and lodging was provided for him at Capt. Edward Yarboro's residence.

This house is still standing, on East Main Street, a few doors east of the Public Square, and nearly opposite the entrance of Meroney's Hall. The house is now marked by a set of semi-circular stone steps. Many have supposed that Washington stood on those steps and addressed the people. It is almost a pity that this is not the truth, but the fact is that those stone steps were placed there since 1830, by Sam Jones, who kept a hotel there. But the President did occupy that house for a night, and he did stand on steps where those semilunar steps now stand. And as he stood there the people from all the country around stood packed and crowded in the street, gazing with reverence and admiration at the soldier and patriot who was "first in the hearts of his countrymen." And as the people gazed the President stood bareheaded, while the afternoon sun illumined his hoary locks. And this was what he said: "My friends, you see before you nothing but an old, gray-headed man." Lifting his hand, with his handkerchief he shielded his head from the rays of the sun, in silence. That night there was a grand ball given to the President at Hughes' Hotel, attended by the prominent gentlemen and ladies of Salisbury and vicinity—Maxwell Chambers and his wife, Spruce Macay, Esq., Adlai Osborne, Esq., Capt. John Beard, Edward Chambers, Joseph Chambers, Lewis Beard, Hugh Horah, Edward Yarboro, Miss Mary Faust, Mrs. Kelly (née Frohock), Mrs. Lewis Beard, Mrs. Giles, Mrs. Torrence, and many others whose names are no longer preserved in a vanishing tradition. There is still in the county a relic of this ball—a brown satin dress, worn by Mrs. Lewis Beard—the daughter of John Dunn, Esq. It is in the possession of Mrs. Mary Locke, granddaughter of Col. Moses A. Locke, and great-granddaughter of the lady who wore it. How far the "Father of His Country" participated in the amusements and festivities of the occasion, tradition saith not. It was probably a mere occasion for a reception on his part, and we may well imagine that the "old, gray-headed man," as he claimed to be, husbanded his strength by retiring early, and thus securing the rest needful to fit him for his next day's journey to Salem. Captain Beard and his Company of "Rowan Light Horse" escorted the Presidential party as far as Salem.

As the reader has incidently learned the names of a few of the citizens of Salisbury one hundred years ago, it will probably be of some interest, especially to those of antiquarian tastes, to have a list of the principal householders of our city in those early days. Fortunately the mayor of the city, Capt. John A. Ramsay, has succeeded in securing a number of the old records of the "Borough of Salisbury," the earliest dating back as far as 1787. On the twelfth of March of that year, Messrs. Maxwell Chambers, Michael Troy, John Steele, and John Blake were duly qualified as town commissioners, and Matthew Troy as Justice of police. James McEwen was elected clerk, and Thomas Anderson, constable. The records are quite fragmentary, those of several years being lost. In 1793, the commissioners adopted several ordinances. One ordinance forbade the citizens to allow their hogs or goats to run at large in the streets, and any person was allowed to kill any hog or goat so found, and the owner sustained the loss. Another ordinance forbade the keeping of any hay, oats, straw, or fodder in dwelling-houses. Another ordinance required each house-holder to keep on hand, for use at fires, a number of leather water buckets, holding not less than two gallons each. And in this connection we have the first list of householders of Salisbury, graded according to the number of buckets they were supposed to be justly required to furnish. As the Chinese mandarin is graded by the number of buttons, and the Turkish pasha by the number of "tails" he wore on his cap, so the Salisbury citizen was graded by the buckets he was required to keep on hand. Richmond Pearson was expected to keep four, and Dr. Anthony Newnan three. The following were rated at two each, viz.: Richard Trotter, Joseph Hughes, Conrad Brem, Tobias Forrie, Michael Troy, Andrew Betz, John Patton, Lewis Beard, Henry Giles, Edward Yarboro, David Cowan, Albert Torrence, Charles Hunt, William Alexander, Maxwell Chambers, M. Stokes, John Steele, William Nesbit, Peter Fults, and Michael Brown. The following householders were let off with one bucket each, viz.: Henry Barrett, Robert Gay, Matthew Doniven, Richard Dickson, Daniel Cress, George Lowman, John Mull, Hugh Horah, George Houver, Charles Wood, Fed. Allemong, David Miller, Mr. Stork, George Moore, John Beard, Mrs. Beard (widow), Leonard Crosser, Martin Basinger, Peter Faust, John Blake, Henry Young, John Whith, George Kinder, Jacob Utzman, Barna Cryder, William Hampton, Samuel Dayton, and Charles Shrote. It seems that at a subsequent meeting of the commissioners, Mr. Pearson at his own request was reduced to the grade of two buckets, and Dr. Newnan, Peter Fults, and Evan Alexander to the grade of one bucket. These commissioners enacted strigent laws against "Bullet Playing"—whatever that was—horse racing, and retailing liquors on the streets. The taxes for 1793 were four shillings (50c.) on every hundred pounds ($250.00) value of town property, and four shillings (50c.) on every white poll that did not hold one hundred pounds (£100) value of town property. It was certainly not much of a privilege to be a poor man in Salisbury, in those days.

According to the above list there were fifty householders in Salisbury in 1793. It has been usual to estimate an average of five inhabitants to each family. This would make a population of two hundred and fifty. But besides these white families, there were a few families of free negroes as well as the household servants in the various wealthier families. There were also a number of ordinaries, or village inns, in the borough, with their attendants and boarders. From these sources we may suppose there might be counted probably one hundred and fifty or two hundred more, making a total population of four hundred, or four hundred and fifty, in Salisbury at the close of the last century.

About the close of the Revolutionary War, in 1782, the records of the Inferior Court show the following licensed ordinary keepers in Salisbury, viz.: David Woodson, Valentine Beard, Archibald Kerr, Gasper Kinder, William Brandon, and Joseph Hughes. In those days the Inferior Courts fixed the tavern rates. The following are the rates of 1782: For a half-pint of rum 1s. 4d; do. of whiskey 8d; do. of brandy 1s.; one quart of beer 8d; for breakfast 1s.; for dinner 1s. 6d; for supper 1s.; for a quart of corn 2d; for hay or blades per day for a horse 1s.; for lodging per night 6d. A shilling was 12½ cents. According to these rates, a dinner, supper, breakfast, and lodging, not including any spirits or horse feed, would amount to the sum of fifty cents. And, speaking of money, we notice that the commissioners begin, about 1799, to speak about dollars and fourths of a dollar, instead of pounds, shillings, and pence, indicating the substitution of the Federal currency for the sterling. About this time an ordinance was adopted disallowing sheep to run at large in Salisbury between eight in the evening and sunrise in the morning. The same year an "order" is directed to be published in *The Mercury,* thus indicating that a paper of that name was published in town. The location and the size of a market-house engaged the attention of the commissioners for several years. At different times it was ordered to be built on three different sides of the courthouse. In 1803 it was ordered to be erected on Corban Street southwest of the courthouse, between the courthouse and the next cross street; to be thirty-two feet wide, and to be set on eight or more brick pillars. In 1805 the commisisoners resolved to issue forty-two pounds and ten shillings (£42/10) in bills of credit, and employed Francis Coupee to print the bills. In 1806 they required every dog to be registered, and allowing every family to keep one dog free of tax laid a tax of one dollar on each surplus dog. Provided a dog should become mischievous, the magistrate of police was to issue a warrant against him, and the constable was to kill him. None of these laws, however, were to apply to dogs "commonly called foists or lap dogs."

In 1811 the following citizens were divided into classes for the purpose of patrolling the town:

1. Samuel S. Savage, captain; Peter Brown, John Murphy, Ezra Allemong, James Huie, John Trisebre, Jacob Smothers, and William Hinly.

2. George Miller, captain; John Utzman, John Wood, John Smith, John Bruner, Christian Tarr, and Horace B. Satterwhite.

3. Moses A. Locke, captain; John Faris, Henry Crider, Abner Caldwell, William Moore, George Rufty, and Henry Poole.

4. Jacob Crider, captain; Joseph Chambers, Peter Bettz, Edwin J. Osborne, Hugh Horah, Archibald Ruffin, and Samuel Lemly.

5. John Smith (hatter), captain; Lewis Utzman, George Utzman, Robert Blackwell, Epps Holland, Benjamin Tores, and Peter Crider.

6. Henry Sleighter, captain; Jacob Utzman, Daniel Jacobs, Abraham Brown, Andrew Kerr, Epps Robinson, William Horah.

7. Robert Torrence, captain; Alexander Graham, Micahel Brown, Horace B. Prewit, George Goodman, James Wilson, Robert Wood.

8. William Hampton, captain; John Albright, Willie Yarboro, Jacob Stirewalt, John L. Henderson, John Fulton, and William C. Love.

9. William H. Brandon, captain; Benjamin Pearson, Michael Swink, Francis Marshall, Joshua Gay, Abraham Earnhart, John Giles.

10. Daniel Cress, captain; Abraham Jacobs, Peter Coddle, George Bettz, William Dickson, David Nesbit, Stephen L. Ferrand.

11. Thomas L. Cowan, captain; Joseph Weant, James Gillespie, William Pinkston, Francis Coupee, William Rowe, and William Davenport.

12. Francis Todd, captain; Thomas Reeves, Jeremiah Brown, Henry Ollendorf, Henry Allemong, George Vogler, and Charles Biles.

These were the able-bodied men of Salisbury in 1811—sixty-nine years ago.

CHAPTER XXI

FAMILIES LIVING ON THE YADKIN RIVER ONE HUNDRED YEARS AGO

Amid the ever-shifting scenes of domestic and social life, it is extremely difficult to get a picture of any one neighborhood. During the period of current life, events are regarded as of so little importance, and they are so numerous and crowded, that nobody takes the time and trouble to make a record of passing events. But when a generation or two has gone by, and children or grandchildren would love to know the history of their ancestors, only fragments remain. Now and then a curious chronicler arises, and by searching into records in family Bibles, old wills and deeds, and by the aid of some survivor of past generations stranded on the shores of time, succeeds in sketching an outline of the old days. But the picture can never be complete, and seldom absolutely accurate. With such aids as these, the author of these pages proposes to give a running sketch of the people who lived in a part of Rowan County at the close of the last century.

About six miles northeast of Salisbury, where Grant's Creek pours its yellow waters into the Yadkin, there was a large farm and spacious dwelling, owned by Alexander Long, Esq. Somewhere about 1756, there appeared in Rowan County a man who is designated in a deed, dated October 7, 1757, as John Long, gentleman. He purchased a tract of land—six hundred and twenty acres—on the ridge between Grant's Creek and Crane Creek, adjoining the township land. In 1758 he received a title from the Earl of Granville for six hundred and eight acres on the "Draughts of Grant's Creek." Also six hundred and forty acres on Crane Creek, adjoining his own. Also six hundred and four acres on Second Creek; besides some town lots in Salisbury—altogether between twenty-five hundred and three thousand acres of land. According to records on minutes of the Inferior Court for 1756, p. 400, John Long had some transactions with William and Joseph Long, of Lancaster County, Pa.—perhaps brothers, or other relatives of his. According to deeds and letters of administration, his wife's name was Hester. These were the parents of Alexander Long, Esq., of Yadkin. In the year 1760, the Cherokee Indians were on the warpath, and Col. Hugh Waddell was stationed with a regiment of infantry, at the new village of Salisbury, for the protection of the western settlements. Tradition says that John Long was killed by the Indians in an expedition against a settlement of them in Turkey Cove, on the North Fork of the Catawba River, not far from Pleasant Gardens. The records of the Inferior Court of 1760, p. 293, have this entry: Upon motion of Mr. Dunn, ordered that Hester Long, relict of John Long deceased, have administration of the estate of her late husband, John Long [and that] Martin Pipher, John Howard, and Thomas Parker be bound in six hundred pounds (£600). She took the oath of administratrix." Tradition states that Hester Long afterwards married George Magoune, by whom she was the mother of a daughter who became the wife of Maxwell Chambers. The Court records of April, 1763, p. 461, have this entry: "William Long vs. George Magoune et uxor., administrator of John Long." Alexander Long, probably the only child of John Long, was born January 16, 1758, and became heir to the vast area of fertile lands entered and purchased by his father. When he became of age he added to this large estate. In 1783 he purchased a tract on both sides of the road from Salisbury to Trading Ford, and in 1784, he entered six hundred and sixty-five acres on the north side of the Yadkin River. He first married a sister of Gov. Montford Stokes, by whom he had one daughter, named Elizabeth, who became the wife of Alexander Frohock, Esq., who was the sheriff of Rowan County. He was married a second time to Miss Elizabeth Chapman, a lady from Virginia, October 12, 1786. Besides his extensive landed estate, Alexander Long was the owner of a hundred or more slaves, and had a valuable ferry over the Yadkin at the mouth of Grant's Creek, besides valuable fisheries on the river. In those days the Yadkin abounded with shad, and immense quantities were caught in Mr. Long's fisheries. He had a large family of sons and daughters—John, Alexander, William, Richard, James, Nancy, Maria, Rebecca, Harriet, and Carolina.

The second son, Dr. Alexander Long, late of Salisbury, whose memory is still fresh in the minds of our citizens, spent the larger part of his life in Salisbury. He was for many years the leading physician in the county, and his practice was very extensive. He married Miss Mary Williams, of Hillsboro. At the organization of the Presbyterian Church of Salisbury, Dr. Long became one of its original members, and one of its first ruling elders. He continued to be an elder until his death in 1877, in the eighty-ninth year of his age. Maria Long, daughter of Alexander Long, Esq., became the wife of the late Michael Brown, of Salisbury, so long a prominent merchant and ruling elder of the Presbyterian Church.

The houses of Dr. Long and Michael Brown were for many years the abodes of a bountiful hospitality. Ministers and agents for religious objects always found there a cordial welcome and a generous entertainment. Harriet, another daughter of Alexander Long, was married to the late George Brown, for a long period a leading merchant of Salisbury. Rebecca Long married Capt. Edward Yarboro. The others were all well known, and exerted an influence in their day. In the large family of Alexander Long, Sr., we have an element of Rowan society as it existed at the close of the eighteenth and beginning of the nineteenth century. The family burying-ground of the Longs was on a high bluff near the river bank, a short distance below the ferry.

2. The next plantation on the Yadkin, and just below the Long place, was originally called the "Stroup Place," and in late years, the "Bridge Place." It was owned in those early days by Lewis Beard, son of John Lewis Beard, one of the first settlers of Salisbury. Some misunderstanding having arisen between Mr. Long and Mr. Beard concerning the right of the latter to keep a ferry on his lands, Mr. Beard secured from the Legislature the right to build a bridge over the river on his own lands. He therefore secured as an architect, Ithiel Towne, and erected a magnificent bridge, at a cost of thirty thousand dollars. For many years this bridge stood there, and spanned the stream, affording passage at all heights of the river. It was known in later years as "Locke's Bridge." Its piers may still be seen rising in their ruins above the waters, from the railroad bridge a half-mile below.

Lewis Beard married Susan, the daughter of John Dunn, Esq., of Salisbury. Of their children, Mary married Major Moses A. Locke, for many years president of the bank in Salisbury. The grandchildren of Major Locke still reside at the Bridge place, near the river. Christine, another daughter of Lewis Beard, married Charles Fisher, Esq., a lawyer of Salisbury. From 1818 until his death in 1849, for nearly forty years, Charles Fisher was a leading man in Rowan County in public affairs, serving often in the State Legislature, and several times in the United States Congress. His son, Col. Charles F. Fisher, was a leading man. He volunteered at the beginning of the late war, and fell in the first battle of Manassas, courageously fighting in front of his regiment. Another child of Lewis and Susan Beard, was Major John Beard, who died about five years ago at his home in Tallahassee, Fla.

3. The third plantation on the Yadkin, going down the stream, was owned by Valentine Beard. It was afterwards known as Cowan's Ferry, and at present as Hedrick's Ferry. Valentine Beard was a Continental soldier in the Revolutionary War, and fought at the battles of the Brandywine and Germantown, and others, under General Washington. He married Margaret Marquedant, of Philadelphia, and at the close of the war settled at this place. Valentine Beard had three daughters. Elizabeth married Benjamin Tores. Maria married Dr. Burns, of Philadelphia, who was a sea captain. Dr. Burns settled in Salisbury about 1819, and remained a few years, when he returned to Philadelphia. Dr. Burns' daughter, Margaretta, married the late Horace Beard of Salisbury, and their descendants still reside here.

Next below the place last named was one called the "Island Ford" place, including the island of one hundred acres lying above Trading Ford. This island is probably the one that is called the "Island of Akenatzy," in the journal of Lederer's explorations, as found in Hawks' History of North Carolina. This place belonged to Lewis Beard, who owned the bridge above.

4. The next place, still going down, was the property of Capt. Edward Yarboro, of Salisbury. The house, occupied by tenants or overseers, stood just back of where St. John's mill now stands. Captain Yarboro lived in Salisbury, and had three daughters and two sons. Sally Yarboro was the second wife of William C. Love, and the mother of William and Julius Love. She and her husband lie buried just in the rear of Meroney's Hall. Nancy Yarboro married Colonel Beatty, of Yorkville, S. C., and Mary married Richard Long. Edward Yarboro, Jr., was the owner of the Yarboro House in Raleigh, and gave his name to it.

5. Just below Trading Ford, on a high bluff, stood the residence of Albert Torrence. The house is still conspicuous from afar, and has been named of late years by a poetical friend, "The Heights of Gowerie." It was from these heights that Lord Cornwallis' artillery cannonaded General Greene, while writing his dispatches in the cabin on the other side of the Yadkin. Albert Torrence, an Irishman, chose this airy situation for his residence, and from the edge of the bluff he could watch the windings of the silver stream, dotted with a cluster of beautiful islets, and beyond could see lying the fertile farms of the famed Jersey Settlement. Albert Torrence married Elizabeth Hackett, of Rowan County. In this family there grew up four sons and one daughter. Hugh, the eldest son married a

GEN. JOHN STEELE

First Comptroller of the Currency under Washington

[From a Minature by Poole]

Miss Simonton, of Statesville, and died early. Albert married a daughter of Judge Toomer, of Fayetteville, and settled in that city. James died young. Charles married first Miss Elizabeth L. Hays, of Rowan County, and after her death, Miss Philadelphia Fox, of Charlotte. His residence was southeast of Charlotte, on the Providence Road, about a mile from the Public Square. The daughter of Albert Torrence married William E. Powe, of Cheraw, and settled at the Bruner place, five miles east of Salisbury, on the Chambers' Ferry Road, where they reared a large family of sons and daughters, only two of whom remain in Rowan—Dr. Albert Torrence Powe, and his sister, Mrs. Hackett, who reside at the family homestead. At the organization of the Presbyterian Church in Salisbury, Albert Torrence became a member, and one of the first bench of elders. His remains, with those of his wife and several of their children, and of Mr. Powe, are sleeping in the English graveyard in Salisbury, under broad marble slabs, near the entrance. Albert Torrence died in 1825, aged seventy-two years.

6. Next to the Torrence place was the farm of Gen. John Steele, of Salisbury. General Steele was the son of William and Elizabeth Steele, and was one of the most distinguished native-born citizens of Salisbury. His mother's maiden name was Elizabeth Maxwell, and she was a native of West Rowan. She was first married to Mr. Gillespie, by whom she had a son and daughter, as mentioned on a former page. Her son, John Steele, was born in Salisbury, November 1, 1764, and was educated in the schools of the town. He commenced life as a merchant, but soon turned his attention to farming, in which he was eminently successful. In 1787 he became a member of the Legislature of North Carolina. In 1790 he was a member of the first Congress of the United States under the Constitution. He was appointed by General Washington, first Comptroller of the Treasury of the United States, which office he held until 1802, when he resigned, though solicited by Mr. Jefferson to continue. He occupied many other prominent stations, and filled them all with faithfulness and success. On the day of his death—August 14, 1815—he was elected to the House of Commons of North Carolina. A singular story is told of a circumstance that occurred at his death. During the time he was comptroller he presented to his native town a clock—the one now on the courthouse—and a bell. The night of General Steele's death, the clock commenced striking, and continued to strike many hundreds of times, until it was run down. Hugh Horah, a watchmaker, had the clock in charge, but he could do nothing with it. It was doubtless, all

things considered, a singular coincidence, and calculated to beget a superstitious awe in the minds of the people. In 1783, John Steele married Mary Nesfield, of Fayetteville. Three daughters lived to grow up and marry. Ann married Gen. Jesse A. Pearson. Margaret married Dr. Stephen L. Ferrand, and was the mother of Mary, the wife of the late Archibald Henderson, Esq.; and Ann, who married the late John B. Lord, Esq., afterwards the late Rev. John Haywood Parker, and lastly T. G. Haughton, Esq.

Eliza, daughter of Gen. John Steele, married Col. Robert MacNamara, a native of Ireland, but for a time a prominent citizen of Salisbury. Colonel MacNamara's children are all dead except Louise, now in a convent, and Eliza, who married Dr. Lynch, of Columbia, S. C. General Steele erected the house occupied by the late Archibald Henderson, Esq. There he died, at the age of fifty, and near his residence he was laid to his rest, where a memorial stone, consecrated by conjugal and filial affection, testifies to his character "as an enlightened statesman, a vigilant patriot, and an accomplished gentleman." General Steele's wife survived him for many years. Salisbury has special reason to be proud of the exalted character and faithful services of her honored son. Second to a sense of duty, there is probably no higher incentive to the faithful discharge of public trusts than the hope of transmitting an honored name to posterity; but if posterity forgets their honored ancestors, then neither the dread of shame nor love of honor is left to inspire men to an honorable course of life.

CHAPTER XXII

DISTINGUISHED MEN IN ROWAN

Before leaving this part of the History of Rowan County it is necessary that the reader should become acquainted with a number of distinguished men who made their homes in Salisbury for a longer or shorter time. One of these was a permanent citizen; the others tarried here for a season. Among these we mention first

Waightstill Avery, Esq.

The *University of North Carolina Magazine* for 1855 contains a sketch of Mr. Avery, and his private Journal for 1767; and Colonel Wheeler's Sketch of Burke County contains a brief biography, from which we condense the following account.

Waightstill Avery was of Puritan stock, and was born in Norwich, Conn. He completed his literary studies at Princeton College, in 1776. From this place he went to Maryland, and studied law under Littleton Dennis, Esq. It is stated that he was tutor for a year in Princeton. This was probably his last year as a student, and he was doing double duty, and at the same time was reading law, for we find him in the beginning of 1767 setting out for North Carolina. His journal shows that he was a diligent student of history and law after he began his course as a lawyer here.

On the fifth of February, 1767, he rode into Edenton, N. C. On the third of March he reached Salisbury, and made the acquaintance of Associate Judge Richard Henderson, Samuel Spencer, Esq.—afterwards Judge Spencer, John Dunn, Esq., Alexander Martin, Esq.—afterwards Governor Martin, William Hooper, Esq., Major Williams, and Edmund Fanning, Esq. Colonel Frohock entertained him at his plantation two miles from Salisbury, and Avery describes his house as "the most elegant and large within one hundred miles." On the first Sunday after his arrival he "heard the Rev. Mr. Tate preach." After going to Hillsboro he journeyed to Wilmington, and thence to Brunswick, where he obtained from Governor Tryon license to practice law in this Province. From Brunswick he passed by Cross Creek, and thence to Anson Courthouse. Anson Courthouse was not then at Wadesboro, but at a place called Mount Pleasant, about a mile west of the Pee Dee River, and a short distance below the Grassy Islands. Here Avery took the attorney's oath, April 13,

1767, and the next day began his work by opening a cause against a hog thief. From Mount Pleasant he went to Mecklenburg, met Adlai Osborne, Esq., and on Sunday, April 23, heard Rev. Joseph Alexander preach—probably at Sugar Creek. Here he engaged board with Hezekiah Alexander. On the fourth of May we find him again in Salisbury, where he engaged a year's board with Mr. Troy at twenty pounds (£20) a year, deducting for absence. On the sixteenth of May "he rode out five miles to Dunn's Mountain, in order to enjoy an extensive prospect of the country." At the August term of Rowan Court he was employed in no less than thirty actions. Again in November he was in Salisbury, and was chosen King's Attorney, in the absence of Major Dunn. During this year Mr. Avery practised law at Salisbury, Anson Courthouse, Charlotte, and Tryon Courthouse, and at once obtained a large number of clients. In 1775 and 1776 he was a member of the Provincial Congress, and was appointed on the committee to revise the statutes of the Province. In 1778 he was made Attorney-General of the State, and shortly thereafter he married and moved to Jones County. But finding that his health was impaired by the climate of the eastern country, in 1781 he removed to Burke County, and settled on a beautiful and fertile estate on the Catawba River, known by the name of Swan Pond, afterwards the home of his son, Col. Isaac T. Avery.

Waighstill Avery devoted himself to his profession, but was chosen to represent Burke County in the Legislature a number of times. He was industrious and methodical, and he was the owner of the most extensive and best selected library in Western North Carolina. "He died in 1821 in the enjoyment of an ample estate, the patriarch of the North Carolina Bar, an exemplary Christian, a pure patriot, and an honest man."

In 1778, Mr. Avery married Mrs. Franks, a widow lady of Jones County, near Newbern, by whom he had three daughters and one son. The son, Col. Isaac T. Avery, occupied the paternal estate at Swan Pond, and reared a large family there, among whom were the late Col. Waightstill W. Avery, Col. Moulton Avery and Judge Alphonso C. Avery, now on the bench of North Carolina. These all deserved well of their country, but their history belongs to Burke, and not to Rowan County.

Hon. Spruce Macay

As early in the year 1762 we have accounts of the Macay family in Rowan County. In that year James Macay obtained from Henry

McCulloh a grant of four hundred and thirty acres of land on Swearing Creek, near the Jersey Meeting-house. This was part of a vast body of land, amounting to one hundred thousand acres, which George II, in 1745, granted to Henry McCulloh, Esq., of Turnham Green, County of Middlesex, England. These lands are described as situated in the Province of North Carolina, lying on the "Yadkin or Pee Dee River or branches thereof," and called Tract No. 9. This tract lay in Earl Granville's division of land, but the Earl and his agents recognized McCulloh's title, and the fact is recited at large in many old grants. On this tract James Macay settled and reared his family.

In 1775, William Frohock executed a deed to James Macay, Esq., Benjamin Rounceville, and Herman Butner, trustees of the United Congregation of the Jersey Meeting-house, consisting of the professors of the Church of England, the Church of Scotland, and the Baptists, for three acres and twenty poles of land, including the meeting-house and the burying-ground. The witnesses to the deed are James Smith and Peter Hedrick, and the land was part of a tract devised by John Frohock to his brother, William Frohock. Though the meeting-house had been standing since 1755, it appears that they had no legal title until the above date. If we may judge from the order of the names, compared with the order of denominations, we would conclude that Macay represented the Episcopalians, Rounceville the Presbyterians, and Butner the Baptists.

Spruce Macay was probably a son of James Macay. At all events he was from that neighborhood, and was buried there, with others of his family. At that early period, the Rev. David Caldwell, D.D., was conducting his classical school, on Buffalo, in Guilford County —then a part of Rowan, about forty miles from the Jerseys. Thither young Spruce Macay was sent for his literary training. He probably read law under John Dunn, Esq., of Salisbury, or it may be Waightstill Avery, who practised in these Courts. He was licensed to practice law about the beginning of the Revolutionary War, and devoted himself with energy to his profession, and soon became such a proficient that students came to him for instruction. In 1776, William R. Davie, just graduated at Princeton College, commenced the study of law in Salisbury, and the current opinion is that his preceptor was Spruce Macay. His residence was on lot No. 19, of the West Ward, the property now owned by Mrs. Nathaniel Boyden, and his law office was in front of his dwelling on Jackson Street. In 1784, Mr. Macay had another pupil, who was in after years honored with the highest office in the United States. This was Andrew Jackson. Parton, in his Life of Jackson says: "At Salisbury, he (Jackson) entered the law office of Mr. Spruce Macay, an eminent lawyer at that time, and, in later years, a judge of high distinction, who is still remembered with honor in North Carolina." In 1790, Spruce Macay was appointed Judge of the Superior Courts of law and equity.

By his marriage he became connected with a family distinguished as lawyers and judges in North Carolina. He married Fanny, the daughter of that eminent jurist of Colonial times, Judge Richard Henderson, and sister of the Hon. Archibald Henderson of Salisbury, and Judge Leonard Henderson of the Supreme Court of North Carolina. By this marriage Judge Macay had one child, a daughter named Elizabeth, who married the Hon. William C. Love, of Salisbury, and was the mother of the late Robert E. Love, Esq., of Salisbury. After the death of his first wife, Judge Macay married Elizabeth Hays, of Halifax, N. C., by whom he had three children—Alfred Macay, who died early, in Salisbury; Fanny, who married George Locke, son of Richard Locke, and moved to Tennessee; and William Spruce Macay, who first married Miss Belle Lowry, daughter of Richard Lowry, Esq., of Rowan; and after her death Miss Annie Hunt, daughter of Meshack Hunt, Esq., of Yadkin County, and granddaughter of Hon. Meshack Franklin. The only daughter of this union, Annie, died recently, and with her death the family became extinct in this county.

Judge Macay bought the Frohock lands and mills, near Salisbury, on Grant's Creek, and owned lands in Davidson County. By inheritance with his wife, by industry and economy, he accumulated a large estate. He died in 1808, and his remains lie interred in the graveyard of Jersey Meeting-house, in Davidson County, by the side of his kindred.

Gen. William Richardson Davie

Another distinguished gentleman who resided for a season in Salisbury was William Richardson Davie, afterwards Governor of the State of North Carolina. General Davie was born at Egremont, England, but came to America at five years of age, and was adopted by his maternal uncle, the Rev. William Richardson, the Presbyterian pastor of the Waxhaw and Providence Churches. Davie was graduated at Princeton College in 1776, and the same year commenced the study of law in Salisbury—it is believed under the direction of Spruce Macay, Esq. In 1779 he raised a Company of

GEN. ANDREW JACKSON AT THE AGE OF FIFTY

cavalry, principally in the "Waxhaws," of which he was lieutenant. After the battle of Stono, where he was wounded, he returned to Salisbury and resumed his studies. In 1780, Davie raised a Company of horse in Rowan County, which he led in the battle of the Hanging Rock, and with which he confronted the British in their northward march at Charlotte, where he and his "Rowan Boys" made a brilliant display of courage. He was with General Greene at Guilford Courthouse, Hobkirk's Hill, and Ninety-Six. After the war he began his professional career, as a brilliant and powerful orator and statesman. He was on the committee that fixed the location of the University of North Carolina. The gigantic poplar tree is still standing in the University Campus, under which General Davie was resting when his negro servant reported that he had found a fine spring near by, and lots of mint growing by its side, and that he thought that was the very place for the college. As Grand Master of the Masonic Fraternity, in October, 1793, General Davie laid the cornerstone of the college, while Dr. Samuel E. McCorkle, of Rowan, made the address. In 1798, Davie was elected Governor of North Carolina, and the succeeding year was appointed ambassador to France. It is said that he was introduced to Napoleon as General Davie, and that the haughty emperor sneeringly remarked in an audible aside, *"Oui, Generale de melish."* His mission to France was the close of his public life. On his return he bought certain articles of costly furniture, and fitted up his residence in handsome style. Being a candidate for office shortly after, his opponent taunted him in public with aping the aristocracy of the old world, and so excited the prejudices of the people as to defeat him. He became disgusted with politics, and retired to his estate of Tivoli, near Landsford, S. C., where he died in 1820. He was regarded as the most polished and graceful orator in North Carolina, in his day. Had he not quit public life at the early age of forty-seven, he might have shone as a star of the first magnitude along with Jefferson, Madison, Monroe, John Q. Adams, Burr, and Crawford. But such is public life, where the demagogue often supplants the patriot and the statesman.

Andrew Jackson

Foremost among the distinguished men who resided for a season in Salisbury was Andrew Jackson. The reader, acquainted with his public career as a soldier and a statesman, will not object to a brief account of his early life, and especially of his sojourn in Salisbury. In 1765, Andrew Jackson, with his wife, two sons, and three neighbors—John, Robert, and Joseph Crawford—emigrated from Carrickfergus, Ireland, to America, and settled in the "Waxhaws," on the boundary between North and South Carolina. While some of the company settled in South Carolina, Jackson settled on Twelve Mile Creek, in Mecklenburg (now Union) County, N. C. In the spring of 1757, Andrew Jackson died, and in a rude farm wagon his body was carried to the Waxhaw Church and deposited in the graveyard. The family did not return to their home on Twelve Mile Creek, but went to the house of George McKemie, a brother-in-law, not far from the church, and a quarter-mile from the boundary of the States, but in North Carolina. There Andrew Jackson, the younger, was born, the night after his father's funeral, March 15, 1767. Evidence for all this, most conclusive and convincing was collected by Gen. Samuel H. Walkup, of Union County, in 1858, and may be found in the first volume of Parton's Life of Jackson. Three weeks after his birth, his mother removed with the family to the residence of her brother-in-law, Mr. Crawford, in South Carolina. Here Andrew grew up, wild, reckless, daring, working on the farm, riding horses, hunting, going to old-field schools, and picking up a little education here and there. He also attended a school of a higher grade at Waxhaw Church, kept by Rev. Dr. Humphries, and he claimed to have attended the Queen's Museum College, in Charlotte, N. C. In these schools he acquired the rudiments of an English education, and perhaps "a little Latin and less Greek." Though only fifteen years old at the close of the Revolution, young Andrew Jackson took part in several skirmishes and other adventures in his neighborhood. At the close of the war he was an orphan, without brother or sister—without fortune—a sick and sorrowful orphan. After a year or two of a reckless career, he began to look at life in earnest, and prepare for it. He taught school for a while, and gaining a little money he came to Salisbury in 1785, and entered as a law student in the office of Spruce Macay, Esq. He lodged in the "Rowan House," but he studied in the office of Mr. Macay, along with two fellow-students—Crawford and McNairy. The reader may remember this little office on Jackson Street, as it stood until four years ago, immediately in front of the residence of the Hon. Nathaniel Boyden. Parton describes it as "a little box of a house fifteen by sixteen feet, and one story high," and built of "shingles," i.e., a framed and weatherboarded house, covered with shingles. This little house was purchased by an enterprising individual and carried to Philadelphia to the Centennial Exposition, in 1876, as a speculation, though it proved to be a very poor investment. While Jackson certainly devoted a good part of his time to study, yet he was no doubt, as Parton describes him, "a roaring, rollicking fellow, overflowing with life and spirits, and rejoicing to engage in all the fun that was going." He played cards, fought cocks, ran horses, threw the 'long bullet' (cannon ball, slung in a strap, and thrown as a trial of strength), carried off gates, moved outhouses to remote fields, and occasionally indulged in a downright drunken debauch." Upon a certain occasion the three law students and their friends held a banquet at the tavern. At the conclusion it was resolved that it would be improper that the glasses and decanters that had promoted the happiness of such an evening should ever be profaned by any baser use. Accordingly they were smashed. The same reasoning led to the destruction of the table. The chairs and the bed were all broken and torn to splinters and ribbons, and the combustible parts heaped on the fire and burned. Of course there was a big bill to settle next day. But it is said that Jackson's landlord was fond of cards, and that Jackson won large sums from him, which were entered as credits against his board bill. Jackson was certainly not a model young man, and not one in ten thousand young men who begin life as he did ever attain to distinction. But there was in him indomitable will, tireless energy, and unflinching courage. He was always willing to "take the responsibility," and he moved on to his aims with a purpose that could not be turned aside. After spending less than two years in the office of Spruce Macay, Jackson completed his studies for the bar in the office of Col. John Stokes, a brave soldier of the Revolution. After this he lived a while at Martinsville, Guilford County, and from that place he removed to Tennessee, in 1788, and settled in Nashville. The reader may follow his course in the legal profession, in the Indian wars, in the battle of New Orleans, in the Presidential chair, by perusing the racy and readable volumes that record his life by James Parton; but these sketches of him must close at this point.

CHAPTER XXIII

OLD FAMILIES OF ROWAN

While the territory now comprehended in Rowan County was a part of Anson County, or further back still, while it was a part of Bladen County, there were settlers in this region. It was in 1745 that Henry McCulloh obtained his grant of one hundred thousand acres of land on the Yadkin and its tributaries. This was probably about the beginning of the settlement. The deeds and grants between this date and 1753, if recorded, would be registered in these counties. Hence it is not always possible to determine the date of the settlement of a family by the date of its oldest deed, since the oldest deeds may have been registered elsewhere. But among the earliest grants registered here are those of the

Brandon Family

This family came to Rowan from Pennsylvania, but they were originally from England, where for many centuries the Brandons played a conspicuous part in public affairs, as every reader of English history knows.

Upon coming to Rowan County they settled in three different neighborhoods. In 1752, John Brandon obtained a grant of six hundred and thirty acres of land from Earl Granville upon the waters of Grant's Creek. In the same year Richard Brandon obtained a grant of four hundred and eighty acres on the South Fork of Grant's Creek. In 1755, John Brandon purchased from Carter & Foster, Lot No. 4, in the South Square of Salisbury, adjoining the Common, and near the courthouse—near where the stocks and pillory then stood. This was near what was known as Cowan's Corner, now Hedrick's Block. It is not certain whether the above-named John and Richard Brandon were brothers, or father and son, or more distant relations.

Another member of the family, William Brandon, said by tradition to be the youngest son, purchased from James Cathey, in 1752, a tract containing six hundred and forty acres on Sill's Creek, beyond Thyatira Church—then Cathey's Meeting-house. He also procured a grant of three hundred and fifty acres adjoining the meeting-house lands and between the lands of John Sill and James

Cathey. William Brandon married a Miss Cathey. He was perhaps a brother of John Brandon of Grant's Creek.

Another branch of the Brandon family settled on the north side of Fourth Creek. Here James Brandon, in 1760 and 1762, ob tained grants from Granville and deed from Patrick Campbell for one thousand five hundred and ninety-two acres of land. Among the Brandons of Fourth Creek there was one George Brandon whose will, dated 1772, names the following persons, to wit: His wife Marian, his sons John, George, Christopher, and Abraham (the latter residing at Renshaw's Ford on South River), and his daughters Jane Silver, Mary McGuire, Elinor Brandon, and Sidney Witherow. Of these families the writer has no knowledge.

With regard to the Brandons of Grant's Creek, we have more definite historical and traditional knowledge.

John Brandon appears among the Justices who presided over our County Courts in the year 1753, along with Walter Curruth, Alexander Cathey, Alexander Osborne, John Brevard, and others. We would infer from this fact that he was somewhat advanced in life, and of prominence in his neighborhood and the county. When the Rev. Hugh McAden passed through Rowan, he stopped a night with Mr. Brandon, whom he styles "His Own Countryman," that is from Pennsylvania, where McAden was born. From a deed dated 1753, we learn that John Brandon's wife's name was Elizabeth.

John Brandon had three sons, namely: Richard, William, and John. Richard Brandon married Margaret Locke, the sister of Gen. Matthew Locke. The children of Richard Brandon and Margaret Locke were John Brandon, Matthew Brandon, and Elizabeth Brandon. The latter is the fair maiden who furnished the breakfast for General Washington, and who married Francis McCorkle, Esq. John and Matthew Brandon resided in the same neighborhood.

Col. John Brandon, brother of Matthew, and son of Richard named above, resided about five miles southwest of Salisbury, on the Concord Road. Among his children was the late well-known Col. Alexander W. Brandon, who resided in Salisbury, and died here about the year 1853. Col. Alexander W. Brandon never married. While in Salisbury he boarded with his nephew, James Cowan, in the old historic "Rowan House," where General Jackson once boarded (the house now owned by Theodore F. Kluttz, immediately opposite the Boyden House). Colonel Brandon possessed a considerable estate, was a general trader, a dealer in money, notes, and stocks. By his will be provided that his body should be laid in Thyatira churchyard among his kindred, and left four hundred dollars to the elders of the church, as trustees, for the purpose of keeping the graveyard in repair. He also bequeathed three thousand dollars to Davidson College for the education of candidates for the ministry, besides legacies to his nephews, Thomas Cowan, James L. Cowan, James L. Brandon, Leonidas Brandon, Jerome B. Brandon, George Locke; and to his brother, John L. Brandon. Colonel Brandon was an upright, steady, moral man, of fine appearance and dignified demeanor.

Besides Alexander W. Brandon, John Brandon left a son named John L. Brandon, and two daughters. One of the daughters, named Sally, was married to James Locke, son of Gen. Matthew Locke, and after his death was married to a Mr. Dinkins, of Mecklenburg. The other daughter, named Lucretia, was the first wife of Abel Cowan, Esq., of Thyatira.

To return a generation or two, we find that Richard Brandon had another son, besides Col. John Brandon, whose name was Matthew. This Matthew Brandon was the father of two daughters. One of these daughters, named Elizabeth, became the wife of Gen. Paul Barringer, of Cabarrus, and the mother of the late Hon. D. M. Barringer, Gen. Rufus Barringer, Rev. William Barringer, Victor C. Barringer, Mrs. Wm. C. Means, Mrs. Andrew Grier, Mrs. Dr. Charles W. Harris, and Mrs. Edwin R. Harris. All these were well-known and honored citizens of Cabarrus and Mecklenburg Counties.

The other daughter of Matthew Brandon, named Elvira, became the wife of the Rev. James Davidson Hall, then pastor of Thyatira Church, and left no children.

Not far from Thyatira Church, many years ago, there lived two brothers named John Brandon and James Brandon. They were the sons of William Brandon, who settled there as early as 1752. Wm. Brandon's first wife was a Cathey, the mother of John and James. After her death he married a Widow Troy, of Salisbury, and moved to Kentucky. From William Brandon and his second wife there descended in the second generation a family of Davises. Two ladies of this name, granddaughters of William Brandon, lived for a while in Salisbury with Miss Catherine Troy, afterwards Mrs. Maxwell Chambers. One of these young ladies married George Gibson, and moved to Tennessee. The other died in Salisbury, after a short residence here.

John Brandon, the son of William Brandon, of Thyatira, married Mary, the daughter of Major John Dunn, of Salisbury. This couple died childless. Their residence was on the west side of Cathey's Creek, a mile from Thyatira Church. The place was known of late years as the residence of Dr. Samuel Kerr, and still later as the home of our fellow-citizen, James S. McCubbins, Esq. The other son of William Brandon, known as Col. James Brandon, married Esther Horah, sister of Hugh Horah, and aunt of the late William H. Horah. He resided near Thyatira Church in his early married life. After the Revolutionary War he was "entry-taker," and lost nearly all his property by the depreciation of continental money in his hands. In his latter days he lived in what is now Franklin Township, where William R. Fraley now resides. Col. James Brandon died about 1820, and left a number of children.

1. Among these was a son named William Brandon, who was a merchant in Salisbury, and kept his store about the place now occupied by Enniss' drug store. He never married, and died young, about the same time that his father died.

2. Priscilla Brandon married William Gibson, and their children were Dr. Edmund R. Gibson, late of Concord, James Brandon Gibson, now an elder of Thyatira, George Gibson, who moved to Tennessee, now dead, and Mrs. Margaret G. Smith, now living with James G. Gibson.

3. Margaret, who never married, died about 1828.

4. Clarissa Harlowe, who married Thomas Kincaid. These were the parents of Mrs. Mary Ann Bruner, Mrs. Jane E. Fraley, and William Mortimer Kincaid, Esq.

5. Sophia Gardner, who never married, and died in 1846.

6. Mary, who married William Hampton of Rowan. Their children were Nancy Reed, the wife of Hon. Philo White; Margaret Gardner, wife of Montfort S. McKenzie, Esq.; Mary Ann, wife of John C. Palmer, of Raleigh; and James, who died young.

7. Elizabeth, who married Francis Gibson. Their children were Clarissa, the wife of Benjamin Julian, of Salisbury; Esther, the wife of Jesse P. Wiseman, Esq.; and Emmeline, the wife of Rufus Morrison.

Of the Brandons it may be remarked that they were a thriving, industrious, and prosperous family in their day, devoting their chief attention to agriculture and local affairs. Some of them wore the military titles of the day, and were doubtless leaders of public opinion in their neighborhoods, resembling the English country squires, who took deeper interest in the sports and institutions of the country than in national affairs. Though the Brandons did not generally aspire to legislative and judicial honors, yet some of them were elevated by their fellow-citizens to places of trust and dignity. Matthew Brandon, son of Richard, and brother of the second John, represented Rowan County four times in the House of Commons, and once in the Senate, of North Carolina. Col. Alexander W. Brandon was once a member of the House of Commons.

Though they were generally men of substance they did not seem to desire for their sons a college education, preferring that they should walk in the peaceful avocations of an independent farmer's life. But they were a race possessed of intellectual force, and many of the scions of this house have achieved success as scholars, as lawyers, legislators, and divines. These branches of the family are scattered over many counties of North Carolina, though the historic name of Brandon has almost disappeared from the land of their forefathers.

John Phifer and George Savitz

On the headwaters of Grant's Creek in the neighborhood of the present village of China Grove, there dwelt in the early times two families very closely connected. About 1760, John Phifer, with five brothers, came from Pennsylvania and settled in Rowan and Cabarrus (then Mecklenburg) Counties. The family is said to have been of Swiss origin, and the name was originally written Pfeiffer. In 1763, John Phifer married Catherine, the daughter of John Paul Barringer, and sister of Gen. Paul Barringer, late of Cabarrus. He settled about a mile south of China Grove, and their union was blessed with two children—Margaret and Paul B. Phifer. While only seven years old, little Margaret Phifer performed a deed of heroism worthy of commendation. Some ruffian Tories and British soldiers visited her home, and with lighted torches ascended the stairs with the purpose of setting the house on fire. Little Margaret fell on her knees and, throwing her arms around the nearest of the marauders, implored him to spare their home. Their hearts were melted by the tender pleading of the child, and they withdrew and left the house standing. This child, growing up, became the wife of John Simianer, of Cabarrus County, and the mother of Mrs. Adolphus L. Erwin, of McDowell County. The son, Paul B. Phifer, married and died early in life, leaving two sons, both of whom removed to the Southwest. One of these sons, Gen. John N. Phifer, had an only son who was graduated at the University of North Carolina.

He was lieutenant in the late war and has been widely known as Brig.-Gen. Charles Phifer. His father, Gen. John N. Phifer, represented Cabarrus County in the Senate of North Carolina in 1818.

It is due to the memory of Col. John Phifer, the elder, to say that he was a conspicuous and leading man in his day, and acted in the foreground of the great movement which terminated in our glorious independence. Though originally settling in Rowan County, it appears that he had such interests in Cabarrus (then Mecklenburg County) as drew him into coöperation with the patriots of Mecklenburg, and his name is found appended to the Mecklenburg Declaration of 1775. But he found an early grave, passing away during the first years of the Revolutionary War, and after a few years, his widow (Catherine, daughter of John Paul Barringer) became the wife of George Savitz, commonly called "Savage." In 1768 Richard Brandon executed a deed to George Savitz for a tract of land on both sides of Grant's Creek, above a certain mill pond. In 1778, George Savitz, Jr., and his wife Catherine, executed a deed for a tract of land on McCutcheon's Creek, a branch of Coldwater, and by purchasing a tract here and there the Savitzes became the proprietors of a large body of land adjoining the Brandons and Lockes, on the head streams of Grant's Creek, in the region of the present village of China Grove. From these deeds we learn that John Phifer had died before 1778, for at that period George Savitz, Jr., had married Katrina, his widow, that is Catherine, the daughter of John Paul Barringer. Here George Savitz and his wife lived, in the house that was saved from the torch by little Margaret Phifer. That house was about a half-mile west of the place where the two churches, Lutheran Chapel and Mount Zion, now stand. The old church stood near the graveyard, west of the railroad, and was popularly known as Savage's Church. Here the Lutherans and German Reformed worshiped together. After the disruption of the Lutheran Church, in 1819, the adherents of Dr. Henkel built a church a mile west, and still later the Lutherans built a house where the Chapel now stands, and the German Reformed where Zion Church stands. But to return. George Savitz, Jr., and Catherine, his wife, had two daughters, named Mary and Catherine. Mary was first married to Charles McKenzie (afterwards she was the wife of Richard Harris, still living). Three children were born to this couple—the late Montford S. McKenzie, Esq.; Maria, who became the second wife of Abel Cowan; and Margaret, the wife of the late John McRorie, of Salisbury.

Catherine Savitz, the other daughter, married Noah Partee, Esq., and resided at the home place. Their children were Hiram and Charles Partee, who moved to the West, and have recently died. A daughter of Noah and Catherine Partee, named Elizabeth, was married to the late George McConnaughey, of Rowan. Another daughter, named Maria, married the late Major Robert W. Foard, of Concord, and still survives. Still another daughter was married to the late Robert Huie, of Mississippi, and resides in Concord.

The Savitz family were of German lineage, and with the industry and prudence characteristic of that race they amassed a large amount of property. They were originally adherents of the Lutheran Church, though their descendants have entered different churches—some Presbyterians, some Methodists, and some Episcopalians. The Brandons on the other hand, though English, and having an affinity for the Church of England, appear as a general rule to have been Presbyterians. One or more, however, of the family of Richard Brandon were adherents of the Episcopal Church. The Brandons of Cathey's Creek, especially Col. James Brandon's family, were earnest Presbyterians. Thyatira in those days was the great rallying point of the Presbyterians. In the earlier years of this century there was not a church of any denomination in Salisbury. The old Lutheran Church had gone down, and the Methodists, Presbyterians, and Episcopalians had not yet organized their churches. Thyatira was the center for the English people.

While the fertile lands lying on the tributaries of the Yadkin were rapidly taken up by the eager immigrants from Pennsylvania, or rather by the Scotch-Irish and Germans, who came through Pennsylvania to Carolina, many drifted on further, attracted by the no less fertile lands of the beautiful Catawba. Here the Davidsons, Brevards, Whites, Winslows, and others gathered in the neighborhood of Beattie's Ford, and on both sides of the river. This region was peopled quite early, their title deeds dating from 1752 and onward. Among these was

The Family of the McCorkles

A member of this family, Francis Marion McCorkle, of Tennessee, has gathered up the traditions of this family, and his manuscript furnishes the basis of this article.

There lived in Scotland, during the troubles arising from the efforts of Charles Edward, the Pretender, to seize the throne, a family of McCorkles that sought a safer and quieter home in Ireland. Here the parents died, and a son of theirs, named Matthew McCorkle, married a lady by the name of Givens. Ned Givens, a brother of Mrs. McCorkle, was quite a character in his way. At the age of fourteen Ned entered the army and was redeemed by his father at great cost. He soon re-enlisted and was a second time redeemed by his father for a large sum, and assured him that if he repeated the project he should take his chances. About this time Matthew McCorkle and his wife were about to remove to the American Colonies, and Ned, not yet tired of adventures, proposed to go with them, but his father refused to let him go. When, however, McCorkle arrived at the port from which he was to sail, to his surprise he found Ned there awaiting his arirval, and determined to go. His persistence was rewarded, for McCorkle paid his passage, and the party arrived safely in Pennsylvania, and after a short stay there proceeded to North Carolina and entered lands near Beattie's Ford, some in Mecklenburg, and some in Rowan (now Iredell). Here Matthew McCorkle and Ned Givens both settled down, and each of them raised large families, and there they ended their days. Givens had already showed that he had a strong will, and he was reputed to have had an ungovernable temper. From him were descended some of the most reputable families of South Iredell, as for instance the family of Whites.

Matthew McCorkle had two sons, Thomas and Francis, and several daughters. One of these sons, Francis, married Sarah Work, by whom he had five children. As his family increased he entered more lands. The second entry was on the west side of Catawba River, on one of the tributaries of Mountain Creek, in the limits of the present County of Catawba. Here he started a farm, planted an orchard, and by industry and skill began rapidly to accumulate property. He was said to have been a man of amiable disposition and of a fine personal appearance (or florid complexion, auburn hair, and about six feet in height).

When the Revolutionary War came on Francis McCorkle promptly took his place on the side of the patriots. In 1774, he was appointed a member of the Committee of Safety of Rowan, along with John Brevard, Matthew Locke, and others. (See Wheeler's Sketches, Vol. 2, page 360.) Though full thirty miles from his home, he is recorded as present in Salisbury at the regular meetings of the committee, and is named in the records as the captain of a Company. He was in the battles of King's Mountain, Ramsour's Mill, Cowpens, and Torrence's Tavern. His patriotic course excited the animosity of the Tories, and he was in consequence frequently compelled to keep away from his home to escape their vengeance. A

John S. Henderson

morning or two before the battle of Ramsour's Mill, Francis McCorkle and a man by the name of Smith rode out before day to learn the whereabouts of the Tories, knowing that they were in the neighborhood. Arriving at a neighbor's house near the head of the creek about daylight, they inquired of the lady if she knew where the Tories were. She replied that she was expecting them every moment. Upon this the party wheeled and rode home in a hurry to arrange matters. After brief preparation they left home, and were scarcely out of sight before the Tories arrived, and searched the house from garret to cellar for McCorkle. They found there some salt, which they appeared to want, and left word if McCorkle would come and bring them some salt all would be well, but if not they would come and destroy everything in his house. Instead of joining them, McCorkle and Smith hastened to the patriotic soldiers that were centering at Ramsour's Mill, and were in the battle there.

The tradition of the McCorkle family is that Colonel Locke, a friend of Francis McCorkle, fell in the battle of Ramsour's Mill. Dr. Foote states that he was killed at the Kennedy place, near Charlotte, and Dr. Caruthers says he fell at Torrence's Tavern. Dr. Foote is evidently mistaken, for it was Lieut. George Locke, a brother of Colonel Francis, that fell at Charlotte. It is probable also that the McCorkle tradition is a mistake, since Tarleton, in his Memoirs, according to Caruthers, preserves a letter written by General Greene to Col. Francis Locke, about the time of the affair at Cowan's Ford, dated Beattie's Ford, January 31, 1781. But the battle of Ramsour's Mill was fought on the twentieth of June, 1780, seven months before this time. Besides, there is no record of any administration upon his estate, but there is a will of Francis Locke on file, dated 1796, with the known signature of Col. Francis Locke. He doubtless survived until this date. But to return. After the battle of Ramsour's Mill, Smith returned and reported that McCorkle was killed. But to the great joy of the family he soon rode up alive and unharmed. He then ventured to sleep in his own house for a few nights. But about the third night he was suddenly awakened by the sound of horses' hoofs. Hearing his name called, he answered, and was told to get up and come to the door. He requested time to put on his clothes, but with abusive words they told him it was no use, as they intended to kill him. They then asked him "whom he was for?" He replied that he did not know whether they were friends or foes, but if he had to die, he would die with the truth in his mouth—he was for liberty. He was then told to put on his clothes, that they had more of his sort, and they would slay them all together. He went with them, but when he arrived at the main body, he was agreeably surprised to learn that they were all Whigs, and that they had met for a jollification after the battle of Ramsour's, and wished to have him in their company.

After the British crossed the Catawba at Cowan's Ford, McCorkle made a narrow escape. He was in the affair at Torrence's Tavern, with his friend Smith, and these two were either acting as a kind of rear guard, or were sent back to reconnoiter, but before going far they were discovered by the British, and wheeling attempted to rejoin their comrades. Smith's horse bolted through the woods, and he was killed. The enemy pursued McCorkle until he came up to the little band of Whigs, who had formed in Torrence's Lane. The little party fought the British troopers under Colonel Tarleton, until the smoke became so dense that they could not tell whether they were among friends or enemies. As the smoke cleared off a little, McCorkle discovered that he was among the redcoats, and putting his hands on a stake-and-ridered fence he leaped through just as three or four sabers struck the rail above him. They all retreated and made good their escape—none being killed except Smith, before named. Several British soldiers were killed and buried east of the Featherston House. McCorkle bore the title of Major, whether won during the war or after the war in the militia is not known. He survived all the dangers of the war, and returned to his peaceful home, and was respected and esteemed by his neighbors. His wife died after the war, and some time about 1794 or 1795 he was again married. His second wife was Elizabeth Brandon, daughter of Richard Brandon, and niece of Matthew Locke. This was the lady that furnished the breakfast to General Washington in 1791 as he passed through Rowan County. By his first marriage to Miss Work, Major McCorkle had two sons, Matthew and Alexander Work. These men lived on Mountain Creek, but never married. Alexander W. McCorkle was a man of wealth and of fine judgment and business talents. He was frequently called upon to advise his neighbors in business affairs, and to aid them in making deeds and conveyances.

By his second wife (Elizabeth Brandon), Major McCorkle had several children.

1. Wm. B. McCorkle, who was a merchant in Wadesboro for about forty years. This son married Mary, the daughter of William Marshall, of Anson County. This William Marshall and his father, James Marshall, and his son, Clement Marshall, were leading men of Anson County, and represented their fellow-citizens often in the Legislature. (See Wheeler's History of Anson.) The children of

William B. McCorkle were: James Marshall McCorkle, Esq., of Salisbury; Dr. John R. McCorkle, of Mooresville; William A. McCorkle, of Jefferson County, Tenn.; and his daughters, Sarah, Mary, Cornelia, and Caroline.

2. The second son of Francis McCorkle by his second wife was Francis McCorkle, who lived on Mountain Creek, and married Elizabeth Abernathy. Their children were: Matthew Locke McCorkle, Esq., of Newton; Thomas, David, and Fanny. David died during the war, in the Confederate army.

3. Another son was named Thomas, who moved to Georgia.

4. Another son of Maj. Francis McCorkle was John H., who moved to Tennessee. His son, Dr. Francis Marion McCorkle, collected the principal facts of this article.

5. A daughter named Elizabeth married Jephtha Sherrill, and was the mother of Henderson Sherrill, who lived in Hickory Nut Gap for a long time. He served in the Legislature.

6. A daughter named Agnes married John Kirk, and lived in Lincoln County.

Besides the old families already mentioned, who came to Rowan County at its first settlement, there were others who came after the War of the Revolution, and near the close of the century. Among the most distinguished of these was

The Henderson Family

This family was descended from Samuel Henderson, of Hanover County, Va., whose ancestors were from Scotland, where the name of Henderson was conspicuous among the leaders in both civil and ecclesiastical affairs for several generations. Samuel Henderson married a Miss Williams, whose ancestors came from Wales. A son of this couple was the distinguished Colonial Judge, Richard Henderson, who came with his father to Granville County, N. C., in 1745. Richard read law with his cousin, Judge Williams, for a year, and was then licensed with encomiums upon his talents and acquirements. He soon rose to the highest ranks of his profession. He was appointed a Judge of the Superior Court, and sustained his dignified position with fidelity and honor during the exciting and dangerous period of the Regulation up to the time when the troubles of the country closed the courts of justice. After an honorable and eventful career, he closed his life in Granville County in 1785.

By his marriage with Elizabeth Keeling, he left a number of children, several of whom became citizens of Salisbury. His daughter,

Fanny, as already mentioned, became the wife of Judge Macay. His son Leonard was distinguished for his knowledge of the law, and became Chief Justice of the Supreme Court of North Carolina. But the son that became the honor and pride of Rowan was the

Hon. Archibald Henderson

He was born in Granville County, August 7, 1768, and was educated in his native county, and studied law with his relative, Judge Williams. He came to Salisbury about 1790, and soon rose to eminence in his profession. Judge Murphy, in 1827, said that he was the most perfect model of a lawyer that our bar had produced. From an elaborate eulogy, written by Hon. A. D. Murphy, and found in Colonel Wheeler's Sketches, we glean the following characteristics. He was a man of great dignity of character, and held himself above the little passions and prejudices of men. He delighted in studying the constitution and jurisprudence of his country, and his knowledge assumed a scientific cast. He had great respect for authority and glorified in the fact that he lived under a government of laws. When he entered a Court of Justice he felt his responsibilty as an expounder of the law, and the guardian of the rights of his clients. To his associates at the bar he was courteous, and to the younger members of his profession he was especially kind and indulgent, rendering them aid when he could in the management of their cases. His speeches were generally brief, pointed, and conclusive, and in great causes his eloquence was irresistible. He did not badger witnesses, as third-rate lawyers are in the habit of doing, but was as polite and decorous to them as to the Court. As he advanced in life he became more accustomed to interpret the laws by the rules of common sense, and lost reverence for artificial rules, being desirous to strip off the veil of mystery from every branch of the law, and root out all the remains of a ridiculous pedantry that so often makes the rules of justice unintelligible to the common mind." It is related that, in 1818, when the Legislature created the Supreme Court of North Carolina, Archibald Henderson was spoken of as one of the Justices, along with John Lewis Taylor and John Hall. Having an extensive and lucrative practice at the bar, and taking special delight in the active duties of an advocate, he went before the Legislature, of which he was a member, and courteously declined the honor, at the same time assuring them that his brother, Leonard Henderson, was better qualified for the duties and responsibilities of that office than himself, and that it would be more con-

MR. A. H. BOYDEN

genial to his tastes. The Legislature thereupon accepted his declination, and elected his brother in his stead.

Archibald Henderson represented his district in Congress from 1799 to 1803, and the Town of Salisbury three times in the General Assembly. He was married to Sarah Alexander, daughter of William Alexander, of Cabarrus, and granddaughter of Col. Moses Alexander, of Colonial times. Her brother, the Hon. Nathaniel Alexander, of Mecklenburg, was elected Governor of North Carolina in 1805, and is represented as a worthy member of a family yet fruitful in talent and patriotism. From this marriage of Archibald Henderson with Sarah Alexander there sprang two children—the late Archibald Henderson, of Salisbury, and Jane Caroline, now Mrs. Judge Boyden.

Archibald Henderson studied at Yale College and at the University of Virginia. Returning home, he settled down near Salisbury. Possessed of an ample estate, and being of a quiet disposition, he did not feel the necessity or possess the disposition to enter into any of the active and stirring professions of life, but devoted his attention to reading and management of his estate. He served his fellow-citizens as a magistrate, and for a while as a member of the Governor's Council. A staunch and intelligent Democrat, his opinions had great weight with his political party.

He married Miss Mary Steele Ferrand, a granddaughter of Gen. John Steele, and lived at the seat of General Steele, near Salisbury. His children were: Lieut. Leonard Henderson, who was killed at the battle of Cold Harbor in Virginia; John Steele Henderson, Esq., now a member of the Salisbury bar; Richard Henderson, a lieutenant in the United States Navy, now in active service; and Mary, still at home. Archibald Henderson died within the present year (1880), and his remains were interred beside his father's grave in the Lutheran graveyard in Salisbury.

Jane C. Henderson, daughter of the Hon. Archibald Henderson, was first married to Dr. Lueco Mitchell, from the eastern part of the State. Doctor Mitchell was a surgeon on the *Caroline* during the siege of New Orleans, in the War of 1812—a fine physician and a courteous and public-spirited gentleman. He was an old-line Whig, and took a prominent part in the political affairs of his day. After the death of Dr. Mitchell, his widow became the wife of the

Hon. Nathaniel Boyden

then a successful lawyer in full practice. Mr. Boyden was a native of Massachusetts, born in Franklin Township, August 16, 1796, and graduated at Union College, New York, in 1821, and the next year removed to North Carolina and settled in Stokes County, and for a while engaged in teaching school. He studied law and was married to Ruth Martin, the daughter of Hugh Martin, Esq., of Stokes County. Our fellow-citizen, John A. Boyden, Esq., and the late Mrs. Ruth Nesbit, wife of Dr. A. M. Nesbit, and Nathaniel Boyden, Jr., are children by this marriage. Mr. Boyden represented Stokes County in 1838, and in 1840, in the Legislature. After the death of his first wife, he removed to Salisbury, in 1842. Here he rose rapidly in popular favor, and represented his adopted county several times in the Legislature, and his District in the Congress of the United States. He was an industrious, enterprising, and successful lawyer, and clients flocked to him wherever he practiced law. He possessed a wonderful memory, retaining in his mind not only the law bearing upon the case, but all the testimony, however voluminous, without noting it on paper. His eloquence was peculiar, always arresting attention, and his audience were always sure that he was saying something to the point. At the close of the late war he was again elected to the Congress of the United States, and in April, 1871, he was elected one of the Judges of the Supreme Court of North Carolina. After a long and active life, having filled many posts of honor, and exerting an influence over the minds and acts of his fellow-men, he fell asleep November 20, 1873. By his second marriage he left one son, Mr. Archibald Henderson Boyden, now doing business in Spartanburg, S. C.

A brother of the Hon. Archibald Henderson and Judge Leonard Henderson, named John Lawson Henderson, resided in Salisbury for a number of years. He was also a lawyer, and resided on the lot once owned by John Dunn, Esq., now by P. P. Meroney. His practice was not as extensive as his brother's, and for a number of years he was Clerk of the Supreme Court of North Carolina. He spent much of his time in Raleigh, where he died and was buried.

Another distinguished member of the Henderson family residing in Salisbury, was Dr. Pleasant Henderson. Dr. Henderson was the son of Major Pleasant Henderson, of Chapel Hill. Major Pleasant Henderson was the son of Samuel Henderson, of Granville County, and the brother of the Colonial Judge Richard Henderson, and the cousin of the Hon. Archibald Henderson, of Salisbury. The children of Col. Pleasant Henderson, were Dr. Alexander Henderson of Salisbury; Eliza, the wife of Hamilton C. Jones, Esq.; William, and Tippoo Sahib. The latter name, together with the fact that Edward Jones, of Chatham, called a son of his, Hyder Ali, recalls a state of feeling with which we are now unfamiliar. Tippoo Sahib and Hyder Ali were two brave and powerful East Indian chiefs, who resisted the English authority in Hindustan, and so great was the animosity of many of our people against England, in the days immediately preceding and during the war of 1812-14, that these two men gloried in calling their sons after these fierce heathen chieftains, simply because they were England's enemies. Dr. Pleasant Henderson was for a long time the most popular physician in Western North Carolina. Handsome, genial, polite, skillful in his profession, a jovial companion, and generous to a fault, the people loved him dearly. He lived for a long time unmarried, but at last married a lady as genial and accomplished as himself, Rebecca Wimbish, of of Virginia. He died about 1850, and his remains lie in the Oak Grove Cemetery, in Salisbury. No monument marks the spot where he sleeps, and perhaps nobody knows where his grave is. He left no children, and his widow married Judge Mills, of Texas.

Dr. Alexander Henderson was a widower when he came to Salisbury, leaving a couple of daughters with their mother's relatives, near Raleigh, to be educated. He afterwards married a Miss Wimbish, sister to his brother's wife. After practicing his profession here for a number of years, he removed to Alabama.

Eliza Henderson married as before stated.

Hamilton C. Jones, Esq.

Many of our citizens remember this genial gentleman, who passed from our midst only a few years ago. His country home was Como, three miles south of Salisbury, on the Concord Road. From Colonel Wheeler's Sketches we learn that Mr. Jones was a native of Virginia, born in Greenville, in 1798, and graduated from the University of North Carolina in 1818, in the same class with President James K. Polk, Bishop Greene, Robert Hall Morrison, D.D., and other distinguished men. He read law with Judge Gaston at Newbern, and soon entered public life as a member of the Legislature, serving a number of terms. For some years he was Solicitor and reporter for the Supreme Court of North Carolina. While engaged in public affairs he exercised a great influence, and his speeches were listened to with attention by all. In July, 1832, Mr. Jones started *The Carolina Watchman,* in the interest of the Whig Party, and continued to edit the same for a period of seven years. His paper rendered efficient service, and at one time he was invited to transfer it to Raleigh, but declined to do so. In 1839 he sold the paper to Pendleton & Bruner, and the last-named editor has continued, with two or three short suspensions, to edit and publish *The Watchman* ever since—a period of forty-one years.

As a humorist, Mr. Jones was not often excelled, possessing an inexhaustible fund of anecdotes, and the power to relate them by word or by pen in a manner peculiarly and irresistibly ludicrous. By his marriage with Eliza Henderson, he left five children—Col. Hamilton C. Jones, a lawyer and brave soldier in the late war, now practicing his profession in Charlotte; Capt. Martin Jones; Martha, married to Mr. Tate, of Morganton; Julia; and Alice, married to Mr. Broadnax, of Rockingham County. Mr. Jones died a few years ago (1887) and the home where he so long lived passed into other hands. A short time ago the residence was consumed by fire, and nothing but the trees and the outbuildings mark the spot once so well known among us.

Another family of Old Rowan was

The Pearson Family

Richmond Pearson, the founder of this family, was a native of Dinwiddie County, Va., and came to North Carolina at nineteen years of age, and settled in the Forks of the Yadkin, then Rowan, now Davie County. At the breaking out of the Revolutionary War, Richmond Pearson was a lieutenant in Captain Bryan's Company, and settled the political affinity of his Company by whipping his captain in a fist fight, as related in a previous chapter. Captain Pearson was present when Cornwallis crossed Cowan's Ford on the Catawba, in 1781, and witnessed the fall of the brave Gen. William Davidson. He was a merchant and a planter, and at an early day succeeded in navigating the Yadkin River. He is said to have established a combined land and water route, as follows: From his mills on the South Fork, by boat down the Yadkin to the Narrows; thence by land below the Grassy Islands; then again by the river to Sneedsboro, which was then a rival of Cheraw. Perhaps when the Yadkin is opened as far as Bean's Shoals, or Wilkesboro, for light draught steamers, according to the plan now undertaken, it will be found that communication may be practicable to the sea by water, and thus reduce the freights now exacted for heavy articles on the railroad.

Richmond Pearson was twice married. His first wife was Miss Hayden, and she bore him three sons and a daughter, namely: Gen. Jesse A. Pearson, Hon. Joseph Pearson, Richmond Pearson, and Elizabeth.

By his second marriage Richmond Pearson had six children—Sarah, Eliza, Charles, Richmond, Mumford, Giles N., and John Stokes Pearson. Most of these children occupied prominent and responsible positions in their day. Jesse A. Pearson represented Rowan County in the Legislature five times. In 1814, he was colonel of a regiment that marched against the Creek Indians under Gen. Joseph Graham. He was first married to a daughter of Gen. John Steele, and afterwards to a Mrs. Wilson, whose daughter by a former husband was the first wife of Archibald Carter, Esq., of Davie.

Hon. Joseph Pearson was a lawyer, represented the borough of Salisbury in the House of Commons, and was a member of Congress from 1809 to 1815.

Richmond Pearson, though never in public life, was an active, enterprising man. He is celebrated for having passed over the falls of the Yadkin in a boat, with two companions. Nobody else is known to have attempted this hazardous enterprise.

But the most distinguished of the family was Richmond M. Pearson. He was born in 1805, prepared for college by John Mushat, at Statesville, and graduated at the University of North Carolina in 1823. He studied law under Judge Henderson, and was licensed to practice in 1826. From 1829 to 1832 he represented Rowan County in the House of Commons. In 1836, he was elected Judge of the Superior Court, and in 1848 he was transferred to the Supreme Court of North Carolina. In 1866, he became Chief Justice, with William H. Battle and E. G. Reade as Associate Justices. In 1870, under the Shoffner Bill, Governor Holden ordered George W. Kirk, with a considerable body of troops, to march into Alamance, Orange, and Caswell Counties. Many arrests were made, and among others those of Josiah Turner and John Kerr, afterwards Judge Kerr. When applied to for writ of habeas corpus for some of these imprisoned citizens, Judge Pearson promptly granted it, but declined to attach Kirk for disobeying it, declaring that the "judiciary was exhausted." Though the decision bore severely upon the prisoners, it is difficult to see how a Judge could enforce the writ, with the Governor in command of the troops of the State, and hostile to the rights of the citizen. In January, 1878, Chief Justice Pearson died on his way to Raleigh to hold the January term of the Supreme Court. Moore in his History says of him, that "His strong native ability, profound learning, and long judicial career have made him immortal in legal circles. It is probable that he was the profoundest jurist ever born in Rowan County.

For a number of years, Judge Pearson resided at Richmond Hill, near Rockford, in Surry County. There he conducted a law school, and students from all parts of the State flocked to his school for instruction.

Giles N. Pearson, a younger brother of Chief Justice Pearson, was also a lawyer by profession, and resided in Mocksville. He married a daughter of Anderson Ellis, Sr., of Davidson County, a sister of Governor Ellis. He died in 1847, leaving a wife and five children, several of them still surviving.

Gov. John W. Ellis

was a native of Davidson County, then Rowan, and was born on the twenty-third of November, 1820. The family of the Ellises, for several generations, lived in the famed Jersey Settlement, on the eastern banks of the Yadkin, and several of them accumulated fortunes. Anderson Ellis, Sr., gave to his children the advantage of a good education, and most of them became prominent and useful citizens. John Willis was early sent to a classical school, taught by Robert Allison, Esq., at Beattie's Ford. After spending a season at Randolph-Macon College, in Virginia, he went to the University of North Carolina, where he was graduated in 1841. His legal studies were pursued under Judge Pearson. He opened a law office in Salisbury, and by his diligence and talents soon won a place in public confidence. He bore the reputation of a hard student, and the passer-by would see the light of Ellis' lamp until long after midnight. Two years after his licensure he was chosen to represent Rowan County in the House of Commons, and he continued in that place until 1848, when he was elected Judge of the Superior Court, when only twenty-eight years of age. He held this important post with credit to himself and honor to the State until 1858, when he was elected Governor of North Carolina over John Pool, of Pasquotank. The issue between Ellis and Pool was what was called the *ad valorem* system of taxation, a system defended with great ingenuity by Pool and the Whigs, but which failed to carry the Party into power. When, in 1861, President Lincoln called upon Governor Ellis for troops to serve against South Carolina, the Governor called for twenty thousand men—not to help to reduce South Carolina, but for whatever side the Convention of North Carolina should take. The Convention met and passed an ordinance of secession, May 20, 1861. Governor Ellis devoted all his energies to meet the demands of the hour. But his health failed him, and he resorted to the Red Sulphur Springs, in Virginia, to restore his strength. But the flame of life flickered only a moment longer, and he died on the seventh of July, 1861, only a few weeks after the battle of Big Bethel, when Gen. (then Col.) D. H. Hill met and defeated Gen. B. F. Butler. Thus it was that his brave spirit departed from earth just as the storm of war began to burst over the devoted South. His remains sleep in quiet, in Oak Grove Cemetery, in Salisbury, where a shaft of polished marble marks his resting-place.

Governor Ellis first married Mary, only daughter of Hon. Philo White, a scion of the Brandon stock, and her remains lie by the side of his, under another marble shaft.

He was married a second time to Miss Daves, a lady of Newbern, N. C., and left two daughters.

The Caldwell Family

In the eastern part of Iredell County, then Rowan, there lived a hundred years ago a substantial citizen by the name of Andrew Caldwell. He was of that study, Scotch-Irish stock that peopled so much of this region of the country. He married Ruth, the second daughter of the Hon. William Sharpe. He was a leading man in his county and often represented his fellow-citizens in the Legislature. He had a number of children, among them three sons widely known, viz.: Hon. David F. Caldwell, Hon. Joseph P. Caldwell, of Iredell, and Dr. Elam Caldwell, of Linctolnton. But we are more particularly interested in Hon. D. F. Caldwell, so long a citizen of Rowan County.

David Franklin Caldwell

was born in 1792, and pursued his literary course at Chapel Hill. He studied law with the Hon. Archibald Henderson, of Salisbury, and entered public life as a member of the House of Commons from Iredell, in 1816, where he served several years. After a time he removed to Salisbury, and in 1829, 1830, and 1831 represented Rowan in the Senate of North Carolina. He was Speaker of the Senate in 1829. After this he pursued his profession as a lawyer with eminent success for a number of years. In 1844 he was promoted to the position of Judge of the Superior Courts of North Carolina.

Judge Caldwell was a stern, but impartial judge, and presided with great dignity, keeping the witnesses, jurors, and lawyers in good order. Many anecdotes are told of his eccentricities, all leaning to the side of simplicity, kindness, order, and decency. A lawyer, then quite young, was sick during the Court in Washington, and was visited very kindly by Judge Caldwell. At a Court the next week, the young lawyer, still quite feeble, managed to attend, and when a case was called in which he was interested, rose to speak. "Sit down, Sir," said the Judge, in his sternest tones. The lawyer sat down, as if thunderstruck. In a moment, however, he rose again to speak, and was told to sit down, in still more terrible tones. Again he sat down, not knowing what it all meant. Then the Judge said, "You are not able to stand up, and I will hear you from your seat." The lawyer was amazed at the unexpected turn of affairs, and knowing that he would not be allowed to stand, addressed the Judge from his seat. Upon a certain occasion, it is related, a young lawyer took his seat inside the bar dressed in peculiarly dandyish style. The Judge surveyed him from head to foot, and muttered to himself, "Hair parted in the middle," "Mustache," "Ruffled shirt," "Striped vest," "Straps," "Pumps." Then in thundering tones, "Get out of the bar!" Some older lawyer arose and informed the Judge that the young man was a lawyer, and had a right to a seat in the bar. "I beg pardon," said the Judge, "but I did not think that any lawyer had so little sense as to dress in that way."

Upon another occasion, the Judge asked a lawyer for a chew of tobacco. The lawyer handed him a piece of plug, bitten all around. The Judge turned it around and around in his hand, and remarked aloud, "Why don't you cut off your tobacco, like a gentleman, and not gnaw it off in that indecent way?"

Judge Caldwell had a high respect for honest labor. One day while passing the premises of a minister, he saw him with his coat off, spading his garden. Lifting his hat in the old-time fashion of courtesy, he said: "Saint Paul used to labor with his own hands, and I am glad to see one minister who is not ashamed to follow his example."

His second wife lies buried under the lecture-room of the Presbyterian Church in Salisbury. For many years Judge Caldwell was in the habit of lifting his hat reverently every time he passed the corner.

In 1858, being then sixty-eight years of age, he felt it his duty to resign his seat on the judicial bench, unwilling to continue until he would become unfit for his duties. He died, in 1867, at the age of seventy-seven, and his remains, unmarked by a monument, are lying beside the resting-place of his first wife, near the monument of the Hon. Archibald Henderson.

Judge Caldwell was twice married. He first married Fanny, the daughter of William Lee Alexander, Esq., and niece of Hon. Archibald Henderson. Their children were, William Lee, Archibald Henderson, Elizabeth Ruth, who married Col. Charles Fisher; Richard Alexander Caldwell, Esq., Dr. Julius Andrew Caldwell, and Fanny McCoy, married to Peter Hairston, Esq. After the death of his first wife, he married Mrs. Rebecca M. Troy, née Nesbit, the widow of the late Matthew Troy, Esq., and the half-sister of the late Maxwell Chambers, Esq. Her remains are interred beneath the Presbyterian lecture-room, near to Mr. Chambers' grave. She was an earnest Christian woman, of a meek and quiet spirit. During her widowhood, she and her half-brother, Maxwell Chambers, lived east of town, where Capt. John Beard now lives. Afterwards, they purchased and lived in the residence where Mrs. Dr. Joseph W. Hall now lives. At the same time, Mrs. Troy, the mother of Matthew Troy, and her daughter, Catherine Troy, lived in the house where R. J. Holmes now resides, on Innes Street.

The Chambers and Troy Families

We have already drifted into some account of one or two members of these families, but a fuller account may be interesting. During the Revolutionary War, Maxwell Chambers, the elder, resided in Salisbury. He lived on the place where Mr. S. H. Wiley's residence now stands. Lord Cornwallis made his headquarters in this house, in 1781. Maxwell Chambers was the treasurer of the Committee of Safety for Rowan, in 1775-76, and was a true patriot, though he once fell under the censure of the Committee for raising the price of powder, and it was ordered that he be advertised as an enemy of his country. After the war he lived at Spring Hill, about two miles east of Salisbury, where he raised a large family. He was married to the daughter of George Magoune, who had married Hester Long, the widow of John Long, and mother of Alexander Long, Esq. Maxwell Chambers had nine sons, named William, Maxwell—who was graduated at Chapel Hill in 1809, Henry, Joseph, Samuel, Edward, Thomas, Otho, and John. Henry became a lawyer, and Maxwell a physician; the others were farmers. They all died early in life, some of them unmarried, and it is not known that any of their descendants are now living in this county. The late William Chambers was a son of Edward Chambers, but left no children. John Chambers married Panthea Troy, sister of Matthew Troy, Esq., and of the late Mrs. Maxwell Chambers.

Maxwell Chambers

the younger, was a distant relative of the family already mentioned, and was the son of Joseph and Mary Chambers, of Salisbury. Beneath the lecture-room of the Presbyterian Church in Salisbury, there are ten graves, nine of them covered with marble slabs, and one marked by a headstone. As there is historical matter inscribed on those slabs, and as the general public never see these inscriptions, I will give the epitaphs in substance. Commencing next to the wall, we find the first monument and the oldest, with this inscription:

1. William Nesbit, died November 22, 1799, aged sixty-four years.

2. Adelaide Fulton, daughter of John and Mary Fulton, died at two weeks of age.

3. Mary Fulton, died January 5, 1806, aged forty-five years.

(a) She was first married to Joseph Chambers, by whom she had one son, Maxwell Chambers.

(b) She was next married to William Nesbit, and had two children, David M. and Rebecca M. Nesbit.

(c) She was again married, to John Fulton, and had one child, Adelaide Fulton.

4. David M. Nesbit, son of William and Mary Nesbit, died October 19, 1811, aged twenty-five years.

5. Henry M. Troy, son of Matthew and Rebecca M. Troy, died July 8, 1824, aged eleven years, eleven months, and fifteen days.

6. Laura Troy, daughter of Matthew and Rebecca M. Troy, died November 16, 1828, aged eighteen years, one month, one day.

7. Rebecca M. Caldwell, second wife of Hon. D. F. Caldwell, died November 28, 1855, in the sixty-fifth year of her age.

8. Panthea Jane Daviess, daughter of Robert and Anne Daviess, of Mercer County, Ky., died May 20, 1835, aged sixteen years.

9. Catherine B. Chambers, consort of Maxwell Chambers, and daughter of Matthew and Jane Troy, died November 27, 1852, aged sixty-seven years, seven months, and three days.

10. Maxwell Chambers, died February 7, 1855, aged seventy-five years, one month, and fourteen days.

From the above figures we gather that Maxwell Chambers was the son of Joseph and Mary Chambers, and was born on the twenty-third of January, 1780. Tradition states that he was born in the house now the residence of Thomas J. Meroney, on Main Street. His early education was probably secured in Salisbury, and he entered into business here with his uncle, a Mr. Campbell, from which we infer that his mother's maiden name was Campbell. After conducting business here for awhile, Mr. Campbell and Mr. Chambers went to Charleston and set up in mercantile business there. Here Mr. Chambers laid the foundation of his fortune, and after awhile he returned to Salisbury and lived with his widowed half-sister, Mrs. Rebecca M. Troy. After a time he married Miss Catherine B. Troy, the daughter of Matthew Troy the elder, and sister of Matthew Troy the younger. It is said that an attachment had long existed between this couple, but Mr. Chambers had thought himself too poor to marry in his younger days. But when he had amassed a considerable fortune, of perhaps one or two hundred thousand dollars, and she being the owner of about thirty thousand dollars, they considered themselves in proper circumstances to marry, though both were somewhat advanced in life. They settled at the Nesbit place, on Innes Street, now the home of R. J. Holmes, and here they ended their days. Mr. Chambers never entered into regular business again, but became a general trader, and attended to the management of his large estate. He was eminently successful in accumulating property, and at his death had amassed a fortune of nearly a half-million dollars. He made arrangements for the removal and liberation of all his slaves at his death, and these plans were faithfully carried out by his executors, and between thirty and forty slaves were sent to the Northwest, and started in life in their new home. Besides legacies to many of his kindred and friends, and to the church of his choice, he left a residuary legacy to Davidson College, which would have amounted to two hundred and fifty thousand dollars if the College had obtained all he intended for it. But owing to the limitations of its Charter, the College could not receive the whole amount, and a considerable sum went to his heirs that were next of kin.

The inscription on the marble slab that covers his remains is probably as fair a delineation of character as was ever put upon a monument, and it is here given:

"In his business he possessed the clearest foresight and the profoundest judgment.

"In all his transactions he was exact and just.

"In social life, dignified, but confiding, tender, and kind.

"In his plans, wise, prudent, and successful.

"In his bestowments his hand was not only liberal but often munificent.

"In the close of his life he set his house in order, willed his soul to God, and the greater part of his estate to the cause of education, through the church of his choice."

Mr. Chambers was not promiscuously liberal, but only to the objects he considered worthy, and in his own way. Upon a certain occasion a poor man had his house burned down, and the next day some friend took around a subscription paper for his benefit. The paper was somewhat ostentatiously presented to Mr. Chambers, but he utterly refused to subscribe. He was of course severely criticized for his illiberality; but while the critics were handing his penuriousness around, Mr. Chambers quietly ordered one of his servants to get ready a cart, and he and his good wife filled it with flour, meal, lard, bacon, bed-clothing, and other things to the value of nearly fifty dollars, perhaps equal in value to the gifts of all the others combined, and the poor man found himself richer than he had been before the fire. Mr. Chambers never mixed business and charity together. He would give and take the last cent due in a trade, and when he chose to give, he gave liberally. His good wife, familiarly known as "Aunt Kitty," was the soul of kindness. She was an earnest and devout Christian, and full of faith and good works. To her pastor, living on a salary rather small, and with a large family, and many visitors, she made weekly, and sometimes daily donations, amounting in the year to some hundreds of dollars. For some years before her death she was blind, but still patient, submissive, and charitable. Her portrait, with that of her husband, hangs in the parlor of the manse in Salisbury, as perpetual memorials of their benefactions.

Rowan County has been the home of a number of other distinguished men, of whom but little mention can be made without swelling these Memoirs beyond the limits assigned. Among these, brief mention must be made of

Hon. John Giles

He was a native of Salisbury, and a descendant, by his mother's side, of the early lawyer, John Dunn, Esq. He was graduated from the University of North Carolina in 1808. He studied law, and settled in his native town, where he practiced his profession for more than thirty years. The name of Jack Giles, as he was familiarly called, was known in the whole western part of the State. He was the clerk of the Rowan Superior Court for many years; and was elected to Congress from his district in 1829, but was compelled to decline because of ill health. He never married, but maintained

COL. CHAS. F. FISHER

his mother and his sisters handsomely while he lived. One of his sisters was the second wife of John Fulton, after whom one of the streets of Salisbury is named, and also the Salisbury lodge of Freemasons. But the last race of the Gileses and Fultons has been laid in the grave.

Hon. William C. Love

represented the Salisbury District in Congress in 1815. He was a Virginian by birth, and reared at the University of that State. He studied law and removed to Salisbury, where he first married Elizabeth, a daughter of the Hon. Spruce Macay, by whom he had one child, the late Robert E. Love, Esq. His second wife was Sally Yarboro, daughter of Capt. Edward Yarboro, and granddaughter of Alexander Long, Esq., of Yadkin Ferry, by whom he had two children, William and Julius Love. William C. Love and his second wife both lie buried in the private burying-ground of the Yarboro family in Salisbury, just in the rear of Meroney's Hall, on the spot where the hotel for colored people now stands.

The Fisher Family

The Hon. Charles Fisher was a native of Rowan County, and was born October 20, 1779. His father came to North Carolina before the Revolution, and was an officer of militia during the war. The subject of this notice was educated by Rev. Dr. John Robinson, of Poplar Tent, and by the Rev. Dr. McPheeters, of Raleigh. He studied law and obtained license to practice, but soon abandoned the bar for the more stirring scenes of political life. He enjoyed the confidence of the people of Rowan County as fully as any man who ever lived in the county, and they delighted to honor him with every office for which he ever asked their suffrages. In 1819 he represented Rowan in the State Senate, and in the same year was elected from the Rowan District for Congress. After this term he again served Rowan County in the State Legislature, and was a member of the Convention of 1835, called to amend the State Constitution. In 1839 he was again elected to Congress, over Dr. Pleasant Henderson, though the latter was a most popular man, and the champion of a Party supposed to be in the majority. Mr. Fisher was one of the most active and energetic men in the State, and an unyielding advocate of State rights against Federal encroachments and usurpations.

Near the close of life he became a member of the Evangelical Lutheran Church, and strove to discharge his duty to his Creator, as he had endeavored to do his duty to his country.

After a long and honored and useful life, he died far away from home, in Hillsboro, Miss., on the seventh of May, 1849. No monument marks his grave. His ashes should rest here, in one of the cemeteries among the honored dead of Rowan. Mr. Fisher married Christiana, daughter of Lewis Beard, Esq., of Salisbury, by whom he had several children. One son died in infancy. His daughter Mary married a Mr. Hill, and removing to Georgia died there a few years ago. Christine, another daughter, still resides in Salisbury. His other son

Col. Charles Frederick Fisher

was the noble son of a noble sire. He was born in Salisbury in 1816. His preparatory education was conducted in the classical schools of Salisbury, and from them he was transferred to Yale College. He never studied any of the professions, but devoted his attention to agriculture and mining, and for several years was associated with Dr. Austin in the publication of *The Western Carolinian.* In 1854-55, he was a member of the State Legislature from Rowan County. He succeeded the Hon. John M. Morehead as president of the North Carolina Railroad, in 1855, and continued to preside over the interests of that great State enterprise, with eminent skill and ability, until 1861.

When the alarm of war rang throughout the land in 1861, Mr. Fisher at once proceeded to raise and equip a regiment at the head of which he took the field in the early part of July. This regiment, the Sixth North Carolina, had been ordered to Winchester, Va., where it was in the command of Gen. Joseph E. Johnston when the army of the Shenandoah was ordered to Manassas to reinforce General Beauregard. Owing to a wreck on the line of railway, there was a delay in the transportation of the troops which threatened disaster, and gave Colonel Fisher an opportunity to render an important service by repairing the track with the aid of the trained railroad men who composed a large part of his command. As a reward for his efforts, the Sixth Regiment was allowed to embark on the next train that left for Manassas, and reached there in time to be ordered into battle by General Beauregard at the most critical period of the action, when their help was greatly needed, shortly after two o'clock in the afternoon. Colonel Fisher then led his regiment almost immediately to the brilliant charge on Rickett's Battery, which destroyed and captured that formidable artillery, and proved the turning point of the battle. From that minute, as the official reports clearly prove, the Federal army went down to defeat, but Colonel Fisher himself died in the hour of his triumph,

Mrs. Frances Christine Fisher Tiernan
(christian reid)

falling gloriously in the charge in which he was leading his men. In an address on this subject, delivered in Charlotte, N. C., on October 12, 1901, Hon. John S. Henderson says: "The ground where the Sixth Regiment fought and destroyed McDowell's most formidable batteries marked the extreme point of the Federal advance towards Manassas. This is the truth of history, and Colonel Fisher fell in the forefront, at the time when the tide of battle had been first turned back, and victory had been assured to the Confederate army by the heroic and successful fighting of himself and the Sixth Regiment."

It was a gloomy day in Salisbury when the remains of her chivalrous son were brought home, and sorrowfully laid in their resting-place in the Salisbury cemetery (Lutheran graveyard).

Colonel Fisher married Elizabeth Ruth Caldwell, oldest daughter of Hon. David F. Caldwell, in July, 1845, by whom he had several children, who were left in the orphanage to the care of his sister, Miss Christine Fisher. The names of these children are Frances, Annie, and Frederick. Miss Frances Fisher, under the *nom de plume* of Christian Reid, has achieved an enviable reputation as a writer of elegant fiction. Her volume, entitled the "Land of the Sky," possesses the merit of being a faithful delineation of the choicest scenery in Western North Carolina, elegantly and attractively written. This charming book has been the means of attracting many visitors to our beautiful mountains, and has rendered it quite fashionable for tourists to visit this region, where the loftiest mountains east of the Mississippi stand grouped together in stately grandeur.

The Craig Family

The traditions of this family relate that their ancestors came direct from Scotland to Rowan County, without stopping, as most of the families did, in the Northern States. They were adherents of "Prince Charles" in his efforts to regain the throne of his fathers, and after the fatal battle of Culloden, April 16, 1746, they deemed it expedient to seek safety in America.

The name "Craig," in the Scottish dialect, signifies a sharp, high rock or crag, and was probably given to the family, or assumed by them, because their hall or castle was situated upon some high rock, thus securing safety to life and property in the days of violence and lawlessness. In the sixteenth century John Craig was one of the Scottish Reformers and a coadjutor of John Knox. It was John Craig that proclaimed the banns of marriage between Queen Mary and James Bothwell, but he openly denounced their union. Sir

Thomas Craig, of Aberdeenshire, was a distinguished lawyer and Judge, who lived from 1538 to 1608, and through his oldest son, Sir Lewis Craig, he left descendants, among whom are several well-known names in the list of Scottish lawyers. It is impossible at this day to connect the Rowan family with that of the Reformer or Jurist, but these historical personages living three hundred years ago in Scotland show that the name comes down from olden times. The Rowan family seem to have been adherents of the Church of England, as is evinced both by family tradition and from existence of an old Book of Common Prayer, Cambridge edition of 1766, still in the possession of the family, with family records on its flyleaves.

About one and a half miles from the Trading Ford, near the road leading to Salisbury, is a place still known as "Craige's Old Field," where the ruins of old chimneys are still to be seen. Here Archibald Craige and Mary, his wife, settled about 1750. The title deeds taken out before the establishment of Rowan County are not registered here, but were probably registered at old Anson courthouse, at Mount Pleasant. But as early as 1756 we find deeds from James Carter and Hugh Foster, Township Trustees, to Archibald Craige, for lots in Salisbury. In 1758 there is a deed from Carter & Foster to Mary Craige. In the files of inventories in the Clerk's office we learn that Archibald Craige died May 20, 1758, and that Mary Craige administered on his estate. In 1764 there is the first mention of James Craige as the purchaser of some lots in Salisbury, and in 1779 there is the record of a grant from the State to James and David Craige for five hundred acres of land on the south side of the Yadkin River. Summing up their grants and purchases we find that James and David Craige were the owners, jointly and severally, of nearly two thousand acres of land on the main Yadkin, the south fork of the Yadkin, and Abbott's Creek. Putting these traditions and records together, we conclude that Archibald and Mary Craige were the founders of the Rowan family; that when Archibald Craige died, in 1758, his sons being too young, his widow became administratrix of the estate, and that the two sons—James, the elder, and David, the younger—were grown men before the Revolutionary War. James was the purchaser of land in 1764, and must have been twenty-one years old at that time. In a bundle of settlement papers near the close of the Revolution we find the name of James Craige as Sheriff of Rowan County. We do not find that he ever married here. Perhaps he removed to some other part of the country.

From the record in the old Prayer Book we learn that David Craige was married to Polly Foster, July 23, 1776, nineteen days

Burton Craige

after the Declaration of Independence. Hugh Foster, one of the township trustees, writes himself as a farmer, and perhaps Mrs. David Craige was his daughter. This David Craige is the one mentioned in Colonel Wheeler's Sketches (Vol. 1, page 80), as a lieutenant in Capt. William Temple Cole's Company in 1776. Colonel Wheeler further states that David Craige "was distinguished for his bravery and patriotic daring" in those stirring times. But the history of those daring deeds has been allowed to sink into oblivion, with those of his brave companions in the great struggle for independence. He died in November, 1784.

The children of David and Polly Craige, as recorded in the old Prayer Book, were: James Craige, born February 2, 1778; David Craige, born January 27, 1780; Lucy and Mary, born April, 1782; and Thomas Craige, born August 5, 1784.

James Craige settled on the old Mocksville Road, six miles from Salisbury, where some of his descendants are still residing.

Thomas Craige lived near Dr. Chunn's place, not far from the old Mocksville Road, and married Susan Jones, the sister of Judge Rowland Jones, late of Louisiana. He died in 1845, and left two children—Thomas, who died in Shreveport; and Mary, who is still living and teaching in St. Louis, Mo.

David Craige, Jr., married his cousin, Mary Foster, and lived on the south fork of the Yadkin, at the place now the residence of James Hudson. His children were: Robert Newton, Samuel, John, and Burton Craige. Robert Newton Craige lived at the home of his father, on South River, and died just before the late war, leaving two daughters. Samuel left two children—Sally, who married Robert Chunn and moved to Arkansas; and Clitus, who was killed at the battle of Cedar Run in Virginia. John Craige left two sons and a daughter, the latter of whom, Miss Bettie Craige, lived with her uncle, Hon. Burton Craige, in Salisbury, for a number of years.

Hon. Burton Craige

the youngest son of David Craige, Jr., was born in Rowan County, March 13, 1811, at the family residence on the south fork of the Yadkin, a few miles above the point, or junction of the two rivers. His early days were spent on the farm and in attending the schools which the neighborhood afforded. About 1823-25, he attended a classical school taught in Salisbury by the Rev. Jonathan Otis Freeman. From this school he went to the University of North Carolina, where he was graduated in the Class of 1829. Returning to Rowan, he for three years edited *The Western Carolinian,* and studied law under David F. Caldwell, Esq., and was licensed in 1832. The same year of his licensure he was elected to the Legislature from the Borough of Salisbury. The Borough embraced nearly the same territory comprised in the present Salisbury Township, and was a relic of the old Colonial times when Newbern, Edenton, Wilmington, Bath, Halifax, and Salisbury were each entitled to a representative in the Assembly. The convention which met in Raleigh, June 4, 1835, to amend the constitution of North Carolina, abolished Borough representation, and the counties thenceforth sent representatives according to population. In the old Borough system the free negroes were allowed, by sufferance, without specific legal right, to vote at elections, but under the revised constitution this was forbidden. Mr. Craige was wont to describe with much zest how the different political Parties under the old system were in the habit of herding and penning the free negroes, and low white voters also, in the "Round Bottom" and elsewhere, guarding, feeding, and treating them for several days before elections, and then marching them into town and "voting" them en masse. Sometimes the opposite Party would make a raid upon one of these pens, at the last moment, and carry off their voters in triumph. These abuses, among other things, led to the abolition of the Borough system.

In 1834, Mr. Craige was elected to the Assembly by the County of Rowan. In 1836 he was united in marriage to Miss Elizabeth P. Erwin, daughter of Col. James Erwin, of Burke County, and great granddaughter of Gen. Matthew Locke, of Rowan. The same year Mr. Craige, being in a feeble state of health, visited Europe, and being much benefited returned home and devoted himself to the practice of his profession. During these years he gathered around him a host of friends, and his practice in the Courts of Rowan was extensive. He possessed those qualities that endeared him to the people—plainness of speech, simplicity of manners, and familiarity in intercourse, without the semblance of condescension. He remembered the names and the faces of people, and the humblest man whom Mr. Craige had ever known would approach him with perfect assurance of recognition and cordial greeting. I do not know that Mr. Craige was peculiarly successful as a farmer himself, but he could talk of farming and of all the interests of the farmer with far more intelligence, fluency, and accuracy than the farmer could himself. He was as perfectly at ease in the homes of the humblest as he was polite and courteous in the parlors of the rich and fashionable. He was thus eminently qualified for a successful politician, and when in 1853 he received the nomination for Congress, he was

elected, as he was also in 1855-57-59; and he was a member of Congress when the late war began. When the convention of North Carolina was called, in 1861, to determine the course North Carolina should pursue, Mr. Craige was sent there from Rowan County, and on the twentieth of May he offered the Ordinance of Secession, which was adopted, and which placed the State of North Carolina along with her sister States of the South in the great struggle against the Federal Government. By this convention he was chosen as a member of the Confederate Congress, along with W. N. H. Smith, Thomas Ruffin, T. D. McDowell, A. W. Venable, J. M. Morehead, R. C. Puryear, and A. T. Davidson. After this he retired to private life, though watching with eager interest the mighty struggle in which his country was embarked. And when at last the flag which bore the blazonry of the "Stars and Bars" was furled, he declined to take any further part in national affairs. He would not apply for the removal of his "disabilities." He still practised his profession, studied the history and recounted the deeds of former days, and sought repose from the strife of public affairs in the bosom of his family. He died in Concord, in the house of his son-in-law, Mr. A. B. Young, where he had gone to attend the Cabarrus Court, December 30, 1875. His remains were laid to rest in Oak Grove Cemetery in Salisbury.

In stature Mr. Craige was herculean—six feet six inches in height, and of corresponding proportions. Fearless and positive in the assertion of his convictions, and with a mien and physical form that might have awakened the envy and excited the fear of the bravest knight of the days of chivalry, he instinctively commanded the respect of his associates, while at the same time he charmed them with his frank, affable, and jovial disposition.

Mr. Craige left three sons and two daughters who, with their mother, still survive.

James, the eldest, was a cadet at West Point, at the opening of the war, but he returned in haste to his home, entered the Confederate army, and rose to the rank of Major in the infantry.

Kerr, the second son, was in the University of North Carolina when the war began, but entered the calvary service in Gen. Rufus Barringer's brigade. He served through the war, and is now a lawyer in Salisbury.

Frank, the youngest, also entered the Army and served through the war. He now resides in Tennessee.

His elder daughter is the wife of Mr. Alfred B. Young, of Concord, and his younger, the wife of Mr. John P. Allison, of Concord.

The Stokes Family

The Hon. John Stokes lived in Rowan County (now Davie) near Richmond Hill, the residence of Richmond Pearson. He was a colonel in the Revolutionary army, and lost his right hand in the affair of Buford's defeat in the Waxhaws. He had a silver cup or "fist" made, which he wore, and in his speeches at the Bar he would sometimes bring down this silver fist with a ringing sound.

He married Elizabeth, the daughter of Richmond Pearson, and half-sister of the late Chief Justice Pearson. He had a son named Richmond Pearson Stokes, who was also a lawyer. Colonel Stokes was at one time United States District Judge. He died in 1801.

Gov. Montford Stokes

was for a long period a resident of Rowan County. He was born about 1760, and was in the Revolutionary army, and was taken prisoner near Norfolk in 1776, and confined for several months in a prison ship. For a number of years he was Clerk of Rowan Superior Court, and Clerk of the State Senate. He was elected by the General Assembly to the United States Senate, but declined to serve. In 1816 he was again elected Senator of the United States, and served until 1823. In 1831 he was appointed by General Jackson, Indian Agent in Arkansas. He removed to that State, and died there in 1842.

The historian of North Carolina, Colonel Moore, says of him, that "Few men were so popular as he, and his wit and humor were unceasing in their flow." Governor Stokes removed from Salisbury about 1812, and settled in Wilkesboro. He was first married to Mary, the daughter of Col. Henry Irwin, who fell at the battle of Germantown. By her he had one daughter, named Adelaide, who became the wife of Henry Chambers, of Rowan. Also a son named Montford S. Stokes, who was a Major of the North Carolina Regiment in the War with Mexico. At the opening of the late War between the States, Montford S. Stokes was Colonel of the First North Carolina State Troops. Colonel Stokes was killed at Ellyson's Mill, near Richmond, June 26, 1862.

His second wife was Rachel Montgomery, the daughter of Hugh Montgomery, of Salisbury. By her he had several children—Hugh M. Stokes, David Stokes, Thomas Jefferson Stokes, and several daughters.

CHAPTER XXIV

THE WAR OF 1812-14

In tracing the history of Rowan County, it will not be expected that we shall enter into a detail of the great public affairs of the United States. And yet we must glance at them in order to account for events that took place in this county. The Barbary States, on the north coast of Africa, for a while obstructed the commerce of the United States in the Mediterranean Sea, and this led to a war with Tripoli, in 1803, in which Commodore Preble, Lieut. Stephen Decatur, and Commodore Barron took a conspicuous part, and brought the Bashaw to make a treaty of peace, which was concluded in 1805. But this matter was scarcely settled when a greater difficulty arose. England and France were then at war, and the United States became involved in regard to her commerce. By "Orders in Council," the English government declared all vessels conveying produce from the United States to Europe legal prizes. Again, in 1806, England declared several European ports in a state of blockade. Napoleon, by his "Berlin Decree" and "Milan Decree," forbade the introduction of English goods into any part of Europe, and confiscated the cargoes of all such vessels as should submit to be searched by the English. But England was in need of sailors, and as many of them were supposed to be employed on American ships she insisted upon searching the ships of the United States. In vain did America protest. The "Queen of the Seas" held our power in contempt, and continued to search all American vessels by force. As the only course left, the Congress of the United States passed the "Embargo Act," by which all United States trading vessels were prohibited from leaving their ports. This Act operated not only to the disadvantage of England, but was disastrous to the shipping interests of this country. All foreign commerce was destroyed, and the people were left to their own resources. Coffee and tea, silks, broadcloths, ribbons, and all such commodities, became as rare as they were in the late Confederate States. This caused distress and murmuring, especially in New England, where most of the shipping was owned. In the meantime, President Jefferson went out of office, and James Madison was inaugurated in 1809. Soon after Madison's inauguration the British Minister at Washington gave assurance that England's "Orders in Council" would be revoked. Upon this Mr. Madison issued a Proclamation—April 19, 1809—that the non-intercourse Act would be suspended after the tenth of the following June. This Proclamation produced great joy throughout the whole country, and the wave of gladness rolled over the land and reached the quiet town of Salisbury. The citizens of Rowan had a general parade in Salisbury, followed by an illumination at night. Capt. John Beard had an immense framework, something like old-time warping bars, erected in front of his house, with candles blazing on every part of the structure. At the foot of it was a table filled with decanters and bottles containing choice liquors, and all his friends were invited to drink to the general joy. Mr. Edward Chambers, son of the elder Maxwell Chambers, made a speech to the ladies, in which he assured them that now the embargo was raised they would have less work to do, inasmuch as they could purchase goods from Europe. But all this joy was premature. The good news had hardly reached the most distant parts of the country before President Madison was assured that the British Minister had exceeded his instructions, and that the "Orders in Council" would not be revoked. And so the President at once issued another Proclamation countermanding the first. And so matters went on, English ships searching American vessels wherever found, with now and then a naval battle.

In the meantime two remarkable natural phenomena occurred that filled the minds of many of our people with foreboding fears. The first of these was the appearance of the celebrated comet of 1811. This comet was the most remarkable in appearance of all that have been seen in the present century. While its nucleus was only four hundred and twenty-eight miles in diameter, it had a tail one hundred and thirty-two millions of miles in length, and had it been coiled around the earth like a serpent, it would have wrapped around it more than five thousand times. This comet has a period of thirty-three hundred and eighty-three years, and had not visited our heavens since B.C. 1572. Then it may have heralded the birth of Moses, and Amram and Jochebed may have gazed at it in wonder, and the cruel Pharoah may have beheld it with terror, from the banks of the Nile. Be this as it may, many of the people of Rowan County were very much frightened at its terrible appearance, and regarded it as the harbinger of evil. It appeared in June, 1811, and continued to blaze in the western sky until November. It is related that late one afternoon in November, a terrible explosion was heard, like a peal of thunder. But the sky was clear and serene. After this the comet was seen no more. Of course there was no connection between the explosion and the disappearance of the comet, but the common people naturally connected them together.

On the eleventh of December another remarkable event occurred. At two o'clock in the morning an earthquake occurred, that shook the houses, toppled brick from the chimneys, and caused hanging furniture to sway backward and forward like a pendulum, and the water would splash out of vessels that stood on the floor. The period of agitation lasted from November until April, 1812. Sometimes there would be two or three shocks in a day, and then only one every two or three weeks. Some of the people would feel as if seasick, and all of them had awful apprehension of some dreadful catastrophe impending.

Meanwhile public affairs were drifting towards a declaration of war. The ultimatum of the British government was referred in Congress to the Committee of Foreign Relations, of which John C. Calhoun was chairman. The Committee reported in favor of a declaration of war. The bill to this end was adopted by Congress, and received the signature of President Madison in June, 1812. The plan of the war, on the part of the United States, was to seize the British Provinces in Canada. This was looked upon as an easy method of bringing England to terms, while little was expected from the infant navy. As it turned out, the navy of the United States made a brilliant record of heroism, while disaster after disaster characterized the land forces.

But to return to Rowan County, we learn that the military spirit pervaded the whole community in 1812 and 1813. Great volunteer meetings were held, and companies and regiments paraded in the streets of Salisbury. Patriotic speeches were made, and volunteers stepped into the ranks of the recruiting officers. Barracks were erected on the eastern side of Crane Creek, on the plantation owned by the late Samuel Reeves, and the barracks were under the command of Col. James Welborn, of Wilkes County. Most of the companies were sheltered in cabins erected for the purpose, but it is remembered that Captain Cloud's Company, from Stokes County, preferred to live in tents. Capt. Jerry Cloud was the father of the Hon. J. M. Cloud, and died near Norfolk, in the encampment with his Company, from the ravages of disease superinduced by measles.

Besides Colonel Welborn, in command, the officers were Captain Ward, Lieutenant Dearing, and Paymaster Glenn. I suppose the proper title for the barracks would a "Camp of Instruction." Recruits of volunteers and enlisted men came here from all Western North Carolina, from South Carolina, and from Georgia. Here they were drilled, embodied, and sent off to the army on the borders of Canada. Some of them went to Sackett's Harbor. They marched to Portsmouth, in Virginia, and went thence in transports as near to Lake Champlain as they could go by water. The camp remained in active operation until late in 1813. When news of a victory by Commodore Perry, or Capt. Isaac Hull, or the defense of Fort Meigs by the gallant Harrison, or any other encouraging news came, the event was duly celebrated at the barracks, or by a feast or dance in some of the parlors of the town. There may have been thanksgiving services in some of the churches in the country, but Salisbury had no church and no minister in those days.

While the war was raging on the northern frontier, the Creek Indians in Georgia and Alabama took up arms against the white settlers. The celebrated Tecumseh made a visit to the Southern Indians in the spring of 1812, and excited them to resistance. The white inhabitants on the Alabama River, in August, 1813, having taken refuge in Fort Mimms, in the Tensaw Settlement, were attacked by the Indians, under their chief, Billy Weatherford, and out of the three hundred men, women, and children there assembled, only seventeen escaped. This was August 30, 1813. In this massacre, Dr. Spruce Macay Osborne, son of Col. Adlai Osborne, then a surgeon in the army, was killed. This unprovoked massacre aroused the whole country, and an army of thirty-five hundred men was raised, chiefly in Tennessee, and placed under the command of Gen. Andrew Jackson. In the meantime, the militia from the Salisbury Congressional District were ordered to rendezvous in Salisbury on the first day of January, 1814, in order to raise a regiment to march against the Creek Indians. It rained and snowed all that day, but notwithstanding the weather the militia flocked in, and were sheltered for the night in the houses of the Salisbury people. On the next day they were transferred to the barracks, and the work of enlistment went on. Some volunteered, others were "detached," until a regiment was formed, which was placed under the command of Col. Jesse A. Pearson. Gen. Joseph Graham was his superior officer in command of the expedition. To this regiment the ladies of Salisbury, headed by Mrs. Moses A. Locke, presented a handsome flag of blue silk, bordered with fringes and tassels of gold. In the center it bore the emblem of the United States, the eagle, painted by Wayne Evans, the son-in-law of Barna Krider. Upon it was also painted a motto composed by Mrs. Locke, as follows: *"Let not the rage of war obliterate honor and humanity towards the females of our savage foe."* This flag was presented to the regiment by Mr. John Lewis Beard, son of Capt. John Beard, in behalf of the ladies, at the old race-track. The Rowan Company in this regiment was commanded by Capt. Jacob Krider, of Salisbury. James Gillespie was a lieutenant, and John Faust, ensign. Many hearts were sad in Rowan County when this regiment marched out of Salisbury towards Alabama. But, aside from the fatigues and dangers of the march, they were never in peril. While they were on their way to join General Jackson, that intrepid chief had met and annihilated the Creek warriors at Tohopeka, in the Horseshoe Bend of the Tallapoosa River. This was March 27, 1814. After this victory the submission of the Indians was complete, and our troops had nothing to do but to turn around and march home again. Very few incidents of this expedition have been handed down. Tradition, however, relates Captain Krider's method of reducing a refractory and disorderly soldier into good behavior. He had such a soldier in his Company and he used all the plans he could think of for this soldier's reformation. At last, while encamped on the banks of one of the Georgia or Alabama rivers, a new idea struck the captain. He had a forked stake driven down near the bank of the river, and procuring a long pole, he tied the refractory soldier to one end of it by his hands and feet, something after the style of a dip net, and balancing the pole on the stake, he caused him to be let down into the water. As this was about May, in a warm latitude, it first seemed to amuse the soldier, and he laughed at the experiment. But his open mouth caused him to ship too much water, and as the process of dipping went on inexorably and seemed about to be endless, he was at last subjugated, confessed his errors, and promised to give no more trouble. He kept his promise. The names of Captain Krider's Company are on file in a printed volume in the clerk's office in Salisbury.

In the meantime the war was drawing to a close, and a treaty of peace was agreed upon at Ghent, December 24, 1814, ratified by the Prince Regent of England, the twenty-eighth of the same month, and by the United States, the seventeenth of February, 1815. The ratification of the treaty was celebrated in Salisbury on the fourth of March, 1815, by processions, speeches, and by a monster ball. The people danced all night, and at sunrise the next morning Mr. Hugh Horah rang the courthouse bell as a signal for breaking up.

At the close of the war, everything settled down into the peaceful routine of life. But the flame of patriotism burned brightly in the hearts of the people. Having made sacrifices to maintain their rights as a free people, they endeavored to keep themselves reminded of the value of their heritage. Hence they celebrated two national festivals annually. One of these was the twenty-second February, the birthday of Washington. The death of this eminent man occurred on the fourteenth of December, 1799, and for a quarter of a century afterwards there were many still living who had seen the "Father of His Country." His distinguished services were not forgotten, and the people loved to do honor to his memory. It is a pity that the lapse of nearly a century has so far displaced his image from the memory of our people that they have forgotten even to notice the day.

The other anniversary was the Fourth of July. Upon this occasion the Declaration of Independence was read, patriotic speeches were made, toasts were drunk, and as a matter of course the ceremonies wound up with a ball, at some spacious hall or public parlor.

From these scenes we will turn to some of another character, in our next chapter.

CHAPTER XXV

AFRICAN SLAVERY

The history of society in Rowan County would not be complete without a glimpse at the system of domestic slavery as it existed here from the first establishment of the county. The early settlers were slaveholders, and on the register's volumes you will find here and there a "Bill of Sale" for a negro slave, and in the volumes of Wills you will see how the fathers of the early days bequeathed the negro man Pompey, or Cæsar, or Ned, or Joe, to one son, and Scipio, or Hannibal, or Cato, or Adam to anther son, while their daughters received bequests of negro girls and women, by the names of Bet and Sal, Luse and Dinah. The question may sometimes have been raised in their minds whether it was right to hold men and women in perpetual slavery; but when they opened their Bibles and read how Abraham bought slaves and had slaves born in his house; and how Moses, by divine direction, provided for the release and redemption of Hebrew slaves, but left no provision for the release of the slave of foreign birth, but allowed him to be bought and sold at the will of their masters; and when they read how slavery was recognized by Christ and his apostles, their doubts as to the rightfulness of the institution in the sight of God vanished. They did not feel themselves responsible for its introduction among them. That had been accomplished a hundred years and more before their time, when the Dutch sold slaves to the Virginians at Jamestown, in 1620, or when citizens of Massachusetts, in 1636, built a slave ship at Marblehead and sent it to Africa for slaves. Barncroft relates that the representatives of the people ordered the negroes to be restored to their native land, and imposed a fine twice the price of a negro upon anyone who should hold any "black mankind" to perpetual service. He, however, ingeniously admits that the law was not enforced, and that there was a disposition in the people of the colony to buy negroes and hold them as slaves forever (History United States, Vol. 1, Chapter 5). Stephens, in his History, states that many of the most prominent men of the Colony of Massachusetts purchased slaves out of the first cargo brought from Africa, in 1638, in the Marblehead slave ship, "Desire."

As population drifted into North Carolina, slavery came along with it—from Virginia, from Pennsylvania, and from more Northern States. And when, in time, it was discovered that slavery was an unprofitable institution in the bleaker regions of New England, and the moral sentiments of the people began to recognize it as unlawful as well as unprofitable, many of the slaves were sold off to more genial latitudes. The mild climate, the fertile soil, and the unreclaimed wilderness of North Carolina furnished an inviting field for the employment of slave labor. And in general, just as fast as the early settlers accumulated enough money to purchase a slave, it was expended in that way. This was peculiarly the case with the English and Scotch-Irish settlers, and the immigrants from Virginia, but not so prevalent among the German settlers, though many of them also followed the same practice. As stated before, the records of the early days of Rowan show the presence of slaves in the county. At the first census, in 1790, there were 1,839 negroes in the county, including the territory now embraced in Davidson and Davie, as well as Rowan. In 1800 there were 2,874 negroes. In 1830 the number had increased to 6,324. The separation of Davie and Davidson Counties reduced the number to 3,463 in 1840, and it rose to 4,066 in 1860. In the last-named year the white population of Rowan was 10,523, or about two and one-half whites to each negro.

The character of Rowan County slavery was generally mild and paternal. On a few plantations, probably, where a considerable number of slaves were quartered, and it was necessary to employ an overseer, there was severity of discipline, and hard labor; for the overseer himself was a hireling, and it was important for his popularity that he should make as many barrels of corn and as many bales of cotton as possible, with the least outlay of money and provisions. But even then the overtasked or underfed slave had access to his master, either directly or through the young masters and mistresses, who felt a personal interest in the slave, and would raise such a storm about the ears of a cruel overseer as would effectually secure his dismissal from his post. The slave represented so much money, and aside from consideration of humanity, the prudent and economical owner could not afford to have his slave maltreated and his value impaired. There was of course room for abuse in all this, and there were heartless and tyrannical masters, and there were oppressed and suffering slaves, just as there is tyranny and oppression in every form of social existence in this fallen and ruined world.

But with many families, where there were only a few slaves, the evils of servitude were reduced to a minimum. The slave was as warmly clothed, as securely sheltered, and as bountifully fed as his master. He worked in the same field, and at the same kind of work, and the same number of hours. Sometimes the clothing was coarser and the food not so delicate; but often the clothing was from the same loom and the food from the same pot. The negro had his holidays too—his Fourth of July, his Christmas, and his General Muster gala day. And where the family altar was established, evening and morning the negroes, old and young, brought in their chairs and formed a large circle around the capacious hearth of the hall-room, while the father and master priest opened the big family Bible, and read the words of life from its sacred pages. And when the morning and evening hymn were sung, the negroes, with their musical voices, joined in and sang the "parceled lines" to the tune of Windham or Sessions, Ninety-fifth or Old Hundred. They worshiped in the same church with their masters, comfortably seated in galleries constructed for their use, and when the Lord's supper was administered, they came forward and sat at the same tables where their masters had sat, and drank the sacred wine from the same cups.

In all this we are not affirming that there was social equality, or that the slave was always contented with his lot in life. No doubt he often chafed under the yoke of bondage, and sometimes when his master dealt hardly with him he ran away, and hid in the swamps and thickets, sustaining life by stealing, or by the aid of his fellow-servants who sympathized with him and who faithfully kept his secret from his master. Our weekly newspaper used to have pictures of fugitive negroes, with a stick over their shoulders, and with a bundle swinging to it, and the startling heading in large capitals "RUNAWAY." Something after this style:

And many a time white children on their way to or from school, would almost hold their breath as they passed some dark swamp or deserted house, when they remembered that a RUNAWAY had been seen in the neighborhood. Generally the runaway got tired of lying out in a few weeks, especially if winter was near, and voluntarily came home and submitted to whatever punishment was decided upon.

Occasionally there were cruel hardships suffered by them. When the thriftless master got in debt, or when the owner died and his estate was sold at vendue, or if the heartless master chose, the negro husband and wife might be separated, or parent and child might be sold from each other, one party falling into the hands of a negro trader, and carried off to Alabama or Mississippi. Such cases occurred at intervals, and under the laws there was no help for it. But in all such cases the feelings of humane and Christian elements of the community were shocked. Generally, however, arrangements were made to purchase, and keep in the neighborhood, all deserving negroes. As sales would come on it was the habit of the negroes to go to some man able to buy them and secure their transfer to a desirable home. Sometimes, however, all this failed, and the "negro trader" having the longest purse would buy and carry off to the West husbands or wives or children against their will. Older citizens remember the gangs of slaves that once marched through our streets with a hand of each fastened to a long chain, in double file, sometimes with sorrowful look, and sometimes with a mockery of gayety. The house of the trader was, perhaps, a comfortable mansion, in some shady square of town. Near the center of the square, and embowered in trees and vines, was his "barracoon," or prison for the unwilling. There a dozen or two were carefully locked up and guarded. Other cabins on the lot contained those who were submissive and willing to go. On the day of departure for the West the trader would have a grand jollification. A band, or at least a drum and fife, would be called into requisition, and perhaps a little rum be judiciously distributed to heighten the spirits of his sable property, and the neighbors would gather in to see the departure. First of all one or two closely covered wagons would file out from the "barracoon," containing the rebellious and unwilling, in handcuffs and chains. After them the rest, dressed in comfortable attire, perhaps dancing and laughing, as if they were going on some holiday excursion. At the edge of the town, the fife and drum ceased, the pageant faded away, and the curious crowd who had come to witness the scene returned to their homes. After months had rolled away the "trader's" wagons came back from Montgomery, Memphis, Mobile, or New Orleans, loaded with luxuries for his family. In boxes and bundles, in kegs and caskets, there were silks and laces, watches and jewelry, ribbons and feathers, candies and tropical fruits, wines and cordials, for family use and luxurious indulgence, all the profits of an accursed traffic in human flesh and blood, human tears and helpless anguish and oppression. This was the horrible and abominable side of this form of social institution. It was evil, wretchedly evil. But it had and has its counterpart in the social evils of the poorer classes of all ages and all lands. Multitudes today, by inexorable necessity, by poverty and the demands for certain kinds of service, are as hopelessly enslaved by circumstances as these were by law. This is not alleged as an excuse or apology for a crying evil, but only as an intimation that he who is without sin may consistently throw stones at the vanished specter of African slavery in the Southern States. And glad are we that the specter has vanished from our fair land.

CHAPTER XXVI

FOLKLORE

The population of Rowan County, it has been truthfully said, was made up of almost all the nations of Europe. There were English, Welsh, Scotch, and the ever present Scotch-Irish, the pure Irish, the French, and Germans from the upper and lower Rhine, the Palatines and Hessians, with now and then a Switzer or Italian. These all brought their own peculiar habits, prejudices, and national superstitions. And when these were all mingled together, and supplemented by the belief in spells, charms, and fetishes of the African race, there was a little of almost every superstition under the sun. Let us catch a glimpse, before it vanishes forever, of this undercurrent of

Popular Superstition

as it existed a few generations ago, and may still exist in certain localities in Rowan County. It is but the reiteration of a well-known historical fact, when we assert that all nations and peoples have had their superstitious beliefs and practices; and it is no discredit to the inhabitants of Rowan to say that they shared with their contemporaries in the popular superstitions of the day. Prominent among these was the

Belief in Witches

No man was ever burnt in Rowan County for witchcraft, as they were in some counties claiming to be more civilized. But this was owing, either to the superior charity of the people, or to the fact that they supposed themselves able to overmatch the witches with countercharms. A witch was generally supposed to be an old woman in league with the devil, and able to do wonderful things by Satanic agency. The usual way to become a witch was to go down to the image dimly outlined in the water, pledge the soul to Satan, upon condition of his rendering them the help needed. After this compact the witches could do wonderful things, such as riding on broomsticks through the air, transforming themselves into black cats, rabbits, and other animals. Walking along the road late in the evening, a man alleged that he saw three women sitting on a log beside the road. As he looked at them, the women suddenly melted from view, and three antlered deer galloped off in their stead. The witch or wizard was supposed to have power to transfer corn from the horse-trough of his neighbor to his own horse, and while his neighbor's horses got poor and lean, his own were sleek and fat. To see a rabbit hopping about a barn suggested the presence of a witch making arrangements to abstract the corn from the horses, or the milk from the cows. But an old-fashioned shilling, with its pillars of Hercules, nailed in the horse-trough, was supposed to break the spell and keep the corn in the trough. The only way of killing the witch rabbits and black cats was by using a silver bullet. The rabbit would vanish, but the witch at home would suddenly die of heart disease or apoplexy. In the meantime, the witches were supposed to use a peculiar kind of a gun, which was simply a glass phial, open at both ends, and a bullet made of knotted and twisted hair. This bullet possessed the wonderful property of penetrating the flesh of an animal without making any hole in the skin. It was alleged that such bullets were found, and animals often, being skinned, would show the hole through which these bullets went.

It was believed that witches rode on the necks of horses at night, and their knotted stirrups were sometimes seen in the manes of the horses. In these cases, they assumed the form of rabbits. A story used to be related of the mistake of an inexperienced witch in trying to increase the amount of butter at a churning. She took her cream, and measured it into her churn by the spoonful, repeating at each dip, "a spoonful from that house," and "a spoonful from that house." Unfortunately, speaking in German, she got the word for ladle instead of spoon, and so said, "a ladleful from that house." As a consequence, when she began to churn, the cream began to swell up as the ladelfuls came in, until the churn was full and it ran over and flooded the room. At that juncture a neighbor walked in, and found her unable to account for the abundance of cream, and in her confusion she divulged the embarrassing secret.

Spells and Charms

Intimately connected with this witchcraft was the beliefs in spells and charms. This was very common among the negroes, and perhaps continues to this day. Nothing was more common than to account for certain obscure diseases as the result of a "trick." The sick person was said to be "tricked." This was supposed to be done in various ways, but very frequently by making some mixture of roots, hair, parings of fingernails, and other ingredients, tying the compound up in a cloth, and laying it under a doorstep, or piece of wood or stone where the victim had to tread, or perhaps was put into the spring or well. In such emergencies the only refuge was a "trick doctor" or conjurer, who knew how to brew a medicine, or repeat a charm more potent than the spell laid on. Such "trick doctors" were to be found in the memory of persons still living. They were generally men of a shrewd, unscrupulous character, who managed to delude the minds of the gullible victims of trickery. He who was weak enough to believe in the "trick," was not hard to be persuaded and imposed upon by the conjurer. Marvelous stories were told of the skill of these conjurers. So potent was the skill of one of these that he needed no lock on his crib or smokehouse. All he did was to draw a circle in the dust or earth around his premises, and the thief who dared enter that magic circle would be found standing there next morning, with his bag of stolen meat or corn on his shoulder. One of these conjurers was believed to have the power of taking some straws and turning a thief's track upside down, and compelling him to come and stand on the reversed track. The premises of a man with such a reputation were generally safe without lock or key. To do them justice, the conjurers were generally very moderate in their charges, seeming to find their reward in the reputation which they achieved among their neighbors. And their countercharms and potions were generally innocent, and only calculated to work upon imagination. Sometimes they used real remedies, supplementing them with certain passes and motions. For instance, many years ago, a boy cut his foot badly with an ax. The wound was loosely and awkwardly bound up, and the blood continued to flow, until the lad was like to die. In this emergency a neighbor was sent for about midnight to staunch the blood by "using" for it. He came promptly, and carefully unbound the foot, washed off the clotted blood, adjusted the lips of the wound, and bound on it the fleshy scrapings of sole leather. After this, he took another sharp tool, a drawing knife, and made various passes over the foot, at the same time muttering some cabalistic words—perhaps a verse from the Bible. The remedy as a whole was eminently successful, but the patient was disposed to attribute the cure to the careful adjustment, and the astringent properties of oak bark absorbed in tanning by the scrapings of the leather, rather than to the magic "passes" and the muttered words.

It was believed that if witch rabbits sucked the cows it would cause them to give bloody milk. The remedy for this was to milk the cow through a knothole of a piece of rich pine plank, and the reader may have seen, as the writer has, such pieces of plank, with a knothole in them, hanging up beside the kitchen, and ready for use at any time. In those days a worn horeshoe nailed over the door was regarded as a spell against witch power, and the cause of good luck. At present it has become the fashion to form many ornaments after the horseshoe pattern as a symbol of good luck. Some persons believed that if a rabbit ran across the road from the right to the left hand, it foreboded bad luck, but if from the left to the right, good luck. To catch the first glimpse of the new moon through the branches of the trees was a token of trouble during the next month, but if seen in the open sky the first time it was the harbinger of a prosperous month. For a funeral procession to stop before getting off the premises or plantation was a sign that another funeral would soon take place from the same house. But the great embodiment of signs was the moon, and in many families scarcely anything of importance was undertaken without first inquiring whether it would be in the "dark" or the "light" of the moon. The Salem almanac was and is an institution that no prudent believer in the signs would think of dispensing with. Corn, potatoes, turnips, and beans, in fact everything, must be planted when the sign is right, in the head, or the feet, or the heart, in Leo or Taurus, in Aquarius or Pisces, in Gemini or Cancer, according as large vegetables or many vegetables are desired. Briars are to be cut and fence foundations laid exactly in the right sign, or success is not expected. In fact, attention to the signs frequently superseded attention to the seed and the soil, and the proper method of cultivation, and has probably done much to retard agricultural progress.

There is a charm in the mysterious that fascinates the untutored mind; and many would rather be skillful in discerning the signs than prudent in bestowing productive labor.

It would be an endless task to enumerate all the superstitious notions that have floated through the popular mind, and that have been the theme of serious conversation and meditation among the people, in the century and a half that has passed since this region was peopled. With many, these superstitions have been but a fancy, a curious theme of discussion, not seriously believed. But others have been the slaves of these unfounded notions, and have been made miserable by the howling of a dog, or the ticking of a "death watch" in the wall. As the light of education and religion is more widely diffused, this slavery has passed away, and there are probably few today who are willing to confess their belief in the notions that still linger in their minds as traditions of their fathers.

CHAPTER XXVII

THE CHURCHES OF ROWAN

The early settlers of Rowan County were religious people, and in many instances the enjoyment of perfect liberty of conscience was the great object which they were seeking when they were making for themselves a home in the Western world. The poor Palatines had endured much suffering in their home on the Rhine, and been driven forth to seek shelter for their families in foreign lands. They, or their descendants, found a resting-place in Eastern Rowan. The Scotch-Irish fled from the North of Ireland, in consequence of disabilities imposed on them for the sake of their religion. They found a home in the fertile lands of Western Rowan; and with them they brought an intense love for their own peculiar doctrines and forms of worship.

Presbyterianism in Rowan

is older than the organization of the county, not only in the affections and doctrines of the settlers, but in the form of organized presbyterian congregations. On pages forty-six and forty-seven of the first volume of deeds in the Register's office, we find it recorded that, on the seventeenth of January, 1753, John Lynn and Naomi Lynn gave a deed for twelve acres of land, more or less, on James Cathey's line, in Anson County, "to a congregation belonging to ye Lower meetinghouse, between the Atking River and ye Catabo Do., adhering to a minister licensed from a Presbytery belonging to the old Synod of Philadelphia." This deed was witnessed by Edward Cusick, John Gardiner, and William Brandon. On the eighteenth of January, 1753, a similar deed for twelve acres more, "on James Cathey's north line," was conveyed to the same congregation. From this we learn that there was an organized congregation of Presbyterians at this point, capable of purchasing land, and its popular name was the "Lower Meeting-house." The second name by which it was known as "Cathey's Meeting-house," doubtless because in the neighborhood of the Catheys. Its third and present name was and is Thyatira. Whether it was an organized church, with its regularly ordained elders, at that early day, we have no means of determining. It is probable that some of the first settlers—the Catheys, Brandons, Barrs, Andrews, Grahams, or Nesbits—were ordained elders before leaving Pennsylvania, and exercised their office in planting a church near their new homes.

A second thought suggested by the name, "Lower Meeting-house," is that there was at that date an "Upper Meeting-house," or perhaps more than one. The "Upper" one would naturally be looked for higher up the principal streams—the Yadkin and Catawba—and was no doubt to be found in the settlement where Statesville was afterwards built, and which was afterwards divided into the three churches of Fourth Creek, (Statesville), Concord, and Bethany. These four churches of Rowan, with seven churches of Mecklenburg, constituted the eleven historical churches of Western North Carolina, whose boundaries were defined, and whose organization was completed, by the missionaries, Rev. Messrs. Spencer and McWhorter, in 1764. The latter is the date generally assigned as the time of their organization, but most of them are really a dozen or perhaps twenty years older, or contemporaneous with earliest settlement.

From the History of Fourth Creek Church, written by Rev. E. F. Rockwell, we learn that Fourth Creek was gathered into a congregation at least as early as 1751, and their place of worship was fixed upon as early as 1756. The Rev. John Thompson came into this region as early as 1751, and settled near Center Church. He preached at Fourth Creek, and various other stations in Rowan County, for about two years, and it is said the people came twenty or twenty-five miles to his appointments. "From the Davidson Settlement and the region of Beattie's Ford, they came; from Rowan, the Brandons, the Cowans, the Brawleys. Sometimes he baptized a score of infants at once." He had one preaching station near where Third Creek Church is, one at Morrison's Mill, one near the present site of Davidson College. As Cathey's Meeting-house (Thyatira) was established about this time, or earlier, no doubt John Thompson preached at that place also.

From a manuscript of Fourth Creek congregation, drawn up by Hon. William Sharpe in 1773, it appears that there were one hundred and ninety-six heads of families, one hundred and eleven different names, residing within ten miles of Fourth Creek Church, and belonging to the congregation. The number of persons, at the usual estimate of five to a family, would be nearly one thousand. Out of these were formed, in later days, the churches of Fourth Creek, Concord, Bethany, Shiloh, Bethesda, Third Creek, Fifth Creek, Tabor, and Clio, or parts of them, now numbering one thousand and ninety-seven members. But though these were in Old Rowan they are now in Iredell County. Cathey's or Thyatira is the mother church of modern Rowan Presbyterians. In 1753, two missionaries were sent by the Synod of Philadelphia to visit Virginia and North Carolina, with directions to show special regard to the vacancies between the Yadkin and Catawba. The names of these ministers were McMordie and Donaldson. In the fall of 1755, the Rev. Hugh McAden made a tour through North and South Carolina, preached at Cathey's Meeting-house, and was solicited to remain, but declined. The same year, the Rev. John Brainard and the Rev. Elihu Spencer were directed by the Synod of New York to supply vacant congregations in North Carolina, but there is no report of their visit. For ten years after this, there is no record of any laborer in this region, but the congregations still held together and awaited the arrival of a minister. In 1764 the Synod of Philadelphia sent the Rev. Messrs. Elihu Spencer and Alexander McWhorter to form societies, adjust the boundaries of congregations, ordain elders, and dispense the sacraments. It was at this period that the seven churches of Mecklenburg, and the two churches of Rowan—Fourth Creek and Thyatira—were definitely established. The next year, 1765, Fourth Creek and Thyatira united in a call for the services of the Rev. Elihu Spencer, and the congregations sent wagons, accompanied by elderly men, all the way to New Jersey to move his family to Rowan. It is said that he declined to come because the messengers refused to pledge themselves to restore his wife to her friends in the event of his death at an early day. It was eight years more before Thyatira obtained a minister. In 1772, the Rev. Mr. Harris, of whom we know nothing further, took charge of the church, and remained about two years. In 1778, the Rev. James Hall became pastor of Fourth Creek, Concord, and Bethany Churches, and in 1777 the Rev. Samuel Eusebius McCorkle was ordained and installed pastor of Thyatira Church. Mr. McCorkle was born in Lancaster County, Pa., in 1746, and came with his parents to Rowan in 1756. He was prepared for college under the Rev. David Caldwell, of Guilford, and was graduated from Princeton in 1772. He was licensed by the Presbytery of New York in 1774, and then preached two years in Virginia. After preaching about eight years in Thyatira, he commenced a classical school, about a mile east of the church, which he called "Zion Parnassus Academy." This school was eminently useful, and Dr. McCorkle's students were thoroughly drilled, and six of the seven graduates of the first class from the University of North Carolina were Dr. McCorkle's pupils. Forty-five of his students entered the ministry, and many of them became lawyers, judges, and officers of the State. The signal success of his pupils in achieving eminence arose from his faithfulness in discouraging young men who were destitute of respectable talents from following any of the learned professions.

In 1795, the trustees of the University of North Carolina elected Dr. McCorkle Professor of Moral and Political Philosophy and History, with the view of his acting as president. General Davie, it seems, objected to the arrangement, and this caused Dr. McCorkle to decline the place. In 1796, the Rev. Joseph Caldwell was elected to the chair of Mathematics, and presiding professor, and for forty years guided the institution in its career of usefulness. But Dr. McCorkle did not cease to labor for the advancement of the infant University. He made many excursions to raise funds for its endowment, was present at the laying of the cornerstone of the first building, and made an address upon that occasion. He did not cease to love the University to the end of his life. On the second of July, 1776, the Rev. Samuel E. McCorkle was married to Margaret Gillespie, of Salisbury, the daughter of the patriotic Mrs. Elizabeth Steele, who relieved the distress of General Greene, in Salisbury, by the timely supply of money. She bore him ten children, six of whom survived him, and some of their descendants are still living in Thyatira. Dr. McCorkle received his death warrant in the pulpit, being stricken with palsy while conducting the services of the sanctuary. He lingered on for a number of years, unable to fulfill the duties of the ministry, except by patient suffering for the Master's sake. On the twenty-first of June, 1811, he was called to his reward, and his body was laid in the Thyatira graveyard.

About 1792, Third Creek and Unity Churches in Rowan were organized, and about the same period, Joppa, now Mocksville Church, in Davie County. The Rev. Joseph D. Kilpatrick, from the Waxhaws in South Carolina, was the first pastor of these churches, that were cut off from Thyatira, Fourth Creek, and Bethany Churches. In the revivals of 1802-03, Mr. Kilpatrick was an active participant, and warm sympathizer. He labored in this field until March, 1829, when he was called to his rest. His remains are interred in the graveyard of Third Creek Church. Two of his sons, Abner and Josiah, became ministers, and two of his daughters married ministers—one the Rev. Mr. Kerr, and the other the Rev. Mr. Porter. Four or five of Mr. Porter's sons became ministers. The revival of 1802-03 had great effect upon the western neighborhoods of Thyatira, and they began to desire a separate church. Dr. McCorkle did not sympathize with the camp-meeting movement, but only tolerated it. On the other hand a part of his congregation was fully under its influence. In 1805, Back Creek was erected into a separate church. At its organization it possessed an eldership of peculiar excellence, and it has sent out some ministers of the gospel whose labors have been greatly blessed. In 1824, Prospect Church, in the southwestern corner of Rowan, was organized, mainly from Center congregation, but partly from Back Creek. In 1829, Franklin Church, four miles north of Salisbury, was organized in vacant ground adjoining Thyatira, Third Creek, and Unity. All these churches have been served by a succession of devoted ministers.

The ministers of Thyatira after Dr. McCorkle, were the Rev. Messrs. Bowman—a son-in-law of Dr. McCorkle—John Carrigan, James Stafford, James D. Hall, A. Y. Lockridge, S. C. Alexander, B. S. Krider, S. C. Pharr, and J. A. Ramsay.

Back Creek has had for ministers, Joseph D. Kilpatrick, A. Y. Lockridge, Thomas E. Davis, S. C. Alexander, W. B. Watts, Robert Bradley, A. E. Chandler, and J. A. Ramsay.

Bethphage Church, originally in Rowan, midway between Thyatira and Poplar Tent, was organized in 1795, and had for its ministers the Rev. John Carrigan, the Rev. James Stafford, Rev. James E. Morrison, Rev. Walter W. Pharr, and Rev. William W. Pharr, all natives of Rocky River congregation.

Third Creek was served by the following ministers: Rev. Messrs. Joseph D. Kilpatrick, Josiah Kilpatrick, A. Y. Lockridge, J. M. H. Adams, S. B. O. Wilson, G. D. Parks, G. R. Brackett, William A. Wood, R. W. Boyd, and A. L. Crawford.

Unity Church was served by Rev. Messrs. Joseph D. Kilpatrick, Franklin Watts, William A. Hall, Jesse Rankin, B. S. Krider, G. R. Brackett, William A. Wood, E. F. Rockwell, and R. W. Boyd.

Prospect Church has enjoyed the ministerial labors of various ministers, among whom are Rev. Messrs. Walter S. Pharr, John LeRoy Davies, John E. McPherson, E. D. Junkin, W. B. Watts, Robert Bradley, Romulus M. Tuttle, William H. Davis, P. T. Penick, and F. P. Harrell.

Joppa (or Mocksville Church), formerly in Rowan, was founded by the Rev. Joseph D. Kilpatrick. After him came the Rev. Franklin Watts, William A. Hall, Jesse Rankin, B. S. Krider, R. B. Anderson, B. L. Beall, William M. Kilpatrick, S. S. Murkland, G. M. Gibbs, and A. L. Crawford.

Franklin Church, founded by the Rev. Franklin Watts in 1829, had for its ministers the Rev. Messrs. William A. Hall, Jesse Rankin, B. S. Krider, James D. Hall, B. L. Beall, S. C. Pharr, A. L. Crawford, and R. W. Boyd.

These churches at the present time have for their pastors the ministers last named in the above rolls, and embrace a membership of nine hundred and forty, with children in the Sabbath Schools numbering seven hundred and forty-six. This estimate includes the Salisbury Church, but excludes Bethphage and Mocksville, as lying outside of Rowan County.

The Salisbury Church

The town of Salisbury lies between the settlements of the Scotch-Irish and the "Pennsylvania Dutch" or Germans. To the east and south lay the great body of the German settlers; and to the north and west the Scotch-Irish predominated. The population of the town was a mixture of these two races, interspersed with Englishmen, Frenchmen, pure Irish and Scotch. Among the early inhabitants we find a good many names that are suggestive of Presbyterian affinities. These people had no church of their own, but such as were church members belonged to Thyatira. Dr. McCorkle, having married the daughter of Mrs. Elizabeth Steele, the half-sister of Gen. John Steele, was early brought into connection with the Salisbury people, and frequently preached in the courthouse, or in the Lutheran Church, as most convenient. In 1803-04, Dr. James McRee, of Center Church, preached in Salisbury once a month, and from 1807 to 1809, the Rev. John Brown, D.D., was principal of an Academy in Salisbury, and preached regularly there one-half of his time, giving the other half to Thyatira. This was during the time that Dr. McCorkle was prostrated by paralysis. Dr. Brown was called to the presidency of the South Carolina College, and afterwards became president of Athens College, Georgia, and there ended his life. Between the years of 1809 and 1819, the Rev. Samuel L. Graham, the Rev. Parsons O. Hays, and perhaps others, preached for a while in Salisbury. During all this time there were not enough Presbyterian Church members in Salisbury to justify an organization; at least, such was the opinion of these members and visiting preachers. But in 1820 there came as teacher to Salisbury, a man who entertained a different opinion. This was the

Rev. Jonathan Otis Freeman, M.D.

He soon began to agitate the subject of church organization, and before the close of the year he collected a body of thirteen members, and had them organized into a church, and ordained Alexander Torrence, Thomas L. Cowan, and Dr. Alexander Long as ruling elders.

In *The Western Carolinian,* published by Bingham & White, of the date of August 7, 1821, appeared the following notice: "The sacrament was administered in the NEW CHURCH in this place for the first time, on last Sabbath, by the Rev. Mr. Freeman, assisted by the Rev. Mr. Robinson, of Poplar Tent congregation." The "New Church" was not a new house of worship, but the newly organized Presbyterian Church of Salisbury, which had probably been organized on the Saturday preceding—August 4, 1821. The church building was not finished until five years later. The church was composed of the following thirteen members: Albert Torrence, Elizabeth Torrence, Hugh Horah, Mary Horah, Thomas L. Cowan, Elizabeth Cowan, Dr. Alexander Long, Mary Long, John Fulton, Charity Gay, Mary T. Holland, Ann Murphy, and Margaret Beckwith. Tradition reports that the church was organized in the old Lutheran Church, standing on a spot just inside of the present Lutheran graveyard. The graves of Mr. and Mrs. Cowan are on the site of the old church. For several years this church had no home, but worshiped either in the courthouse or in the Lutheran Church. Weekly prayer meetings were held in private houses, and from this originated the custom in this church of kneeling at its prayer meetings instead of standing as is practiced in other Presbyterian Churches. Dr. Freeman remained in Salisbury until 1826, when he removed to Raleigh, N. C. Just before leaving, he laid the cornerstone of the present church building, with appropriate services. During his stay of five years the following persons were added to the church: Michael Brown (1823), Isabella Maria Brown, Jane Troy, Catherine B. Troy, Elizabeth Murphy, Elizabeth Giles, Susan Giles, Margaret Dickson, Mary Gay, Mary Ann Reeves, Jane Trotter, Joseph Hall, Dr. John Scott, William Curtis, Mrs. Curtis, with seven colored persons. All these have passed away from earth. Thirty-five were gathered into the church under Dr. Freeman's administration. Of Dr. Freeman, the founder of the Salisbury Presbyterian Church, not very much is now known. Jonathan Otis Freeman was born in Barnstable, Mass., April 6, 1772. He was probably educated in his native State, studied medicine and took his degree of Doctor of Medicine. He married Mary Crocker, of his native town, December 10, 1794. He removed to North Carolina in 1805. At a meeting of Concord Presbytery, held in Salisbury, September 27, 1821, the Rev. Jonathan O. Freeman produced testimonials of his dismission from the Presbytery of Orange, and was received as a member of Presbytery. He had come to Salisbury some time before, for he closed a session of his school in Salisbury early in the year 1821, as published in *The Western Carolinian.* Dr. Freeman remained in Salisbury until the fall of 1826, when he removed to Raleigh. After this he labored in the bounds of Orange Presbytery and in Virginia for a number of years. He was an excellent teacher of the classics, and a number of our prominent men, as Hon. Burton Craige and Dr. Joseph W. Hall, were prepared for college by him. He died in Washington, N. C., in 1835, in the sixty-third year of his age.

Dr. Freeman's son, Edmund B. Freeman, was clerk of the Supreme Court of North Carolina, from 1836 to 1868, thirty-two years.

The Rev. Jesse Rankin, a native of Guilford County, was invited to Salisbury as principal of the Academy and supply to the church. He came in January, 1827, and remained until about the close of 1830, four years. During the period of his ministry here there were twenty-seven additions to the church, an average of nearly seven each year. For the first fifty years of its existence there was an addition of four hundred and six persons to its communion, an average of eight each year. From 1831 to 1836, the Rev. Thomas Espy and the Rev. P. J. Sparrow served the Salisbury and Thyatira Churches, each one year. Mr. Espy died, April 16, 1833, and his remains were deposited in the Lutheran graveyard in Salisbury, where a marble slab commemorates his life and labors. Mr. Sparrow was called from the Salisbury Church to the Professorship of Languages in Davidson College, whither he went in 1737. He afterwards became president of Hampden-Sidney College. He died a few years since near Pensacola, Fla. In the year 1832, a remarkable revival of religion occurred in this church, under the preaching of the Rev. A. D. Montgomery, by which many were added to the church. From 1836 till 1845, the Rev. Stephen Frontis was pastor of this church, and forty-four were added to the church during his ministry. Mr. Frontis died a few years ago, and sleeps in the graveyard of Prospect Church. On the first of February, 1846, the Rev. Archibald Baker, a native of Robeson County, became pastor of the church and continued until 1859, a period of thirteen years, and one hundred and fifty-six communicants were added under his ministry. Mr. Baker was a devout, earnest, and amiable servant of the Lord, and his memory is still cherished by the older members of the church. He was stricken down while speaking in Center Church, in his native county, and died in the harness.

On the third Sunday of November, 1860, the Rev. Jethro Rumple began his work as pastor of the Salisbury Church, and continued

DR. J. J. SUMMERELL

until the present time. During the twenty years of his ministry there have been two hundred and forty additions to the church.

In closing this sketch there are two or three facts that may interest the reader. The first is, that from the beginning this church maintained a well conducted Sunday School, in which many of the most devoted members of the congregation were teachers. The principal superintendents of the Sunday School have been, Thomas L. Cowan, J. J. Blackwood, Colonel Samuel Lemly, D. A. Davis, Philip L. Sink, William Murdock, J. J. Bruner, Samuel H. Wiley, and J. D. McNeely. Most of those who are now members of the church were once pupils in the Sunday School, and received their early religious impressions in that nursery of the church.

Another element of success in the church has been its earnest and faithful office-bearers, embracing many of the most highly esteemed and influential citizens of the town. The ruling elders have been as follows:

Albert Torrence, Thomas L. Cowan, Dr. Alexander Long, Michael Brown, Samuel Lemly, Philip L. Sink, D. A. Davis, J. J. Bruner, William Murdock, Thomas McNeely, Dr. J. J. Summerell, J. S. McCubbins, Julius D. McNeely, E. H. Marsh, R. A. Knox, and Orin D. Davis. The deacons have been Julius D. Ramsay, J. J. Summerell, M. D., Obadiah Woodson, John D. Brown, James S. McCubbins, J. A. Bradshaw, John A. Ramsay, John M. Horah, Julius D. McNeely, E. H. Marsh, J. K. Burke, T. B. Beall, R. A. Knox, Theodore F. Kluttz, Samuel H. Wiley, W. L. Kluttz, and Hugh M. Jones.

Another element of success has been that the church has had few and brief periods of vacancy, and very little serious internal dissension. Upon the departure of one pastor the congregation speedily agreed upon and secured another, and the work thus went on without intermission.

Another characteristic of the church is that it has always diligently fostered schools and colleges. Its early ministers were teachers, and in later days it has maintained excellent male and female academies where every child in the congregation has free access for ten months in the year. As a result many of the youth have been prepared for the higher schools and colleges, where they have received the benefits of a liberal education, and have been enabled to enter the liberal professions, and grace the cultivated circles of society.

Within the past ten years the following sons of this church have entered the ministry of the Presbyterian Church: Rev. William H. Davis, now laboring in Henderson County; Rev. John W. Davis, missionary in Soochow, China; Rev. Branch G. Clifford, in Unionville, S. C.; Rev. J. A. Ramsay, in Rowan County, N. C.; Rev. J. H. N. Summerell, in Cabarrus County, and K. P. Julian, now in his last year at the Theological Seminary. Bryant D. Thomas, who was received into this church between 1826 and 1830, became a minister and preached in the West. He died a few years ago.

Third Creek Church sent out a number of useful ministers, among whom were Abner and Josiah Kilpatrick, sons of Rev. Joseph D. Kilpatrick; William H. Johnson, B. S. Krider, William A. Wood, and R. Z. Johnston. Among the ministers born in Back Creek, were Silas Andrews, J. Scott Barr, John A. Barr, and R. W. Shive of Mississippi. The Presbyterian Churches of Rowan have been served by more than fifty different ministers, and have sent out probably not more than twenty-five or thirty into the work, and not more than a half-dozen of these who have served her churches have been natives of Rowan County.

President Polk's Forefathers and Thyatira Church

James K. Polk, eleventh President of the United States, was born in Mecklenburg County, November, 1795. His mother was Jean, daughter of James Knox, of Rowan County. This James was the son of John Knox, who was a native of Scotland, born about 1708, and who went from Scotland to Ireland with other emigrants, by invitation of the King of England, to constitute a balance of power against the insurgent Irish Catholics. He married an Irish Presbyterian, Jean Gracy, whose mother's name was Jean Sinclair, a relative of the mother (a Sinclair) of John Knox the Reformer.

This John and Jean came with other immigrants to America, about 1740, and were among the early settlers of Rowan County, buying six hundred acres of land on the south side of Third Creek, for thirty-seven pounds, ten shillings (£37/10), which land had been granted by Earl Granville to James Stewart.

For more than one hundred and fifty years an old stone stood in the Thyatira Churchyard, inscribed as follows:

HERE THE BODY LYS OF
JOHN KNOX
WHO DECEASED OCTOBER YE 25, 1758
AGED FIFTY YEARS
ALSO HERE LYS THE BODY OF
JEAN KNOX
HIS WIFE
WHO DECEASED SEPTEMBER 18, 1772
AGED SIXTY-FOUR YEARS

JAMES K. POLK

This stone is now fitted into a new one, with this inscription:

IN MEMORY OF
JOHN KNOX
1708-1758
AND HIS WIFE
JEAN GRACY
1708-1772
NATIVES OF SCOTLAND
ALSO THEIR SEVEN SONS
SOLDIERS OF THE AMERICAN REVOLUTION
WILLIAM SAMUEL
JAMES
(GRANDFATHER OF PRESIDENT JAMES KNOX POLK)
ABSALOM JOHN
JOSEPH BENJAMIN
AND THEIR DAUGHTER
MARY
ERECTED BY THEIR DESCENDANTS
MAY 20, 1911

So it comes about that from Rowan stock was produced a President, which fact we hope the good old county may repeat at an early date.

THYATIRA CHURCH AND KNOX MEMORIALS

CHAPTER XXVIII

LUTHERANISM IN ROWAN

The Lutheran Church in Rowan County is composed chiefly, but not exclusively, of the descendants of those German settlers who began to occupy the county about 1745. Fortunately for the history of this people, the Rev. Dr. Bernheim, in his book, entitled "History of the German Settlers and of the Lutheran Church in the Carolinas," has gathered up and preserved the traditions and documents that tell the story of their settlement and religious life. The author of these pages had intended that this chapter should be written by a minister or layman of the Lutheran Church, but succeeded only in securing a very brief but most interesting Sketch of Organ Church, by the Rev. Samuel Rothrock. For the general account he is indebted to Dr. Bernheim's interesting volume, which has been freely used in composing this chapter.

St. John's Lutheran Church in Salisbury is entitled to the distinction of being the oldest Lutheran congregation organized in the Province of North Carolina.

In the year 1768, John Lewis Beard, a wealthy citizen of Salisbury, and a member of the Lutheran Church, was bereaved by the death of a daughter, and her body was interred in a lot of ground owned by her father. To prevent her remains from being disturbed by the march of civilization, Mr. Beard executed a deed for the lot, containing one hundred and forty-four square poles, to a body of trustees of the Evangelical Lutheran congregation, of the township of Salisbury, allowing ministers of the High Church of England to occupy it when not used by the Lutherans. Upon this lot, now known as the Lutheran graveyard, or Salisbury Cemetery, the congregation soon after erected a log church, or block-house. All this was in preparation for some minister whom they expected in time to obtain. Five years later, in 1773, the Rev. Adolph Nussmann, a ripe and thorough scholar, and devoted and self-sacrificing Christian, was induced to come from Germany to Rowan County. After laboring in Salisbury and Organ Church for a short time, Mr. Nussmann removed from Salisbury and took charge of Buffalo Creek Church—St. John's—in Mecklenburg, now Cabarrus. At the same time that Mr. Nussmann came from Germany, Mr. Gottfried Ahrend came over as schoolmaster. As ministers were much needed, and Mr. Ahrend was qualified, he was ordained to the work of the ministry in 1775. As he preached at Organ Church—then called Zion's Church—from 1775 to 1785, it is probable that part of his time was devoted to the Salisbury Church. In 1785, Mr. Ahrend removed from Rowan to Lincoln County. For twelve years these two Lutheran ministers, with the Rev. Mr. Beuthahn, a German Reformed minister, labored among the German population of Rowan, Cabarrus, Lincoln, Catawba, Iredell, Davidson, Guilford, and other counties. At this time the Rev. Mr. Harris, and after him the Rev. Samuel E. McCorkle, was preaching to the Presbyterians at Thyatira, Rev. James Hall in Iredell, and Rev. David Caldwell in Guilford. These seven were breaking the bread of life to the thousands of people in this vast region.

Soon after the arrival of Messrs. Nussmann and Ahrend, the Revolutionary War opened, and for nearly eight years all correspondence with the Fatherland was cut off, and the congregations and ministers of Rowan were left to their own resources. No ministers, no books, no material aid or sympathy came to cheer them. Besides this, Mr. Nussmann was persecuted by the Tories, and forced to seek safety by hiding himself in a secure retreat, not far from his residence on Dutch Buffalo. At the close of the war, Mr. Nussmann reopened correspondence with friends in Germany, and in 1787 the Lutheran Church in North Carolina was put into connection with the parent church. A supply of books was obtained from Helmstadt, in the Duchy of Brunswick, and a call for several ministers to labor in North Carolina was preferred by Pastor Nussmann to Dr. Velthusen. In 1787, the Rev. Christian Eberhard Bernhardt, a native of Stuttgard, was sent to Rowan. His first charge was on Abbott's Creek, Davidson County, where he labored for a year. He afterwards labored for several years in Stokes, Forsyth, and Guilford Counties, and in 1800 removed to South Carolina.

The year 1788 was signalized by the arrival in Rowan of one who may be called the apostle of the Lutheran Church in Rowan. This was the Rev. Carl August Gottlieb Storch. He was sent out by the Helmstadt Missionary Society, and was a native of Helmstadt, and educated at the University of that city. Upon his arrival he took charge of the Salisbury, Pine, and Organ Churches. The Pine Church—now called Union—he soon resigned, and the next year began to preach in the "Irish Settlement," once a month, for which he was promised thirteen or fourteen pounds, about thirty-five dollars. His salary for the two churches of Salisbury and Organ was eighty pounds (£80), paper money, equal to two hundred dollars. The fees for funerals and marriage ceremonies averaged one dollar each, and may have amounted to fifty dollars annually, the whole amounting to nearly three hundred dollars. With the simple habits of those early days, and the cheapness of the necessaries of life, this salary of three hundred dollars was more liberal than the average minister's salary of these days. Besides having charge of these churches, Mr. Storch had charge of a small German school in Salisbury, and gave instructions in Hebrew to some pupils in the Salisbury Academy. Whether he realized any income from the schools is not known. Not long after this he married Miss Christine Beard, daughter of John Lewis Beard, and lived in the house on the corner of Main and Franklin Streets. After this he removed to what is now known as the Chilson place, one and a half miles east of Salisbury. A few years afterward he gave up the Salisbury Church, and moved ten miles south of Salisbury, on the New Concord Road, convenient to his three churches, Organ, Savitz's, and Dutch Buffalo. Here he spent the remainder of his life. On the twenty-seventh of March, 1831, Dr. Storch died, aged nearly sixty-seven years. His dust reposes in the graveyard of the Organ Church, where a suitable stone marks the spot and commemorates his life and labors. He was a ripe scholar, familiar with the Hebrew, Greek, and Latin languages, and it is said that he could converse fluently in five or six different tongues. Abundant in labor, crowned with honors, and rich in the affection of his people, he departed full of faith and hope in the Redeemer. His long service of more than forty years, including the critical period of his people's transition from the use of the German to the use of the English language, did much to preserve Lutheranism from decay and extinction in Rowan County. It is because of his labors, doubtless, that the Lutherans are, at the present day, equal in numbers to all other denominations together in this county.

But to return. A few months after Mr. Storch's arrival, in 1788, Rev. Arnold Roschen, a native of Bremen, was sent to North Carolina by the Helmstadt Mission Society, and upon his arrival began his labors on Abbott's Creek, now in Davidson County.

We may mention in passing that, in 1791, the present massive stone church was erected for the Organ congregation, and an organ of excellent quality was built by Mr. Steigerwalt, one of the members of the church. As this organ was the first and only instrument of the kind in the county it gave the name to the church, which it retains to this day.

In 1794, the Lutheran pastors, Nussmann, Ahrend, Roschen, Bernhardt, and Storch, ordained to the work of the ministry Robert Johnson Miller, obliging him to obey the "Rules, ordinances, and customs of the Christian Society called the Protestant Episcopal Church in America." This was a singular proceeding, but the request was made by Mr. Miller, and a congregation in Lincoln County which desired his services, and it is said was counseled by the Presbyterians. Mr. Miller afterwards sought and obtained Episcopal ordination at the hands of Bishop Ravenscroft.

The number of Lutheran ministers in North Carolina was reduced by the death of Mr. Nussmann in 1794, the removal of Mr. Bernhardt to South Carolina in 1800, and the return of Roschen to Germany the same year. Dr. Storch was however reinforced by the Rev. Adam N. Marcand, who became pastor of St. John's Church, Cabarrus, in 1797. He however remained but two years. In 1801, the Rev. Philip Henkel, from Virginia, took charge of the Guilford pastorate. Thus far the church seems to have depended upon foreign supplies for the pulpit. But a change was taking place that looked toward a home supply. On the second day of May, 1803, the Rev. Messrs. Gottfried Ahrend, Robert J. Miller, C. A. G. Storch, and Paul Henkel, with a number of elders and deacons, met in Salisbury, and formed the North Carolina Synod of the Lutheran Church. From this time the work went on more systematically. From the annual report of the Rev. Paul Henkel, in 1806, we learn the state of the church in North Carolina at that date.

In Orange and Guilford Counties there were three Lutheran churches and one "joint" church—that is Lutheran and German Reformed—served by Philip Henkel. In Rowan, east of the Yadkin, there were three "joint," and one Lutheran churches, served by Rev. Paul Henkel, afterwards by Ludwig Markert. In the vicinity of Salisbury three strong Lutheran churches enjoyed the ministry of the Rev. C. A. G. Storch for nearly twenty years. This report represents that about twenty years previous to that time there had been a tolerably strong German congregation in Salisbury, but as the German people and their language were changed into the English, the German worship soon became extinct. The three strong churches mentioned in the report, were doubtless the Pine Church—now Union, the Organ Church, and Savitz's—now Lutheran Chapel—once called the Irish Settlement. The report goes on to state that near Buffalo Creek, Cabarrus, there is one of the strongest Lutheran churches, served by the Rev. Mr. Storch. About eighteen miles west of Salisbury—I suppose near the present Troutman's depot—there was another Lutheran church. Also in Lincoln County there were eight or nine German congregations, mostly "joint," served by the Rev. Mr. Ahrend. There were churches also in Wilkes, Stokes, and other counties.

In 1805 the Synod ordained Philip Henkel to the full work of the ministry, and licensed John Michael Rueckert and Ludwig Markert. At a meeting of the Synod, October 22, 1810, held at Organ Church, there were present ten ministers and a number of lay delegates. This Synod ordained Gottlieb Schober as a Lutheran minister. Mr. Schober continued to be a member of the Moravian Church to the end of his days, while at the same time he was a Lutheran minister and pastor of several Lutheran churches. These excusable irregularities, such as the ordination of Miller and Schober, give evidence of a fraternal feeling between the different churches of that day, and became necessary because of the great scarcity of laborers in the whitening harvests on all sides.

At this same Synod of 1810, Jacob Scherer and Godfrey Drehr were licensed, and the limited license of Cathechists Rueckert and Jacob Greison were renewed. Twenty-three churches were reported, of which three were in Rowan.

In 1811, the North Carolina Synod, endued with the true spirit of missions, sent out several exploring missionaries to learn the condition of the Lutheran congregations in South Carolina, Virginia, Tennessee, and Ohio. The Rev. Messrs. Miller, Franklow, and Scherer were the missionaries, and they traveled and preached the gospel in distant regions. In 1813, David Henkel, J. J. Schmucker, and Daniel Moser were licensed to preach the gospel. In the year 1814, it is estimated that there were twenty-one ministers in the Synod of North Carolina, including those laboring in South Carolina; and eighty-five in the whole United States.

The remainder of the history of the Lutheran Church, so far as these sketches propose to give it, will be found in a brief and interesting account of the Organ Church, prepared by its present pastor, the Rev. Samuel Rothrock, to which will be added a sketch of St. John's Church, Salisbury, since its reorganization, and a general statement as to the ministers, churches, and number of communicants as they now exist.

Organ Evangelical Lutheran Church

The first organization of a congregation at this place dates back more than a century. The original members were Germans, few in number, but devotedly attached to the church of their choice. The services, and records in the church-book, were all in the German language. From the German church-book, which is well preserved, we gather the principal items in relation to the history of this congregation. The following is a translation from the records of the church-book, and in the translation the German orthography of names is preserved, and the present English orthography thrown in parentheses.

TRANSLATION

In the year A.D. 1774, the following members of our congregation commenced to build the so-called Organ Church, viz.:

Georg Ludwig Siffert (George Lewis Sifford), Wendel Miller, Peter Edelmann (Eddleman), Johannes Steigerwalt (John Stirewalt), Philip Gruss (Philip Cruse), Peter Steigerwalt (Stirewalt), Michael Guthmann (Goodman), Christoph Bless (Christopher Pless), Leonhard Siffert (Sifford), Jacob Klein (Cline), Anton J. Kuhn (Anthony J. Koon), Georg Heinrich Berger (George Henry Barger), Christoph Guthmann (Christopher Goodman), Johannes Rintelmann (John Rendleman), Johannes Eckel (John Eagle), Bastian Lenz (Bostian Lentz), Jacob Benz (Bentz), George Eckel (George Eagle), Franz Oberkirsch (Francis Overcash), Johannes Jose (John Josey), Heinrich Wenzel (Henry).

A majority of the aforementioned members united in the year 1772, and resolved to solicit for themselves a preacher and school-teacher from the Hanoverian Consistory in Germany. For in their time, North Carolina, together with all the other now free American States, were under the King of England, who was likewise Elector of Hanover. Christoph Rintelmann (Christopher Rendleman) and Christoph Layrle (Christopher Lyerly), were sent to London as deputies from the congregation, from which place they journeyed to Hanover, and through Gotten, the counselor of the Consistory, obtained a preacher and school-teacher, viz.: as preacher, Adolph Nussmann; and for school-teacher, Gottfried Ahrend. Both arrived safely in America in the year 1773. At this time there was but one common church for Reformed and Lutherans equally, the so-called Hickeri (Hickory) Church. One year the new pastor preached in this church, but some disharmony arose, and a majority of the Lutherans resolved to build for themselves an own church, and thus organized Organ Church. But before this church was built, Nussman left the congregation and devoted himself to Buffalo Creek. Whereupon, the congregation, which before had one church and one school-teacher, but now no preacher, procured the aforementioned Gottfried Ahrend to be ordained to the office of preacher in the year 1775. He served the congregation until 1785, when he devoted himself to Catawba River, residing in Lincoln County until the close of his life. For two years Nussmann served the congregation again, but he left the church for the second time. From 1787 to 1788, the congregation had no preacher. Gottfried Ahrend came once in a while. In 1788, at the desire and petition of Nussmann, a preacher, viz.: Charles Augustus Gottlieb Storch, was sent from Germany, who, according to Nussmann's assignment, was to go to Stinking Quarter, in Orange County. Various circumstances transpired that he did not wish to go to Stinking Quarter, but resolved to take charge of the congregation at Organ Church and the one in the town of Salisbury. He entered his services in the former on the twenty-sixth day of October, 1787, i.e., the twenty-third Sunday after Trinity; and in the town the second Sunday of November, i.e., the twenty-fourth Sunday after Trinity in the same year. The congregation at Organ Church promised their preacher a yearly salary of forty pounds (£40), North Carolina currency. The number of those who subscribed to the salary, as well as to the new church regulations, amounted to seventy-eight persons.

The new church regulations referred to above, very concise and wholesome in their nature, were introduced and adopted on the first day of January, 1789, are upon record in the church-book, but are not here translated.

The following ministers have been the successive pastors of Organ Church:

Rev. Adolphus Nussmann from 1773, to 1774, one year; Godfrey Ahrend, 1775 to 1785, ten years; Adolphus Nussmann, 1785 to 1787, two years. The church was now vacant for one year, and was visited occasionally by Rev. Gottfried Ahrend.

Rev. Charles A. G. Storch, from 1788 to 1823, thirty-five years; Daniel Scherer, 1823 to 1829, six years; Jacob Kæmpfer, 1829 to 1832, three years; Henry Graber, 1832 to 1843, eleven years; Samuel Rothrock, 1844 to 1866, twenty-two years; W. H. Cone, from January 1, 1866, to May, 1866, four months; William Artz, May 1, 1866,————; Samuel Rothrock, from July 1, 1868, to January 1, 1869, six months; Revs. S. Scherer and W. H. Cone, from January 1, 1869, to January 1, 1870, one year; W. H. Cone, January 1, 1870, to May 1, 1873, three years and four months; W. R. Ketchie, from June, 1873, to January, 1874, seven months; P. A. Strobel, from January 1, 1874, to October 1, 1875, one year and eight months; Samuel Rothrock, from January 1, 1876, and still pastor, December, 1880.

St. John's Church, Salisbury

Though this is the oldest Lutheran church in North Carolina, there was for a considerable period such a decline as almost amounted to extinction. Still there were Lutherans here, and they owned a lot and building that were used by occasional ministers of their own faith as well as by other denominations. In 1822, steps were taken to secure its reorganization. The Rev. Gottlieb Schober, president of the Synod that year, addressed a letter to the Lutherans of Salisbury urging them to gather up their forces, re-constitute their church, and claim their property. This letter had the desired effect, for the adherents of the church met, and a paper was drawn up by the Hon. Charles Fisher pledging the signers to reorganize the church. This paper was dated September 20, 1822, and was signed by the following persons, viz.: John Beard, Sr., Charles Fisher, Daniel Cress, Peter Crider, John Trexler, John Beard, Jr., Peter H. Swink, Moses Brown, John H. Swink, Bernhardt Kreiter, Lewis Utzman, H. Allemong, M. Bruner, John Albright, and Henry Swinkwag. Efforts were at once made to secure a minister, but without success. About this time a fence was placed around the graveyard, which had lain for some time in a neglected condition. In 1825, the work of reorganization was begun again, and Messrs. John Beard, Sr., George Vogler, and Moses Brown were elected elders, and Messrs. Nathan Brown, George Fraley, and Henry C. Kern, deacons. During the following year, 1826, the church was successful in its efforts to secure the Rev. John Reck, of Maryland, as pastor. He found but fourteen members at his arrival; but the next year there were thirty members in full communion. Mr. Reck remained with the church five years, and his labors among them were greatly blessed. In 1831, the pastor resigned and returned to Maryland. "After this time the congregation had such a continued and rapid succession of ministers, besides having been at times unsupplied with the stated means of grace, as not to be enabled to command the influence which the regular ministration of a permanent pastor might have given it."

The following roll of its pastors is made up, partly from the pages of Dr. Bernheim's History, and partly from the recollection and memoranda of Mr. B. F. Fraley, and is believed to be accurate.

1. Rev. John Reck, 1826 to 1831.
2. Rev. Mr. Tabler.
3. Rev. William D. Strobel, D.D.
4. Rev. Mr. Rosemuller.
5. Rev. Edwin A. Bolles, of South Carolina, in 1835.

6. Rev. Samuel Rothrock, first time, 1836.
7. Rev. Daniel Jenkins.
8. Rev. John D. Sheck, of South Carolina, 1840.
9. Rev. J. B. Anthony, 1844 to 1846.
10. Rev. J. H. Coffman, 1848.
11. Rev. Daniel I. Dreher.
12. Rev. Samuel Rothrock (second time).
13. Rev. Levi C. Groseclose, 1860 to 1865.
14. Rev. N. Aldrich, of South Carolina, 1865 to 1867.
15. Rev. Simeon Scherer, 1867 to 1872.
16. Rev. William H. Cone, of Virginia, 1870 to 1872.
17. Rev. J. G. Neiffer, of Pennsylvania, 1872 to 1876.
18. Rev. T. W. Dosh, D.D., of South Carolina, 1876 to 1877.
19. Rev. W. J. Smith, of Maryland, 1878———.

If to these nineteen we add the names of Nussmann, Ahrend, and Storch, we have a succession of twenty-two ministers that have served this church during the one hundred and nine years of its existence, an average of one minister for every five years. The church now numbers one hundred and fifty-two members, and it has been greatly strengthened in members and in resources within the last dozen years.

The present condition of the Lutheran Church in Rowan County —its churches, ministers, and membership—as gathered from the Minutes, is as follows:

The Rev. Samuel Rothrock's charge, Organ Church and Ebenezer, has three hundred members.

Rev. W. J. Smith's charge, St. John's, Salisbury, has one hundred and fifty-two members.

Rev. W. A. Lutz's charge (in Rowan), St. Enoch's Church, has three hundred and three members.

Rev. B. S. Brown's charge, Lutheran Chapel, Center Grove, and St. Paul's, has four hundred and eighty-six members.

Rev. R. L. Brown's charge, Union and Christiana, has two hundred and forty members.

Rev. H. M. Brown's charge, Bethel and Christ's Church, has one hundred and fifteen members.

Rev. V. R. Stickley's charge, St. Luke's, Salem, and Grace Church, has one hundred and eighty-one members.

Rev. J. A. Linn's charge, St. Peter's, St. Matthew's and Luther's Church, has three hundred and fifty members.

Rev. Whitson Kimball's charge (in Rowan), St. Stephen's and Gold Hill, has one hundred and fifty members. The whole making nine ministers, nineteen churches, and 2,277 communicants.

To this may be added, the Rev. J. C. Moser, a member of the Tennessee Lutheran Synod, and his three churches—Mount Moriah, St. Marks, and Phanuel—embracing one hundred and seventy-five members.

The whole summing up ten ministers, twenty-two churches, and 2,452 members. According to these statistics the Lutherans have more ministers in Rowan than the Presbyterians, Methodists, Episcopalians, and Missionary Baptists combined, and probably nearly as many churches and communicants as all the other white churches in the county. In fact, a large part of the strength of Lutheranism in North Carolina is concentrated in Rowan County.

THE INTRODUCTION AND GROWTH OF METHODISM IN ROWAN COUNTY

BY REV. H. T. HUDSON, D.D.

The Approach of Methodism Into the Rowan Section

In 1780, the Yadkin Circuit was formed, having only twenty-one members. Andrew Yeargan was the first circuit preacher sent to this new field. The church records no clue as to the boundaries of this circuit, but tradition says it embraced Stokes, Davidson, Rowan (then including Davie County), and the Surry regions. About this time the pioneers of Methodism began to preach at various points in Rowan. There being no church edifices, they were obliged to preach in private houses, barns, schoolhouses, and under bush arbors.

In 1783, Yadkin Circuit is reported as having three hundred and forty-eight members, in growth of three hundred and sixty-two in three years. In 1784, the Salisbury circuit is entered upon the minutes of the Conference, being organized into a separate pastoral charge, Jesse Lee being its pastor. Mr. Lee says he found a "society of truly affectionate Christians" in the town of Salisbury. When this society was organized he does not state, but likely it was formed between the years of 1780 and 1783.

Mr. Lee says, in his Journal: "In entering upon this field of labor, he was greatly encouraged at meeting large congregations of anxious hearers at all of his appointments. Gracious influences attended his preaching, to the comfort of believers and the awakening of sinners; his own soul was greatly blessed while striving to bless others." While preaching "at Hern's" his own soul was filled so full of love that he burst "into a flood of tears, and there were few dry eyes in the house." "At C. Ledbetter's the hearers were much wrought upon." "At Cole's the congregation was so large we had to go under the shade of trees, and the friends wept greatly." "At Jersey Meeting-house, Colonel G.'s wife came to me, and began to cry and say, I am the worst creature in the world; my heart is so hard I don't know what to do—and begged me to pray for her."

"At Costner's an old man rose up and spoke in a melting manner with tears streaming from his eyes: I am almost ready to depart this life, and am not ready to die, and you may judge how I feel."

The force and pathetic power of Mr. Lee's sermons may be seen from these brief extracts from his Journal. Only one church edifice is mentioned—The Jersey Meeting-house, located somewhere on the eastern side of the Yadkin River. The church in which the old pioneers preached most was the temple of nature. Its roof was the blue firmament, its floor the green earth, swept by the winds—its lamp the radiant sun—its seats the rocks, stumps, and logs. The voice of the preacher mingled with the free songs of the birds, the splash of the rippling streams, the neighing of horses tied in the bushes, and the cries of penitent souls.

Jesse Lee

was one of the eminent Methodist pioneers, "a man of vigorous though unpolished mind, of rare popular eloquence and tireless energy, an itinerant evangelist from the British Province to Florida." He labored as presiding elder thirty-five years, was chaplain to Congress, the first Methodist American Historian of his church, begged money in the South to build the first Methodist church in the New England States, where he became the chief founder of Methodism. He was the peer of Asbury and Dr. Coke in talent and fruitfulness. He died gloriously shouting, "Glory, Glory, Glory," in 1816; and was buried in the city of Baltimore.

The prominence of Methodism in Salisbury and the region round about seems to be indicated from the fact that Bishop Asbury preached in that town, 1785, and held two annual Conferences there —one in 1786, and the other in 1787—the first Conference held in the western part of the State.

Hope Hull followed Mr. Lee on the Salisbury circuit, in 1785. He was a man of singular power in the pulpit, and shares the honor of laying the foundation of Methodism in this region. On one occasion, he was invited by way of fun-making to a ball. He went—was invited to dance. He took the floor, remarking: "I never engage in any kind of business without first asking the blessings of God, *so let us pray.*" Down he went upon his knees, and such a prayer rolled out from his eloquent lips as shook the whole party with terror. The gay dancers were thunderstruck. Some fled from the house, others began to pray for mercy. Hull arose from his knees, gave out an appointment to preach there four weeks hence, and quietly retired. When the appointed time came around, Hull was there, and preached a most effective sermon to a large congregation. From that prayer in the ballroom a wide extended revival began and spread in all directions.

Introduction of Methodism into Davie County, which was then a Part of Rowan

"Beale's Meeting-house was probably the first Methodist church built in this section. It is said to have been built during the Revolutionary War, in 1780. It was located on the 'Old Georgia Road,' near Anderson's Bridge over Hunter Creek. 'Timber Ridge,' a schoolhouse located between Smith Grove and Olive Branch, was one of the early preaching places for the Methodists in Davie County. 'Whitaker's Church' also claims to be the first. So the old church four miles east of Mocksville, known as the 'Dutch Meeting-house,' is put down as among the first in all that country." "Bethel Church," first located about a mile east of Mocksville, afterwards moved to Mocksville, is one of the old churches built in the country.

It is very likely that Andrew Yeargan, sent on the Yadkin circuit, 1780, was the first regular pastor of all that section known as the "Forks of the Yadkin," and laid the foundation of the churches already mentioned. At this period the country was sparsely settled, the people rude and almost wild as the native deer. At Beale's Church, tradition says the preacher, growing warm during his sermon, walked down into the congregation and laid his hand upon the head of an old man, saying, "My friend, don't you want to go to heaven?" To which the frightened man replied: "Man, for God's sake, go off and let me alone; I don't live about here, I came from away up in the mountains." At the same church, in 1795, a quarterly meeting was held, and to the question: "How much of the preacher's salary has been paid?" Charles Ledbetter, the pastor, presented one pair of socks as the full amount up to that time.

John Cooper, Enoch Matson, George Kimble, Henry Ogburn, William Connor, Lemuel Green, Barnabas McHenry, followed Yeargan, and did a good work in establishing Methodism in this section. After these came such men as Reuben Ellis and John Tunnel, men of gifts and piety. About this time, James Parks appears as a preacher and teacher. He had charge of the first Methodist school founded in this section, and known as "Cokesbury School." It was located on the Yadkin River near Phelps' Ferry. This school after a short period was discontinued, and the house used for a church. Parks moved to Jonesville and established a school there. He had four sons who became ministers, one of whom, Martin P. Parks, became one of the most brilliant pulpit orators of his day.

In 1800, Yadkin circuit numbered four hundred and seventy-nine members, and Salisbury circuit four hundred and ninety-four —nine hundred and seventy-three in the two. The year of 1799 is famous for the introduction and prevalence of camp-meetings. They began in the West under the united labors of the McGee brothers—one a Methodist, the other a Presbyterian minister. At this date, these mammoth meetings were union meetings of the Methodists and Presbyterians. Drs. James Hall and L. L. Wilson often labored in them. The first camp-meetings held in Davie were in 1805, at Olive Branch Church, and at Walnut Grove on Dutchman's Creek. At these meetings great revivals broke out and swept over the country as fire in dry stubble. The result was the membership of the church grew rapidly, and new church edifices sprang up all over the Yadkin Valley. Schoolhouses and a higher grade of civilization followed in the wake of the enlightening gospel.

In 1807, Iredell circuit, embracing Iredell County, was set off from the Yadkin and Salisbury circuits, into a new pastoral charge. As the gospel spread, other circuits were formed. In 1831-33, Stokes, Randolph, Davidson, and Wilkes circuits were formed. In 1834, Salisbury and Lexington constituted a pastoral charge, Thales McDonald being pastor. In 1836, Salisbury was made a station, R. O. Burton being pastor. In 1836, Mocksville circuit is made. In 1845, Jonesville circuit was set off. In 1848, Taylorsville was set off, and in 1850, Forsyth. The formation of these pastoral charges indicates the growth of Methodism in the valley of the Yadkin. Just one hundred years ago, Methodism entered this section and began its work of evangelization, with the capital in hand of twenty-one communicants and one preacher. Out of this mustard seed so small in beginning has grown a gospel tree, whose fruitful branches spread over a large scope of country.

The Results

Salisbury station, Salisbury circuit, Mooresville circuit, Mocksville and Davie circuits, Iredell, Alexander, Wilkes, Yadkin, Surry, Mount Airy, Davidson, Stokes, Forsyth, Winston, Uwharrie, Statesville, Statesville circuit, and the pastoral charges which have grown out of the original circuits of Salisbury and Yadkin with thirty-seven local preachers, 8,200 members, 4,294 Sunday-school scholars, one hundred four churches, seven parsonages—the churches and parsonages valued at $88,650. These charges paid, in 1876, for religious purposes, $9,219.40.

Methodist Ministers Born and Reared in Rowan County

Rev. Moses Brock

was a native of Rowan, now Davie County; joined the Virginia-North Carolina Conference in 1820. For more than forty years he bore a conspicuous part in building up Methodism in Virginia and North Carolina. When the occasion called out his full strength, "he was eloquent and eminently successful" as a preacher. He was naturally witty, full of good humor, eccentric, and original. He finished his useful days in Tennessee, where he died in good old age.

Rev. Richard Neely

was a native of Rowan, born 1802, entered the Tennessee Conference in 1821. He was a successful missionary among the Cherokee Indians. Died 1828. "He was a man of good mind, pleasing manners, a pious and useful minister."

Rev. John Rich

a native of Davie, born 1815, joined conference in 1840. "A peerless preacher and sweet-spirited Christian." Died in Davidson County in 1851.

Rev. S. M. Frost, D.D.

born in Davie, joined conference in 1846. He labored many years in North Carolina as an eminent minister and successful teacher. He is now living and preaching in Pennsylvania.

Rev. L. L. Hendren

born in Davie in 1822, joined conference in 1845. He is now an influential member of the North Carolina Conference, and one of the most promient presiding-elders in the connection.

Rev. H. T. Hudson, D.D.

born in Davie 1823, entered conference in 1851, and is now pastor of the Methodist Church at Rockingham, N. C.

Rev. Abram Weaver

a native of Rowan, entered conference in 1851, located in 1860, moved to Missouri, and joined the Baptist Church.

Rev. James F. Smoot

born in Davie, joined conference in 1856, located in 1875, is now a teacher in Iredell.

Rev. S. D. Peeler

born in Rowan, entered conference in 1854, is now pastor of Yadkin circuit.

Rev. Calvin Plyer

born in Rowan, entered conference in 1861, located in 1873, is now living in Salisbury.

Rev. Wm. C. Wilson

born in Davie, entered conference in 1863, is still a minister in good standing, though at present is without any pastoral charge, because of family afflictions.

Rev. Wm. C. Call

born in Davie, joined conference in 1867, is now in charge of Snow Hill circuit.

Rev. Leonidas W. Crawford

born in Rowan, entered conference in 1868, and is now stationed in Salisbury.

Rev. James Wilson

born in Davie, entered conference in 1871, is now in charge of Mount Airy Academy.

After this brief and imperfect sketch, the writer desires to append a few remarks.

First, the late Peter Doub, D.D., did more than any other minister to instill the peculiar doctrines of Methodism into the minds of the people living in Rowan and Davie Counties. He preached all over this country for many years to vast assemblies attending the camp-meetings and quarterly meetings.

Rev. John Tillett did more than any other man in putting down intemperance and distilleries in Davie County. Rev. Baxter Clegg was the most useful and successful teacher. Out of his academy, located at Mocksville, came many useful ministers, lawyers, physicians, and citizens. Methodism, both in Rowan and Davie, is also much indebted to such ministers as: Revs. J. W. Childs, Abram Penn, James Reid, Joseph Goodman, S. D. Bumpass, William Barringer, N. F. Reid, D.D.—all gone to their heavenly reward; and a host of others whose names we have not space to mention.

THE METHODIST CHURCH OF SALISBURY

The Rev. J. J. Renn, late pastor of the Salisbury Methodist Episcopal Church, writes concerning its history as follows:

The Rev. Peter Doub, D.D., was presiding elder in this district during the years 1825-29. During these four years 2,738 souls were converted at meetings which he held in person, and more than seven thousand in the bounds of the district. About that time ministers from both the Virginia and South Carolina Conferences preached occasionally at the courthouse in Salisbury, among whom were Moorman, Travis, Tate, Stork, Martin (who is still living in South Carolina), and others. This, with the deep revival influence then working, resulted in the building of a Methodist church in the town of Salisbury.

The first Methodist church in Salisbury was organized in November, 1831, with thirteen members, four of whom are still living (1880), viz.: Miss Adelaide Clary (now Mrs. Rowzee), of Salisbury; John C. Palmer, now of Raleigh; and James Glover and wife, now of Davidson County. One name of the others is lost. The rest were Mrs. John C. Palmer, Mrs. Mary Hardy, Miss Margaret Shaver, Mrs. Slater, Mrs. Samuel Fraley, Alexander Biles, Mrs. Eunice Cowan, and Miss Sarah Bailey.

This church was in the Virginia Conference. Charles P. Moorman was the first preacher in charge. The first Quarterly Conference was appointed to be held in the courthouse, in November, 1832, but the Presbyterian brethren kindly offered the use of their church, which was gratefully accepted, and so the first Methodist Conference ever convened in Salisbury was held in the Presbyterian church, presided over by that singular man, "the stern, the inflexible, the devoted, the self-poised, the brave, the witty, the fearless Methodist preacher, Moses Brock," who was at that time presiding elder of the district.

At that Quarterly Conference, money was raised, and a comfortable wooden church was completed early in the following year (1833). With the exception of one year, the church was a part of the Salisbury circuit, until 1845. In 1834 it was made a station, and served by Rev. R. O. Burton. It then went back to the circuit. During this time (between 1833 and 1845), it had for pastors Revs. Messrs. T. McDonald, Tinnen, Yarrell, and others. Rev. Thomas S. Campbell traveled this circuit in 1835.

In 1845, it became a permanent station, with Rev. S. Milton Frost, pastor. The presiding elder was the Rev. Joseph Goodman. This year there was an extensive revival, and about seventy-five were added to the church. There was another revival in 1848, under Rev. L. Shell, which greatly strengthened the church.

EPISCOPACY IN ROWAN COUNTY

BY JOHN S. HENDERSON, ESQ.

England is the only European country which failed to establish her church, in all its perfectness, amongst her colonies. In Spanish America, as early as 1649, Davila estimates the staff of the Spanish church to have been—one patriarch, six archbishops, thirty-two bishops, three hundred forty-six prebends, two abbots, five royal chaplains, eight hundred forty convents, besides a vast number of inferior clergy. Religion was almost entirely neglected in the early settlement of the American colonies of England. Some form of the Christian religion was nominally patronized, and established by law in each colony—but very little attention was paid to giving to the people full and genuine religious privileges. The non-Episcopalians were generally much better off than their brethren of the Church of England. The latter were never allowed to have in any colony either a synod or a bishop. There was no power of obtaining Episcopal ordination in America. Candidates for the ministry were required to cross the Atlantic to receive Holy Orders. This was both costly and full of peril. One in five of all who set out returned no more. It is stated that, in the year 1724, about twenty young men, graduates from Yale College, who wished to obtain Episcopal ordination, being discouraged at the trouble and charge of going to England, either abandoned the ministry altogether, or accepted non-Episcopal ordination. The non-Episcopal denominations each possessed their own system in perfection. "It is hard," was the complaint of the "Churchmen" or "Episcopalians" at the time, "that these large and increasing dispersions of the true Protestant English Church should not be provided with bishops, when our enemies, the Roman Catholics of France and Spain, find their account in it to provide them for theirs. Even Canada, which is scarce bigger than some of our provinces, has her bishops, not to mention the Moravians, who also have theirs. The poor church of America is worse off than any of her adversaries. She has nobody upon the spot to comfort or confirm her children—nobody to ordain such as are willing to serve." The colonies were all nominally under the jurisdiction of the Bishop of London, who lived more than three thousand miles away, and who never pretended to visit America at all. Nearly all the Episcopal ministers were missionaries in the pay of the Society for the Propagation of the Gospel in Foreign Parts. So far as religious advantages were concerned North Carolina seems to have been somewhat worse off than any other colony, but there was more religious liberty and toleration—and there never was any such thing known here as religious persecution. All Christian denominations, during the seventeenth and the greater part of the eighteenth centuries, believed that some form of Christianity should be established by law as the church of the State. Such a thing as the perfect religious toleration and freedom we now enjoy was then unknown anywhere. The Church of England, until the period of the Revolution of 1776, was the religious establishment of the Province of North Carolina, and up to that date there was no period when the adherents of that church did not constitute at least one-half of the population. But there were very few clergy. In 1764, Governor Dobbs reported that there were then but six clergymen in the Province, although there were twenty-nine parishes, and each parish contained a whole county. Governor Tryon, in 1767, in his report of the state of religion in the Province, "observed with pleasure that religion was making a very regular progress." He recommended "the greatest caution in the choice of gentlemen sent over as ministers, the inhabitants of this Province being strict inquisitors into the moral character and behavior of the clergy; and that the latter will attract but little esteem and do but little good if their lives are not truly exemplary and agreeable to their profession." In 1770, the number of the clergy had increased to eighteen, while the population of the Province probably exceeded two hundred thousand.

I have been unable to ascertain whether there ever was a fully organized parish in Rowan County before the Revolutionary War. Rowan was erected into a county and parish in 1753, and the name of the latter was

St. Luke's Parish

Before the year 1768, it is probable that ministers of the Church of England may have occasionally visited the county, but there is no tradition that any minister of that church had theretofore been located in the parish. This seems to be plain from the following extract of a petition from sundry inhabitants of the county of Rowan.

"To the Governor, his Majesty's Honorable Council, and the House of Burgesses of North Carolina:

"The petitioners complain: 1. That his Majesty's most dutiful and loyal subjects in this county, who adhere to the liturgy and profess the doctrines of the Church of England as by law established, have not the privileges and advantages which the rubrics and canons of the church allow and enjoin on all her members. That the Acts of Assembly calculated to forming a regular vestry in all the counties have never in this county produced their happy fruits. That the county of Rowan, above all counties in the Province, lies under great disadvantages, as her inhabitants are composed almost of all nations of Europe, and instead of uniformity in doctrine and worship they have a medley of most of the religious tenets that have lately appeared in the world; from dread of submitting to the national church, should a lawful vestry be established, elect such of their own community as evade the Acts of Assembly and refuse the oaths, whence we can never expect the regular enlivening beams of the Gospel." Williamson, in his History of North Carolina, from which I have copied the above (p. 258), makes the following comments of his own: "The petitioners go on to pray that means be taken for compelling persons chosen vestrymen to take the oaths prescribed, or such other means as may produce a regular lawful vestry.' There were thirty-four subscribers to the petition; six of them made their marks, and some of the other signatures are hardly legible. When thirty-four such persons could propose that six or seven hundred should be taxed for their accommodation, they certainly had need of gospel that teaches humility." The "humility" which these petitioners had need of was universally lacking in the Christianity of those times. But it is doubtful whether these petitioners proposed to do what Williamson charges them with—that is to "tax" other people "for their accommodation." The proposition to lay a tax does not seem to be even implied from any of the language of the petition. Because they wished a "lawful vestry" is no proof that they desired the vestry to levy and collect taxes for religious purposes. And because some of the petitioners "made their marks" is no proof that they were utterly ignorant, uninfluential, and disreputable. A great many very respectable and intelligent people in those times were unable to read or write. I have been unable to ascertain the names of the signers of this petition. I think probable, however, that it was chiefly signed by residents of the town of Salisbury, and that it therefore represented but a mere fraction of the "church people" of the county. The date of this petition is not given, but I am inclined to think it must have been some time between the years 1764 and 1768. Salisbury, according to the current tradition, was originally settled by a few English churchmen from the cathedral city of Salisbury in England, and owes its name to that circumstance.

It is impossible to estimate the number of people in the county who were adherents of the Established Church—but I think it probable that they amounted to at least one-fourth or one-third of the whole population. A great many of the old families were undoubtedly members of the Church of England. Nearly all the English people and their descendants naturally belonged to that Church. So did the Welsh. More than half of the Protestants of Ireland have always owed allegiance to the same religious faith. I think it probable that the following-named persons, living in this county before the Revolution, were Church of England people: John Frohock, William Giles, Matthew Locke, Maxwell Chambers, James Macay, John Dunn, William Temple Coles, Benjamin Boothe Boote, James Carter, Hugh Forster, William Churton, Richard Viggers, William Steele, Thomas Frohock, Matthew Troy, James Kerr, Daniel Little, Alexander Martin, Francis Locke, James Dobbin, Alexander Dobbin, Arichibald Craige, David Craige, James Brandon, John Nesbit, Anthony Newnan, James Smith, and Richmond Pearson. The Howard family were also here then, and were members of the English Church.

Very little is known about the efforts that were made to organize Episcopal congregations in this county during the period before the Revolution. The tradition is that the Rev. Theodore Drane Draig came to Salisbury in the year 1768 or 1769, and almost immediately succeeded in having a chapel erected in the Jersey Settlement, about nine or ten miles east of Salisbury—somewhere near where Dr. William B. Meares now resides. Dr. Draig remained here about four years, but failed to organize the parish upon a legal and permanent foundation. "For on Easter Monday, 1770, when an election, according to the then law of the Province, was to be held for the purpose of electing vestrymen, the Presbyterians set up candidates of their own and elected them, not with any design that they should act as vestrymen but solely for the purpose of preventing the Episcopalians from electing such as would have done so." The Rev. Robert J. Miller relates this anecdote on the authority of Dr. Anthony Newnan, John Cowan, Sr., and others of the old people of Salisbury. Mr. Miller makes the following comments of his own: "This (election and its consequences) caused much bitter animosity to spring up between the parties, and so, much discouraged the reverend gentleman. Perhaps the approach of the Revolutionary War had its influence also, but be that as it may, after a four years' fruitless effort to organize an Episcopal congregation in this section, he left it as he found it, without any." Dr. Draig was a great friend of Mr. John Dunn, who is said to have been instrumental in persuading him to come to this parish. The usual place for holding the services in Salisbury was the large house of Mr. Dunn, situated on what is now the northeast corner of Innes and Church Streets—on the same lot where Mr. Philip P. Meroney resides. Mr. Dunn is said to have been a good Churchman. His house was decorated with evergreens as regularly as Christmas Day would come.

Governor Tryon, being in Salisbury on the twentieth day of May, 1767, went into the office of John Frohock, Clerk of the County Court and Register, "and examined all the registry books, and fully approved of the method they were kept in. Colonels Palmer and Waddell were in company with the Governor. Colonel Palmer found lying in one of the books a copy of a call to the Rev. (Richard) Sankey, read it to the Governor, and at His Excellency's request, took it with him to take a copy thereof." (See Register's book 6, p. 397.) The clerk's office was then kept in the house of Mr. William Steele. I think that this call may have been made by a vestry of St. Luke's Parish. Elections for vestrymen were held every three years, and I suppose the polls were usually opened at the proper times. It is probable, therefore, that elections were held on Easter Monday, in the years 1758, 1761, 1764, 1767, and 1770. Mr. Sankey seems to have been in Rowan as early as the year 1758—for on the fifth day of September, 1758, he married John Braley to Sarah Carruth, of Rowan County (Register's book 7, p. 302). He is said to have been a Virginian and a Presbyterian. But I think it probable that he had received Episcopal ordination. I can find out nothing satisfactory about him. He must have returned to Virginia before the date of Governor Tryon's visit.

In those days the feeling was well-nigh unanimous that the Christian religion must be established and maintained as the law of the State. Nothing proves this more plainly than the "instructions" given to the delegates from Mecklenburg County in 1775.

"13. You are instructed to assent and consent to the establishment of the Christian religion as contained in the Scriptures of the Old and New Testaments, and more briefly comprised in the Thirty-nine Articles of the Church of England, excluding the thirty-seventh article, together with all the articles excepted and not to be imposed on Dissenters by the act of toleration, and clearly held forth in the Confession of Faith compiled by the Assembly of Divines at Westminster, to be the religion of the State, to the utter exclusion forever of all and every other (falsely so-called) religion, whether Pagan or Papal, and that the full, free, and peaceable enjoyment thereof be secured to all and every consistent member of the State as their inalienable right as free men, without the imposition of rites and ceremonies, whether claiming civil or ecclesiastic power for their source, and that a confession and profession of the religion so established shall be necessary in qualifying any person for public trust in the State. If this should not be confirmed, protest and and remonstrate.

"14. You are instructed to oppose to the utmost any particular church or set of clergymen being invested with power to decree rites and ceremonies, and to decide in controversies of faith, to be submitted to under the influence of penal laws. You are also to oppose the establishment of any mode of worship to be supported to the opposition of the rights of conscience, together with the destruction of private property. You are moreover to oppose the establishing an ecclesiastic supremacy in the sovereign authority of the State. You are to oppose the toleration of the Popish idolatrous worship. If this should not be confirmed, protest and remonstrate."

It is somewhat remarkable that the North Carolina patriots of 1776 never protested against any evils out of the existing religious establishment. This is conclusive proof that they did not consider an established church an evil at all; and that the ecclesiastical laws then on the statute books must have been very mildly and rarely enforced.

All persons holding office in the Province of North Carolina before the Revolution were required, in addition to the usual oath of office, to take certain oaths appointed by Act of Parliament for the qualification of public officers, and to repeat and subscribe "the test." The latter oath made the renunciation of the doctrine of transsubstantiation a necessary qualification for office. The declaration seems to have been repeated and subscribed every time the Court met. I find the following entry on one of the old Superior Court dockets:

"North Carolina, Salisbury, to wit:

"I, A. B., do declare that I do believe in my conscience that there is not any transsubtantiation in the sacrament of the Lord's Supper, or in the elements of bread and wine at or after the consecration thereof, by any person whatsoever, etc.

"(Signed): James Hassell, C. J.
Edmund Fanning, A. J.
William Hooper
freland burn
his
Michael x burn
mark

"September Superior Court, 1767."

I never knew before that Edmund Fanning, the Hillsboro Tory, was an Associate Judge of the Superior Court. Wheeler does not mention the fact in his "Sketches." Fanning presided over the Court at Salisbury frequently, as the records abundantly prove.

I have not been able to locate the exact spot where Dr. Draig's chapel was, in the Jersey Settlement. Miss Chrissie Beard says "the congregation drank out of Mrs. Kelly's spring." She thinks it was very near the spot where Dr. Meares now lives. I have heard from several sources that there is a deed on record conveying a lot of land to certain trustees for the use of the Episcopal Church—supposed to be the very ground where the Jersey chapel was built—but I have not yet been able to find the deed referred to, not knowing the names either of the grantor or of the grantees.

Among the names of the old ante-Revolutionary Churchmen was Alexander Martin, who lived in Salisbury until Guilford County was erected. He had a brother who was a clergyman of the Church of England, and lived in Virginia. The former was quite a distinguished man. He was a prominent lawyer by profession, and was frequently commissioned by the crown to hold the District Court at Salisbury. He presided over the Court which was held on the first day of June, 1775, during the sitting of which Captain Jack passed through on his way to the Continental Congress at Philadelphia, with the Mecklenburg "Resolves" of the thirty-first of May. He was a colonel in the Continental Army, and fought under LaFayette at the battle of Brandywine. He was elected Governor of the State in 1782, and again in 1789. He was also Governor in 1781, during the enforced absence of Governor Burke, who had been captured by the Tory Colonel Fannen, of Chatham. He never married. The last office he held was that of United States Senator, to which he was elected in 1799. He died in 1807.

The Revolutionary War dispersed nearly all the Episcopal congregations in the State. The majority of the clergy, being Englishmen by birth and sympathy, and being deprived of all means of support, returned to the land of their nativity. "Still there were some four or five ministers who remained steady at their posts, ever ready to administer the ordinances of the Church and consolation to all who applied for them at their hands. These were the Rev. Messrs. Pettigrew, Cuppels, Blount, and Micklejohn; perhaps also, the Rev. Mr. Taylor, in Halifax. Seed was yet left, and a few praying Simeons and Annas still remained." (See letter of Rev. Mr. Miller, published by Rev. Dr. Hawks, dated April 15, 1830.)

I think it doubtful whether any of these clergymen ever extended their ministrations further west than the county of Orange, where Mr. Micklejohn resided. For many years after the war of the Revolution the children and friends of Episcopacy, few in numbers and feeble in influence, lived in a state of religious destitution and in a condition of despondency bordering on despair. It was not until the year 1790 that an effort was made to revive their drooping spirits. A convention met in Tarboro, organized a "standing committee," and elected delegates to the General Convention. Shortly thereafter, the Rev. Dr. Halling, of Newbern, obtained the necessary credentials, and was ordained by Bishop Madison, of Virginia. A second convention was held in Tarboro in the year 1793; and a third was held in the same town on the last Wednesday in May, 1794; when and where the Rev. Charles Pettigrew was elected Bishop of the Diocese of North Carolina. For some reason satisfactory to himself the Rev. Mr. Pettigrew never made application for consecration. "It is a melancholy reflection," says the Rev. Mr. Miller, "for me to be obliged to say that no beneficial effects resulted from all these efforts to revive the spirit and cause of Episcopacy in the State of North Carolina. Yet such was the fact. They were by no means commensurate with the wishes and hopes of its real friends; for the prospect rather became more dense in gloom. Under the pressure of many complicated difficulties, our wonder will cease that the efforts of the few remaining friends of the Episcopal Church in this State had so little effect, and that a declination instead of a revival took place. The clergy were not only discouraged and dispirited, but were obliged in most cases to turn their attention to other objects in order to procure the necessaries of life. Twenty-three years the stream of time rolled along, and no star appeared in any quarter of our horizon to cheer the gloom that had enveloped our hopes and our spirits. From 1794 to 1817, all was dark and dreary, yet the great Redeemer had not forgot his gracious promise. It was then that the daystar from on high visited us in mercy, when two heavensent heralds of the everlasting Gospel came to Wilmington and Fayetteville, and there laid the foundation of the restoration of the Episcopal Church and cause in North Carolina." The "heralds" referred to were the Rev. Messrs. Adam Empie and Bethel Judd.

I cannot better describe the growth and progress of Episcopacy in Rowan County than by giving brief biographical sketches of the ministers who have officiated within its bounds. I will first begin with the name of

Robert Johnstone Miller

He was a Scotchman by birth, and was born and brought up, until his fifteenth year, in the Episcopal Church of Scotland, under the ministry of the venerable Bishop Rail, who was upwards of eighty years old when young Miller left Scotland and came to America. At what time he came to this country I do not know; probably a short time before the Revolutionary War. He resided in Virginia for some years, and about the year 1784 connected himself with the Methodists, who, Mr. Miller says, at that time professed to be members of the Episcopal Church. In the same year he "rode with Dr. Coke to a conference in Franklin County, this State." Dr. Coke was an ordained priest of the Church of England who had previously been ordained a bishop by Wesley. Mr. Miller says that, although dissatisfied with the Methodist system—he himself being thoroughly persuaded of the truth of the Apostolic Succession—he nevertheless continued with them through the year 1785, in the Tar River circuit, where in some measure he lost his health; for the recovery of which he came up into the western part of the State. He says that during his continuance with the Methodists they always treated him with respect, and when he withdrew himself from any connection with them, in 1786, "they publicly declared that they had no charge against him whatever, and that it was his own voluntary act, in consequence of his disapprobation of their system and rules." About this time the people of the congregation of Whitehaven, comprehending Whitehaven and the lower and upper Smyrna, in Lincoln County, applied to him to take charge of them as a congregation, in the capacity of a lay-reader merely. The people of his congregation were chiefly immigrants from Pennsylvania and Virginia. They were a mixed people—German, English, Irish, and some Scots originally; but at that time very destitute of any regular religious instruction. The most of them and their fathers were and had been members of the Episcopal Church. Mr. Miller agreed to become their public reader, to catechize their children, and to bury their dead. Both he and the congregation mutually resolved and agreed to adhere to the Episcopal Church, to which they were alike bound by the strong ties of heredity prepossession, and of love and affection strengthened by conviction. A congregation was organized, church wardens and a vestry were chosen, and an act of incorporation obtained from the General Assembly. Prayer books were scarce. The congregation had a few English ones, and he procured two of the first edition from Philadelphia. He also had printed in Salisbury a catechism, to which he added an explanation of the two covenants, and the feasts of the Christian Church, together with some religious terms not generally understood. The most of the congregation were under the necessity of receiving the sacraments from the hands of a Lutheran minister who lived in the vicinity. With him, Mr. Miller formed an intimate acquaintance, and with his ministerial brethren also who lived in the adjacent counties of Rowan, Guilford, and Randolph. Mr. Miller says they pressed him with the plea of necessity to accept ordination from their hands, mentioning that the Rev. Dr. Pilmour had done so during the time of the Revolutionary War. A number of Presbyterian clergy with whom he was intimate recommended the same course; and his congregation earnestly requested him to accept such ordination, assuring him that they would be perfectly satisfied with his ministrations. He consented to receive, ordination from them, not as a Lutheran minister, but as an Episcopalian. In the letters of orders which they gave him, they bound him to be subject to the discipline and rules of the Protestant Episcopal Church in the United States. In administering the ordinances and offices of the Prayer book, Mr. Miller says he paid as strict attention to the rubrics as circumstances and situation would admit.

In the year 1803, at the request of the congregation and of the Lutheran ministry and their congregations, and after several consultations held for the purpose, a convention met in Salisbury, and formed a union and constitution, which adopted the leading features of the General Constitution of the Protestant Episcopal Church in the United States. Under this constitution, which was drawn up by Mr. Miller as aforesaid, he continued in union with the Lutherans until the year 1818. He says, "our success in introducing order and regularity throughout our charges, and in extending their boundaries, was far beyond any expectation entertained by us at the commencement." In the year 1794, Mr. Miller was invited by the Episcopal clergy of the State to attend the convention which assembled at Tarboro in May of that year, and was also furnished with a certificate that he had been elected a member of the standing committee of the Diocese. Mr. Miller attended the convention, and took with him a member of the laity of Whitehaven Parish, who represented the parish in the convention. The organization of the congregation of St. Michael's Church, Iredell County; Christ Church, Rowan County, and St. Luke's Church, Salisbury, arose in some measure at least from Mr. Miller's labors amongst them for more than thirty years, before either parish was received into regular union with the Diocese. Mr. Miller says, Christ's Church was organized as a congregation during his "connection with the Lutheran Synod; and St. Luke's, Salisbury, by our lamented and venerated Father in God, Bishop Ravenscroft, Monday, September 8, 1823. Miss Chrissie Beard—now in her eighty-second year—one of the most highly respected ladies of Salisbury, says Mr. Miller also preached at a log church, about five miles above town, on the old Wilkesboro Road. This church was built for Mr. Miller by Mrs. Elizabeth Kelly, John Howard, and other neighbors; and Episcopal services were frequently held there. The same lady also says that she remembers perfectly well that her uncle, Lewis Beard, when she was a child, went to Charleston, and brought back with him a number of catechisms, which were eagerly sought for and highly prized by all the Episcopal families, who studied them attentively themselves, and made their children learn them. The introduction of these catechisms must have been some time about the year 1806. In 1818 the long declining and almost obliterated cause of Episcopacy began to revive in this State. "In that year," says the Rev. Mr. Miller, "the beloved and Rev. Adam Empie, who was then the rector of St. James' Church, Wilmington, and one of the honored and principal instruments under God of the blessed and I may say glorious work, entered into a correspondence with me touching my standing in the Church, and the state of religion in this section of the country. To him I stated my situation, and that of the people then under my care, and their and my connection with the Lutherans. This union was from first to last our own individual act. And at the time when I was ordained by them, I had expressly reserved my right and liberty, with those under my care, to return and unite in full union and without any impediment, with the Episcopal Church, whenever it should please God to revive her in this State." The result was that he attended the fifth annual Convention of the Diocese, held in Raleigh, April 28, 1821. It was the third convention over which Bishop Richard Channing Moore, of Virginia, had presided. Mr. Miller, at this convention, was ordained by Bishop Moore, a deacon and priest—the first in the morning and the second in the evening of the same day, to wit: May 2, 1821. It is reported that when Bishop Moore read Mr. Miller's certificate of ordination, he said to him, *"you belong to us."* This anecdote is told as if Mr. Miller for the first time then conceived it his duty to obtain Episcopal ordination. But it is plain from what has been said that he had never faltered in his purpose to obtain Holy Orders from the Church of his fathers, whenever a favorable opportunity presented itself. He had never ceased to consider himself a member of that Church. I have not access to the earliest journals of the Diocese, but I have no doubt Mr. Miller became a candidate for Orders shortly after the correspondence with the Rev. Mr. Empie began.

The Rev. Mr. Miller, even after he had resolved to obtain Episcopal ordination, still continued to administer the sacraments, and to preach to the congregations under his care.

There is an old record of Christ Church, in the handwriting of Mr. Miller, from which several of the first leaves are missing. From this it appears that Mr. Miller was in the habit of administering the holy rite of confirmation to all who would receive it at his hands. He administered confirmation for the first time in Christ Church, Rowan County, some time previous to the year 1820. The record concerning it is missing. The date of his second confirmation is the third Sunday in April, sixteenth day, 1820, when he confirmed twenty-four persons.

The following record is preserved of the early communions in the same church.

Fourth communion, date not given, fifty-one communicants; fifth, April 16, 1820, forty-four communicants; 1820, fifty-eight; 18—, number not given.

The next communion was after Mr. Miller had received Episcopal ordination, November 4, 1821—thirty-six communicants, with this note—"day very unfavorable, a number that had given in their names unable to attend. Collected $2.96 1-4. (Signed) Robert J. Miller, Rector."

Fourth Sunday in May, 1822, entered as the Seventh communion —though it must have been the ninth—twenty-four communicants; eight (?), July 3, 1823, forty-eight communicants; tenth (?), Sunday, August 21, 1825, fifty-one communicants. At the convention of 1821, Christ Church was admitted into union with the Diocese. Allmand Hall attended as the first delegate. This gentleman was the ancestor of quite a number of distinguished Episcopal families in North Carolina. One of his daughters married Mr. Chambers McConnaughey of this county. Mrs. McConnaughey is still living, and has always been a devoted Christian and churchwoman. One of her daughters married Dr. John L. Henderson, whose family reside in Concord, and are members of the new Episcopal congregation there. Another daughter married Dr. Thomas Hill, recently a vestryman of St. Luke's Parish, but who has removed to Goldsboro. A daughter of Mr. Allmand Hall married Dr. William McKoy, of Clinton, Sampson County, the father of the Hon. Allmand A. McKoy—one of the most capable and acceptable Judges of the Superior Court now on the bench.

The Rev. Mr. Miller removed to Burke County, and took up his residence at St. Mary's Grove, a short time before the year 1821. During that year St. Andrew's Church was organized as a parish, and Mr. Miller became its rector. Notwithstanding his removal to Burke County (now Caldwell), Mr. Miller did not entirely lose sight of his flock in Iredell, Rowan, and Lincoln Counties, but for several years continued to make periodical visitations from time to time of the congregations and families committed to his care. He is remembered with great affection and esteem by some of the older people—as coming down on such occasions, preaching at the little churches and other places, catechizing the children and baptizing a great many, distributing the bread of life to the faithful, visiting the Episcopal families as he had opportunity, and like some other old gentlemen of that day wearing the old-fashioned knee-breeches.

St. Peter's Church, Lexington (then of Rowan), was admitted into union with the Diocese at the (Raleigh) convention of 1822—delegate, Alexander Caldcleugh. The delegate from Christ Church was Benton A. Reeves.

The eighth annual convention of the Diocese assembled in Salisbury, in the old Lutheran Church, in the spring of 1823—seven clergymen being present. The Revs. Gottlieb Shober and Daniel Scherer, and Col. Henry Ratz, delegates from the Lutheran Synod, were in attendance as honorary members of the convention, in pursuance of articles of agreement between the convention and the Synod. The delegates from Christ Church were John Cowan, Benjamin Lightell, and Samuel Fleming; from St. Peter's Church, Lexington, James R. Dodge, Dr. William R. Holt, and Dr. Willliam Dobson.

The Rev. John Stark Ravenscroft, of Virginia, was elected the first Bishop of North Carolina. He was consecrated to the Episcopate May 23, 1823. On Saturday evening, September 6, 1823, Bishop Ravenscroft preached on Confirmation in the old courthouse in Salisbury (services being held there by request). On the next day he preached, both morning and evening, in the Lutheran Church; administered the Holy Communion to about forty persons—one-third of whom were colored; and confirmed thirteen persons, among whom were Miss Chrissie Beard, Mrs. Eleanor Faust, Mrs. Susanna Beard, Mrs. Elizabeth Kelly, Mrs. Mary Beard, Misses Camilla and Loretta Tores, Mrs. Mary Locke, and Misses Margaret Burns, Mary Hampton, and Mary Todd.

At this, his first visitation, Bishop Ravenscroft organized the parish, on Monday evening, at the house of Mrs. Susanna Beard, on Innes Street, between Main and Church Streets, just opposite the present residence of Mr. R. J. Holmes. The old house is now occupied by Mrs. Rutledge and family.

On September 14, 1823, the Bishop visited Christ Church, confirmed fifty persons, and administered the Holy Communion to sixty-three persons. Doubtless a good many of those who had been previously confirmed by Mr. Miller were again confirmed by the Bishop.

St. Luke's Parish was admitted into union with the Diocese at the (Williamsboro) convention of 1824, and Dr. Lueco Mitchell attended as a delegate. Dr. Stephen L. Ferrand, the father of Mrs. Mary S. Henderson, and of Mrs. Ann Haughton, deceased, attended the (Washington) Convention, April 21, 1825, as a delegate from the same parish. Bishop Ravenscroft reported that he had visited Christ Church on the thirteenth and fourteenth of October, 1824, and "though the weather was bad, preached to good congregations." On the second day he was assisted by Mr. Miller, administering the Holy Communion to thirty-eight persons. Returning to Salisbury, after service by Mr. Miller, on Saturday the sixteenth, he preached on the seventeenth, being Sunday, confirmed eight persons, and administered the communion to sixteen persons, assisted by Mr. Miller. "In the afternoon divine service was again performed. The congregations respectable, both forenoon and afternoon." On the eighteenth, the Bishop left Salisbury, in company with Mr. Miller, and on the nineteenth, at the house of Mr. Mills, in Iredell, he confirmed five persons. Mr. Mills' family formed the Episcopal part of the former joint Episcopal and Lutheran congregation of St. Michael's, which the Bishop had visited in the year 1823. Mr. Mills' family afterwards constituted the main strength of the Episcopal parish of St. James. The Bishop reached Mr. Miller's "hospitable mansion" on the twenty-first. On the twenty-fourth, in St. Andrew's Church, Burke County, eighteen persons were confirmed, "a numerous congregation" being present. On the twenty-sixth, he preached at St. Peter's Church, Lincoln County, to a small congregation, and on the twenty-seventh, in the same church, confirmed seven persons. Mr. Miller assisted in the service. On the twenty-eighth and twenty-ninth, he officiated at Symrna, without any appearance of interest on the part of the few who attend."

On the thirtieth and thirty-first he officiated at Whitehaven, assisted by Mr. Miller, and confirmed nine persons, and "administered the Holy Communion to a small number of serious people." On the fourth of November he performed divine service again at Whitehaven, preached on the subject of Confirmation, and administered that rite to seven more persons.

The Bishop, in his address to the convention of 1825, said "that he was happy to be able to state that the principles of the church and of pure religion were gaining ground among her members, among whom there were not a few whose zeal was coupled with knowledge and whose faith was manifested by their works, and in general more consideration was given to the subject. In the western section of the Diocese the prospect was very discouraging, though not without hope. With the exception of the congregation at Wadesboro, under the care of the Rev. Mr. Wright, which was second to none in any Diocese for soundness in the faith and exemplary holiness; and the congregation of Christ's Church, Rowan, which is numerous and regular, and in the main sound as Episcopalians, though not without exceptions; and a few recently organized in Salisbury, there is nothing at present to be depended upon. In the immediate neighborhood of the Rev. Mr. Miller, they have commenced retracing their steps, and will in time, I trust, recover from the paralyzing effect of the attempt to amalgamate with the Lutheran body, and the unjustifiable conduct of some of the missionaries heretofore employed, in abandoning the Liturgy altogether in their public services. In Lincoln, the effects are most visible, and likely to be most injurious; yet had we the means of giving and continuing to them the services of a faithful clergyman, my hope is good for the revival of the church even there. Some very influential men are engaged in the cause, and there is sufficient ability, could it be roused into action, to give it success."

November 13, 1825, the Bishop visited Christ Church, Rowan, where he preached and administered the Holy Communion to fifty-six white and three colored communicants.

Mr. Miller made a report to the convention at Hillsboro, May 18, 1826, covering a period of two years:

Baptisms—St. Andrews, Burke County, 21; In Iredell and Rowan, 85; In Lincoln, 35; On Johns and Catawba Rivers, 11. Total, 152.

Communicants—St. Andrew's, 15; Christ Church, 50; Whitehaven, 17; Smyrna, 7; Mr. Mills', 17. Total, 106.

Marriages, 5; burials, 12; paid to Bishop's salary, $20.00; candidates for confirmation at St. Andrew's, 11.

Mr. Miller attended the convention at Salisbury in the year 1829. His report shows that he was confining his labors almost exclusively to the little parish of St. Andrew's. He made another report to the convention at Washington, in 1834, in which he stated that, although enjoying in other respects a good state of health for one of his years, he was very often prevented from attendance on the appointments that were made for him by sudden and severe attacks of a painful complaint with which he was afflicted. He died early in the summer of 1834, having lived a long life full of years and usefulness in the service of his Master. He was a truly pious, sincere Christian—and notwithstanding his apparent inconsistencies of conduct was devotedly attached all his life to the Church of his baptism; and he was instrumental in a larger degree than any other one person in keeping alive a knowledge of Episcopacy in the western part of the State. Wherever he went, his ministrations were always welcome. Mr. Miller's descendants are numerous, one of whom—Miss Amanda Haigler—is the wife of Mr. Lewis V. Brown, late of Salisbury, but now of Denton, Tex.

Bishop Ives, in his address to the convention of 1835, thus alludes to the death of this venerable and saintly servant of God:

"I notice with unfeigned sorrow, the death, during the past year, of the Rev. Robert Johnstone Miller, of Burke County, a clergyman of whom we may emphatically say, for him to live was Christ and to die is gain. Brethren of the clergy, let us follow his example of humility, of faith and patience, that ours may be his crown of eternal glory, through him who has washed us from our sins in his own blood."

It was through the instrumentality of Mr. Miller that fraternal relations were established between the Lutheran Synod and the Episcopal Convention, by a mutual interchange of delegates from one to the other for several years previous to the consecration of Bishop Ravenscroft. Before the Revolution, the Swedes and German Lutherans in the American colonies, almost without exception, are understood to have conformed to the Episcopal Church. In a report made to the Bishop of London, in 1761, the number of "church people" in Pennsylvania is put down at sixty-five thousand, of whom forty thousand were said to be Swedish and German Lutherans "who reckon their service, etc., the same as that of the Church of England" (Wiberforce, American Church, 133).

The Rev. Robert Davis, whose history is unknown to the writer, officiated in this section of the State, coöperating with Mr. Miller, in the years of 1821-23. I find his name included in the list of the clergy for North Carolina, in Sword's Almanac for the year 1822, the whole number of clergy being put down at nine, among whom were the Revs. Richard S. Mason (Newbern), and William Hooper, professor in the University of North Carolina.

About the year 1794, a number of Episcopal families removed from Maryland to the western part of Rowan, among them two families of Barbers, and other families by the names of Gardner, Chunn, Harrison, Alexander, Lightell, Mills, Swan, Reeves, Burroughs, etc. The Rev. Richard W. Barber, of Wilkesboro, is descended from Elias Barber the patriarch of one branch of the Barber family, and the Rev. Samuel S. Barber, of Hyde County, is descended from Jonathan Barber, the patriarch of the other branch.

Mr. Chunn was the grandfather of the Chunns of this county, Mrs. Susan W. Murphy, Mrs. Betty Murphy, and many others. The late Archibald Henderson was often heard to remark that the Rev. Thomas F. Davis—afterwards Bishop of South Carolina—said to him, that Mr. William Chunn—the father of Mrs. Susan W. Murphy—was "God's gentleman," meaning thereby that he was endowed by nature with all the graces and genuine characteristics of a true, cultured, Christian gentleman—a very high compliment indeed, coming from such a man as Bishop Davis. Mr. Samuel R. Harrison, of Salisbury, and many others are descendants of those who first came out with the Maryland colony, and the Turners, of Rowan and Iredell, are also descended from one of this colony. Mr. Charles Nathaniel Mills, with his family, removed soon after his arrival to Iredell County—where his descendants, including a portion in the Northwestern States and a few in Salisbury, now number several hundred. The Rev. Hatch Dent, an Episcopal clergyman, and an uncle of the Barbers, came out with this colony. He purchased six hundred and sixty-one acres of land in Mount Ulla township, where Dent's Mountain is situated—being that part of the Boyden and Henderson plantation called "the Dent Tract." The reverend gentleman remained but a few years. Parson Dent and Jonathan Barber had married two Misses Swan—aunt and niece—and the parson, on returning to Maryland, left his nephew in charge of this tract of land just mentioned, giving him the use of it rent-free for ten years.

Jack Turner, whose wife was a Dent, was the father of Wilson and Joseph Turner and others. Wilson Turner (brother of Jack), was the father of Wilfred Turner and others. Samuel Turner came into the county ten or twenty years later than the first colonists.

Had Parson Dent made Rowan his permanent residence, and if he had been ordinarily zealous and successful in his ministrations, it is believed by many that the Episcopal Church would have been at this time numerically as strong as any religious denominations in the county. An opportunity presented itself at that early day which can never occur again. The Rev. Thomas Wright, of Wadesboro, visited St. Luke's Salisbury, and Christ Church, Rowan County, thrice each during the year ending April 21, 1825. He reported at that time six communicants at St. Luke's, and fifty-eight at Christ Church. On the twenty-fourth of November of the same year, Mr. Wright accepted a call to the rectorship of these two parishes. His salary was fixed at five hundred dollars—one-half of which was assured by the vestry of Christ Church. The contract on the part of Christ Church with St. Luke's was signed by William Cowan, John Swan, and David Cowan. On the twenty-seventh, Bishop Ravenscroft preached in the courthouse in Salisbury, which the Bishop said "was more convenient to the inhabitants generally than the church, situated at the extreme end of town"—in the old Lutheran cemetery. At this time there seems to have been some misunderstanding between the Lutherans and Episcopalians, about the claim of the latter to use the old church building. The Bishop thus alludes to it in his Journal: "An interference in appointments took place, which gave me the opportunity to press upon the members of the church the necessity of providing a place of worship for themselves. And though the present building has been erected almost entirely at the expense of Episcopalians, yet as the ground was originally given for a free church, and each denomination has an equal right to the use of it, I recommend to surrender it altogether, and rent some convenient place for present use until they could provide the means of erecting a suitable building for themselves." In his first report to the convention at Hillsboro, May 18, 1826, Mr. Wright returns the number of communicants at Christ Church at sixty-four, and at St. Luke's, eleven. In January, 1826, Mr. Wright took charge of these congregations, reserving five Sundays in the year for his former flock (in Wadesboro). He reports: "our prospects in the parish of St. Luke's, though not flattering, to be as good as ought to be expected under the existing circumstances. The brethren of Christ Church in general are of one mind and spirit; and walking themselves in the old paths and the good way, will induce others also to follow in their steps. They have recently raised the frame of a new building, sixty by forty feet."

Samuel Fleming attended the convention at Hillsboro as a delegate from Christ Church. In his report to the Newbern Convention, May 17, 1827, Mr. Wright said that "there was reason to hope that the friends and members of the church in his charge have not only increased in number, but are advancing in zeal and knowledge, growing in grace and holiness."

The new building of Christ Church was consecrated by Bishop Ravenscroft, July 17, 1827, in the presence of a large concourse of people, the customary deed having been executed on the day previous. The Bishop was assisted in the services by the Revs. Thomas Wright, R. S. Miller, and William M. Green. The latter is now the venerable and beloved Bishop of Mississippi. This church was situated about twelve miles west of Salisbury, near the Statesville Road—about one mile below the point where Third Creek station on the Western North Carolina Railroad is now located. In his report of this consecration, to the Fayetteville Convention, 1828, the Bishop speaks of the congregation of Christ Church as a "large body of worshipers, the second in number of communicants in the Diocese." On the fifteenth day of September, 1827, Moses A. Locke, Charles Fisher, and John Beard, Jr., as executors of Lewis Beard, executed and delivered to John McClelland, James Martin, Stephen L. Ferrand, Thomas Chambers, Edward Yarboro, and Edward Cress, vestry of the Episcopal congregation of St. Luke's Church, a deed in fee for Lot No. 11—one hundred and forty-four square poles—in the town of Salisbury—now the east corner of Church and Council Streets. The following clause is inserted in the deed:

"And in case at any time hereafter the congregation of St. Luke's shall dissolve, then the right to said lot shall vest in the Episcopal Bishop of the Diocese of North Carolina, and his perpetual successors, in trust for the said congregation of St. Luke's when it shall revive." (Registered in Book No. 30, p. 8.) The lot is said to have been presented by Major John Beard, Jr., a very devoted churchman who removed to Florida, where he resided for many years, having died only a few years ago.

The present church building was erected in the year 1828, the Rev. Francis L. Hawks being the architect. Mr. John Berry was the contractor and builder. Mrs. Mary N. Steele, widow of Gen. John Steele, gave the ground to make the bricks, and burned them. Before the church was consecrated, the Masonic Fraternity assembled there and organized "Fulton Lodge"—the Rev. W. M. Green (now Bishop) meeting with them. The building was consecrated by Bishop Ravenscroft, in July or August, 1878, assisted by the Revs.

Messrs. William M. Green, Thomas Wright, Philip B. Wiley, and John H. Norment. The services "formed an object of much interest to some, and of curiosity to more." About this time, Mr. Wright ceased to be the rector of Christ Church, owing to the disinclination of the latter to continue their union with the church at Salisbury upon its original footing—and "that large and important and able congregation"—in the language of Bishop Ravenscroft—remained for some time without a regular pastor.

The thirtenth annual convention met in St. Luke's Church, Salisbury, on Saturday, May 23, 1829. The lay delegates from Christ Church were Charles Mills, Benjamin Harrison, David Cowan, and Dr. W. H. Trent. From St. Luke's Parish were James Martin, Romulus M. Saunders, Edward Yarboro, and John Beard, Jr. Thomas F. Davis, Jr., afterwards rector of the parish and Bishop of South Carolina, was present as a lay delegate from St. James' Church, Wilmington. E. J. Hale was present as a lay delegate from St. John's Church, Fayetteville. During the morning service on the first day of the session, the sacrament of baptism was administered to four adults; and at night to four infants. Mr. Wright reported fifteen communicants at St. Luke's and seventy at Christ Church, and said "Fears are entertained by some of the vestry that they cannot maintain a clergyman, even with the aid of Christ Church. Perhaps an unmarried man, who could combine secular with clerical duties, or who would divide his time between the two churches of Rowan and the congregation at Wadesboro, might be supported. The few members of the Female Episcopal Society have wrought diligently, and have been able to defray the expense of painting the church and procuring cushions, etc., for the pulpit, reading desk, and altar. By the exertions chiefly of one lady, eighty-five dollars have been presented for the purpose of purchasing a bell." "The members in general of Christ Church are more confirmed in their attachment to the Church, and a few of them have obviously advanced in knowledge, zeal, and holiness." On Sunday morning, the Bishop preached from Romans 10:14. The sermon was published by request of the convention, and was entitled, "Revelation the Foundation of Faith." The Rev. Philip B. Wiley was ordained priest, and the communion was administered to fifty-one persons. Evening service was performed by the Rev. G. W. Freeman. The Rev. Mr. Wright was elected one of the delegates to the General Convention. During the temporary retirement of the Bishop Romulus M. Saunders, a lay delegate, was called to the chair. The Bishop's salary was fixed at one thousand dollars per annum, commencing from June 11, 1829.

From Mr. Wright's report to the convention of 1832, I extract the following: "A few years ago the congregations in Rowan had a name to live, and were dead; but by the grace and mercy of God they have revived, arisen from the dust, and been in some measure purified, and now our principles are better understood than at any preceding period. Our services are attended by those who love them; and the blessed Gospel is, in general, honored by the holy walk of such as profess to believe it." Bishop Ives, in his address, speaks of "the faithful and self-denying labors of Mr. Wright in St. Luke's Parish having been very inadequately repaid." He reported the congregation of Christ Church, "as to its spiritual state, seeming to be prosperous." On Wednesday the thirtieth of May, 1823, Bishop Ives visited St. Luke's Church, officiating on Thursday, Friday, and Saturday ensuing, preaching to unusually serious and attentive congregations, and confirming ninety-two persons. "It was a circumstance of unusual gratification to myself," says the Bishop, "as it must have been to the worthy and devoted servant of God who was about leaving this scene of his self-denying labors, to observe among those who on this occasion publicly professed their faith a number of the most deservedly influential gentlemen of the place, and among all a spirit of increasing solemnity. Among the gentlemen then confirmed were Judge James Martin, John Beard, William Howard, and Major John McClellan.

The Rev. Mr. Wright removed from Salisbury, with his family, to Tennessee, towards the close of the year 1832. He was for a short time a student of the law. He was born in Wilmington; ordained deacon about the year 1821, and ordained priest in 1823 or 1824. He married a sister of Bishop Green, and raised a large family of children. He lived in the old MacNamara house, on Main Street (near the Western North Carolina Railroad), next door to the Misses Beard. He was a most devoted herald of the cross —full of years and piety, and abounding in missionary labors. During the time he was at Salisbury he officiated constantly in the parishes of Rowan County, and frequently and regularly visited Wadesboro, fifty-six miles away. He occasionally visited the Mills Settlement in Iredell County, Mocksville, and Wilkes County. He accompanied Bishop Ravenscroft for days at a time whenever the latter was on his visitations. He is said to have built up the first Episcopal congregation of Memphis. He is remembered with great admiration and affection by his old parishioners in this State.

The Rev. John Morgan

Mr. Wright's successor, must have arrived in Salisbury the latter part of November, 1832. He reached Oxford, on his way, on Saturday, the twenty-fourth, and there met Bishop Ives, and assisted the latter in his Sunday services. Mr. Wright and his family did not leave Salisbury until after his arrival. Mr. Morgan was an Englishman by birth and education, and was never married. Bishop Ives visited St. Luke's Church, Friday, June 14, 1833, and confirmed seven persons. "He was highly gratified to mark so many indications of spiritual improvement." I extract the following from Mr. Morgan's report to the convention of 1834: Baptisms, twenty-six; communicants, twenty; Christ Church baptisms, twenty; communicants, seventy-six; Charlotte baptisms, seven; communicants, three; Iredell County baptisms, ten. His field included Charlotte and Lincolnton, which he visited every fifth week. "We have ordered an organ; the ladies deserving the credit of it. The congregation of Christ Church is decidedly improving in regard to the number of those who regularly attend, and I trust in knowledge, grace and zeal." The same organ has continued in use at St. Luke's to this very day. It was built by Henry Erben, of New York. The original price was seven hundred dollars, but he reduced the charge to five hundred dollars. Mr. Morgan removed to Maryland some time the latter part of the year 1835. He lived to a good old age, dying on Staten Island in 1877. He was fond of accumulating rare and beautifully bound books, and he took great pride in showing his books to those who called to see him. He was a very charitable man—spending his money, however, without discrimination. He paid a visit to England shortly after leaving here, in company with the late Hon. Burton Craige. I heard the latter say that Mr. Morgan was in the habit of dropping a gold guinea ($5) into the box for the poor every time he entered a church, while other people were dropping in pennies or shillings. Mr. Craige said he repeatedly remonstrated with him about such reckless extravagance, telling him that, at the rate he was going on, the legacy which he had lately inherited would soon be exhausted. But his remonstrances had very little effect. He is said to have given his own overcoat to a man who was shivering in the cold, and rode home himself without one. Before leaving the State, Mr. Morgan, in December, 1834, gave up the rectorship of St. Luke's Church, in order to confine himself more closely to his other fields of labor. About that time he reports the number of communicants at Salisbury at twenty-three; Christ Church and Iredell, one hundred and ten; Burke County, seventeen; Charlotte, two. On Friday, September 24, 1834, the Bishop confirmed at Christ Church thirty persons.

Mr. Morgan labored with great zeal and success, and was greatly beloved and respected by his parishioners—in fact, by all who knew him.

He was succeeded in the rectorship of St. Luke's by the

Rev. William W. Spear

in January, 1835. Mr. Spear had been ordained deacon, July 25, 1834, at Hillsboro. The ordination sermon was preached by the Rev. George W. Freeman. Mr. Spear was an educated gentleman. He went to school in Salisbury to the Rev. Jonathan Otis Freeman, a Presbyterian minister, and pastor of the Presbyterian congregation in Salisbury. The latter was a brother of the Rev. George W. Freeman, who was then rector of Christ Church, Raleigh, and afterwards the Bishop of Arkansas. The Rev. G. W. Freeman ministered to Bishop Ravenscroft during his last hours. He was born in Massachusetts in the year 1789 (?).

The Rev. Jonathan O. Freeman was a celebrated instructor. Numbers of the old people in Salisbury of all denominations were baptized and instructed by him, including many Episcopalians. His son, E. B. Freeman, of Raleigh, and Clerk of the Supreme Court, adopted the religion of his uncle, and became a communicant of the Episcopal Church.

Mr. Spear, after becoming a candidate for Holy Orders, entered the General Theological Seminary, in New York, where he completed his preparatory theological studies. He remained in Salisbury about a year, when he removed to South Carolina. He afterwards went North, where he became a distinguished divine. He is still living in the city of Philadelphia. His parents were English people, who came to this State shortly before or after his birth. He married Miss Emily Ewing, of Philadelphia, who is said to have been a beautiful woman. During his rectorship, Mr. Spear and his wife boarded in the family of the late Judge James Martin, who lived in the same house now occupied by the Rev. J. Rumple.

Miss Maria Louisa Spear, an elder sister of the Rev. Mr. Spear, also resided in Salisbury for a few years. She was born in Paddington, England, April 12, 1804, and died near Chapel Hill, January 4, 1881. She educated, both directly and indirectly, her own brother and sisters, and became a prominent and useful teacher of many young ladies; and all her pupils have retained through life a grateful sense of the value of her literary instructions and religious influence.

Mrs. Mary S. Henderson and Mrs. Sarah J. Cain were in their childhood pupils of Miss Spear. When Miss Spear was in Salisbury, she lived in the family of the Rev. Mr. Wright. Miss Ellen Howard was an infant at that time. Miss Spear thought her a beautiful child, and used to remark what a pretty picture the child would make. Miss Spear is said to have been a very fine artist.

She was one of the very first persons confirmed by Bishop Ravenscroft, and became an intimate friend and active helper of her pastor, Mr. Green, of Hillsboro, now the venerable Bishop of Mississippi, who has recently spoke of her as an "incomparable woman." Mrs. Cornelia P. Spencer, of Chapel Hill, herself a Presbyterian, and a sister of the Rev. Charles Phillips, D.D., thus lovingly writes about Miss Spear in an obituary article in *The Church Messenger* of January 27, 1881:

"Miss Maria Spear, having been born an Englishwoman, remained an Englishwoman all her life, possessing some of the most valuable representative characteristics of that nationality. She was thorough, she was sincere, she was quiet, she was conservative, and she was a staunch and devout churchwoman. Her love for the Episcopal Church, and her delight in its service, was in her blood. She has been teaching in North Carolina for fifty-six years, and of the many who have been instructed by her, and the many friends who have loved and esteemed her, not one, perhaps, could this day remember in her an inconsistency or an indiscretion or an unkindness. Miss Maria Spear passed out of life on the same night in which her beloved and revered Bishop Atkinson was released from his suffering forever. Together they passed into glory."

I extract the following from Mr. Spear's report to the convention of 1835: The connection with Christ Church "was dissolved, with the hope that each of these congregations would be able to support a minister residing among themselves. In Salisbury, the experiment has succeeded to a degree; though it is not probable that the present plan can long continue. A large and influential family, with other individual members, have removed to the West, and most of the remainder who are interested in our cause are anticipating the same result. The Sunday School has recently been opened, though that part of the town open to us does not afford more than twenty scholars. Junior and senior Bible classes are held in the week, attended, I believe, with serious feeling." Communicants, seventeen. He also occasionally officiated at Charlotte and Lincolnton.

The Rev. M. A. Curtis, then missionary deacon, located at Lincolnton, occasionally ministered to the Rowan congregations after the resignation of Mr. Spear. He afterwards became the beloved rector of St. Matthew's Church, Hillsboro, where he died a few years ago. He was a man of great piety and learning. The Rev. C. J. Curtis, editor of *The Church Messenger,* is a son of his, and the Rev. W. S. Bynum, of Winston, married one of his daughters.

Sunday, July 24, 1836, Bishop Ives preached, baptized six infants, confirmed six persons, administered the Holy Communion, and examined the children in the catechism, in St. Luke's, Salisbury.

The next rector of the congregation of Christ Church and St. Luke's was the

Rev. Thomas F. Davis, Jr.

He took charge in November, 1836. The congregations had been suffering from the want of regular religious services, and from the removals of some of the most valuable members of St. Luke's. Mr. Davis, in his report to the convention of 1837, prayed to "Almighty God to pour upon these congregations the abundance of his heavenly grace. Their pastor cannot but feel his own insufficiency, and deplore the small apparent fruit of his labors."

In 1838, the communicants at St. Luke's were eighteen; at Christ Church, seventy-eight. One of the largest families connected with St. Luke's Church had removed to the West during the previous year. Mr. Davis reported "the condition of the church in Salisbury as not encouraging." "Christ Church was gradually gaining strength." The delegates to the convention of 1839 from St. Luke's, were John B. Lord, William Locke, and Charles K. Wheeler—the two former attended. Mr. Davis reported twenty-one communicants at St. Luke's, and for Christ Church, ninety-one. Confirmations at the latter twenty-one (July 14 and 15, 1838). "There has been a much larger and more interested attendance upon divine ordinances than heretofore. An increased interest in the church then certainly is accompanied with an increased degree of attention to the Word of God. The people of St. Luke's, entirely of their own accord, have almost doubled the pastor's salary, and have in every respect exhibited towards him a kind and affectionate regard." "The children of Christ Church are well acquainted with the Church catechism." "At Mills' Settlement, Iredell County, communicants, eighteen. The cause of the Church is on the advance in this part of the country."

The twenty-fourth convention of the Diocese met in St. Luke's Church, Salisbury, Wednesday, May 13, 1840. St. Andrew's

Church, Rowan County, was admitted into union with the convention. Vestrymen were Philip Rice, Jacob Correll, Samuel Turner, Joseph Turner, and John Watson. Delegates to convention, Joseph Owens, William Heathman, Samuel Turner, and John Watson. From St. Luke's, A. Henderson, John B. Lord, Charles A. Beard, William Chambers. From Christ Church, J. E. Dobbin, William Chunn, Thomas Barber, Joseph Alexander. Among the names of many other lay delegates I find the following: Dr. John Beckwith, Raleigh; Thomas S. Ashe, Wadesboro. Convention sermon was preached by Rev. G. W. Freeman, D.D.

The Bishop reported that he had visited Salisbury on the fourth, fifth, sixth, and seventh of July, 1839, preached five times, catechized the children, and confirmed four persons. He stated that it had been an object with him during the year to visit every communicant, and to cathechize every baptized person of suitable age in the Diocese, where there is no clergyman or established congregation; and this object he had nearly accomplished.

Mr. Davis was chairman of the committee on the state of the Church and wrote a very eloquent and encouraging report—in which this sentence occurs: "Not captivated by the specious but seducing influences of the day, the Church has remembered always that to her the object of divine faith is her adorable Redeemer and Head; her only law a simple and entire submission to his will and acquiescence in his appointments. She has ceased not to teach and to preach Jesus Christ." Mr. Davis' report to the convention shows the following as the condition of his charge: Communicants—St. Luke's, twenty-five; Christ Church, one hundred; Iredell County, seventeen. The ladies of St. Luke's had lately realized two hundred and forty dollars from a Fair.

The first confirmation at St. Andrew's Church was on August 30, 1840, when the Church was consecrated. Eleven persons were confirmed. Communicants reported to the convention of 1841: St. Andrew's, 29; Christ Church, 92; St. Luke's, 26; confirmations at the latter, 9. Lexington, Mocksville, and Huntsville, had been visited. Rev. C. B. Walker, deacon, had become an assistant minister to Mr. Davis. Bishop Ives, in his address to the convention of 1842, thus alludes to the field of labor under the charge of Mr. Davis. "The counties of Rowan, Davie, Iredell, Davidson, and Surry come under the charge of another faithful Presbyter, with his associate deacon. The missionaries here deserve great attention, and claim, although they have hitherto received compartively nothing, a share of your bounty. They have been able to sustain themselves only by limited private means." The delegates elected to the convention of 1844, from St. Luke's, were John W. Ellis, John B. Lord, William Locke, and Archibald H. Caldwell.

Mr. Davis removed to Camden, S. C., the latter part of the year 1846, after a continuous residence in Salisbury of ten years. He was admired, respected, and beloved by all who knew him. The parish records of St. Luke's Church before the rectorship of Mr. Davis are lost, and the records kept by him are incomplete. Mrs. Jane C. Mitchell (now Boyden) is the first name among the list of confirmations, September 9, 1837. The last name is Charles F. Fisher, September, 1846. Among the baptisms is this entry: "July 24, 1844, James Alexander Craige and George Kerr Craige, infants of Burton and Elizabeth Craige, Catawba County." Among the burials are the following names: November, 1841, Mr. George Baker; August 22, 1843, Mrs. Mary N. Steele; January 24, 1844, W. D. Crawford." Among the marriages are the following: 1843, Dr. George B. Douglas and Miss Mary Ellis; July, Mr. Charles F. Fisher and Elizabeth Caldwell; November, Mr. N. Boyden to Mrs. Jane Mitchell; Dr. R. Hill to Miss M. Fisher. The record of marriages before the year 1843 has not been preserved.

Thomas Frederick Davis was born near Wilmington, February 8, 1840; was a brother of the Hon. George Davis, once a member of the Confederate Cabinet, as Attorney-General, and was educated at the University of North Carolina. Among his seniors were Bishops Green (of Mississippi), and Otey (of Tennessee); while among his classmates were also Bishop Polk of Tennessee, the Rev. Dr. Francis L. Hawks, and Judge William H. Battle. He studied law and was admitted to the bar, and practiced in Wilmington and the neighboring counties for several years. His first wife was Miss Elizabeth Fleming, of Wilmington, who died in the year 1828. He was shortly thereafter confirmed, and admitted to the Holy Communion. He immediately became a candidate for Holy Orders, and was ordained deacon by Bishop Ives, November 27, 1831. In 1832, he was ordained priest. The first years of his ministry were spent in hard missionary work. The towns of Wadesboro and Pittsboro were one hundred miles apart, and in each of these he gave services on the alternate Sunday, driving in a conveyance from one to the other during the week. He had now married again, his second wife being Ann Ive Moore, also of Wilmington. She was in the habit of accompanying him in his missionary drives; and when the question was once asked where they lived, the answer was truly given in these words: "On the road." He afterwards became rector of St. James'

Church, Wilmington, and remained so for about three years. But he was not long in working himself down. The city missionary work was constantly engaging his attention, and among the poor, the sailors, and the strangers, he was ever ready to do his Lord's service. He then removed to Salisbury, and occupied during his residence there the house previously owned by Judge Martin, the same known now as the "Presbyterian manse," where the Rev. J. Rumple resides. While Mr. Davis remained rector of St. Luke's, a number of young theological students were guided by him in their studies, among others the Rev. Edwin Geer, who married Margaret Beckwith, a daughter of Dr. John Beckwith and wife, Margaret Stanly, at one time residents of Salisbury, but then of Raleigh. Mrs. Geer was the sister of the present Bishop John W. Beckwith, of Georgia, and both she and her brother were children of Margaret Beckwith, one of the original thirteen members of the first organized Presbyterian congregation of Salisbury. From Salisbury Mr. Davis removed to Camden, S. C., and became rector of Grace Church. He labored there faithfully for nearly six years. In May, 1853, he was elected Bishop of South Carolina. He was consecrated in St. John's Chapel, New York, October 17, 1853. Bishop Atkinson, of North Carolina, was consecrated at the same time and place. More than thirty Bishops were present. The Bishop-elect of South Carolina was presented by Bishop William M. Green, of Mississippi, and George W. Freeman, of Arkansas. Bishop Davis gradually became totally blind. In 1858, he visited England and the continent of Europe, and consulted the highest medical and surgical authorities. He could not be relived. He never murmured, but bore his trial meekly, patiently, and cheerfully. He died in Camden, December 2, 1871. He was a wise Bishop, a true Christian, a great divine, and a sincere, pure, good man.

The next pastor of the congregations in Rowan County was the

Rev. John Haywood Parker

The statistics of his first report, to the convention of 1847, are: Communicants—St. Luke's Church, 30; St. Andrew's, 49; Christ Church, 89; Mocksville, 9; Lexington, 6; Mills' Settlement, 17; Huntsville, 4.

Mr. Parker endeavored to supply all the stations lately served by Mr. Davis and his assistant, Mr. Charles Bruce Walker. The removal of the Rev. Mr. Davis to South Carolina was a great shock to Bishop Ives. He thus alluded to the subject in his report to the convention: "That such priests as the Rev. Thomas F. Davis should be allowed, with the most heartfelt reluctance, to leave the Diocese, and for no other reason than the want of necessaries of life, is to my mind a problem on all Christian grounds beyond the possibility of solution. No circumstance during the fifteen years of my Episcopate has tended so much as this to fill me with sadness and apprehension." The Diocesan Convention met in St. Luke's Church, Salisbury, May 24, 1849, and again on May 27, 1857. The delegates elected to the last-named were William Murphy, Charles F. Fisher, Benjamin Sumner, and Luke Blackmer, from St. Luke's Church; Thomas Barber, Thomas Barber, Jr., Jacob F. Barber, William Barber, Jonathan Barber, Matthew Barber, R. J. M. Barber, and William F. Barber, from Christ Church; George Mills, John A. Mills, Henry M. Mills, Franklin Mills, Andrew Mills, Israel Mills, George Mills, Jr., and Charles Mills, from St. James' Church, Iredell County. In 1858, Mr. Parker reported the communicants at St. Luke's to be 74. He departed this life, September 15, 1858, in his forty-sixth year, having been born January 21, 1813. He was baptized, November 7, 1841, by Rev. Thomas F. Davis, rector of St. Luke's Church; was ordained deacon, May 31, 1846, and priest May 10, 1847, by Bishop Ives.

He was married on the................day of..................................18........ to Miss..who lived only a few months. On January 25, 1854, he was married to Mrs. Ann Lord, widow of the late John B. Lord, and daughter of the late Dr. Stephen L. Ferrand. The ceremony was performed by the Rev. Joseph Blount Cheshire, of Tarboro, who was a brother-in-law of Mr. Parker. Mr. Theophilus Parker is the only surviving child of this union. The Rev. John H. Parker was a faithful servant of Christ, and was greatly beloved by his flock. The parish paid him the honor to erect a handsome marble shaft over his remains, which were buried near the church where he officiated so constantly and acceptably for more than eleven years. His walk and conversation in this world was that of a humble obedient, patient, and God-fearing follower of Christ; and "he died the death of the righteous."

During the years 1847-48, or portions thereof, the Rev. Oliver S. Prescott, then a deacon, was the minister in charge of the congregations of Christ Church and St. Andrew's, Rowan County, and of St. Phillip's Church, Mocksville. He reported to the convention of 1848 that there were eighty-seven communicants at Christ Church; forty-seven at St. Andrew's; seventeen at the Mills' Settlement; and nine at St. Philip's Church, Mocksville. In the last-named Church he said "that the Holy Days had been observed, and during Lent daily prayers were said." He was ordained priest by Bishop Ives, and removed to Massachusetts. He is now, and has been for many years, rector of St. Clement's Church, Philadelphia, where he has built up a numerous, charitable, and most self-denying congregation. He is thoroughly devoted to his calling, and his parishioners are wonderfully attached to him. He is identified with the so-called "ritualistic party."

During the next few years the same congregations were ministered to by the Rev. James G. Jacocks, who was succeeded in the year 1854 by the

Rev. George Badger Wetmore

The latter is still ministering with great acceptability to the congregations of Christ Church and St. Andrew's in Rowan County, and of St. James' Church in Iredell County. He now resides in Thomasville, N. C., and is building up an Episcopal congregation in that growing and important town. The writer is indebted to the Rev. Dr. Wetmore for many useful facts mentioned in this sketch relating to the Episcopal churches and families of this county.

The Rev. Thomas G. Haughton succeeded Mr. Parker as rector of St. Luke's, in November, 1858. He resigned the sixteenth day of July, 1866; and shortly thereafter abandoned the ministry. He died in the month of October, 1880, in the town of Salisbury. He was married on the twentieth day of February, 1860, to Mrs. Ann Parker, widow of the late Rev. John H. Parker, by the Rev. George B. Wetmore, D.D. Thomas Ferrand Haughton, now in his sixteenth year, is the only child of this union.

The next rector of St. Luke's was the

Rev. John Huske Tillinghast

who assumed charge in the spring of 1867. He ministered with much zeal and self-denial until June 14, 1872, when he removed to Richland County, S. C., where he is now officiating very acceptably to several county congregations. He is remembered with great regard and affection.

He was succeeded, July 1, 1872, by the

Rev. Francis J. Murdock

who was born in Buncombe County, N. C., March 17, 1846; ordained deacon in St. Luke's Church, Salisbury, September, 1868, and priest in St. Paul's Church, Edenton, May, 1870. He is the incumbent of the parish at the present time (January, 1881).

The following statistics of St. Luke's Parish may prove of interest to the curious. Under Mr. Davis, confirmations, 33; baptisms, 90. Under Mr. Parker, confirmations, 35; baptisms, 105. Under Mr. Haughton, confirmations, 29; baptisms, 110. Under Mr. Tillinghast, confirmtaions, 36; baptisms, 53. Under Mr. Murdock, confirmations, 132; baptisms, 123. During Mr. Murdock's rectorship of eight years, the communicants have increased more than one hundred per cent. The number of communicants in the county is 224; of which there are at St. Luke's, 118; at Christ Church, 72; and at St. Andrew's, 34. The whole number of Episcopal Church people is about seven hundred. The largest confirmation class under Mr. Davis—May 16, 1840—numbered nine, including John B. Lord, Mrs. Ann Lord, Misses Julia Beard, Christian Howard, and others. Some of the names in the other classes are William Chambers, Charles Wheeler, William Locke, William Murphy, Marcus Beard, Samuel R. Harrison, Eliza Miller, Jane Wheeler, Ellen Woolworth, Ellen Howard, Rose Howard, Mary S. Henderson, and Augusta M. Locke. .Mr. Parker's largest class numbered 12—March 28, 1858—including John Willis Ellis, Louisa M. Shober, Julia Ann Blackmer, Alice Jones, Sarah H. Mitchel, Ann Macay, and Ellen Sumner. Some of the names in the other classes are Mary Murphy, Julia Long, Helen B. Bryce, Sophie Pearson, Mary McRorie, Laura Henderson, Jane A. Howard, Luke Blackmer, Nathaniel Boyden, James Murphy. Mr. Haughton's largest class numbered eleven—January 29, 1860—including Archibald Henderson, John M. Coffin, Fanny Miller, H. C. Jones, Jr., Frances C. Fisher. Some of the names in the other classes are Mary Locke, J. M. Jones, Elizabeth Vanderford, Henrietta Hall, Annie McB. Fisher, Alice L. Pearson. Mr. Tillinghast's largest class—November 21, 1869—numbered eight, including Laura C. Murphy, John R. Ide, Julia Ide. Some of the names in the other classes are Robert Murphy, Jr., Charlotte C. Mock, Anna May Shober, Lewis Hanes, Mary E. Murphy, Leonora Beard, May F. Henderson. Mr. Murdock's largest class—October 6, 1873—numbered thirty-four, including Francis E. Shober, Jr., William C. Blackmer, William Howard, A. J. Mock, and Fanny Kelly. Some of the names in the other classes are Walter H. Holt, Charles F. Baker, Peter A. Frercks, Belle Boyden, Joseph O. White, Annie Rowzee, Caroline McNeely, Penelope Bailey, Clarence W. Murphy, Annie Cuthrell, George A. Kluttz, and Lillian Warner.

Some of the most influential and distinguished names which have adorned the annals of Rowan County have been communicants or adherents of the Episcopal Church. I have already spoken of the ante-Revolutionary period. Between that period and the year 1823, when Bishop Ravencroft made his first visitation to Salisbury, the following may be confidently claimed as friendly to Episcopacy, to wit: Maxwell Chambers, Matthew Troy, Anthony and John Newnan, Thomas Frohock, Lewis Beard, Spruce Macay, Alfred Macay, Matthew and Francis Locke, Joseph and Jesse A. Pearson, John L. and Archibald Henderson, John Steele, William C. Love, and many others.

Since the year 1823, many of the most distinguished citizens of the State have either been communicants of St. Luke's Church or members of its congregation. John W. Ellis was a member of the General Assembly, a Judge of the Superior Court, and Governor of the State. Richmond M. Pearson became Chief Justice of the State; and Nathaniel Boyden became a member of Congress and an Associate Justice of the Supreme Court. James Martin, Jr., Romulus M. Saunders, and David F. Caldwell were Judges of the Superior Courts. Mr. Saunders was also Attorney General of the State, and Minister Plenipotentiary to Spain. John Beard, Jr., Thomas G. Polk, Charles F. Fisher, John A. Lillington, John B. Lord, A. H. Caldwell, Stephen L. Ferrand, John L. Henderson, Richard H. Alexander, William Chambers, H. C. Jones, have been members of the General Assembly, in one House or the other; and many of them have occupied other important public stations. Archibald Henderson was a member of the Council of State under Governors Reid and Ellis. I have not included in the above list any persons now living. A large majority of the persons named were communicants.

St. Luke's congregation has nearly always embraced persons in every walk and station in life—mechanics, merchants, lawyers, doctors, farmers, and working men of various kinds. Although now greatly reduced in worldly means and property, it is stronger than at any previous period of its history, and its numbers are on the increase. In prosperity as well as adversity, its greatest strength and reliance—from human point of view—has ever been a constantly increasing band of intelligent, devoted, faithful, and noble-minded Christian women.

GERMAN REFORMED CHURCH

For the origin of the German Reformed Church we must look to the mountains of Switzerland, where Ulric Zwingle began to preach the gospel in its purity, about the same time that Luther raised his voice for Christ in Germany. As there were differences of opinion between Zwingle and Luther upon the subject of the "real presence" in the Lord's Supper, as well as upon some of the other doctrines of grace, the adherents of the two reformers did not unite in the same body. After the death of Zwingle, his followers fell naturally in with the churches that were founded and nurtured by Calvin. In Germany, as well as in Switzerland, the Reformed Church is Calvanistic in faith and Presbyterian in church government. The Heidelberg Catechism is their symbol, and they practice the rite of confirmation, though by many this rite is regarded as little else than the ceremony of admitting candidates who give evidences of conversion to full communion.

The German Reformed Church in the United States dates its origin to about 1740, and was formed by immigrants from Germany and Switzerland, who settled in the eastern portion of Pennsylvania. About this time the tide of German immigration flowed southward, and along with the Lutherans who came to Rowan from 1745 and onward were many of German Reformed Church affinities.

Lower Stone, or Grace Church

lying in the center of the German population of Eastern Rowan is the parent of all the German Reformed Churches in Rowan County. The fathers and mothers of these inhabitants came into this region along with the Lutheran settlers about 1750, and their descendants may still be found on or near the old homesteads. The names of the Reformed families were Lingle, Berger, Fisher, Lippard, Peeler, Holshouser, Barnhardt, Kluttz, Roseman, Yost, Foil, Boger, Shupping, and others still familiar in that region.

According to the custom of these early days, the settlers united in building a joint or union church. The first church erected by the Lutherans and Reformed jointly was a log church situated about six miles northeast of the present Lower Stone Church, which was called St. Peter's Church. From a want of harmony or other unknown cause a separation took place, and the Lutherans built the Organ Church, and the Reformed built the Lower Stone Church. Both these churches were of stone work, and were named, one from its organ, and the other from the material of its building. The land for the Lower Stone Church was purchased from Lorentz Lingle for two pounds (£2), proclamation money. The deed bears the date of 1774, and conveys the land to Andrew Holshouser and John Lippard for the use of the "Calvin congregation." The Reformed Church was distinguished from other denominations in these early days by the fact that they were followers of the great reformer of Geneva, John Calvin, who perfected the reformation that was begun in Switzerland by Ulric Zwingle. The site of this church is about four miles west of Gold Hill, on the Beattie's Ford Road. The first structure was of logs, but they were not long content with so humble a building, judging rightly that a house erected for the worship of God ought to be superior to their own dwellings. The Lutherans had just completed their house of stone, and in the year 1795 the Reformed Church set about the erection of their church of the same material. The cornerstone was laid in 1795, under the pastorate of the Rev. Andrew Loretz. Col. George Henry Berger, who was a prominent member of the Rowan Committee of Safety before the Revolution, and Jacob Fisher, were the elders of the Church at this time, and were most active in the erection of the new church. But many trials and discouragements obstructed the good work, and it was not until November, 1811, sixteen years after the cornerstone was laid, that the building was completed and dedicated to the worship of God. In the services of that occasion Pastor Loretz was assisted by the Rev. Dr. Robinson, then and for many years the beloved pastor of the Presbyterian Church of Poplar Tent.

Previous to the pastorate of the Rev. Mr. Loretz there were different pastors, whose names are unknown. The Rev. Mr. Beuthahn resided in Guilford County, organized churches, and preached among them, but supported himself chiefly by teaching a German school in the southeast corner of Guilford County.

Rev. Samuel Suther

was one of the early German Reformed ministers in Guilford, Rowan, and Cabarrus. Governor Tryon, in his Journal for 1768, relates that while he was at Major Phifer's in Mecklenburg (now Cabarrus), on Sunday, the twenty-first of July, he "heard Mr. Luther, a Dutch minister, preach." No doubt this is a misprint for Mr. Suther, since there is no evidence that such a minister as Luther was here, and there is evidence of the presence of a Rev. Mr. Suther. He was sent out from the old country to preach to the German Reformed people in the Carolinas, and was pastor of the Guilford charge during the Revolutionary War. Mr. Suther was a man of learning, and an uncompromising patriot during the struggle for American freedom. His residence was a mile from the battleground of the Regulators in Alamance, May 16, 1771. During the Revolution he was an outspoken patriot, and so obnoxious to the Tories that he was often compelled to hide himself from their vengeance. It is said that there was but one single Tory in his entire charge. Captain Weitzell, a member of Mr. Suther's Church, commanded a Company in the battle of Guilford Courthouse, that was made up of members of the Reformed Church. The records of Lower Stone Church mention Samuel Suther as its pastor in 1782, and that he had removed thither from Guilford County. This was in the days of Tory ravages, when Col. David Fanning and his troop of marauders struck terror into the region that extends from Guilford to Cumberland County. As he had many enemies around him, he found it expedient to remove to a more peaceful region. The date of his death and the place of his burial are unknown to the writer. There are a number of families by the name of Suther residing in and near Concord.

The records of Lower Stone Church show that after Pastor Loretz's time for many years the church was served by the loving, gentle, and patient servant of God, the Rev. George Boger. Mr. Boger was succeeded in 1831 by Dr. B. Lerch, who came among this people in the early days of his ministry, finished his course here, and his dust now rests in the adjoining graveyard.

Mr. Lerch was succeeded by the Rev. John Lantz, who, after a few years, removed to Catawba County, and from thence to Hagerstown, Md., where he finished his earthly labors in 1852.

Mr. Lantz was succeeded by the Rev. Thornton Butler, who had associated with him for a short time the Rev. Gilbert Lane. Mr. Lane removed to New York, and in 1868 the Rev. Mr. Butler removed to Illinois and there died. The next pastor of the Lower Stone Church was the Rev. J. C. Denny, of Guilford. Mr. Denny was educated for a Presbyterian minister, and was licensed by Orange Presbytery. Seceding from the Presbyterians, he was received and ordained by the German Reformed Classis, and served some of their churches in Rowan County for a number of years. Finding at length the German Reformed Church not congenial to his tastes, he again seceded, and was received into the Baptist Church, and is still a Baptist. The Lower Stone Church, after Mr. Denny's secession, was served for a while by Professors Clapp and

Foil, of the Catawba College, and for the last few years by the Rev. R. F. Crooks, who is now pastor.

Mount Hope

formerly called St. Paul's is an offshoot of Lower Stone or Grace Church. The church was organized about 1835 or 1840, from members of the Reformed and Lutheran Churches living in the neighborhood of Holshouser's Mill, now known as Heilig's Mill. The land for the church was given by Andrew Holshouser, a member of the Reformed Church. In 1866 the church was removed about three miles further south, to a point on the New Concord Road, seven miles south of Salisbury. Here a new brick church sixty by forty feet has been erected. The congregation was served first by the Rev. John Lantz. The Rev. Thornton Butler became pastor in 1852, and served them until 1857. He had associated with him for a while the Rev. Gilbert Lane. Mr. Butler was succeeded by the Rev. J. C. Denny, and he by the Rev. P. M. Trexler, and he, in 1878, by the Rev. John Ingle, who is the present pastor.

Shiloh Church

of the Reformed Classis was organized March 19, 1871, by Rev. J. C. Denny, with seventeen members, and has now thirty-four members. The pastors of this church have been Rev. J. C. Denny, from March, 1871, to March, 1873; Rev. P. M. Trexler, from March, 1873, to March, 1876; Rev. J. C. Denny, from March, 1876, to January, 1878; Rev. John Ingle, from January, 1878.

St. Luke's Reformed Church

was organized December 31, 1871, by Rev. P. M. Trexler, with twenty members, and now has forty-five members. Rev. P. M. Trexler was pastor from December 31, 1871, to June, 1877; Rev. John Ingle, from January 1, 1878, to present time.

Mount Hope, Shiloh, and St. Luke's are offshoots of Lower Stone (Grace Church).

Mount Zion Reformed Church

is situated ten miles south of Salisbury on the Concord Road. Next to Lower Stone it is probably the oldest Reformed Church in the county. For many years this church worshiped in the same house with the Lutherans at "Savage's." But when the Lutherans erected a new church, about forty years ago, the German Reformed erected a new church also near the old site, and named it Mount Zion. They have lately erected a second handsome brick church. This church has been served by a succession of ministers, in many cases the same who served the Lower Stone Church. The Rev. P. M. Trexler is the present pastor. The author regrets that his efforts to get accurate statistics of this church have failed, and that he is compelled to give such a general account of it.

Rowan County contains three charges of the German Reformed Church: Central Rowan, Rev. John Ingle pastor, 139 members; West Rowan, Rev. P. M. Trexler pastor, 290 members; East Rowan, Rev. R. F. Crooks pastor, 433 members. Pastors 3, Churches 5, members 862. From the total membership we must subtract about 145 members who belong to Mount Gilead Church, in Cabarrus County.

THE BAPTIST CHURCHES OF ROWAN

According to Benedict's "History of the Baptists," the oldest church of this denomination in America is the First Baptist Church, of Providence, R. I. Roger Williams, having been banished from Massachusetts by the General Court, by a decree adopted in November, 1635, because he taught that the civil magistrate ought not to interfere in cases of heresy, apostacy, and for other offenses against the first tables of the law, wandered into the region outside the jurisdiction of Massachusetts, and the following year laid the foundations of the city of Providence. In the course of three years a number of families cast in their lot with Williams, and in March, 1639 he and Ezekiel Holliman and ten others, met to organize a church. The whole company regarded themselves as unbaptized, and as they knew none to whom they could apply for baptism, they appointed Mr. Holliman to baptize Mr. Williams, and he in turn baptized Mr. Holliman and the ten others. The families of these first members probably also belonged to their church, and in a short time they were reinforced with twelve other members. From this beginning this denomination gradually spread abroad through New England, and in the middle colonies. The growth was not rapid, for at the expiration of the first hundred years it is estimated that there were but thirty-seven Baptist churches in America, and probably less than three thousand members. At this period, however, there began an era of extraordinary growth. In 1740, George Whitefield began to preach in Boston, and multitudes were converted to God. Many of these converts became Baptists, and were called "Separates" or "New Lights." Seven of the "Separates" organized the Second Baptist Church, of Boston, and their views spread abroad.

In 1754, Shubeal Stearns, with eight families and sixteen members, set out from Boston for the South. After halting for a while in Virginia, they settled ultimately on Sandy Creek, in Randolph County, N. C. They were of the "Separate," or "New Light" order of Baptists. They were not, however, the first Baptists in North Carolina. As far back as 1727, Paul Palmer gathered a Baptist Church at a place called Perquimans, on the Chowan River. About 1742, one William Sojourner led a colony from Berkeley County, Va., and established a Baptist Church on Kehukee Creek, in Halifax County, N. C. But the Sandy Creek Church, under Shubeal Stearns, was the first organization of the kind in Western North

Carolina. In 1854, the Baptists of North Carolina were visited by the Rev. John Gano, the Rev. Benjamin Miller, and the Rev. Peter P. Vanhorn, who were sent South by the Philadelphia Association. When the Rev. Hugh McAden, a Presbyterian minister, visited North Carolina in 1755, he found a Mr. Miller—he says—a Baptist minister, preaching and visiting in the Jersey Church. By his labors and those of the Rev. Mr. Gano, a Baptist Church was established in the Jersey Meeting-house, that has continued from that day to this. Mr. McAden expressed the fear that the Presbyterians, who seem to have been the most numerous previous to that time, would soon become too weak to call or support a minister. His fears have been realized.

About 1768 or 1770, the Rev. Mr. Draige, an Episcopal minister, effected an organization of the Episcopal Church in the "Jerseys," but that church too ceased, in time, to occupy the field. The Baptists remained in possession, and the Jersey Church became the parent of nearly all the Baptist Churches of Rowan. There were other Baptist Churches, a hundred years ago, on the Uwharrie River, on Abbott's Creek, and in Surry County. But for three quarters of a century this denomination made little progress in the present limits of Rowan. The churches as they now exist, as well as can be ascertained, originated as follows:

Flat Creek

is a Primitive Baptist Church, and is situated in the edge of Rowan, near the Stanly line, on the Yadkin River, and was considered an old church forty years ago. It is probably an offshoot of the Sandy Creek Church of Shubeal Stearns. The membership is small.

Corinth

is situated at Morgan's muster ground, about fourteen miles east of Salisbury, about four miles from the Yadkin. It was organized in 1808, from converts of a meeting held by the Rev. Messrs. Morton, Carter, and Lambeth. This church has the largest membership—about one hundred—of any Baptist Church in the county, and has a neat and comfortable house of worship. Rev. Mr. Hodge is the pastor.

Mount Zion

was organized, in 1867, from converts of the same meeting. This church has about twelve members, and worships in an arbor, eleven miles from Salisbury, beyond Dutch Second Creek. Rev. J. C. Denny preaches there.

Gold Hill

Church was organized in 1871. This church owns a house, but its membership is not very large. Rev. J. B. Stiers was their first preacher. After him the Rev. Mr. Stokes preached to them a while.

Trading Ford

Church was established as a branch of the Jersey Church in 1756, and was served by the Rev. William Lambeth for fifteen years, beginning in 1853, before the organization, and continuing until 1869. They commenced in the woods, with a schoolhouse and an arbor, but have now a comfortable building of their own, eight miles east of Salisbury, on the Miller's Ferry Road. In the summer of 1870, Elders Bessent, Allison, and one other, met as a Presbytery and organized it a full and separate church. Since Mr. Lambeth ceased to minister to them they have had as ministers, Rev. C. W. Bessent, Rev. W. R. Gwaltny, Rev. S. F. Conrad, and Rev. Mr. Morton.

Salisbury Baptist Church

On the eleventh of August, 1849, the Baptists worshiping in Salisbury were set off as a branch of the Jersey Church, under the ministry of the Rev. S. J. O'Brien, a talented and earnest preacher of the gospel. The next year—April 21, 1850—the Rev. J. B. Soloman became minister in charge, and the following month (May 26) the Branch was constituted a regular Baptist Church, with Mr. Soloman as pastor, and John A. Wierman as church clerk. There were at that time ten white and eight colored members, eighteen in all. In August of the same year, the church united with the Liberty Association. In September, 1851, Mr. Soloman resigned, and the church was vacant until November 6, 1852, when Rev. R. H. Griffith took charge and served until 1854. In 1856, the Rev. J. C. Averitt established a school in Salisbury, and served the church for one year. In 1857, the Rev. William Lambeth, of Salisbury, who had been ordained in 1854, and was preaching at Trading Ford, was chosen pastor of the church. Being destitute of a house of their own, and the war coming on in a few years, the little band was scattered, and services were suspended.

Near the close of the war, the Rev. Theodore Whitefield preached in Salisbury occasionally, but for ten years after this time, no regular services were held by this church. In November, 1876, the North Carolina Baptist Association appointed the Rev. J. B. Boone to labor in Salisbury, and rebuild, if possible, this declining church.

Seven members rallied around him, only seven of the fifty-seven who were here in 1855. On the third of February, 1877, the church was dissolved in order to form a new organization, with others who were to be added by baptism. On the next day twelve others were baptized, and on the following day (February 5, 1877), a Presbytery consisting of the Rev. Messrs. F. M. Jordan, W. R. Gwaltny, Theodore Whitefield, William Lambeth, and J. B. Boone, constituted the Salisbury Baptist Church, with nineteen members. In September following, the church united with the South River Association.

This church does not yet possess a house of worship, but services are held twice a month in a public hall. Nearly two years ago, however, a lot near the courthouse was secured for four hundred dollars. Since that time a more desirable lot, on the corner of Church and Council Streets, adjoining Oak Grove Cemetery, has been secured, and there they expect soon to erect a church.

The present number of members is fifty. Calvinistic in doctrine, congregational in government, of the order called Missionary Baptists, this church holds up the light of the Gospel and points sinners to the Lamb of God.

The materials for this sketch have been collected from Benedict's "History of the Baptists," notes furnished by Rev. J. B. Boone, and recollections of Rev. William Lambeth.

In closing these sketches of the Rowan Churches, it may be remarked that there are a few small Methodist Protestant Churches in the county, and perhaps a Northern Methodist Church or two, but the writer has no facts in possession concerning them. There are also a number of Roman Catholics in Salisbury, who are visited occasionally by priests from Charlotte and elsewhere.

Since their emancipation, the colored people of Rowan have formed themselves into churches in all parts of the county. In Salisbury there are two Baptist colored churches, and one Methodist, and one Presbyterian, with their regular pastors, and each of these denominations have several churches in the county. Some of these ministers, especially in the town, are well-educated, earnest, and pious men, and are laboring to elevate their people, not only by their regular pulpit ministrations, but by means of schools for their daily instruction. They are now working out the great problem of their social regeneration, and accumulating by their efforts materials that may be properly and profitably incorporated in some future History of the Churches of Rowan.

APPENDIX

ROLL OF HONOR

Appendix

Roll of Honor

The following Roll of Honor embraces the names of the officers and privates from Rowan County who served in the Confederate Army, and who continued in service until they were killed, captured, or honorably discharged. There are doubtless a number of other names entitled to a place in this roll, that have not been reported. The compiler has, however, used due diligence in gathering information from all accessible sources. The great body of the names has been courteously furnished by Col. W. L. Saunders and Col. J. McLeod Turner, from the Roll of Honor deposited in the State Capital. Extensive additions have been made to the original roll by surviving officers and privates in Salisbury, under the supervision of Mr. C. R. Barker.

The following abbreviations are employed:

a.—age.
c.—captured.
Capt.—captain.
Col.—colonel.
Cor.—corporal.
d.—died.
d. in p.—died in prison.
d. of d.—died of disease.
en.—date of entrance into service.
h. d.—honorably discharged.
k.—killed.
Lt.—lieutenant.
Ord. Sgt.—ordnance sergeant.
pr.—promoted.
Sgt.—sergeant.
tr.—transferred.
w.—wounded; and a number of others.

PAYMASTER'S DEPARTMENT

Joseph K. Burke, 2d. Lt.; Enrolling Officer; office at Statesville, N. C.
William G. McNeely, Capt., Paymaster of Second Army Corps.
J. C. Swicegood, Confederate States Navy, Charleston, S. C.

QUARTERMASTER'S DEPARTMENT

R. P. Bessent, Capt., Quartermaster Forty-Second Regiment.
William H. Neave; commissioned Bandmaster Army of Northern Virginia.

SECOND REGIMENT CAVALRY

Company B

Privates

Maloney, J. P.; k.

FOURTH REGIMENT CAVALRY

Company E

Privates

Cauble, Henry.
Cauble, John; w. at Gettysburg.
Danis, John.
Hartman, Luke.
Thomas, Charles.

NINTH REGIMENT CAVALRY

Company C

Privates

Cauble, J. D.; en. July 3, 1861; a. 20.

Company F

Officers

Kerr Craige, 5th. Sgt.; en. 1861; a. 18; pr. 2d. Lt. Company I, August 24, 1862.

Privates

Bernhardt, Caleb T.
Bernhardt, Crawford.
Bost, Henry C.
Brown, Pleasant.
Cowan, William L.; en. June 15, 1861; a. 20; d. of d. at Centerville, Va., December 30, 1861.
Fisher Charles H.; en. June 15, 1861; a. 20; w.
Howerton, A. W.; en. June 15, 1861; a. 27.

Johnston, James G.; en. June 15, 1861; a. 22; pr. to 1st. Cor.
Luhn, Gustave J.; en. June 15, 1861; a. 22.
Miller, Henry G.; en. March 20, 1862; a. 25.
Pearson, Charles W.; en. June 15, 1861; a. 22; tr. from Company B, Tenth Virginia Cavalry; pr. to 2d. Lt. Fifth North Carolina Cavalry, February, 1863; pr. to Capt. July, 1864.
Sides, Reuben A.; en. June 15, 1861; a. 21.
Stiller, Charles M.; en. June 15, 1861; a. 24; k.

FIRST REGIMENT ENGINEERS, ARTILLERY AND ORDNANCE OF NORTH CAROLINA STATE TROOPS

Company D (Rowan Artillery)

Officers

John A. Ramsey, Senior 1st. Lt.; pr. to Capt.
William Myers, Junior 1st Lt.
Jesse F. Woodard, Senior 2d. Lt.
William L. Saunders, Junior 2d. Lt.
E. Myers, Senior 2d. Lt.
W. R. Dicks, 1st Sgt.
Edward F. Kern, 2d. Sgt.
I. D. J. Louder, 3d. Sgt.
Silas Sheppard, 4th. Sgt.
Francis Schaffer, Quartermaster-Sgt.; pr. to Lt.
Matthew Moyle, 1st. Cor.
James M. Crowell, 2d. Cor.
William H. Bucket, 3d. Cor.
A. A. Holhouser, 4th. Cor.; pr. to Ord. Sgt.; d. of d.
Jerre Pierce, Artificer.
Zudock Riggs, Bugler; k. at Richmond.

Privates

Agner, H. C.
Baily, John T.; pr. to Sgt.
Baine, David; d. in p.
Basinger, Jere W.; h. d.
Bell, Joseph F.
Black, William H.; d. of d.
Braddy, Benjamin.
Braddy, Moses G.
Brady, David.
Brady, John.

Brady, Joseph.
Bringle, John.
Brown, C. L.
Brown, H. M.
Brown, Richard L.
Bulaboa, Lorenzo; k. by explosion of caisson.
Bunage, James.
Campbell, W.; w. at Malvern Hill.
Carter, John.
Casper, Alex.
Cauble, Henry M.
Clampet, John.
Cranford, W. H.
Cowan, Richard, Jr.
Crowell, H. H.; pr. to Cor.
Crowell, Richard E.
Crowell, Thomas.
Crowell, William.
Daniel, Amos.
Earnhardt, Abram; k. at Malvern Hill.
Earnhardt, James P.
Earnhardt, Robert.
Earnhardt, Thomas M.; w. near Richmond.
Earnhardt, Wiley.
Elkins, Owen L.
Eller, F.; k. accidentally.
Eller, Farley; w.
Eller, Jacob.
Eller, James I.
Eller, Milas.
Eller, William.
Fraley, White.
Frick, Levi.
Frick, Moses; w. at Gettysburg.
Glover, Richard.
Goodman, Tobias; d. of d.
Gorman, James A.
Hardester, John W.; w. at Malvern Hill; w. at Gettysburg.
Hardester, Thomas; d. of d.
Hall, Stockton S.
Hodge, Abram.
Hoffman, Nathan; k. at Gettysburg.

Hoffman, William.
Holshouser, Alex.
Holshouser, C.
Holshouser, Mike.
Holshouser, Rufus; w. at Malvern Hill.
Honbarger, John.
Howard, Andrew M.
Huff, William H.
Irby, William H.
Jackson, Andrew.
Julian, James.
Kepley, Calvin; k. at Sharpsburg.
Kistler, Daniel.
Kistler, Henry R.
Kinney, Calvin S.; d. of d.
Kluttz, Henry
Kluttz, Jacob.
Kluttz, Peter.
Kluttz, Rufus, Jr.
Kluttz, Rufus, Sr.
Lemley, Jacob.
Linn, James F.
Lyerly, Joseph M.
McCombs, William.
May, Calvin.
May, Robert.
Miller, H. M.; k. at Sharpsburg.
Miller, Lawson.
Miller, Rolin.
Miller, Uriah.
Misenheimer, D. I.; k. at Sharpsburg.
Mitchel, J.
Morgan, C. W.
Morgan, Joe.
Oldham, Josiah.
Owen, Henry; k. at Gettysburg.
Parks, Daniel.
Parks, John F.
Parks, Joseph D.
Parks, William.
Peeler, A. L.
Peeler, Alf. M.

Peeler, Daniel.
Pool, H. C.
Richards, John.
Riggs, John.
Rowe, Benjamin C.
Rowe, S. A.
Rufty, Milas A.; k. at Malvern Hill.
Ruth, Andrew J.; w. at Malvern Hill.
Ruth, Lorenzo D.
Seaford, Daniel.
Seaford, Simeon.
Skillicorn, William; w. at Culpeper Courthouse.
Terrell, Thomas; tr. to Navy.
Thomas, Thomas.
Thompson, Thomas.
Trexler, Allen.
Trexler, David; w. at Malvern Hill.
Trexler, Jesse L.
Trexler, Peter M.
Troutman, Daniel, d. in p.
Troutman, Rufus.
Troutman, Rufus; d. of d.
Waller, Crusoe.
Waller, Lewis A.
Weaver, Tobias.
Wilkinson, William.
Woodsman, Solomon.
Works, Isaac.

FIRST REGIMENT INFANTRY

Company H

Officers

James H. Kerr, 2d. Lt.; en. August 23, 1861; w. Ellyson's Mill; d. August 6, 1863.

Privates

R. R. Crawford; en. May, 1861; a. 21; pr. 1st. Lt. Company D, Forty-second Regiment.

SECOND REGIMENT INFANTRY

Company H

Officers

Alexander Murdock, 3d. Sgt.; en. May 27, 1861; a. 30; appointed Ord. Sgt. May 14, 1862; d.

FOURTH REGIMENT INFANTRY

Company B

Officers

James H. Wood, Capt.; en. May 16, 1861; a. 21; pr. Major July 22, 1862; pr. Lt.-Col. May 19, 1864; pr. Col. July 18, 1864; k. at Sniggers Gap, November 23. 1864.

Thomas C. Watson, 1st. Lt.; en. May 1, 1861; a. 22; Com. Capt., July 22, 1862; w. and resigned.

Jesse F. Stancill, 2d. Lt.; en. May 1, 1861; a. 21; pr. Capt.; w. November, 1864; pr. Major.

J. Fuller Phifer, 1st. Sgt.; en. June 12, 1861; a. 19; reduced to ranks at his own request; d. Richmond, January 25, 1863.

B. Knox Kerr, 2d. Sgt.; en. June 3, 1861; a. 25; d. March 26, 1862.

M. Stokes McKenzie, 3d. Sgt.; en. June 3, 1861; a. 22; k. May 31, 1862, Seven Pines.

Joseph Barber, 4th. Sgt.; en. June 3, 1861; pr. Jr. 2d. Lt., February 25, 1863; a. 26; w. (lost right arm), Chancellorsville.

John Hillard, 5th. Sgt.; en. June 3, 1861; a. 24.

Isaac A. Cowan, 1st. Cor.; en. June 3, 1861; a. 21; pr. 2d. Lt. November 15, 1862.

William H. Burkhead, 2d. Cor.; en. June 3, 1861.

Benjamin A. Knox, 3d. Cor.; en. June 24, 1861; a. 22; pr. Sgt. April 25, 1862.

D. W. Steele, 4th. Cor.; en. June 3, 1861; a. 20; d. Richmond, August 20, 1861.

Privates

Alexander, J. L.; en. July, 1861; w. and c. at Sharpsburg.

Anderson, Charles; en. June 3, 1861; a. 19; w. June 22, 1862; d. of w. July 15, 1862.

Barber, Edward F.; en. June 3, 1861; a. 22; pr. 1st. Sgt. March 1, 1863; w. Chancellorsville; k. May 19, 1863.

Barber, James; en. June 3, 1861; a. 25; d. in Salisbury, N. C., August 15, 1862.

Barber, John Y.; en. June 3, 1861; a. 15; tr. Regimental Band, September 15, 1861.

Barber, Robert J. M.; en. June 2, 1861; a. 28; c. in Maryland September 10, 1862.

Barber, Thomas D.; en. June 3, 1861; a. 22; k. Spottsylvania Courthouse, May 12, 1863.

Barnhardt, J. C.

Barringer, William H.; en. July 10, 1861; a. 20; d. of d. at Manassas, September 19, 1861.

Baxter, Hugh; en. June 3, 1861; a. 22; w. Seven Pines; d. of w. July 6, 1862.

Beaver, A.

Beaver, Henry; en. March 3, 1862; a. 53; h. d. and d.

Beaver, J. Martin; en. June 3, 1861; a. 22; h. d.

Beaver, Joe.

Beaver, Joel; en. June 3, 1861; a. 23; d. at Richmond, July 21, 1862.

Beaver, John D.; en. June 3, 1861; a. 20; w. Seven Pines; d. of w. June 15, 1862.

Beaver, Mike.

Beaver, W. A.

Belk, George S.; en. June 12, 1861; a. 23; d. 1864.

Biggers, W. D.; en. June 3, 1861; a. 20; pr. Cor. September 20, 1861; w. Seven Pines, discharged for w. March 24, 1863.

Brandon, Calvin J.; en. June 3, 1861; a. 22; k. near Richmond, June 27, 1862.

Briggs, James; en. June 3, 1861; a. 24; k. March 20, 1862, by accident on Western North Carolina Railroad.

Briggs, Thomas; en. March 13, 1862; a. 21; d. of d.

Burke, James P; en. June 3, 1861; a. 21; w. South Mountain, September 14, 1862; pr. 2d. Lt.

Chunn, William; en. June 3, 1861; a. 17; w. Seven Pines; d. of w. June 12, 1862.

Cowan, D. Stokes; en. June 3, 1861; a. 24; lost left arm at Winchester, Va.; h. d.

Cowan, James F.; en. June 3, 1861; a. 18; w. Seven Pines, lost right arm; h. d. August 11, 1862.

Cowan, John Y.; en. June 3, 1861; a. 18; d. December 9, 1861, at Manassas Junction.

Cowan, Nathan N.; en. June 3, 1861; a. 19; w. Seven Pines.

Cox, Wiley E.; en. June 3, 1861; a. 36; w. Seven Pines; d. of w. June 5, 1862.

Current, A. J.; en. June 24, 1861; a. 26; d. Yorktown, Va., April 22, 1862.

Dismukes, Richmond L.; en. March 4, 1861; a. 37; pr. 1st. Lt. in Company G; resigned.

Donaho, David.

Donaho, Frank.

Donaho, Newberry.

Donnell, J. Irwin; en. June 3, 1861; a. 18; d. Manassas Junction, September 12, 1861.

Douglas, Adolphus D.; en. June 3, 1861; a. 22; d. Manassas Junction, September 12, 1861.

Eller, Edward; en. March 14, 1862; a. 38; d. of d. July 19, 1862, at Danville.

Felker, Alexander; en. June 3, 1861; k. Seven Pines, May 31, 1862.

Gantz, Wiley; en. March 3, 1862; a. 37.

Gillespie, Thomas P.; en. June 14, 1861; tr. Regimental Band, September 15, 1861.

Graham, Cam; k.

Graham, Clay; k.

Graham, R. L.

Gullet, John.

Hall, Richard J.; en. June 3, 1861; d. Lynchburg, Va., May 26, 1862.

Hall, W. W.

Henry, Elam T.; en. June 3, 1861; h. d. for accidental gunshot w. in the hand.

Hilliard, James B.; en. June 3, 1861; a. 22; w. Seven Pines; k. at Chancellorsville, May 3, 1863.

Hix, Calvin J.; en. June 19, 1861; a. 21; pr. Sgt. July 5, 1861; k. Seven Pines, May 31, 1862.

Holdclaw, James H.; en. June 14, 1861; a. 37; w. Seven Pines; det. as nurse at Richmond.

Hughes, James C.; en. June 3, 1861; a. 20; d. at home, August 18, 1861.

Hughey, T. A.; k. Chancellorsville.

Hyde, James C.; en. June 10, 1861; a. 20.

Jordan, Thomas; en. June 3, 1861; a. 31; pr. Cor. April 26, 1862; k. Seven Pines, May 31, 1862.

Kistler, John W.; en. June 3, 1861; a. 23; w. Seven Pines; w. South Mountain.

Kistler, Joseph B.; en. June 3, 1861; a. 25; det. as prison guard; k. 1864.

Lipe, David.

Leazer, John; en. March 3, 1862; a. 18; w. Seven Pines.

Louder, Daniel M.; en. June 3, 1861; a. 29; d. Camp Pickens, Va., October 6, 1861.

Lyerly, Thomas S.; en. June 14, 1861; a. 20; w. at Gettysburg.

McCormick, E. Laf.; en. June 11, 1861; a. 27; det. as brigade blacksmith, August 12, 1862.

McCormick, Hiram S.; en. June 19, 1861; a. 22; det. as Regiment teamster.

McKenzie, W. White; en. June 3, 1861; a. 24; det. hospital steward, August, 1861; d. July 10, 1862.

McLaughlin, Silas M.; en. June 12, 1861; a. 29; h. d. for disease.

Meniss, George W.; en. June 10, 1861; a. 23; w. Seven Pines, June 27, 1862.

Miller, Henry C.; en. June 3, 1861; a. 20; pr. Cor. November 4, 1862; pr. Ord. Sgt.; w. Chancellorsville.

Mills, R. A.; en. June 3, 1861.

Moore, David C.; en. June 10, 1861; a. 19; w. Hagerstown; d.

Moore, William A.; en. June 3, 1861; a. 24; w. Seven Pines; w. Hagerstown; d.

Niblock, Frank K.; k. Seven Pines.

Pachell, Joseph; en. March 3, 1862; a. 18; d. of d., July 5, 1862, in Richmond.

Pinkston, Thomas; en. June 3, 1861; a. 19; k. Seven Pines, May 31, 1862.

Plumer, William F.; en. June 3, 1861; a. 20; w. Seven Pines; d. Richmond, December, 1862.

Rice, Allen G., en. June, 1861; a. 23; d. at camp near Bull Run, September 23, 1861.

Safret, Charles; en. March 11, 1862; a. 24; d. June 27, 1862, at camp hospital.

Safret, Peter; en. March 15, 1862; a. 22; w. South Mountain, September 14, 1862; left on field; sent as nurse to Wilmington.

Safret, Powel; d.

Sears, John W.; en. June 12, 1861; a. 28.

Shinn, J. W.; en. June 12, 1861; a. 30; pr. 1st. Sgt., 1862; d. of d. at home.

Sides, John M.; en. June 3, 1861; a. 26.

Smith, Jef.

Stikeleather, M. W.; en. March 11, 1862; a. 27.

Webb, Abner; k. Seven Pines.
Wilhelm, Jacob; k.

Company K (Rowan Rifle Guards)

ENTERED SERVICE APRIL 19, 1861. REORGANIZED AS COMPANY K, FOURTH REGIMENT INFANTRY, MAY 30, 1861

Officers

Francis M. Y. McNeely, Capt.; en. May 30, 1861; resigned May 31, 1862.

W. C. Coughenour, 1st. Lt.; en. May 30, 1861; a. 25; pr. Capt. May 31, 1862; w. Seven Pines; appointed Inspector-General of Ramseur's Brigade, August, 1863; w. April 4, 1864, Amelia Courthouse.

Marcus Hoffin, 2d. Lt.; en. May 30, 1861; pr. 1st. Lt. May 31, 1862; pr. Capt. August, 1863; appointed Capt. Com. Dept. 1864; w. Seven Pines.

Williams Brown, Jr. Lt.; en. May 30, 1861; resigned November, 1861.

Addison N. Wiseman, 1st. Sgt.; en. May 30, 1861; a. 24; pr. 2d. Lt. 1862; w. December 14, 1862; pr. 1st. Lt. 1863; w. Chancellorsville, May 3, 1863; k. Winchester, September 19, 1864.

Wilburn C. Fraley, 3d. Sgt.; en. May 30, 1861; a. 21; pr. 1st. Sgt. 1862; w. September 19, 1864.

Moses L. Bean, 4th. Sgt.; en. May 30, 1861; a. 20; pr. 1st. Sgt. 1862; pr. 2d. Lt. April 1, 1863; pr. 1st. Lt. September 19, 1864; pr. Capt. February, 1865; w. May 12, 1864.

James Bowers, 1st. Cor.; en. May 30, 1861; a. 21; k. Seven Pines, May 31, 1862, with Regimental Colors in his hands.

John F. Kenter, 2d. Cor.; en. May 30, 1861; a. 23; pr. Q.-M. Sgt. November, 1861; c. Petersburg, Va.

John L. Lyerly, 3d. Cor.; en. May 30, 1861; a. 27; transferred.

James Crawford, 4th. Cor.; en. May 30, 1861; a. 23; elected 3d. Lt. Company B, Forty-second Regiment.

Privates

Baity, Robt. A.; en. May 30, 1861; a. 22; w. Chancellorsville; d. of w. May 3, 1863.

Barger, Paul; en. May 30, 1861; a. 19; k. June 27, 1862, Cold Harbor, Va.

Barringer, John W.; en. May 30, 1861; a. 19; d. in camp, Manassas, Va.
Bassinger, G. H.; en. September 7, 1862; a. 19; c. Sharpsburg; w. Spottsylvania.
Bean, J. W.; en. April 12, 1863; a. 39; w. Spottsylvania, Va.
Beaver, Michael; en. January 12, 1861; a. 21; w. Fredericksburg, December 14, 1862.
Bencini, M. A.; c. September 19, 1864, Winchester, Va.
Blackner, Elon G.; appointed 2d. Lt. Company F, Seventh Regiment.
Bogle, David.
Brown, Peter A.; en. January 14, 1861; a. 24; w. Seven Pines; pr. Cor.
Brown, Stephen A.; k. Cold Horbor.
Bryant, Lindsay; en. May 30, 1861; a. 20.
Buis, W. A.; en. January 14, 1861; a. 28; c.
Carter, Alfred C.; en. May 30, 1861; a. 21; w. June 27, 1862, Cold Harbor; w. Chancellorsville, May 3, 1863.
Carter, E. F. M.; en. September 9, 1862; a. 30; c. Sharpsburg; k. Chancellorsville, May 3, 1863.
Casper, Ambrose; en. March 9, 1862; a. 20; c. Sharpsburg; c. near Richmond.
Casper, James C.; en. January 29, 1861; a. 26; c. near Spottsylvania Courthouse, Va.
Caster, Henry M.; en. July 3, 1861; a. 26; k. Winchester, Va.
Castor, John; en. March 16, 1862; a. 38; c. Sharpsburg.
Cauble, George A.; en. June 25, 1861; a. 22; k. June 27, 1862; Cold Harbor, Va.
Church, N. N.; en. September, 1861; a. 30; d. in hospital.
Colley, Leroy C.; en. May 30, 1861; a. 22; k. September, 1862, Sharpsburg, Md.
Crawford, William H.; appointed 1st. Lt. Company F, Seventh Regiment.
Crooks, Henry W.; en. May 30, 1861; a. 23; d. in camp 1861.
Crowel, John T.; en. September 8, 1862; a. 20; k. Seven Pines.
Crowel, R. E.; en. April 13, 1863; a. 23; w. Spottsylvania, Va.
Cummings, William W.; en. May 30, 1861; a. 19; k. Seven Pines.
Davis, L. M.; appointed Lt. in Company K, Fifth Regiment.
Deaton, John C.; en. May 30, 1861; a. 22; w. Seven Pines.
Durell, William M.; en. May 30, 1861; a. 18; w. May 12, 1864, at Spottsylvania Courthouse.

Eddleman, J. A.; en. March 15, 1862; a. 23; c. Sharpsburg, Md.; c. Fisher Hill, Va.

Eddleman, Jacob A.; en. May 30, 1861; a. 25; k. Seven Pines.

Eller, Nelson A.; en. May 30, 1861; a. 19; w. Seven Pines; c. at Chancellorsville.

Eudie, John J.; en. June 26, 1861; a. 22; tr. to light duty, 1863; c.

Fraley, Jacob L.; en. May 30, 1861; a. 30; k. Spottsylvania Courthouse, May 12, 1864.

Fraley, Jess R.; en. September, 1862; a. 25; appointed Assistant Surgeon, April, 1863.

Freidheim, Arnold; en. June 15, 1861; a. 23; w. Seven Pines; pr. Cor.

Fulk, Edward; en. March 15, 1862; a. 25; d. in hospital.

Gardner, Frank S.; d. in hospital.

Glover, Jeremiah; en. June 29, 1861; a. 18.

Glover, William H.; en. June 26, 1861; a. 25; k. Sharpsburg, Md.

Gorman, W. R.; tr. to Regimental Band; d. at home.

Heilig, Philip A.; en. January 30, 1861; a. 19; w. Seven Pines; k. Spottsylvania Courthouse.

Heirn, David; en. May 4, 1861; a. 30; d. Manassas.

Henderson, C. A.; appointed Assistant Surgeon in Sixth Regiment.

Henderson, Leonard; appointed 1st. Lt. Company F, Eighth Regiment.

Hendricks, James L.; en. May 30, 1861; a. 22; d. Manassas.

Holdhouser, Crawford; c. Sharpsburg, Md.

Holdhouser, Lewis D.; en. March 7, 1862; a. 21; w. Seven Pines; w. May 3, 1863, Chancellorsville.

Holdhouser, Milas M.; en. June 29, 1861; a. 21; c. Sharpsburg.

Holdhouser, Otho; en. May 30, 1861; a. 25; pr. to Sgt.; w. Seven Pines; k. Spottsylvania.

Horah, George; en. May 30, 1861; a. 20; appointed Lt. in Forty-sixth Regiment.

Huff, William H.; en. May 30. 1861; a. 24; tr. to Riley's Battery.

Hunt, M. F.; appointed 2d. Lt. Company E, Fifth Regiment.

Hyer, Charles; en. June 4, 1861; a. 25; in Regimental Band.

Irwin, Joseph C.; May 30, 1861; a. 23; appointed Lt. Fifth Regiment; w. Sharpsburg, Md.

Johnston, Daniel C.; en. May 30, 1861; a. 20; k. Seven Pines.

Jones, Charles R.; en. May 30, 1861; a. 20; appointed Lt. in Fifty-fifth Regiment.

Jones, Hamilton C.; appointed Capt. Company K, Fifth Regiment.

Josey, Wallace; en. March 29, 1862; a. 20; w. June 3, 1864, near Richmond; d. of w.

Josey, Wilson R.; en. May 30, 1861; a. 18; k. Chancellorsville, May 3, 1862.

Kelly, Joseph; en. April 12, 1863; a. 35.

Kerr, James H.; appointed Lt. in First Regiment.

Kyle, Robert G.; en. May 30, 1861; a. 18; pr. Cor.; k. Seven Pines.

Landcherry, R.; en. March 12, 1862; a. 30; d. in hospital.

Lanicr, Benjamin; en. May 30, 1861; a. 18; k. Seven Pines.

Lilly, W. T.; en. May 30, 1861; a. 18; discharged on account of ill health.

Lillycrop, William; en. October 14, 1861; a. 24; w. Mechanicsville, Va.

Locket, John B.; en. May 30, 1861; a. 24; tr. to general hospital as nurse.

Long, Hamilton C.; en. May 30, 1861; a. 25; pr. 2d. Lt. November, 1861; w. Seven Pines; resigned.

Lowrence, Alfred A.; en. May 30, 1861; a. 18; k. Seven Pines.

McCanless, James C.; en. June 29, 1861; w. seven days' fight at Richmond.

McDaniel, J. A.; en. September 22, 1861; a. 20; k. Sharpsburg, Md.

McQueen, A. M.; en. March 20, 1862; a. 27; w. Seven Pines, May 31, 1862; w. December 14, 1862, at Fredericksburg; d. of w.

McQueen, Daniel M.; en. March 21, 1862; a. 32; w. September 14, 1862; d. of w.

McQueen, William; en. May 30, 1861; a. 24; c. Petersburg, Va.

Mahaly, Lewis; en. May 30, 1861; a. 27; w. Chancellorsville, May 3, 1863; d. of w.

Matthews, Bradley; en. July 14, 1862; a. 24; Musician; w.

Mauldin, James; en. March 9, 1862; a. 18; w. Seven Pines; d. of w. August 10, 1863.

Mauney, John; en. June 14, 1861; a. 34; d. in camp.

Meisenheimer, George; c. Sharpsburg, Md.

Miller, Alfred W.; en. July 3, 1861; a. 22; w. September 14, 1862; d. of w.

Miller, Calvin L.; en. July 3, 1861; a. 22; k. May 3, 1863, Chancellorsville.

Mills, Francis M.; en. May 30, 1861; a. 17; w. Seven Pines.

Mitchell, Lueco; appointed Lt. in Riley's Battery.

Moose, W. A.; en. May 30, 1861; a. 26; tr. to Band; d. in hospital.

Morris, William; en. May 30, 1861; a. 26; w. Cold Harbor, June 27, 1863; d. of w.

Mowery, Andrew; en. May 30, 1861; a. 24.

Mowery, William G.; en. May 30, 1861; a. 28; d. in hospital.

Moyer, Daniel; en. May 30, 1861; a. 25; w. Seven Pines.

Murr, William; en. June 22, 1861; a. 22; w. September 19, 1864, Winchester, Va.

Neave, Edward B.; en. May 30, 1861; a. 20; Leader Regimental Band.

Neely, James W.; en. May 30, 1861; a. 20; w. Seven Pines, discharged on account of wounds.

O'Neal, Isaac P.; en. May 30, 1861; a. 25; c. September 16, 1862, Sharpsburg.

Owens, J. T.; en. July 20, 1863; a. 36; k. Spottsylvania, Va.

Parker, William; en. May 30, 1861; a. 18; pr. Cor.; w. Seven Pines; w. Chancellorsville; c. Sharpsburg, Md.

Patterson, Edward; en. May 30, 1861; a. 28; w. Sharpsburg; w. May 19, 1864; tr. to Navy.

Pearson, Eli.

Peden, John T.; en. May 30, 1861; a. 21; pr. Lt. in Fifty-fifth Regiment.

Peeler, W. D. C.; en. March 7, 1862; a. 22; w. Seven Pines; c. Sharpsburg, Md.

Pendleton, Ham Jones; pr. 5th. Sgt. Company F, Seventh Regiment.

Ploughman, Solomon; en. May 30, 1861; a. 27; k.

Rendleman, Lawson M.; en. May 30, 1861; a. 20; k. Seven Pines.

Roberts, Alfred H.; en. May 30, 1861; a. 21; w. near Charlestown, 1864.

Roberts, James W.; en. May 30, 1861; w. Seven Pines; tr. to light duty.

Roberts, R. S.; discharged on account of ill health.

Rowzee, Allison H.; d. in camp, 1861.

Sanders, J. B.; en. April 1, 1863; a. 21.

Smithdeal, William; en. May 30, 1861; a. 19; discharged on account of w. Seven Pines.

Snuggs, George D.; en. May 30, 1861; a. 25; w. Seven Pines; w. Chancellorsville; c. Sharpsburg; w. Snickers' Ford, July 21, 1864.

Snuggs, John; c. April 6, 1865.

Severs, Henry C.; en. May 30, 1861; a. 19; w. Seven Pines; c. 1863; Sharpsburg, Md.

Strayhorn, Samuel; en. May 30, 1861; a. 21; k. Seven Pines.
Thompson, John F.; en. May 30, 1861; a. 19; w. Cold Harbor, June 27, 1862, as Courier.
Thompson, Joseph F; en. May 30, 1861; a. 27; w. December 14, 1862, Fredericksburg; d. of w.
Thompson, N. A.; en. June 19, 1861; a. 18; d. in camp.
Trexler, Hiram A.; en. May 30, 1861; a. 25; d. Manassas.
Troutman, M. B.; en. March 16, 1862; a. 27; w. May 3, 1863, Chancellorsville.
Turner, J. McLeod; appointed Capt. Company F, Seventh Regiment.
Turner, Levi; en. March 7, 1862; a. 21; w. Seven Pines; w. Spottsylvania.
Weant, Matthew J.; en. May 30, 1861; a. 23; w. Seven Pines; tr. to Regimental Band.
Weant, William A.; en. May 30, 1861; a. 20; discharged on account of ill health.
Williams, Henry; en. September 21, 1862; a. 24.
Williams, Richard; en. May 30, 1861; a. 24; pr. to Cor.; w. Seven Pines.
Williamson, Thomas G.; appointed 2d. Lt. Company F, Seventh Regiment.
Winter, George S.; en. January 16, 1861; a 18; k. Seven Pines.
Wise, Henry; en. March 9, 1862; a. 35; w. Seven Pines; d. of w.
Wise, Tobias; en. March 9, 1862; a. 40; w. May 3, 1863, Chancellorsville; d. of w.

FIFTH REGIMENT INFANTRY

Company E

Officers

Samuel Reeves, Capt.; en. May 16, 1861; a. 38; resigned March 8, 1862.
Robert Hendry, 1st. Lt.; en. May 16, 1861; a. 32.
M. F. Hunt, 2d. Lt.; en. May 16, 1861; a. 21; w.
Fred H. Sprague, Jr. 2d. Lt.; en. May 16, 1861; a. 25.
Jonathan Graham, 1st. Sgt.; en. June 6, 1861; a. 30; d. of w. at Williamsburg, Va., May 8, 1862.
John T. Rodman, 2d. Sgt.; en. June 4, 1861; a. 18.
C. L. Reeves, 3d. Sgt.; en. July 3, 1861; a. 35; h. d.
David Morgan, 4th. Sgt.; en. June 28, 1861; a. 22; pr. to 2d. Sgt., May 5, 1862.

James Hendry, 1st. Cor.; en. July 1, 1861; a. 28; w. at Williamsburg; h. d.

John R. Hunter, 2d. Cor.; en. July 1, 1861; a. 43.

Jere M. Miller, 3d. Cor.; en. June 29, 1861; a. 22; w. Seven Pines; k. at Gettysburg, Pa., July 1, 1863.

Daniel Basinger, 4th. Cor.; en. June 14, 1861; a. 22; w. at Gettysburg, Pa.

Privates

Baines, Levi; en. July 8, 1861; a. 22; pr. Sgt.; w. at Cold Harbor; w. at Chancellorsville.

Barrett, J. G.; en. June 18, 1861; a. 18; pr. 5th. Sgt., August 31, 1863.

Basinger, Emanuel; en. June 19, 1861; a. 21; w. at Wilderness and at Gettysburg.

Basinger, Henry; en. June 15, 1861; a. 44; w. at Wilderness and Gettysburg.

Basinger, James J.; en. July 6, 1861; a. 25.

Basinger, John; en. July 1, 1861; a. 31.

Basinger, William A.; en. June 29, 1861; a. 27; k. at Williamsburg, Va., May 5, 1862.

Beaver, Daniel; en. June 29, 1861; a. 30.

Beaver, Monroe; en. June 29, 1861; a. 27; w. at Wilderness.

Beek, William; en. June 11, 1861; a. 21.

Bond, William J.; en. June 1, 1861; a. 23; w. at Gettysburg; pr. to 3d. Sgt. August 31, 1863.

Boyle, John; en. June 5, 1861; a. 18.

Brown, Adam; en. June 9, 1861; a. 30.

Brown, Henry M.; en. July 3, 1861; a. 20; w. at Williamsburg, Va.

Bryant, John J.; en. July 15, 1862; a. 22; d. of d. November 16, 1862.

Carr, William A.; en. April 23, 1861; a. 18; pr. to 2d. Lt. from Company A, Third Regiment, April 13, 1862.

Clodfelter, D. E.; en. June 29, 1861; a. 21; w. at Williamsburg.

Clodfelter, William C.; en. July 1, 1861; a. 26; d. of d. January, 1862.

Clutts, Jere; en. July 3, 1861; a. 22.

Cruse, Munroe; en. June 11, 1861; a. 25; w. at Chancellorsville; pr. Cor., April 30, 1863.

Cunningham, Pat; en. June 5, 1861; a. 18; d. of w. at Gettysburg, July 5, 1863.

Dickens, Thomas; en. July 2, 1861; a. 31.

Duckworth, J. W.; en. July 4, 1861; a. 23.
Duke, George; en. June 11, 1861; a. 18.
Earnhardt, Levi T.; en. July 6, 1861; a. 18.
Ellar, William; en. July 4, 1861; a. 24.
Fight, Samuel J.; en. June 28, 1861; a. 20.
File, Ivy W.; en. June 19, 1861; a. 22.
Gillespie, John; en. June 5, 1861; a. 22; w. at Williamsburg.
Hadley, R.; en. September 1, 1861; a. 22.
Hargaty, Pat; en. June 15, 1861; a. 20; k. at Williamsburg, May 5, 1862.
Hartman, Jacob A.; en. June 29, 1861; a. 19.
Hewitt, D. H.; d. of w. at Gettysburg, July, 1863.
Johnson, Calvin; en. July 2, 1861; a. 30.
Johnson, Green; en. July 8, 1861; a. 18.
Kelly, John; en. June 17, 1861; a. 31; d. of d., May 5, 1863.
Kennerly, George A.; en. July 25, 1861; a. 40.
Kinney, M. L.; en. June 8, 1861; a. 23.
Lane, David; en. July 4, 1861; a. 19.
Lanier, Israel; en. June 17, 1861; a. 23; k. at Chancellorsville, May, 1863.
Long, G. W.; en. June 19, 1861; a. 20; pr. Cor. August 31, 1863; w. at Gettysburg.
McGuire, Mike; en. June 5, 1861; a. 22.
McNellis, Condie; en. June 5, 1861; a. 28.
Mauldin, James; en. June 22, 1861; a. 18.
Medly, William A.; en. July 4, 1861; a. 27; d. of d. August, 1861.
Miller, Calvin; en. June 6, 1861; a. 25.
Miller, D. L.; en. July 6, 1861; a. 21; d. of d., 1862.
Mills, William; en. July 1, 1861; a. 31; d. of d., April, 1862.
Morris, Richland; en. September 1, 1861; a. 26; k. at Williamsburg, May 5, 1862.
Murdy, John; en. June 5, 1861; a. 20; w. at Williamsburg.
Newson, C. C.; en. August 19, 1861; a. 19; w. at Williamsburg and Chancellorsville.
O'Donnel, Francis; en. June 15, 1861; a. 18.
Parker, John; en. July 1, 1861; a. 24; d. of d., 1862.
Parker, William L.; en. July 1, 1861; a. 18.
Parks, James O.; en. July 1, 1861; a. 24.
Parks, Jesse A.; en July 20, 1861; a. 24; w. at Williamsburg and Chancellorsville.
Parnell, Frank; en. June 24, 1861; a. 22.
Patten, A. W.; en. July 15, 1862; a. 22; missing at Sharpsburg.

Peacock, William L. C.; en. June 19, 1861; a. 22.
Pence, Jake; en. July 4, 1861; a. 44.
Porter, James H.; en. June 29, 1861; a. 32.
Rawlins, B.; en. July 4, 1861; a. 43; w. at Seven Pines.
Riggsbey, C. C.; en. July 15, 1862; a. 29.
Riggsbey, William H.; en. July 15, 1862; a. 25.
Robinson, J. M.; en. July 4, 1861; d. at Bull Run, July 25, 1862.
Rufty, G. W.; en. June 13, 1861; a. 18.
Scott, John; en. July 4, 1861; a. 37; pr. to Cor., October 31, 1862; w. at Gettysburg.
Singleton, J. V.; en. July 4, 1861; a. 29.
Sloop, Joel G.; en. July 4, 1861; a. 19; w. at Williamsburg.
Steel, William; en. July 4, 1861; a. 37; pr. to 3d. Sgt., October 31, 1862; k. at Gettysburg, July, 1863.
Stoup, Thomas; en. July 4, 1861; a. 18; d. of d., 1861.
Waller, George; en. June 11, 1861; a. 20; k. at Gettysburg, July 1, 1863.
West, R. C.; en.. April 23, 1861; a. 18; pr. to 2d. Lt. from Company A, Third Regiment, April 13, 1863.
West, S. B.; en. May 16, 1861; a. 26; pr. Capt.
Wilheim, Jesse; en. June 28, 1861; a. 30.

Company K

Officers

Hamilton C. Jones, Capt.; en. May 16, 1861; a. 24; pr. to Lt.-Col. Fifty-seventh Regiment.
J. M. Jones, 1st. Lt.; en. May 16, 1861; a. 27.
L. M. Davis, 2d. Lt.; en. May 16, 1861; a. 22; pr. to Capt.
Joseph C. Irwin, 2d. Lt.; en. June 22, 1861; a. 23.
Cæsar Guttenberg, 1st. Sgt.; en. April 29, 1861; a. 33; w. Chancellorsville.
William T. Fesperman, 2d. Sgt.; en. June 13, 1861; a. 25; pr. to 2d. Lt.
Paul Barringer, 3d. Sgt.; en. July 4, 1861; a. 29; pr. to 1st. Sgt. January 1, 1863.
George Miller, 1st. Cor.; en. June 25, 1861; a. 22.
George Heilig, 2d. Cor.; en. June 5, 1861; a. 25; pr. to 2d. Lt. for gallantry.
Calvin Phillips, 3d. Cor.; en. July 1, 1861; a. 22; d. Richmond, April, 1862.
Franklin D. Julian, Musician; en. July 1, 1861; a. 16.

Privates

Allen, Jasper; en. July 16, 1861; a. 18; k. Gettysburg, July, 1863.
Atkinson, J. H.; en. July 30, 1861; a. 34.
Basinger, John A.; en. August 8, 1862.
Beaver, David; en. July 1, 1861; a. 35.
Beaver, David; en. August 8, 1862.
Beaver, E. M.; en. August 8, 1862; a. 31.
Beaver, H. M.; en. August 8, 1862; a. 28; d. of d. at Strasburg, Va., November 11, 1862.
Beaver, Jeremiah; en. August 8, 1862; a. 27; w. Chancellorsville; d. at home, August 7, 1863.
Beaver, Joseph; en. August 8, 1862; a. 30.
Beaver, L. A.; en. August 8, 1862; a. 23.
Beaver, Rufus; en. August 8, 1862; a. 20.
Beaver, Simeon; en. August 8, 1862; a. 33; d. near Charlestown, W. Va., on march.
Bost, Allison; en. August 8, 1862; a. 19.
Bost, G. M.; en. August 8, 1862; a. 24; d. November 29, 1863; near Gordonville.
Bostian, Aaron; en. August 8, 1862; a. 28; k. July 1, 1863, Gettysburg.
Bostian, A. J.; en. August 8, 1862; a. 31.
Bostian, Andrew; en. August 8, 1862; a. 34.
Bostian, Eli; en. August 8, 1862; a. 32.
Bostian, William; en. August 8, 1862; a. 24.
Bradshaw, Francis; en. February 25, 1861; pr. to Cor. for meritorious conduct.
Bray, J. F.; en. July 15, 1861; fell out of ranks, August, 1862, and never heard from.
Brewer, Elijah; en. July 15, 1862; w. at Gettysburg.
Bringle, L. D.; en. July 1, 1861; a. 18; w. Gettysburg.
Brown, Charles; en. June 12, 1861; a. 30.
Butler, Martin; en. July 12, 1861; a. 25; k. Williamsburg, May 5, 1862.
Carver, Kyle; en. August 22, 1861.
Cash, A. G.; en. August 8, 1862.
Cates, Calvin; en. July 6, 1861; a. 36; d. Richmond.
Cauble, Pleasant; en. June 27, 1861; a. 21; pr. to Cor. February, 1862.
Coan, R. H.; en. July 7, 1861; a. 18; k. Williamsburg, May 5, 1862.
Coleman, J. A.; en. August 8, 1862.

Craven, W. H.; en. July 15, 1862; fell out of ranks August, 1862, and never heard from.

Cress, Absalom; en. August 8, 1862.

Cruse, Joseph; k.

Cruse, Tobias; en. August 8, 1862; k. at Gettysburg, July 1. 1863.

Davis, Jackson; en. July 12, 1861; a. 44; pr. to 5th. Sgt.

Deal, Levi; en. August 8, 1862; w. severely at Gettysburg.

Deberry, Richard L.; en. June 11, 1861; a. 19.

Deberry, William; en. June 18, 1862.

Dolan, Alfred; en. June 8, 1861; a. 21.

Earnhart, Calvin; en. August 8, 1862; d. November, 1862, at Guinea Station.

Earnhart, David; en. August 8, 1862.

Earnhart, Isaac; en. August 8, 1862; k. July 1, 1863, Gettysburg.

Earnhart, J. C.; en. August 8, 1862.

Eller, Charles A.; en. February 7, 1862; w. severely at Williamsburg.

Eller, Hamilton; en. February 7, 1862; w. severely at Seven Pines.

Fesperman, J. H.; en. August 8, 1862.

File, Noah; en. August 8, 1862.

Fink, J. C.; en. August 8, 1862; d. of d., April 1, 1863, at Fredericksburg.

Fink, J. F.; en. June 2, 1861; a. 19.

Fink, J. M.; en. August 8, 1862; d. of d., February 21, 1863, at Richmond.

Fry, Pleasant; en. June 10, 1861; a. 19; pr. to 2d. Cor.; d. of d. at Richmond, August, 1862.

Gardner, J. W.; en. July 15, 1862; d. May 3, 1863, Guinea Station.

Garver, Benjamin; en. July 1, 1861; a. 18.

Garver, John M.; en. July 8, 1861; a. 21.

Hancock, Thomas; en. July 5, 1861; a. 28.

Hardester, E. H.; en. July 15, 1862; fell out of ranks on march to Maryland, and not heard from.

Hardester, L. W.; en. July 15, 1862; w. at Sharpsburg.

Heilig, J. M.; en. August 8, 1862; a. 24; k. July 1, 1863, Gettysburg.

Heilig, Julius; en. June 8, 1861; a. 18; w. Williamsburg and pr. to Cor. for gallantry.

Heilig, J. W.; en. August 8, 1862; a. 31.

Helfer, Edward; en. June 20, 1861; a. 21.

Hill, E. S.; en. July 15, 1862; d. December 31, 1862, Guinea Station.

Hill, Jesse; en. July 15, 1862; fell out of ranks on march to Maryland, and not heard from.

Hill, W. H.; en. July 15, 1862; fell out of ranks on march to Maryland, and not heard from.

Huie, Elias J.; en. June 17, 1861; a. 31.

Jones, Levi; en. August 16, 1861; a. 22.

Jones, R. B.; en. July 15, 1862; a. 40; w. Gettysburg.

Keith, George; en. August 8, 1862; a. 28; k. July 1, 1863, Gettysburg.

Kluttz, Eli; en. August 8, 1862; a. 35.

Kluttz, Joseph; en. August 8, 1862; a. 35; d. December 18, 1862, near Fredericksburg.

Leach, D. W.; en. July 15, 1862; a. 19.

Leach, E. E.; en. July 15, 1862; a. 35; w. Gettysburg; d. of w., July 15, 1863.

Lefler, William; en. June 28, 1861; a. 21; w. Gettysburg.

Lentz, L. B.; en. August 8, 1862; a. 23; d. of d., November 14, 1862; near Winchester, Va.

Lippard, A. L. J.; en. August 8, 1862; a. 21; w. Gettysburg.

Lippard, E. S. P.; en. August 8, 1862; a 32.

Luther, George; en. July 15, 1862.

Maxwell, J. R.; en. June 28, 1861; a. 21.

Miller, Jesse; en. August 8, 1862; a. 34; w., arm amputated.

Moffit, B. F., en. July 15, 1862; a. 19; d. of d., November 1, 1862, Richmond.

Nance, H. H.; en. July 15, 1862.

Nance, J. M.; en. July 15, 1862.

Newell, William G.; en. July 12, 1861; a. 50; d. of d. at Camp Wigfall, Va.

Nichols, Columbus; en. July 5, 1861; a. 19.

Pechel, Miles; en. June 19, 1861; a. 27; d. of d. at Richmond.

Phillips, D. J.; en. August 26, 1861; a. 28.

Porter, Otis; en. August 31, 1861; a. 47.

Potter, James; en. June 21, 1861; a. 41; d.

Powe, Hugh T.; en. August 8, 1862; a. 33; severely w., etc., at Gettysburg, and d. in enemy's hands.

Quinn, Michael; en. July 26, 1861; a. 17; tr. to a South Carolina Battalion.

Rimer, Reuben H.; en. July 2, 1861; a. 22.

Robinson, J. M.; en. August 1, 1861; a. 27; k. May 5, 1862, Williamsburg, Va.

Rose, J. A.; en. August 8, 1862; a. 22; d. of d., March 5, 1863, at home.

Rose, R. A.; en. August 8, 1862; a. 20; d. of d., Farmville, Va., March 26, 1863.

Safrit, Eli; en. August 8, 1862; w. at Gettysburg.

Safrit, Moses; en. May 19, 1863; a. 37; w. Gettysburg; d. of w., July 19, 1863.

Scott, William; en. June 12, 1861; a. 22.

Seaford, Edmund; en. August 8, 1862; w. severely at Gettysburg.

Shupping, John A.; en. June 17, 1861; a. 27.

Sikes, J. P.; en. July 3, 1861; a. 36; d. May, 1862, in enemy's hands, of w.

Snider, W. L.; en. July 15, 1862; fell out of ranks, August, 1862, not since heard from.

Steed, C.; en. July 15, 1862; fell out of ranks, August, 1862, not since heard from.

Stikeleather, Alex.; en. June 30, 1861; a. 21; k. Cold Harbor, June 27, 1862.

Stirewalt, Jacob; en. June 20, 1861; a. 35.

Sugart, W. C.; en. July 15, 1862; w. severely at Gettysburg.

Swink, James; en. June 10, 1861; a. 19.

Thompson, S. G.; en. July 15, 1862; fell out of ranks, August, 1862, not since heard from.

Varner, J. G.; en. July 15, 1862; fell out of ranks, August, 1862, not since heard from.

Wade, Benjamin F.; en. June 14, 1861; a. 28; d. August, 1862, at Camp Wigfall.

Watson, Michael; en. July 25, 1861; a. 16.

West, William; en. July 14, 1861; a. 30.

Winders, Abner; en. June 12, 1861; a. 22; d. of d. at Richmond.

SIXTH REGIMENT

Officers, Field and Staff

Charles F. Fisher, Col.; en. May 16, 1861; a. 40; k. Manassas, July 21, 1861.

A. M. Nesbit, Surgeon; en. May 16, 1861; a. 45; tr. to a Virginia Regiment, July 15, 1861.

Julius A. Caldwell, Assistant Surgeon; en. May 16, 1861; a. 32.

C. A. Henderson, Assistant Surgeon; en. May 10, 1861; a. 26.

Company A

Officers

James C. Turner, Capt.; en. May 16, 1861; a. 22.

Company G

Officers

James A. Craige, Capt.; en. May 16, 1861; a. 20; pr. to Major Fifty-seventh Regiment, July 17, 1862; w.

R. Rush Smith, 1st. Lt.; en. May 26, 1861.

James T. Rosenborough, 2d. Lt.; en. May 26, 1861.

John P. M. Barringer, 1st. Sgt.; en. May 29, 1861; a. 25; k. Seven Pines, May 31, 1862.

David M. Basinger, 2d. Sgt.; en. May 29, 1861; a 23; pr. to 1st. Sgt. November 1, 1862.

William C. Cooper, 3d. Sgt.; en. May 29, 1861; a. 21; d. of w. received at Sharpsburg, September 20, 1862.

George H. Brown, 4th. Sgt.; en. May 29, 1861; a. 20; pr. to 1st. Sgt. July 1, 1863; w. at Second Manassas; w. and c. at Gettysburg.

William Owens, 1st. Cor.; en. May 29, 1861; a. 20; k. May 31, Seven Pines.

Lewis H. Rothrock, 2d. Cor.; en. May 29, 1861; a. 21; pr. 2d. Lt. December 20, 1861; pr. 1st. Lt.

Abram Miller, 3d Cor.; en. May 29, 1861; a. 20.

Richard Graham, 4th. Cor.; en. May 29, 1861; a. 19.

Privates

Allen, Bartley; en. May 29, 1861; a. 28; c. November 7, 1863; Rappahannock Railroad Bridge.

Atwell, Charles F.; en. May 29, 1861; a. 24; pr. Cor. November 3, 1863.

Baker, Joseph N.; en. May 29, 1861; a. 19; c. November 7, 1863, Rappahannock Railroad Bridge.

Barnhardt, John C.; en. March 5, 1862; a. 24; c. at Rappahannock Railroad Bridge, November 7, 1863.

Barnhardt, Julius A.; en. July 9, 1862; a. 19; d. in hospital.

Bencini, Moses A.; en. March 12, 1862; a. 16; tr. to Company K, Fourth Regiment.

Blackwelder, Alex. W.; en. May 29, 1861; a. 23, k. Seven Pines, May 31, 1862.

Blackwelder, Jacob S.; en. May 29, 1861; a. 21; c. July 2, 1863.

Bostian, George W.; en. May 29, 1861; a. 18.

Bostian, John A.; en. June 5, 1861; a. 20; c. November 7, 1863; Rappahannock Railroad Bridge.

Bringle, John; en. May 29, 1861; a. 18; c. November 7, 1863, Rappahannock Railroad Bridge.

Brolly, James; en. May 29, 1862; a. 28; d. of d.

Brown, J. McNeely.

Cauble, William Martin; en. May 29, 1861; a. 23; c. November 7, 1863; Rappahannock Railroad Bridge; w. Seven Pines.

Correll, Joseph.

Correll, Joseph; en. May 29, 1861; a. 29.

Corriher, Amos B.; en. May 29, 1861; a. 19; k. Manassas, July 1, 1861.

Corriher, Jacob R.; en. May 29, 1861; a. 24; k. Manassas, July 1, 1861.

Corriher, Wash. E.; en. May 29, 1861; a. 18; k. Seven Pines, May 31, 1862.

Craige, Clethus; en. March 15, 1862; a. 18; k. at Cedar Run, 1864.

Cress, Thomas; en. May 29, 1861; a. 25; k. Sharpsburg, September 17, 1862.

Dancy, Naphthall L.; en. May 29, 1861; a. 23; k. Manassas, July 1, 1861.

Eagle, Alex.; en. May 29, 1861; a. 33; d. of d. at Liberty, Va., June 20, 1862.

Eagle, Moses I.; en. May 29, 1861; a. 19; d. of d., October 4, 1861.

Edwards, Hannibal.

Edwards, T. L.; en. June 5, 1861; a. 17.

Fesperman, Levi A.; en. May 29, 1861; a. 23; c. Rappahannock Railroad Bridge, November 7, 1863.

Freeze, Caleb; en. September 11, 1861; a. 37; d. of d., Richmond, July 10, 1862.

Freeze, Mike; en. May 29, 1861; a. 19; d. of d., September 4, 1861.

Freeze, Wiley; en. May 29, 1861; a. 18; d. of d., November 26, 1861.

Gibbons, Anderson; en. May 29, 1861; a. 22.

Graham, John C.; en. May 29, 1861; a. 22; c. Rappahannock Railroad Bridge, November 7, 1863.

Graham, Levi A.

Graham, R. Frank; en. May 29, 1861; a. 19; w. at Second Fredericksburg battle; pr. 2d. Cor.

Greene, Fortune; en. March 13, 1862; a. 49; d. at Richmond, July 10, 1862.

Gullet, Andrew J.; en. May 29, 1861; a. 21; w. and c., at Gettysburg, July, 1863.

Hall, James O.; en. May 29, 1861; a. 19; h. d., August 4, 1861.

Hearne, George.

Heilig, John F.; en. May 29, 1861; a. 19; c. Rappahannock Railroad Bridge, November 7, 1863.

Hess, John; en. May 29, 1861; a. 20; k. at Manassas Junction, July 21, 1861.

Holt, James A.; en. May 29, 1861; a. 20; w. below Richmond, Va.

Howard, John; en. May 29, 1861; a. 23; w. and c., Rappahannock Railroad Bridge, November 7, 1863; w. at Manassas.

Johnson, Harrison; en. May 29, 1861; a. 18; c. at Rappahannock Railroad Bridge, November 7, 1863.

Josey, Moses C.; en. May 29, 1861; a. 20.

Josey, W. R.; d. of d. in hospital.

Lee, James.

Lewis, John R.; en. March 19, 1862; a. 39; d. at Richmond, September 1, 1862.

Lipe, Caleb J.; en. May 29, 1861; a. 21.

Lipe, John M.; en. March 3, 1862; a. 18; d. in hospital.

Love, H. C.

Miller, Abram H.; en. May 29, 1861; a. 26; pr. 2d. Lt. December 2, 1862.

Miller, Emanuel; en. May 29, 1861; a. 25; c. Rappahannock Railroad Bridge, November 7, 1863.

Miller, Ebeneezer H.; en. May 29, 1861; a. 22; c. at Rappahannock Railroad Bridge, November 7, 1863.

Miller, Henry W. A.; en. July 1, 1861; a. 21; pr. 2d. Lt. Forty-second Regiment, March 15, 1862.

Miller, H. W.; w. at Manassas.

Miller, Jacob W.; en. May 29, 1861; a. 25; w. at Manassas, July 21, 1861.

Miller, John L.; en. May 20, 1861; a. 20; k. at Sharpsburg, September 17, 1862.

Miller, Martin M.; en. March 5, 1862; a. 28; w. at Gettysburg, July 2, 1863.

Miller, R. A.; en. February 5, 1862; a. 19; c. Rappahannock Railroad Bridge, November 7, 1863.

Miller, William Westley; en. May 29, 1861; a. 19; w. at Seven Pines, May 31, 1862; pr. 4th. Cor.

Morgan, Calvin R.; en. March 3, 1864; a. 18; w. Winchester, Va., both legs broken, one amputated.

Morgan, Moses Levi; en. July 1, 1861; a. 23; k. Gaines' Farm, June 27, 1862.

Morgan, Noah; en. March 3, 1864; a. 18; w. October 18, 1864.

Nance, Shadrack; en. July 1, 1861; a. 27; d. in p.

Noah, George W.; en. July 1, 1861; a. 25; k. Manassas Junction, July 21, 1861.

Overcash, James W.; en. July 1, 1861; a. 24; c. at Rappahannock Railroad Bridge, November 7, 1863.

Overcash, John S.; en. March 19, 1862; a. 21; c. at Rappahannock Railroad Bridge, November 7, 1863.

Owens, Henry C.; en. July 1, 1861; a. 19; pr. to Sgt. November 1, 1862; c.

Owens, Joseph F.; en. July 1, 1861; a. 20; c. at Rappahannock Railroad Bridge, November 7, 1863.

Owens, William R.; en. May 29, 1861; a. 26; k. Seven Pines, May 31, 1862.

Penninger, Wilson; en. March 19, 1862; a. 26; d. in hospital, Richmond.

Pogue, Elias James; en. July 1, 1861; a. 27; c. Rappahannock Railroad Bridge, November 7, 1863.

Porter, William Henry; en. July 1, 1861; a. 23; k. Seven Pines, May 31, 1862.

Redwine, Peter W.; en. May 29, 1861; a. 18; k. at Gaines' Farm, July 27, 1862.

Rendleman, Laurence T.; en. May 29, 1861; a. 19; k. at Seven Pines.

Rendleman, Tobias; w. at Richmond, May 31, 1861.

Ritchie, Charles; en. July 1, 1861; a. 28; c. June 27, 1862.

Ritchie, Henry W.; en. July 1, 1861; a. 20; w. at Sharpsburg, September 17, 1862.

Ritchie, Jacob M.; en. July 1, 1861; a. 27; c. Rappahannock Railroad Bridge, November 7, 1863.

Ritchie, William M.; en. May 29, 1861; a. 23; h. d., October, 1861.

Russel, James W.; en. May 29, 1861; a. 21; w. and c. at Gettysburg, July 1, 1863.

Safrit, Jacob Monroe; en. June 5, 1861; a. 19; k. at Manassas Junction, July 21, 1861.

Setzer, Jason D.; en. June 5, 1861; a. 19; k. Manassas Junction, July 21, 1861.

Sheppard, John; en. May 29, 1861; a. 34; c. at Rappahannock Railroad Bridge, November 7, 1863.

Shinn, William F.; en. September 15, 1861; a. 25; w. at Gettysburg, July 1, 1863.

Shullibarrier, William S.; en. July 1, 1861; a. 19; w. at Sharpsburg, September 17, 1862.

Shuping, Mike; en. May 29, 1861; a. 22; h. d., November 16, 1861.

Shuping, Noah R.; en. May 29, 1861; a. 21; w. at Second Manassas, August 29, 1862.

Sloop, David Alex.; en. May 29, 1861; a. 23; tr. to Regimental Band, December 1, 1862.

Sloop, William J. A.; en. July 1, 1861; a. 18; d. of d., September 15, 1861.

Smart, T. R.

Smith, J.; d. of d. at Ashland hospital, May 6, 1862.

Smith, Jacob S.; en. July 1, 1861; a. 21; k. at Manassas Junction, July 21, 1861.

Smith, James; en. March 19, 1862; a. 30; w. at Fredericksburg, December 13, 1862.

Smith, William A.; en. July 1, 1861; a. 19; k. at Seven Pines, May 31, 1862.

Smith, William H.; w. at Seven Pines.

Smith, W. J.

Spears, J. F.

Sronce, Jacob; d. of d. at Camp Fisher, January 6, 1862.

Starrett, George M.; en. July 1, 1861; a. 19; w. at Seven Pines.

Starrett, John E. D.; en. March 15, 1862; a. 19; c. at Rappahannock Railroad Bridge, November 7, 1863.

Stuart, Thomas R.; en. March 15, 1862; a. 23; c. at Rappahannock Railroad Bridge, November 7, 1863.

Swisher, Alex. C.; en. July 1, 1861; a. 23.

Swisher, Claudius W.; en. March 19, 1862; a. 18; c. at Rappahannock Railroad Bridge, November 7, 1863.

Swisher, J. C.

Thaxton, Thomas C.; en. May 29, 1861; a. 20; w. at Second Manassas, August 29, 1862.
Thomason, Frank W.; en. March 19, 1862; a. 28; d. at Richmond, July 1, 1862.
Thomason, James W.; en. September 13, 1861; a. 23; d. at Montgomery Springs, Va., November 29, 1862.
Thomason, Jesse B.; en. March 19, 1862; a. 20; c. Rappahannock Railroad Bridge, November 7, 1863.
Thomason, John P.; en. September 13, 1861; a. 25; w. at Sharpsburg, September 17, 1863.
Thomason, Pink J.; w. at Richmond.
Trexler, Adam; en. May 29, 1861; a. 22; c. at Rappahannock Railroad Bridge, November 7, 1863.
Upright, Eli; en. May 29, 1861; a. 22; c. Rappahannock Railroad Bridge, November 7, 1863.
Walker, Joseph M.; en. October 15, 1861; a. 21; k. at Fredericksburg, Va., December 13, 1862.
Waters, John.
Wedlock, W.
Wilson, Joseph L.; en. May 29, 1861; a. 21; pr. to Sgt.
Yost, Solomon; en. May 29, 1861; a. 20; pr. to Cor., July 1, 1862.

SEVENTH REGIMENT

Company A

Officers

John G. Knox, 1st. Lt.; en. May 16, 1861; a. 21; pr. to Capt., April 4, 1862.

Privates

Knox, Joseph A.; en. May 29, 1863; a 21; k. at Gettysburg, July 8, 1863.

Company E

Privates

Burwell, Henry; en. August 1, 1862; a. 23; w. at Sharpsburg.
Link, John; en. August 1, 1862; a. 24.
Link, Oliver; en. August 1, 1862; a. 30.
Miller, Jacob C.; en. August 1, 1862; a. 33; w. Spottsylvania Courthouse, May 12, 1864.

Parker, James A.; en. August 1, 1862; a. 18; w. at Sharpsburg; k. Spottsylvania Courthouse, May 12, 1864.

Stokes, Obadiah; en. May 16, 1862; a. 25; d. of d., November, 1862.

Company F

Officers

John McLeod Turner, Capt.; en. May 16, 1861; a. 19; pr. to Major May 3, 1863; pr. to Lt.-Col.; w. in side at Newbern, N. C.; w. in head at Second Manassas; dangerously w. at Fredericksburg, Va., December 13, 1862; w. through right lung and in the head, in foot and through waist, at Gettysburg, July 3, 1863, by which he was permanently disabled.

William H. Crawford, 1st. Lt.; en. May 16, 1861; a. 28; pr. to Capt. Company B, Forty-second Regiment.

John R. Pearson, 2d. Lt.; en. October 10, 1863; k. in front, Petersburg, Va., 1864.

Thomas G. Williamson, 2d. Lt.; en. May 16, 1861; a. 23.

Elon G. Blackmer, 3d. Lt.; en. May 16, 1861; a. 22.

Hamilton, J. Pendleton, 5th. Sgt.; en. June 4, 1861; a. 28; missing in battle of Newbern, N. C.

James C. Johnson, 1st. Cor.; en. July 1, 1861; a. 21.

William C. Fesperman, 4th. Cor.; en. July 8, 1861; a. 22; pr. to 1st. Sgt. October, 1862; w. at Richmond; w. at Fredericksburg, December 13, 1862.

John W. Rough, Drummer; en. July 18, 1861; a. 18.

Privates

Arey, B. C.; en. August 20, 1862.

Ayers, Solomon K.; en. June 21, 1861; a. 21; pr. to Sgt. 1863; for gallantry and good conduct.

Baker, William; en. July 2, 1861; a. 19.

Basinger, B. P.; en. August 20, 1862; w. at Chancellorsville, May 3, 1863.

Basinger, Harrell M.; en. August 20, 1862; c. at Gettysburg.

Blackburn, I. H.

Bostian, Jacob A.; w. at Ream Station.

Brown, James H.; en. June 20, 1861; a. 24; k. at Chancellorsville, May 3, 1863.

Cauble, David M.; en. June 15, 1861; a. 19; pr. to Cor. January 1, 1863; w. below Richmond.

Cline, James; en. October 20, 1861; a. 56.
Coyle, Adam; en. June 3, 1861; a. 19; w. at Chancellorsville.
Deberry, David S.; en. June 13, 1861; a. 17; c. at Gettysburg.
Earnhardt, Lorenzo S.; en. June 13, 1861; a. 18; c. at Gettysburg and exchanged.
Eller, Caleb; en. August 20, 1862.
Eller, Jesse; en. August 20, 1862.
Fight, Henry T.; en. June 8, 1861; a. 21; pr. to Cor. Colorbearer at Gaines' Mill, where w., and w. at Fredericksburg.
File, Eli.
Fleming, Richard.
Graham, Hezekiah C.; en. July 1, 1861; a. 34.
Hagler, Charles W.; en. July 20, 1861; a. 19; w. at Fredericksburg, leg amputated.
Headinger, Wiley; en. June 4, 1861; a. 26.
Hill, Henry G.; en. July 1, 1861; a. 19; k. at Ox Hill, September 1, 1862.
Hooks, George E.; en. June 5, 1861; a. 25.
Johnson, John; en. July 8, 1861; a. 18.
Kinnerly, Charles W.; en. June 15, 1861; a. 20.
Kinnerly, John A.; en. June 6, 1861; a. 23; k. at Williamsport, Md., June 6, 1863.
Kluttz, W. Lawson.
Knox, James G.; en. April 7, 1862; a. 28.
Mills, Woodson D.; en. June 3, 1861; a. 40; k. Ox Hill, September 1, 1862.
Morgan, John G.; en. August 20, 1862.
Myers, John H.; en. June 15, 1861; a. 19; k. at Frazier's Farm, June 30, 1862.
Owens, Giles S.; en. July 3, 1861; a. 22.
Pennington, George B.; en. June 4, 1861; a. 21; w. at Fredericksburg.
Pennington, John.
Phillips, D. V.
Pinkston, T. R.
Quillman, George.
Reid, Calvin; d. of w., received at Battle of Jones' House, October, 1864.
Reid, Jesse; drowned in Yadkin River in sight of his home, returning from Army of Northern Virginia after Lee's surrender.
Reid, Milas.
Ridenhour, A. H.

Rimer, H. F.
Robinson, S. W.
Rowe, Peter.
Rufty, Rufus.
Stokes, W. C.; d. of w., received at Sharpsburg, September 24, 1862.
Swink, Edward.
Turner, W. L.
Watkins, L.
Watson, Albert W.
Wilkinson, John; en. August 10, 1861; a. 30; c. at Gettysburg.
Williamson, E.
Wyatt, Thomas.

EIGHTH REGIMENT

Company F

Officers

Leonard A. Henderson, 2d. Lt.; en. May 16, 1861; a. 19; pr. Capt. November, 1862; c. at Roanoke Island, February 8, 1862; k. while leading his Regiment in a charge at Cold Harbor, June 1, 1864.

Privates

Ashley, Wilburn; en. August 5, 1861; a. 19; w. severely at Roanoke Island, N. C., February 8, 1862.
Bostian, Andrew; en. August 10, 1861; a. 36.
Bostian, Wiley; en. July 20, 1861; a. 21; w. at Roanoke Island, February 8, 1862.
Rogers, A. J.; en. March 4, 1864; a. 17; enlisted on his own accord for forty years.
Sloop, Luther; en. August 4, 1863; a. 18.

Company H

Privates

Earnhardt Crusoe; en. March 3, 1863.
Ketchey, William R.; detailed as Courier for General Clingman.
Kistler, G. C.; en. June 27, 1863.
Patterson, J. E.; k. at Plymouth, N. C., April 20, 1864.

Patterson, S. G.; en. September 1, 1862; w. at Harrison, Va., September 30, 1864.

Company K

Officers

Pinkney A. Kennerly, Capt.; en. July 5, 1861; a. 38.

William H. Howerton, 1st. Lt.; en. July 5, 1861; resigned.

John J. Bell, 2d. Lt.; en. July 5, 1861; a. 56; pr. to 1st. Lt.; w. at Roanoke Island; resigned.

William M. Wilhelm, 2d. Lt.; en. July 5, 1861; a. 33; pr. to 1st. Lt., October 15, 1862.

Wilson W. Morgan, 1st. Sgt.; en. July 5, 1861; a. 32; d. while on sick furlough at Salisbury, N. C.

Stephen A. Shuman, 2d. Sgt.; en. July 5, 1861; a. 16; pr. to 1st. Sgt.; c. Cold Harbor, Va.

John C. Moore, 3d. Sgt.; en. July 5, 1861; a. 26; resigned on own account; c. at Cold Harbor, Va.

S. T. Chafin, 4th. Sgt.; en. July 5, 1861; a. 22; h. d.

Joseph E. Ide, 5th. Sgt.; en. August 1, 1861; a. 44; c. at Cold Harbor, May 31, 1864.

Henry A. Kale, 1st. Cor.; en. August 2, 1861; a. 27; resigned, on detached duty.

William Rainey, 2d. Cor.; en. July 5, 1861; a. 25; tr. to Fifty-seventh Regiment, January 31, 1864.

Philip Ivey Miller, 4th. Cor.; en. August 6, 1861; a. 26; pr. to 2d. Lt. March, 1863; shot through right lung at Plymouth, N. C.; k. at Fort Harrison, Va., September 30, 1864.

Privates

Agner, H. C.; en. August 2, 1861; a. 18; h. d.

Agner, Lewis; en. September 4, 1862; a. 34; w. at Plymouth, N. C., April 20, 1864.

Agner, William; en. July 15, 1861; a. 19; w. Bermuda Hundred, May 20, 1864; k. at Petersburg, August 19, 1864.

Barger, George A.; en. July 15, 1862; a. 17; c. Cold Harbor, May 31, 1864.

Barger, George H.; en. December 17, 1862; a. 27; d. in p.

Barger, Jacob; en. August 23, 1861; a. 21; c. at Cold Harbor, May 31, 1861.

Barger, Moses J.; en. August 28, 1861; a. 21; pr. 2d. Sgt.

Barker, Cicero R.; en. August 12, 1861; a. 13; pr. Drum-Major of Regiment, 1863.

Barnhardt, William A.; w. at Drewry's Bluff, May 18, 1864.

Barringer, David M.; en. September 3, 1861; a. 16; k. in front, Newbern, N. C., February 2, 1864.

Basinger, Andrew; en. July 27, 1861; a. 20; pr. to Cor.; c; d. in p.

Basinger, John; en. August 28, 1861; a. 19; h. d.

Bean, W. Hunter; en. September 14, 1862; a. 25; leg amputated at Bermuda Hundred, May 20, 1864.

Boggs, Peter; en. August 10, 1861; a. 18; h. d.

Brockman, John G.; en. July 20, 1861; a. 51; w. at Plymouth, N. C., April 20, 1864; d. in hospital at Richmond.

Brothers, ...

Brown, Mike; en. December 17, 1862; a. 38; d. of d., April, 1863.

Burriss, Solomon; w. at Drewry's Bluff, May 18, 1864.

Caldwell, Jesse B.; en. August 1, 1861; a. 40; seriously w. at Plymouth, N. C., April 20, 1864.

Canup, Benjamin F.; en. April 14, 1863, d. in p.

Canup, Milas A.; en. April 14, 1863; d. in p.

Clark, James W.; en. December 20, 1862; a. 18; c.

Clark, John; d. in p.

Colley, John T.; en. September 2, 1861; a. 24; c.

Colley, Samuel B.; en. September 2, 1861; a. 20; pr. to Cor.; w. at Battery Wagner, S. C.; w. in two places at Plymouth, N. C., April 20, 1864.

Cranford, Stephen J.; en. July 18, 1861; a. 46; h. d.

Crotser, Joseph; en. July 3, 1862; a. 16; d. of d., August, 1863.

Cruse, Rufus J.; en. July 18, 1861; a. 20; pr. to Cor.; c.; d. in p.

Deal, Charles A.; en. July 14, 1861; a. 28; k. at Plymouth, N. C., April 20, 1864.

Deal, Jacob A.; w. at Bermuda Hundred, May 20, 1864.

Eagle, George; en. August 31, 1861; a. 20; d. of d., December, 1863.

Etheridge, William; en. July 16, 1861; a. 36; w. at Plymouth, N. C., April 20, 1864.

Farr, F. M.; en. July 11, 1861; a. 20; disabled by wounds received at Battery Wagner, S. C.

Gallimore, Roby; w. at Plymouth, N. C., April 20, 1864.

Gates, Jesse C.; w. twice at Plymouth, N. C., April 20, 1864.

Goodman, ...; d. of d.

Harkey, Paul R.; en. July 15, 1861; a. 19; k. at Bermuda Hundred, May 20, 1864.

Hartman, W. F.; en. September 5, 1861; a. 16; d. of d., March, 1862.

Hess, Thomas; k. at Fort Harrison, Va., September 30, 1864.

Hoffman, M. C.; w. at Plymouth, N. C., April 20, 1864.

Holhouser, J. R.; en. July 27, 1861; a. 21; c. at Cold Harbor, May 31, 1864.

Holhouser, Wiley M.; en. August 6, 1861; a. 28; h. d.

Holobough, George M.; en. July 21, 1861; a. 19; c. at Cold Harbor, May 31, 1864.

House, James H.; en. July 14, 1862; a. 30; w. Drewry's Bluff, May 13, 1864.

Jenkins, John W.; en. July 16, 1861; a. 30; pr. to Cor.; w. at Drewry's Bluff, May 13, 1864; w. and c. at Fort Harrison, Va., September 30, 1864.

Johnson, Ransom; k. at Kinston, N. C., March 9, 1865.

Kale, Pinkney, C.; c.

Kestler, Cornelius; w. at Fort Harrison, Va., September 30, 1864.

Kestler, James H.; en. July 22, 1861; a. 21; d. of d.

Kestler, William A.; en. July 22, 1861; a. 19; w. at Plymouth, N. C., April 20, 1864; c. at Cold Harbor, May 31, 1864.

Ketchney, John I.; en. July 31, 1861; a. 22; k. at Plymouth, N. C., April 20, 1864.

Lanning, ...

Lefler, William M.; en. July 25, 1861; a. 31; k. by a fall from railroad bridge at Salisbury, N. C., July, 1862.

Lentz, John.

Linebarrier, John M.; en. August 12, 1861; a. 18; d. of d.

Linebarrier, James; en. November 10, 1862; h. d.

Lucas, John H.; en. July 11, 1861; a. 18; h. d.

Lucas, John; en. November 8, 1861; a. 35; d. of d., November, 1861. 1861.

Lyerly, Alex. M.; en. December 11, 1863; a. 17; c.

McGuire, Thomas; en. August 10, 1861; a. 21; w. at Bermuda Hundred, May 18, 1864.

McKinley, ...; d. of d., August 20, 1864.

Melton, Wallace; en. July 6, 1861; a. 21; tr.

Miller, Crawford A.; en. August 6, 1861; a. 21; d. of d., November, 1862.

Miller, John Wilkes; w. at Fort Harrison, September 30, 1864; w. at Bentonville, N. C., March 19, 1865.

Morgan, Abram; en. July 17, 1861; a. 28; w. at Plymouth, N. C., April 20, 1864.

Morgan, Ivey C.; en. July 17, 1861; a. 21; pr. Cor.; w. seriously at Drewry's Bluff, May 13, 1864.

Morgan, John C.; w. at Fort Harrison, September 30, 1864.

Murph, John L.; k. at Plymouth, N. C., April 20, 1864.

Murph, J. R.; en. July 13, 1861; a. 25; w. at Roanoke Island, February 8, 1862; w. at Bermuda Hundred, May 20, 1864; w. at Bentonville, N. C., March 20, 1865.

Newson, J. E.; en. July 31, 1861; a. 23; c. three times.

Peeler, Moses J.; en. September 14, 1862; a. 20; d. of d., January, 1863.

Plummer, Frank E.; c.

Plummer, William J.; en. November 22, 1861; a. 18; w. at Plymouth, N. C., April 20, 1864.

Price, Thomas; en. September 6, 1861; a. 18.

Propst, Henry M.; en. September 14, 1862; a. 21; c.

Propst, William D.; en. September 14, 1862; a. 34; d. of d. at Wilmington, N. C., June, 1863.

Rainey, John; k. at Plymouth, N. C., April 20, 1864.

Rainey, William; en. August 27, 1861; a. 24; tr. to Fourth Regiment, 1862.

Reeves, Charles; en. November 10, 1862; a. 36; h. d.

Riley, ...

Rimer, John L.; en. July 6, 1861; a. 16; w. at Plymouth, N. C., April 20, 1864.

Rimer, Leonard; en. July 14, 1861; a. 40; h. d.

Rimer, Milton F.; en. November 17, 1861; a. 14; k. at Battery Wagner, S. C., August 31, 1863.

Rowzee, Claudius W.; en. August 27, 1861; a. 25; pr. Hospital Steward in Navy.

Rufty, James R.; en. September 14, 1862; a. 22; detailed as miller.

Sawyer, Robert W.; en. September 6, 1861; a. 15; h. d., but remained on his own account and took a drum until large enough to handle a musket; w. through the hand at Plymouth, N. C., April 20, 1864; and pierced by four balls at Fort Harrison, Va., September 30, 1864; d. in hands of the enemy.

Sawyer, William R.; en. July 6, 1861; a. 18; c. at Cold Harbor, June 1, 1864.

Seaford, W. M.; en. July 31, 1861; a. 25; w. and refused to leave the field at Plymouth, N. C., April 20, 1864; and k. the same day.

Shaver, Abram; en. July 17, 1861; a. 21; d. in p.
Shaver, Alex.; en. July 26; 1861; a. 21; c.
Sheppard, Daniel; en. July 8, 1861; a. 23; d. in p.
Shipton, Hiram; en. August 23, 1861; a. 17; tr. to Engineering Corps, June, 1863.
Sloan, James T.; en. July 6, 1861; a. 20; w. at Roanoke Island, February 8, 1862.
Spears, Josiah W.; en. July 6, 1861; a. 27; d. of d.
Stoner, Alfred; en. August 31, 1861; a. 18; d. of d., November, 1861.
Swink, George R.; en. July 13, 1861; a. 18; w. at Petersburg, Va., June 17, 1864.
Swink, Leslie D.; en. July 15, 1861; a. 18; w. and c. at Cold Harbor, June 1, 1864; d. in p.
Swink, Peter; leg amputated at Plymouth, N. C., April 20, 1864.
Swink, Peter R.; en. July 15, 1861; a. 45; d. of d. at Richmond, Va., August 5, 1864.
Taylor, D. C. S.; c.
Thompson, John; en. July 27, 1861; a. 43; h. d.
Tries, Peter; c.
Weant, Alex. W.
White, James R. H.; pr. Cor.; c.
Wormington, James; en. July 30, 1861; a. 22; w. at Sullivan's Island, S. C.; d. in p.
Wright, William M.; en. July 24, 1861; a. 41; d. in p.
Wyatt, Gilbert I.; en. July 6, 1861; a. 32; k. at Battery Wagner, S. C., August 28, 1863.
Wyatt, James I.; en. July 17, 1861; a. 22; d. of d.
Wyatt, Wilson R.; en. July 6, 1861; a. 32; d. of d., March, 1862.

This entire Company with its Regiment was captured on Roanoke Island, N. C., February 8, 1862; retained as prisoners for two weeks and paroled; exchanged and reorganized at Raleigh, N. C., September, 1862; assigned to Clingman's Brigade, where it remained until its surrender with Gen. Joseph E. Johnston's Army, at Greensboro, N. C., April 26, 1865.

TENTH REGIMENT

Company B

Privates

John S. Henderson.

ELEVENTH REGIMENT (OLD BETHEL)

Company——

Officers

Calvin S. Brown, Capt.

Company K

Privates

Smith, J. L.; en. April 25, 1861; a. 21; pr. to Sgt. Forty-second Regiment.

THIRTEENTH REGIMENT

Company F

Privates

Clomminger, Alonzo; a. 22; k. at Chancellorsville, Va., May 3, 1863.

FOURTEENTH REGIMENT

Company B

Privates

Bemister, Thomas; en. May 1, 1861; a. 25; tr. to Company D, November 30, 1862.

Company I

Privates

Todd, Giles; d. of d., 1863.
Fred C. Fisher; attached to Gen. W. H. F. Lee's Staff.
A. H. Boyden; attached to Gen. R. F. Hoke's Staff.

FIFTEENTH REGIMENT

Company C

Privates

Williamson, P.; en. July 15, 1862; a. 56.

SIXTEENTH REGIMENT

Officers

Benjamin F. Moore; appointed Adjt. April 26, 1862; w. at Mechanicsville, Va.

TWENTIETH REGIMENT

Company A

Privates

Bell, Robert O. B.; en. April 20, 1961; a. 24; d. of d. at Salisbury, N. C., August 5, 1863.

Castor, Daniel; en. March 16, 1862; a. 35; d. of d. at Hanover Junction, Va., April 18, 1863.

Correll, Adam M.; en. June 7, 1861; a. 22.

Deal, George H.; en. June 7, 1862; a. 28.

Fink, D. C.; en. April 20, 1861; a. 27.

Fink, Henry H.; en. May 3, 1861; a. 21.

Gordy, John W.; en. 1862; a. 39; w. at Cold Harbor; k. at Chancellorsville, Va., May, 1863.

Lingle, Alfred; en. March 19, 1862; a. 25.

Patterson, I., Frank; en. June 7, 1861; a. 18; arm amputated at Chancellorsville, Va.

Petchel, Jacob V.; en. June 7, 1861; a. 24; w. at Malvern Hill.

Wensil, Henry A.; en. March 19, 1861; a. 24; w. at Gettysburg. Pa.

TWENTY-THIRD REGIMENT

Company D

Privates

Bringle, Nicholas; en. September 6, 1862; a. 42.

Callicut, Pascal; en. September 6, 1862; a. 23.

Clifford, Branch G.; en. September 6, 1862; a. 18.

Edgerson, John; en. September 6, 1862; a. 28.

Eller, Joshua; en. September 6, 1862; a. 28; w. at Gettysburg.

Eller, Moses; en. September 6, 1862; a. 34; sent to hospital, September 17, 1862; missing.

Eller, Richard E.; en. September 6, 1862; a. 36; d. of d. at Winchester, Va., November, 1863.

Eudy, William C.; en. September 6, 1862; a. 19; d. of d. at Winchester, Va., April 2, 1863.

File, Milas A.; en. September 6, 1862; a. 33.
Hill, Henry; en. September 6, 1862; a. 32.
Lutrick, Alfred N.; en. September 6, 1862; a. 28; d. of d. at Richmond, Va., July 6, 1862.
Stirewalt, Frank A.; en. September 6, 1862; a. 32; w. at Chancellorsville.
Stone, Charles W.; en. September 6, 1862; a. 31.
Misenheimer, M. R.; en. September 6, 1862; a. 30.

Company H

Privates

Eller, Eli; en. September 3, 1862; d. of d. at Richmond, Va.
Eller, James; en. September 3, 1862.
Eller, Samuel; en. September 3, 1862; leg amputated at Gettysburg, Pa.
Frick, John; en. September 4, 1862; k. at Gettysburg, July, 1863.
Lemley, B. T.; en. September 4, 1862.
Lemley, D. A.; en. September 4, 1862.
Vandervort, W. K. G.; en. September 4, 1862; severely w. at Chancellorsville, Va.
Wyatt, G. W.; en. August 1, 1862.
Wyatt, J. E.; en. September 4, 1862.
Wyatt, W. W.; en. September 4, 1862; k. at Gettysburg, Pa., July 1863.

TWENTY-SIXTH REGIMENT

Company I

Privates

Dickson, M. B.; en. September 23, 1862; a. 34.

TWENTY-EIGHTH REGIMENT

Officers

F. N. Luckey; en. September 25, 1861; Assistant Surgeon; pr. to Surgeon, February, 1862.

Company D

Privates

Arey, G. W.; en. March 15, 1862; a. 32; w.
Canup, D. A.; d. of d.

Lyerly, Hartwell.
Malt, Isaac C.; d. of d.
Malt, J. P.; w. at Gettysburg.
Miller, A. D.; k. at Gettysburg.
Parker, B. P.; k. at Sharpsburg.
Parker, John A.; d. of d.

THIRTIETH REGIMENT

Company K

Privates

Dunn, George; en. July 1, 1863; a. 43.
Thompson, James; en. July 1, 1863; a. 37; d. of d. at Morton's Ford, December 12, 1863.
West, William; en. July 1, 1863; a. 40.

THIRTY-FIRST REGIMENT

Company K

Privates

McLaughlin, W. H.; en. May 27, 1863; a. 36.

THIRTY-THIRD REGIMENT

Company C

Officers

Frank B. Craige, 2d. Lt.; en. February 20, 1864; a. 18; pr. to 1st. Lt July 28, 1864.

Company G

Privates

Miller, H. W.; en. September 23, 1864; a. 38.
Owens, W. F.; en. September 23, 1864; a. 35.

THIRTY-FOURTH REGIMENT

Company D

Officers

William A. Houck, Capt.; en. September 9, 1861; a. 35; pr. to Lt.-Col. on reorganization of Regiment; resigned.

John Graham, 2d. Lt.; en. September 9, 1861; a. 37; pr. to 1st. Lt. October 25, 1861; resigned.

John P. Parks, Lt.; en. September 9, 1861; a. 27; pr. 1st. Lt. April 18, 1862; k. below Richmond, June 30, 1862.

Robert S. Cowan, 2d. Sgt.; en. September 9, 1861; a. 22; pr. to 2d. Lt. April 18, 1862; k. below Richmond, June 30, 1862.

James Basinger, 3d. Sgt.; en. September 9, 1861; a. 30; pr. to 2d. Lt. July 20, 1862; d. of w. received at Sharpsburg, September 18, 1862.

P. A. Sloop, 4th. Sgt.; en. September 9, 1861; a. 21; severely w. at Chancellorsville.

W. A. Kilpatrick, 5th. Sgt.; en. September 9, 1861; a. 26; w. at Chancellorsville.

C. K. McNeely, 1st. Cor.; en. September 9, 1861; a. 25; pr. to Lt. July, 1862; pr. to Capt. September 7, 1862.

James B. Parker, 2d. Cor.; en. September, 1861; a. 37.

Edward Sloop, 3d. Cor.; en. September 9, 1861; a. 34; d. of d. at Richmond, July 30, 1862.

Privates

Atkinson, Thomas J.; en. September 9, 1861; a. 21; pr. to Sgt. April, 1862; d. of d.

Atwell, B. M.; en. September 9, 1861; a. 18; d. of w. received at Richmond.

Atwell, George A.; en. September 9, 1861; a. 18; pr. to Sgt.-Major February, 1863; pr. to Lt. Company E; pr. to Capt. August, 1863.

Atwell, George L.; en. September 9, 1861; a. 17; d. of d., April 25, 1863, at Fredericksburg, Va.

Baker, Henry.

Barnhardt, Wiley.

Barnhardt, William; k. at Petersburg, Va.

Bostian, ———.

Brown, Henry T.; en. September 9, 1861.

Clodfelter, John T.; en. September 9, 1861; a. 19; k. at Petersburg, Va.

Corriher, Joel; en. September 9, 1861; a. 25; w.

Dancy, A. L.; en. May 15, 1862; d. of d., September, 1862; at Danville, Va.

Davis, William; d. of d. at High Point, N. C.

Douglas, Augustus; d. of d.

Douglas, Joseph A.

Douglas, Samuel; pr. to 3d. Lt.; d. of d.
Edminston, A. H.; en. September 9, 1861; a. 23; w.
Eller, Green; en. September 9, 1861; a. 29.
Eller, Obadiah; en. September 9, 1861; a. 21; pr. to Sgt., September 1, 1863.
Elliott, William F.; en. September 9, 1861; a. 19; d. of d. in hospital, October 24, 1862.
Ellis, John W.; en. September 9, 1861; a. 20; pr. to Sgt., May 3, 1863.
Foster, George; en. September 9, 1861; a. 16.
Freeland, James.
Frieze, Miles W.; en. September 9, 1681; a. 19.
Glover, James; en. September 9, 1861; a. 17.
Harrill, William; en. September 9, 1861; a. 38; d. of w. received at Richmond.
Hodgins, Martin; leg amputated.
Jamison, M. S.; en. September 9, 1861; a. 37.
Kistler, T. H.; en. September 9, 1861; a. 20; pr. to Cor. July, 1863; w. at Manassas; d. of w. received at Culpeper Courthouse.
Leazer, William A.; en. September 9, 1861.
Lowder, Daniel R.; en. September 9, 1861; a. 18; arm amputated at Ox Hill.
Lowrance, F. A.; en. September 9, 1861; a. 18; pr. to Sgt.; k. at Chancellorsville, May 3, 1863.
Lowrance, J. C.; en. September 9, 1861; a. 20.
McLaughlin, E. C.; en. September 9, 1861; a. 28; w.
McLaughlin, J. H.; en. September 9, 1861; a. 30; w. at Ox Hill; w. at Sheppardstown.
McLaughlin, S. W.; en. September 9, 1861; a. 39.
McNeely, James A.; en. May 15, 1863; a. 29; d. of d.
McNeely, James K.; en. September 9, 1861; a. 35; pr. to Cor.; pr. to Capt.
McNeely, J. R.; en. September 9, 1861; a. 24; k. at Richmond, July 27, 1862.
Martin, J. S. A.; en. September 9, 1861; a. 18; d. of w. received at Mechanicsville.
Miller, Franklin.
Miller, J. A.; en. September 9, 1861; a. 21; k. at Gettysburg.
Miller, J. F.; en. September 9, 1861; a. 25; d. of d.
Overcash, G. M.; en. September 9, 1861; a. 18; w. at Gettysburg; w. at Wilderness.
Overcash, H. F.; en. September 9, 1861; a. 20; d. of d., July 11, 1862, at Richmond.

Overcash, H. J.; en. September 9, 1861; a. 21.
Overcash, H. W.; en. September 9, 1861; a. 23.
Overcash, John J.; en. September 9, 1861; a. 27; d. of d. at High Point, N. C., August 28, 1861.
Overcash, R. A.; en. September 9, 1861; a. 19; pr. to Cor.; w.
Overcash, S. S.; en. September 9, 1861; a. 20; d. of d., August, 1862.
Parks, B. C.; en. September 9, 1861; a. 42.
Pehel, Levi; en. September 9, 1861; a. 41.
Pickler, David; en. September 9, 1861; a. 17; d. of w. received at Richmond.
Seckler, John F.; en. September 9, 1861; a. 40; d. of w. received at Richmond.
Sloan, Junius J.; en. September 9, 1861; a. 25; d. of d., June, 1862, at Richmond.
Stirewalt, J. F.; en. September 9, 1861; a. 22.
Torrence, Samuel; d. of d.
Voils, Jackson; d. of d.
Waggoner, Frank.
Weaver, John M.
Williford, James F.; en. September 9, 1861; a. 20; w. at Richmond.
Williford, John A.; en. September 9, 1861; a. 52.

Company E

Privates

Atwell, G. A.; en. July 29, 1863; pr. to 2d. Lt.

THIRTY-FIFTH REGIMENT

Company I

Privates

McLaughlin, J. H.; en. May 6, 1863; a. 39.

FORTY-SECOND REGIMENT

Company B

Officers

James R. Crawford, Capt.
A. B. Wright, 1st. Lt.
Robert W. Price, 2d. Lt.; w. above Richmond, December 10, 1864.
J. F. Dodson, Jr., 2d. Lt.

J. Smith; en. March 10, 1863; 2d. Sgt.
W. P. Shuford; en. January 17, 1862; 3d. Sgt.
H. A. Harman; en. January 27, 1862; a. 26; 4th. Sgt.; w. at Chafin's Farm.
R. C. Cobb; en. January 27, 1862; Cor.

Privates

Beefie, W. F.; en. January 27, 1862; a. 24; k. at Petersburg.
Beeker, H.; en. January 27, 1862; a. 22; pr. to 4th. Cor.
Blackwelder, W.; en. January 27, 1862.
Boyden, A. H.; det. as Courier for Maj.-Gen. R. F. Hoke.
Brown, H.; en. January 27, 1862; d. at home.
Burns, W.; en. January 27, 1862; w. at Kinston.
Carper, W. C.; en. January 27, 1862.
Cauble, Benjamin; en. January 27, 1862.
Cauble, J. G.; en. March 11, 1863.
Cauble, Mike; en. January 27, 1862.
Cauble, Samuel; en. January 27, 1862.
Clark, J. C.; en. January 27, 1862; tr. to Thirteenth Regiment.
Clomlinger, ————; en. January 27, 1862; tr. to Thirteenth Regiment, Company K.
Connell, J.; en. January 27, 1862; k. at Petersburg.
Connell, J.; en. January 27, 1862; k. at Petersburg.
Correll, J.; en. January 27, 1862.
Coughenour, Thomas A.; en. January 27, 1862; tr. to Regimental Band.
Cowan, B. F.; en. January 27, 1862; w. at Petersburg.
Daniel, W.; en. January 27, 1862; k. at Bermuda Hundred.
Daniel, W. J.
Dillard, J.; en. January 27, 1862.
Dolin, A.; en. January 27, 1862; w. at Blackwater.
Doy, Daniel.
Dry, D.; en. January 27, 1862.
Eagle, P.; en. January 27, 1862; w. at Petersburg.
Eagle, W.; en. January 27, 1862.
Exum, J. W.; en. January 27, 1862; k. at Cold Harbor, May 30, 1864.
Fesperman, George; en. January 27, 1862; d. at home, 1862.
Fink, M.; en. January 27, 1862.
Fry, J. P.; en. January 27, 1862; w. at Petersburg.
Hambry, R. C.; en. January 27, 1862; w. at Kinston.
Hess, George; en. January 27, 1862.

Hess, Levi; en. January 27, 1862.
House, D.; en. January 27, 1862.
House, John; en. January 27, 1862.
House, Thomas; en. January 27, 1862; k. at Cold Harbor.
House, W.; en. January 27, 1862; w. at Bermuda Hundred.
Hunt, Jason; en. January 27, 1862.
Isenhour, J., Sr.; en. January 27, 1862.
Isenhour, J., Jr.; en. January 27, 1862; w. at Petersburg.
Kerr, John; en. January 27, 1862; d. at Tarboro.
Kestler, H. A.; en. March 10, 1863; k. at Cold Harbor.
Kestler, William H.; w. at Bermuda Hundred.
Kiser, J.; en. January 27, 1862; w.
Knox, B.; en. January 27, 1862.
Knox, T.; en. January 27, 1862; k. at Sheppardsville.
Love, W. H.; pr. Drum-Major of Regiment.
McGhee, ———; en. January 27, 1862.
Martin, John; en. March 10, 1863; k. at Petersburg.
Miller, E.; en. January 27, 1862; w. at Richmond.
Mills, N. N.; en. January 28, 1862.
Mills, C.; en. January 27, 1862.
Montgomery, James.
Moore, A. C.; en. January 27, 1862; k. at Petersburg.
Moore, J.; en. January 27, 1862; d. at home.
Moore, S. J.; en. January 27, 1862.
Munroe, Peter.
Overcash, Allison.
Parnell, W.; en. January 27, 1862.
Pennington, David.
Phifer, D.; en. January 27, 1862; w. at Kinston.
Phifer, W.; en. January 27, 1862.
Phillips, C.; en. January 27, 1862.
Pig, Hugh; en. January 27, 1862; w. at Petersburg.
Pig, Ris; en. January 27, 1862.
Reese, C.; en. January 27, 1862.
Reese, W.; en. January 27, 1862.
Richie, M.; en. January 27, 1862; k. at Kinston.
Ruff, J. C.; en. January 27, 1862.
Rumple, W.; en. January 27, 1862; w. at Richmond, December 10, 1864.
Sanders, W.; en. January 27, 1862.
Sharp, R.; en. March 10, 1863.
Shuford, A. L.; en. January 27, 1862; pr. to Ord. Sgt.; w. at Petersburg.

Sipe, J.; en. January 27, 1862; k. at Kinston.
Smith, Theodore; en. January 27, 1862; w. at Cold Harbor.
Stillerell, L.; en. March 10, 1863; k. at Petersburg.
Stillwell, L.; en. January 27, 1862.
Stoner, W.; en. March 10, 1863; w. at Kinston.
Taylor, L.; en. January 27, 1862.
Thompson, S.; en. January 27, 1862; d. in Camp.
Trexler, B. C.; en. January 27, 1862.
Tucker, Daniel; en. January 27, 1862.
Tucker, J.; en. January 27, 1862.
Wade, J.; en. January 27, 1862.
Walton, Allen.
Walton, L. W.; en. March 10, 1863; tr. to Regimental Band.
Walton, R.; en. January 27, 1862; d. at Richmond.

Company C

Privates

Black, John; en. March 18, 1862; a. 42; w. at Petersburg.
Black, Thomas; en. March 1, 1864; a. 18; d. of d., October 1, 1864.

Company D

Officers

Joseph M. Roark, Capt.; en. February 28, 1862; a. 30.
Robert R. Crawford, 1st. Lt.; en. February 28, 1862; a. 22; pr. Capt. November 25, 1862.
Leonidas W. Crawford, 2d. Lt.; en. February 28, 1862; a. 21; pr. to 1st. Lt.; c. at Cold Harbor, June 3, 1864.
Edward A. Rusher, 2d. Lt.; en. February 28, 1862; a. 30; k. at Petersburg.

Privates

Almand, Archibald; en. March 15, 1862; a. 23.
Barringer, Henry; en. March 24, 1862; a. 23; k.
Basinger, Henry; en. March 11, 1862; a. 45; w. severely.
Basinger, John G.; en. March 11, 1862; a. 28.
Boyer, Moses; en. March 24, 1862; a. 22; c. at Cold Harbor.
Bradshaw, Levi; en. March 20, 1862; a. 54.
Casper, Munroe; en. March 15, 1862; a. 21.
Davis, Martin; en. March 24, 1862; a. 41.

Eller, Cornelius; en. March 24, 1862; a. 28; d. in hospital, December 25, 1862.
Eller, David; en. March 24, 1862; a. 28.
Eller, Tobias; en. March 24, 1862; a. 30.
Fulenwider, John; en. March 18, 1862; a. 35.
Hess, Caleb A.; en. March 22, 1862; a. 19.
Hess, William; en. March 22, 1862; a. 30.
Hoffman, Henry; en. March 22, 1862; a. 19.
Holhouser, Jeremiah; en. March 1, 1862; a. 18.
Kestler, George B.; en. March 18, 1862; a. 25.
Kluttz, Levi; en. March 18, 1862; a. 36; d. of d., March 10, 1863.
Koon, Richard M.; en. March 18, 1862; a. 18.
Loftin, Lindsay; en. March 19, 1862; a. 36.
Morris, James; en. March 17, 1862; a. 39.
Pinkston, George W.; en. March 18, 1862; a. 62.
Pinkston, Matthew L.; en. March 18, 1862; a. 35.
Rainey, Isaac A.; en. March 18, 1862; a. 34; c. at Cold Harbor; d. in p.
Sheets, John; en. March 17, 1862; a. 36; d. in hosptial, April 26, 1863.
Shields, Joseph P.; en. July 4, 1862; a. 35.
Smith, Michael; en. March 4, 1862; a. 29.
Trexler, Henry A.; en. March 18, 1862; a. 21.
Troutman, W. G.; en. March 18, 1862; a. 18; w. at Butler's Tower.
Waller, Jesse; en. March 4, 1862; a. 49.
Wilhelm, William A.; en. March 4, 1862; a. 22.

Company G

Officers

James A. Blackwelder, Capt.; en. March 15, 1862; a. 40.
Augustus Leazer, 1st. Lt.; en. March 15, 1862; a. 19.
Henry W. A. Miller, 2d. Lt.; en. July 1, 1861; a. 21; pr. from private in Company G, Sixth Regiment; w. twice.
William L. Atwell, 2d. Lt.; en. July 2, 1861; a. 30; resigned August 8, 1862; re-enlisted as private, March 15, 1864; d. of d., August 3, 1864.
Charles A. Miller, 2d. Lt.; en. May 5, 1862; w. severely at Petersburg.
David A. Atwell, 1st. Sgt.; en. April 11, 1862; a. 19; tr. from Company B.
John A. Hess, 2d. Sgt.; en. March 19, 1862; a. 27.

David M. Cooper, 3d. Sgt.; en. March 19, 1862; a. 29.
Jacob J. Bostian, 4th. Sgt.; en. March 19, 1862; a. 47.
William W. Graham, 5th. Sgt.; en. March 17, 1862; a. 23; k. at Petersburg, July 30, 1864.
Alphonzo L. Atwell, 1st. Cor.; en. March 29, 1861; a. 21.
John C. Leazer, 2d. Cor.; en. March 29, 1862; a. 21.
John W. Rumple, 2d. Cor.; en. March 29, 1862, tr. to Regimental Band.
James F. Rumple, 3d. Cor.; en. March 29, 1862; a. 30.
John C. Wilhelm, 4th. Cor.; en. March 29, 1862; a. 21; pr. to 1st. Cor.
Jesse H. Albright, Musician; en. March 15, 1861; a. 28; d. of d. at Weldon, N. C., March, 1863.
George A. Cooper, Musician; en. March 17, 1862; a. 18.

Privates

Allman, Nelson; en. May 30, 1862; a. 17.
Atwell, James A.; en. May 19, 1862; a. 46.
Atwell, John C.; en. May 17, 1862; a. 21; d. of d. at Lynchburg, Va., August 15, 1862.
Atwell, Joseph E.; en. January 1, 1864; a. 18.
Atwell, O. W.; en. May 19, 1862; a. 27.
Atwell, William A.; en. January 10, 1863; a. 16.
Baker, John M.; en. March 19, 1862; a. 21.
Blackwelder, Henry C.; en. March 24, 1862; a. 18.
Blackwelder, S. T.; en. May 15, 1862; a. 16.
Brantly, William W.; en. April 25, 1862; a. 30; pr. to Cor.; pr. to Sgt.
Beaver, George F. S.; en. May 5, 1862; a. 22.
Beaver, Jacob H.; en. November 6, 1862; a. 18; k. near Fort Fisher, N. C., December, 1864.
Beaver, Levi A.; en. March 19, 1862; a. 32.
Bostian, Andrew; en. March 19, 1862; a. 37.
Bostian, Jacob J.; en. March 19, 1862; a. 20; k. March 10, 1865.
Bostian, James M.; en. June 6, 1862; a. 17.
Bostian, John M.; en. October 8, 1862; a. 18.
Bostian, William M.; en. March 19, 1862; a. 21.
Brown, George A.; en. March 22, 1862; a. 22.
Brown, James L.; en. May 5, 1862; a. 18.
Brown, John M.; en. March 22, 1862; a. 20.
Brown, Joseph, en. March 27, 1862; a. 24.
Brown, Laurence; en. August 25, 1863; a. 18.
Brown, William L.; en. March 19, 1862; a. 26.

Cleaver, Daniel M.; en. March 27, 1862; a. 16.
Coburn, James; en. March 19, 1863; a. 47.
Cooper, G. A.
Cooper, Joseph E.; en. March 3, 1864; a. 18; k. at Petersburg, July 10, 1864.
Correll, Daniel; en. March 19, 1862; a. 42.
Corriher, Henry C.; en. March 19, 1863; a. 22; pr. to Sgt.
Corriher, James F.; en. March 19, 1863; a. 19; pr. to Cor.
Corriher, Thomas W.; en. March 19, 1962; a. 22.
Deal, Alex.; en. March 19, 1862; a. 33.
Deal, David, en. March 19, 1862; a. 32.
Deal, Franklin W.; en. March 19, 1862; a. 28; d. of w. received at Petersburg, July 30, 1864.
Deal, Jacob, Sr.; en. March 19, 1862; a. 49.
Deal, Jacob, Jr.; en. March 19, 1862; a. 25; d. of d. 1864.
Deal, John A.; en. December 24, 1862; a. 18; k. October 9, 1863, by accident on W. & W. Railroad.
Deal, John L.; en. April 10, 1863; a. 37.
Deal, Samuel; en. March 19, 1862; a. 30.
Deal, W. A.; en. March 19, 1862; a. 33.
Deal, William E.; en. May 1, 1862; a. 31.
Felcher, Archibald W.; en. February 2, 1863; a. 37.
Fesperman, Frederick; d. of d. at Lynchburg, Va., 1862.
Fesperman, John A.; en. September 14, 1863; a. 18.
Fesperman, John M.; en. March, 1862; a. 18; d. of d. at Lynchburg, June 28, 1862.
Fouts, James S.; en. November 3, 1862; a. 18; d. July 24, 1864, of w. received at Petersburg.
Fouts, John D.; en. March 19, 1862; a. 20.
Fouts, William H.; en. March 19, 1862; a. 21; pr. to Cor.
Freeland, William R.; en. December 24, 1862; a. 18.
Freeze, Caleb M.; en. March 19, 1862; a. 28.
Freeze, Henry E.; en. March 19, 1862; a. 30.
Freeze, Ivel J.; en. March 21, 1862; a. 24.
Garver, L. B.; en. March 19, 1862; a. 19.
Hampton, David A.; en. March 19, 1862; a. 20.
Hampton, John W.; en. March 19, 1862; a. 22.
Karriker, Jacob L.; en. May, 1863; a. 32; k. June 18, 1864, at Petersburg.
Karriker, Jacob P.; en. March 17, 1862; a. 19; k. June 18, 1864; at Petersburg.
Karriker, John A.; en. March 3, 1864; a. 18.

Karriker, William A.; en. March 17, 1862; a. 21.
Kluttz, Alex.; en. March 19, 1862; a. 25; d. of d. at Richmond, August 25, 1864.
Kluttz, Jesse A.; en. August 25, 1863; a. 18.
Lawrence, David A.; en. August 14, 1863; a. 18.
Leazer, David M.; en. March 19, 1862; a. 28.
Leazer, James W.; en. May 12, 1862; a. 37.
Leazer, William F.; en. March 19, 1862; a. 21; d. September 21, of w. received at Petersburg.
Leazer, William H.; en. May 1, 1862; a. 26; k. at Newport Barracks, February 2, 1864.
Lipe, E. J.; en. April 10, 1863; a. 26.
Lipe, Jacob S.; en. March 19, 1862; a. 25; pr. to Cor.
Lipe, William A.; en. July 8, 1862; a. 28; w. at Petersburg twice.
Lippard, John T.; en. May, 1862; a. 25.
Litaker, William R.; en. March 19, 1862; a. 38.
Lynch, Andrew J.; en. March 19, 1862; a. 32; d. of. d. July 13, 1864, at Petersburg.
Martin, Levi A. C.; en. August 17, 1862; a. 18.
Miller, Andrew A.; en. March 19, 1862; a. 19.
Miller, John D.; en. August 14, 1863; a. 18.
Miller, Samuel A.; en. July 27, 1863; a. 18; d. of d. at Goldsboro, N. C., October 10, 1864.
Overcash, George F.; en. August 14, 1863; a. 18.
Overcash, Samuel; en. March 19, 1862; a. 27.
Overcash, Soloman W.; en. May 10, 1862; a. 28.
Pechel, A. J.; en. October 17, 1863; a. 18.
Pechel, F. M.; en. March 19, 1862; a. 37; d. of d. at Petersburg, September, 1862.
Pechel, John; en. March 19, 1862; a. 45.
Pechel, Solomon; en. March 19, 1862; a. 35.
Rhimer, Thomas H.; en. March 19, 1862; a. 24.
Richey, John D.; en. March 3, 1864; a. 18.
Richey, John R.; en. March 3, 1864; a. 18.
Ridding, Rufus M.; en. February 20, 1863; a. 37; d. of d. at Goldsboro, N. C., July 31, 1863.
Rogers, George R.; en. March 19, 1862; a. 34.
Rogers, Jeremiah; en. March 19, 1862; a. 20.
Rose, John A.; en. April 24, 1862; a. 29; severely w. at Petersburg.
Sechler, James P.; en. March 22, 1862; a. 33; severely w. at Petersburg, July 8, 1864.
Shulinbarger, J. L.; en. August 14, 1863; a. 19.

Shuping, Absalom A.; en. April 2, 1862; a 28; d. of d. August 13, 1864, at Petersburg.
Shuping, Andrew F.; en. April 5, 1862; a. 22.
Sloop, Henry O., Sr.; en. March 19, 1862; a. 32.
Sloop, Henry O., Jr.; en. March 19, 1862; a. 18; w. at Petersburg.
Smith, Henry C.; en. March 19, 1862; a. 19.
Smith, John W.; en. March 19, 1862; a. 33.
Smith, Joseph W.; en. July 27, 1863; a. 18.
Smith, Samuel; en. March 19, 1862; a. 32; d. of d. at Kinston, N. C., September 14, 1863.
Smith, Thomas H.; en. March 19, 1862; a. 32.
Upright, William; en. April 2, 1862; a. 32.
Walcher, James L.; en. March 19, 1862; a. 20.
Yost, F. M.; en. March 19, 1862; a. 30; d. of d. May 1862, at Salisbury, N. C.

FORTY-FIFTH REGIMENT

Company K

Officers

M. B. Hemphill, 4th. Cor.; en. May 10, 1862; a. 26; pr. to 2d. Cor.

FORTY-SIXTH REGIMENT

Company A

Privates

Buchanan, John; en. April 15, 1863; a. 39.
Cole, J. W.; en. April 15, 1863; a. 19; k. at Petersburg.
Davis, James; en. April 23; 1863; a. 40.
Glover, Charles; en. April 15, 1863; a. 32.
Glover, R. J.; en. April 15, 1863; a. 20.
Goodman, Christopher; en. April 15, 1863; a. 38, d. of d. at home.
Hill, J. L.; en. April 15, 1863; a. 39; k. at Wilderness.
Hodge, Richard; en. April 15, 1863; a. 39; c. at Petersburg, March, 1865.
Leonard, William; en. April 15, 1863; a. 39.
Mahaley, Charles; en. April 15, 1863; a. 37.
Mahaley, Lawrence; en. April 15, 1863; a. 38.
Mesimor, Bedford; en. April 15, 1863; a. 36.
Overcash, Alex.; en. April 18, 1863; a. 30.
Overcash, J. J.; en. April 18, 1863; a. 37.
Overcash, J. W.; en. April 15, 1863; a. 35.

Penninger, Paul; en. April 30, 1863; c.
Rhymer, D. A.; en. April 15, 1863; a. 37.
Ritchie, John; en. April 15, 1863; a. 36; w.
Sides, Levi; en. April 15, 1863; a. 37; c.
Summers, James; en. April 15, 1863.
Ward, B. F.; en. April 15, 1863; a. 34.
Wyatt, R. H.; en. April 15, 1863; a. 28; w. at Wilderness.

Company B

Officers

William L. Saunders, Capt.; a. 26; pr. to Major October 1, 1862; pr. to Lt.-Col. January 1, 1863; pr. to Col. January 1, 1864; w. at Fredericksburg.
Nathan N. Fleming, 1st. Lt.; en. April 3, 1862; a. 36; pr. to Capt. October 1, 1862; w. at Sharpsburg; k. May 5, 1864, at Wilderness.
George Horah, 2d. Lt.; a. 20; pr. 1st. Lt. March 20, 1863; k. May 5, 1864.
William B. A. Lowrance, 1st. Sgt.; en. May 19, 1862; a. 20; pr. 2d. Lt. October 7, 1862; was in Old Bethel Regiment.
John J. Stewart, 2d. Sgt.; en. May 19, 1862; a. 23; pr. to 1st. Sgt. October 7, 1862; pr. to 2d. Lt. April 6, 1863.
Jacob Kluttz, 3d. Sgt.; en. May 19, 1862; a. 36; pr. to 2d. Sgt.; pr. to 1st. Sgt.
L. G. Holhouser, 4th. Sgt.; en. February 13, 1862; a. 24; pr. 3d. Sgt.; pr. 2d. Sgt.
John F. Agner, 5th. Sgt.; en. May 19, 1862; a. 29; arm amputated at Wilderness.
Charles G. Harryman, 1st. Cor.; en. December 20, 1862; a. 33; pr. 4th. Sgt.; pr. 3d. Sgt.; w. at Wilderness.
Benjamin Holhouser, 2d. Cor.; en. February 29, 1862; a. 23; pr. to 5th. Sgt.; d. of d. November 17, 1862.
A. Calib Basinger, 3d. Cor.; en. May 19, 1862; a. 34; pr. 1st. Cor.; pr. 5th. Sgt.

Privates

Barger, A.; en. April 13, 1862; a. 40.
Barringer, A. M.; en. April 13, 1863; a. 37; w.
Basinger, Eli.
Basinger, George; en. March 19, 1862; a. 44; d. of w. received at Wilderness, May 5, 1864.
Basinger, Joe; en. February 15, 1862; a. 17; d. of w.
Basinger, Munroe; en. April 13, 1863; a. 39.

Beaver, Jesse, en. March 19, 1862; a. 35.
Beaver, John P.; en. March 19, 1862; a. 25; k. at Wilderness, May 5, 1864.
Bost, John J.; en. March 22, 1862; a. 20; missing since September 7, 1862.
Bost, Moses A.
Bost, W. H.; en. March 18, 1862; a. 19.
Brandon, R. A.
Brown, John D. A.; en. March 20, 1862; a. 23.
Canup, David S.; en. March 19, 1862; a. 28.
Canup, John; en. March 19, 1862; a. 18; d. of d. at home, November 24, 1862.
Canup, Wiley.
Chandler, David; en. April 8, 1862; a. 37.
Crawford, P. C.; en. April 7, 1862; a. 24.
Dunn, William; en. March 20, 1862; a. 30; c.
Earnhardt, Eli; en. February 19, 1862; a. 23; d. of d. at Petersburg, June 30, 1862.
Eagle, David; en. March 19, 1862; a. 35.
Frieze, David.
Gardner, James; en. April 13, 1862; a. 38.
Goodman, George; en. March 15, 1862; a. 30.
Grady, James; en. March 1, 1862; a. 40; d. at Drewry's Bluff, January 16, 1862.
Grady, William; en. April 1, 1862; a. 18.
Guhn, Abner H.; en. March 15, 1862; a. 30.
Guhn, Milas; en. April 13, 1863; a. 40; d. of d. February, 1865.
Harkey, Christopher; en. March 19, 1862; a. 50; h. d.
Heilig, Green.
Holhouser, A. M.
Holhouser, F. M.
Holhouser, James; en. April 13, 1863; a. 37.
Holhouser, J. R.; en. March 26, 1862; a. 26; d. of d. March 2, 1863.
Holhouser, Paul.
Holhouser, W. P.; en. May 6, 1862; a. 19; d. of d. June 4, 1862.
Honbarger, Eli; en. April 13, 1863; a. 26.
Honbarger, Jacob; en. April 13, 1863; a. 18.
Horah, Rowan; en. March 13, 1862; a. 24; h. d.
Hurley, James O.; en. March 15, 1862; a. 22.
Johnson, William; en. April 13, 1863; a. 28; d. of d. 1863.
Kluttz, Jeremiah; en. April 13, 1863; a. 22.
Kluttz, Tobias; en. March 19, 1862; a. 36; k. at Fredericksburg.
Linn, Thomas I.

Lyerly, Jesse.
Lyerly, Martin; d. of d.
Mahew, Newton; en. May 19, 1862; arm amputated at Wilderness.
Miller, A. W.; en. April 13, 1863; a. 34.
Miller, Daniel; k.
Miller, David; en. May 13, 1862; a. 38; d. of d.
Miller, John; en. April 13, 1863; a. 40.
Miller, John D.
Miller, John Eli; en. March 19, 1862; a. 36.
Miller, Levi; en. April 13, 1863; a. 36.
Misenheimer, C. A.; en. April 13, 1863; a. 36.
Newman, James A.; en. March 19, 1862; a. 25; d. of d. at Drewry's Bluff, June 20, 1862.
Newman, J. P.; en. March 19, 1862; a. 23; d. of d. at Goldsboro, N. C., June 7, 1863.
Owens, H. C.; en. April 22, 1862; a. 20; w. in three battles.
Parks, D. M.; en. April 13, 1863; a. 30.
Peeler, Monroe; en. March 19, 1863; a. 33; d. of d.
Penninger, Tobias; en. March 19, 1862; a. 36.
Phipps, A. A.; en. April 13, 1863; a. 36; h. d.
Pigg, Hugh; en. March 22, 1863; a. 17.
Pless, John L. A.; en. April 13, 1863; a. 18; k. at Wilderness, May 5, 1864.
Powlas, Moses C.; en. March 19, 1863; a. 18; k. at Wilderness, May 5, 1864.
Propst, Valentine.
Rimer, David; en. April 13, 1863; a. 38; d. of d.
Rogers, William.
Rumple, P. A.; en. April 13, 1863; k.
Seaford, Eli; k.
Seaford, Henry.
Shuping, Mike; en. April 13, 1863; a. 21.
Sides, R. A.; en. April 13, 1863; a. 22.
Sloop, Abram; en. April 13, 1863; a. 36; w. at South Anna Bridge.
Stiller, William; en. March 19, 1863; a. 24.
Trexler, Adam; k. at Hatcher's Run, 1865.
Trexler, Rufus; en. March 11, 1863; a. 22; w. at South Anna Bridge.
Waggoner, C. A.; en. March 19, 1862; a. 23.
Waller, Frederick; en. April 13, 1863; a. 38.
Waller, George; en. April 13, 1863; a. 36; d. of d. 1864.
Waller, Jacob; en. March 19, 1862; a. 35.
Waller, John; en. March 11, 1862; a. 36; d. of d. 1864.

Walton, B. T.; en. April 13, 1863; a. 40; d. of d. September 22, 1863.
Weaver, George M.; en. April 13, 1863; a. 38.
West, Thomas W.; en. March 31, 1862; a. 36.
Wilhelm, W. L.; en. April 13, 1863; a. 37.
Williams, M.; en. April 13, 1863; a. 38; d. of d.
Wise, Benjamin; en. March 18, 1862; a. 23; k. at Wilderness, May 5, 1864.
Wise, Pleasant.
Woods, J. B.; en. April 13, 1863; a. 40; d. of d. at Lynchburg, 1863.
Wyatt, R. R.
Wyatt, Wilson M. J.; en. March 15, 1862; a. 20.

FORTY-SEVENTH REGIMENT

Company H

Privates

Elliot, S. L.; en. October 17, 1862; a. 18.
Frieze, Jacob; en. October 17, 1862; a. 38; w. at Gettysburg.
Shuford, F.; en. October 17, 1862; a. 25; d. of d. November, 1863.

FORTY-EIGHTH REGIMENT

Company A

Officers

Thomas J. Witherspoon, 1st. Lt.; en. May, 1861; a. 22; k. at Sharpsburg, September 17, 1862.

Company C

Privates

Elliott, W. A.; en. March 19, 1862; w.

FORTY-NINTH REGIMENT

Company C

Officers

P. B. Chambers, Capt.; pr. to Major; resigned.
Henry A. Chambers; pr. to Capt. from Fourth Regiment.
Giles Bowers, 1st. Lt.; en. March 13, 1862; a. 41.
Charles C. Krider, 2d. Lt.; en. March 19, 1862; a. 27; leg amputated at Petersburg, March 25, 1865.

James T. Ray, 1st. Sgt.; en. March 19, 1862; a. 26.

A. F. Ludwick, 2d. Sgt.; en. March 18, 1862; a. 32; d. of d. May 14, 1862.

Thomas F. Robinson, 3d. Sgt.; en. March 19, 1862; a. 31.

M. A. Noah, 4th. Sgt.; en. March 24, 1862; a. 23; k. at Malvern Hill, July 1, 1862.

Munroe Barger, 5th. Sgt.; en. March 19, 1862; a. 33.

F. H. Mauney, 1st. Cor.; en. April 9, 1862; a. 16; w. at Petersburg and Weldon Railroad.

James F. Watson, 2d. Cor.; en. March 19, 1862; a. 22; d. of d. July 10, 1862.

Simeon W. Hatley, 3d. Cor.; en. March 18, 1862; a. 26; d. of d. July 2, 1862.

Julius A. Lylerly, 4th. Cor.; en. March 19, 1862; tr. to Petersburg and Weldon Railroad.

Privates

Albright, George; en. September 24, 1863; a. 40.

Albright, Mike.

Bailey, Daniel; en. March 18, 1862; a. 37.

Barber, John R.; en. March 19, 1862; a. 24; d. of d.

Barger, Jacob A.; en. March 19, 1862; a. 26.

Beeker, Philip S.; en. March 18, 1862; a. 32; d. of d. at Front Royal, November 20, 1862.

Benson, Samuel; en. March 18, 1862; a. 25; w. at Bermuda Hundred, May 20, 1864.

Bunn, J. C.; en. March 18, 1862; a. 31.

Chambers, R. M.; en. March 19, 1862; a. 22; d. of d. April 23, 1863.

Cole, James B.; en. March 24, 1862; a. 19; w. at Petersburg.

Cook, Thomas M.; en. March 19, 1862; a. 34; k. at Petersburg.

Cress, Lawson; en. September 23, 1863; a. 21; k. at Drewry's Bluff, May 16, 1864.

Daniel, Wiley B.; en. March 18, 1862; a. 24; k. at Drewry's Bluff, May 16, 1864.

Earnhardt, Moses G.; en. March 19, 1862; a. 26.

Elliot, Julius A.; en. March 19, 1862; a. 23.

Felker, William; en. March 19, 1862; k. at Drewry's Bluff, May 16, 1864.

Finch, ——; d. of d.

Frieze, Jacob; en. March 19, 1862; a. 24; k. at Petersburg.

Gallimore, W. B.; en. July 7, 1862; a. 17; k. at Sharpsburg, September 16, 1862.

Geisler, John; en. March 15, 1862; a. 40; pr. to 2d. Sgt.; k. at Weldon Railroad.
Gillean, John N.; en. July 7, 1862; a. 29; d. of d. November, 1862.
Graham, H. C.; en. April 12, 1862; a. 18; d. of d. October 11, 1862.
Graham, Joseph C.; en. September 23, 1863; a. 40.
Graham, Richard S.; en. March 19, 1862; a. 25; d. of d. August 15, 1862.
Hall, Thomas F.; en. April 29, 1862; a. 30.
Harkey, Milas; en. March 24, 1862; a. 21; w. at Petersburg.
Harrison, B. A.; en. March 25, 1862; a. 39; h. d.
Hartman, John B.; en. March 22, 1862; a. 21.
Henly, John D.; en. April 4, 1862; a. 49.
Hill, William J.; en. March 19, 1862; a. 45; k. at Petersburg.
Hoffman, Atlas; en. March 19, 1862; a. 22; d. of d. May 23, 1862.
Holhouser, John; en. March 19, 1862; a. 19; d. of d. May 10, 1862.
Johnson, William; en. March 19, 1862; a. 21.
Jordan, ——; k. at Petersburg.
Kern, Daniel; en. March 21, 1862; a. 21.
Ketchey, Noah.
Lentz, Caleb.
Lentz, Eli C.; en. March 22, 1862; a. 25.
Link, James M.; en. March 22, 1862; a. 28.
Lyerly, Alex.; Regimental Colorbearer.
Lyerly, Isaac; en. July 7, 1862; a. 24.
McCandless, D. A.; en. September 9, 1863; a. 18.
McCandless, James.
McCarn, George W.; en. March 18, 1862; a. 20; w. at Malvern Hill.
Mask, Marion; en. March 19, 1862; a. 28; k. at Petersburg.
Menis, Andrew; en. September 23, 1863; a. 49.
Menis, James F.; en. March 9, 1862; a. 22; d. of d. December, 1862.
Mesamor, George W.; en. March 20, 1862; a. 19.
Miller, Alex. M; en. March 19, 1862; a. 33.
Miller, James; en. September 23, 1863; a. 36; d. of d.
Nash, Abraham; en. March 15, 1862; a. 34.
Nash, Wylie A.; en April 15, 1862; a. 32.
Plummer, Matthew; en. March 19, 1862; a. 24.
Powlas, Jesse.
Ratts, B. R.; en. September 23, 1863; a. 44.
Rice, Joseph A.; en. April 18, 1863; a. 22; d. of d.
Rice, William G.; en. September 16, 1863; a. 18.
Ritchie, George M.; en. March 19, 1862; a. 32; k. at Petersburg.
Robinson, James H.; en. March 19, 1862; a. 28; w. at Petersburg.
Rogers, Henry H.; en. September 23, 1863; a. 18.

Shaver, Alvin W.; pr. to Cor.
Shuping, Andrew.
Sides, Ransom; en. March 18, 1862; a. 31; k. at Petersburg.
Skeen, Jesse; en. March 18, 1862; a. 29.
Smith, John C.; en. May 11, 1862; a. 18; d. of d. March 26, 1862.
Stikeleather, John McC.; en. September 23, 1863; a. 22.
Stone, R. A.; en. March 24, 1862; a. 24; pr. to Cor.
Stone, Robert.
Summers, John.
Terrell, John; en. March 19, 1862; a. 27.
Thomas, James; en. March 19, 1862; a. 32; k. at Petersburg.
Thomason, William A.; en. April 18, 1863; a. 31; w. at Petersburg.
Thompson, Benjamin T.; en. July 7, 1862; a. 20.
Thompson, John N., Sr.; en. March 10, 1862; a. 26; pr. to 1st. Sgt. 1862; pr. to 2d. Lt., December 29, 1862.
Thompson, John N. Jr.; en. March 19, 1862; a. 18; k. at Malvern Hill, July 1, 1862.
Thompson, Thomas L.; en. March 19, 1862; a. 26.
Thompson, William A.; en. March 16, 1862; a. 31; w. at Petersburg.
Thompson, William H.; en. March 18, 1862; a. 22; pr. to 4th. Cor., December 25, 1862; k. at Weldon Railroad, 1864.
Troutman, T.
Watson, D. F.
Watson, James F.; d. of d.
Watson, John B.; en. March 19, 1862; a. 20; k. at Malvern Hill, July 1, 1862.
Watson, Thomas T.; en. March 19, 1862; a. 19; k. at Malvern Hill, July 1, 1862.
Williams, John G.; en. March 18, 1862; a. 21; d. of w. received at Malvern Hill.
Wise, Alexander.
Wise, Edward; en. March 19, 1862; a. 32; w. at Malvern Hill.
Yountz, Julius.

FIFTY-SECOND REGIMENT

Company K

Privates

Padget, Marble S.; en. October 8, 1862; a. 25.

FIFTY-SEVENTH REGIMENT

Company A

Officers

William H. Howard, Capt.; en. July 4, 1862; a. 34.

William C. Lord, Capt.; a. 20; pr. from Seventh Regiment; d. of w. received at Fredericksburg.

A. E. Temple, Capt.; en. July 4, 1862; a. 24; w. at Fredericksburg.

Abner L. Cranford, 1st. Lt.; en. July 4, 1862; a. 21; d. of d. July 2, 1863.

James H. Sloan, 2d. Lt.; en. July 4, 1862; a. 23; d. of d. July 8, 1863.

John H. Hall, 1st. Sgt.; en. July 4, 1862; a. 21.

James A. Houston, 2d. Sgt.; en. July 4, 1862; a. 44; d. of w. received at Fredericksburg.

Stephen W. Miller, 4th. Sgt.; en. July 4, 1862; a. 23; d. of d. January 20, 1863.

W. C. Correll, 5th. Sgt.; en. July 4, 1862; a. 27.

J. W. Thompson, 2d. Cor.; en. July 4, 1862; a. 25; w. at Fredericksburg.

H. G. Cranford, 3d. Cor.; en. July 4, 1862; a. 20.

R. E. Beaver, Musician; en. July 4, 1862; a. 24; w. at Fredericksburg.

J. W. Winders, Musician; en. July 4, 1862; a. 26; w. at Fredericksburg.

Privates

Beaver, A. A.; en. July 4, 1862; a. 26.

Brawley, W. B.; en. July 3, 1862; a. 19; d. of d. February 26, 1863.

Boger, J. W.; en. July 4, 1862; a. 20; d. of d. November 10, 1862.

Boger, R. A.; en. July 4, 1862; a. 20.

Casper, D.; en. July 4, 1862; a. 34.

Deal, A.; en. July 4, 1862; a. 18.

Deal, L. A.; en. July 4, 1862; a. 27.

Emery, W. W.; en. July 4, 1862; a. 37.

Fisher, J. R.; en. July 4, 1862; a. 24; w. at Fredericksburg at First and Second Battles.

Graham, J. W.; en. July 4, 1862; a. 27.

Graham, W.; en. July 4, 1862; a. 29.

Harrison, R.; en. July 4, 1862; a. 30.

Hodges, J. C.; en. July 4, 1862; a. 23.

Hodges, J. H.; en. July 4, 1862; a. 25.

Johnson, J. D.; en. July 4, 1862; a. 19; d. of d. March 16, 1863.

Josey, L.; en. July 4, 1862; a. 28; w. at Second Fredericksburg.
Josey, T.; en. July 4, 1862; a. 31.
Ketchey, J. L.; en. July 4, 1862; a. 24.
Kilpatrick, L. W.; en. July 4, 1862; a. 21; k. at Gettysburg.
Kluttz, A. L.; en. July 4, 1862; a. 24.
Kluttz, C. F.; en. July 4, 1862; a. 22; w. at Fredericksburg, First and Second Battles.
Lyerly, H.; en. July 4, 1862; a. 30; k. at Second Fredericksburg.
McNeely, S. A.; en. July 4, 1862; a. 29.
Menis, J. C.; en. July 4, 1862; a. 26.
Miller, D. A.; en. July 4, 1862; a. 23.
Miller, J. C.; en. July 4, 1862; a. 21.
Miller, J. R.; en. July 4, 1862; a. 22; k. at Fredericksburg, December 13, 1862.
Miller, J. W.; en. July 4, 1862; a. 21; d. of d. February, 1863.
Moore, C.; en. July 4, 1862; a. 29.
Patton, J. M.; en. July 4, 1862; a. 33.
Philips, J. L.; en. July 4, 1862; a. 28.
Ritchie, G. W.; en. July 4, 1862; a. 26.
Ritchie, J.; en. July 4, 1862; a. 29; w. at Fredericksburg.
Ritchie, P. A.; en. July 4, 1862; a. 32.
Rufty, W.; en. July 4, 1862; a. 26.
Rusher, A. W.; en. July 4, 1862; a. 28; w. at Gettysburg.
Shoff, J. C.; en. July 4, 1862; a. 22.
Shoff, O. H.; en. July 4, 1862; a. 19; w. at Fredericksburg.
Shuping, A. A.; en. July 4, 1862; a. 28.
Shuping, W. M.; en. July 4, 1862; a. 26.
Stiller, J. M.; en. July 4, 1862; a. 26.
Walton, M. J.; en. July 4, 1862; a. 30.
Wilhelm, M. S.; en. July 4, 1862; a. 26.
Wise, W. A.; en. July 4, 1862; a. 25; w. at Fredericksburg.

Company C

Officers

John Beard, Capt.; en. July 4, 1862; a. 28.
F. M. Graham, 1st. Lt.; en. July 4, 1862; a. 33; k. at Harper's Ferry, July 5, 1862.

J. W. Miller, 2d. Lt.; en. July 4, 1862; a. 32; pr. Capt., in Company E; c. March 6, 1863.
H. D. Verble, 2d. Lt.; en. July 4, 1862; a. 31; c. at Rappahannock Railroad Bridge, November 6, 1863.
A. M. A. Kluttz, 1st. Sgt.; en. July 4, 1862; a. 26; d. of d. February 24, 1863.
Paul Peeler, 2d. Sgt.; en. July 4, 1862; a. 29; w. at Chancellorsville.
Jacob J. Albright, 3d. Sgt.; en. July 4, 1862; a. 32; c. November 6, 1863.
James S. Graham, 4th. Sgt.; en. July 4, 1862; a. 25; k. May 3, 1863, at Chancellorsville.
Cranford Holhouser, 5th. Sgt.; en. July 4, 1862; a. 28; d. of d. October 19, 1862.
Albert Miller, 1st. Cor.; en. July 4, 1862; a. 28; d. of d.
Alex Peeler, 2d. Cor.; en. July 4, 1862; a. 26; c. November 6, 1863.
Lucius P. Wade, 3d. Cor.; en. July 4, 1862; a. 21; k. at Fredericksburg, December 13, 1862.
John M. Cowan, 4th. Cor.; en. July 4, 1862; a. 20; c. November 6, 1863.

Privates

Albright, Peter; en. July 4, 1862; a. 33; c. November 6, 1863.
Albright, Peter R.; en. July 4, 1862; a. 30; w. at Gettysburg.
Albright, William M.; en. July 4, 1862; a. 32; d. of w. received at Fredericksburg.
Baker, H. J.; en. July 4, 1862; a. 32; c. November 6, 1863.
Barringer, E. J.; en. July 4, 1862; a. 20.
Basinger, John; en. July 4, 1862; a. 33; d. of d.
Beaver, Alex.; en. July 4, 1862; a. 30; w. at Fredericksburg; d. April 10, 1863.
Beaver, Cranford; en. July 4, 1862; a. 28; c. November 6, 1863.
Beaver, J. M.; en. July 4, 1862; a. 32.
Beaver, Tobias; en. July 4, 1862; a. 29; missing at Chancellorsville.
Blackwell, George; en. July 4, 1862; a. 20; d. of w. received at Chancellorsville.
Blackwell, John; en. July 4, 1862; a. 30; w. at Gettysburg.
Bostian, D. M.; en. July 4, 1862; a. 23; c. November 6, 1863.
Bostian, J. A.; en. July 4, 1862; a. 26; d. of d.
Brown, Allen; en. July 4, 1862; a. 18; k.
Brown, Nathan; en. July 4, 1862; a. 25; c. November 6, 1863.
Burgess, A. A.; en. September 15, 1863; a. 51; d. of d.
Carriker, L. B.; en. July 4, 1862; a. 18.
Casper, A. M.; en. July 4, 1862; a. 30.

Castor, H. A.; en. July 4, 1862; a. 30; w. at Harper's Ferry, July 6, 1864.

Castor, J. F.; en. July 4, 1862; a. 24.

Cauble, J. M.; en. July 4, 1862; a. 41; d. of w. received at Chancellorsville.

Clouts, William L.; en. July 4, 1862; a. 30; d. of w.

Colley, J. M.; en. July 4, 1862; a. 25.

Correll, Samuel; en. September 15, 1863; a. 18; d. of d. November 16, 1863.

Criswell, J. D.; en. July 4, 1862; a. 28; d. of d.

Criswell, W. C.; en. July 4, 1862; a. 18.

Earnhardt, A. S.; en. July 4, 1862; a. 24; w. at Gettysburg.

Earnhardt, Benjamin; en. July 4, 1862; a. 34; missing at Chancellorsville.

Earnhardt, Edward; en. July 4, 1862; a. 33.

Eddleman, J. M.; en. July 4, 1862; a. 24; w. at Chancellorsville.

Eddleman, W. C.; en. July 4, 1862; a. 19.

Eddleman, W. H. C.; en. July 4, 1862; a. 19; d. of w. received at Chancellorsville, January 28, 1863.

Eller, John; en. July 4, 1862; a. 28.

Eller, John M.; en. July 4, 1862; a. 24.

Eller, Joseph; en. July 4, 1862; a. 19; d. of d. January 28, 1863.

Fesperman, S. R.; en. July 4, 1862; a. 20; c. November 6, 1863, at Rappahannock Railroad Bridge.

Frieze, George; en. July 4, 1862; a. 20; c. November 6, 1863.

Fry, N. W.; en. July 4, 1862; a. 24; d. of d. January 16, 1863.

Gardiner, J. W.; en. July 4, 1862; a. 20; d. of d.

Gaskey, George; en. December 29, 1862; a. 36; d. of d. May 8, 1863.

Gaskey, Joshua; en. July 4, 1862; a. 23; w. at Winchester, September 19, 1864.

Gillespie, Richard T.; en. November 29, 1862; a. 18; d. of d. February 8, 1863.

Graham, R. F.; en. July 4, 1862; a. 35; c. November 6, 1863.

Graham, W. T.; en. July 4, 1862; a. 30; d. of w.

Goodman, A. M.; en. July 4, 1862; a. 28; k. in works at Petersburg, March, 1865.

Hare, J. M.; en. July 4, 1862; a. 18; c. November 6, 1863.

Hartman, Alex.; en. July 4, 1862; a. 19; c. November 6, 1863.

Heilig, A. H.; en. July 4, 1862; a. 27; w. at Chancellorsville.

Heilig, J. M.; en. July 4, 1862; a. 33; k. at Mount Jackson, November, 1864.

Heilig, Richard; en. July 4, 1862; a. 31; c. November 6, 1863.

Hemrick, George; en. July 4, 1862; a. 20; d. of d. April 15, 1863.

Holhouser, Calvin; en. July 4, 1862; a. 21; d. of d. April 15, 1863.
Holhouser, Eli; en. July 4, 1862; a. 29; c. November 6, 1863.
Holhouser, M. A.; en. July 4, 1862; a. 33; c. November 6, 1863.
Kerr, James Mc.; en. July 4, 1862; a. 27; d. of d. October 14, 1863.
Lawrance, J. S.; en. July 4, 1862; a. 17; c. November 6, 1863.
Lingle, W. A.; en. July 4, 1862; a. 31; w. at Winchester, September 19, 1864; c. twice.
Lipe, S. J.; en. July 4, 1862; a. 33; c. November 6, 1863.
Lyerly, Alex.; en. July 4, 1862; a. 35; c. November 6, 1863.
Lyerly, Charles; en. July 4, 1862; a. 33; c. November 6, 1863.
Lyerly, Jacob; en. July 4, 1862; a. 24; d. of d.
McConnaughey, George C.; en. October 22, 1863; a. 25.
Maloney, J. S.; en. July 4, 1862; a. 28; d. of d.
Maxwell, A. W.; en. July 4, 1862; a. 28; c. October 6, 1863.
Maxwell, John; en. July 4, 1862; a. 32; h. d.
Menis, F. E.; en. July 4, 1862; a. 21; c. October 6, 1863.
Menis, Monroe; en. July 4, 1862; a. 33; c. October 6, 1863.
Miller, C. J.; en. July 4, 1862; a. 23.
Miller, John M.; en. July 4, 1862; a. 20; d. of d. December 22, 1862.
Miller, Joseph; en. July 4, 1862; a. 37; d. of w.
Miller, J. R.; en. July 4, 1862; a. 19; w. at Fredericksburg.
Minsey, William; en. July 4, 1862; a. 16; c. October 6, 1863.
Misenheimer, Morgan; en. July 4, 1862; a. 28; c. February 6, 1865.
Niblock, Alex.; en. July 4, 1862; a. 21; d. of d. June 19, 1863.
Niblock, Benjamin; en. July 4, 1862; a. 35; d. of d. January 22, 1863.
Niblock, Thomas; en. July 4, 1862; a. 27; c. October 6, 1863.
Overcash, Michael; en. July 4, 1862; a. 51; d. of d. May 25, 1863.
Pace, John F.; en. July 4, 1862; a. 18; pr. to Sgt. for gallantry at Fredericksburg.
Peeler, J. A.; en. July 4, 1862; a. 31; c. October, 1863.
Peeler, J. C.; en. July 4, 1862; a. 19; d. of d. May 29, 1863.
Peeler, J. M.; en. July 4, 1862; a. 29.
Peeler, M. M.; en. July 4, 1862; a. 24; d. of d. November 23, 1863.
Peeler, Solomon; en. July 4, 1862; a. 30; c. October 6, 1863.
Penny, J. A.; en. July 4, 1862; a. 20.
Phifer, J. C.; en. July 4, 1862; a. 33.
Phifer, J. Cowan; en. July 4, 1862; a. 35; d. of d. January 9, 1863.
Propst, S. D. M.; en. July 4, 1862; a. 22; w. at Fredericksburg.
Propst, S. M.; en. July 4, 1862; a. 20; d. of d. February 15, 1863.
Rendleman, J. L.; en. July 4, 1862; a. 26; c. November 6, 1863.
Rimer, S. M.; en. July 4, 1862; a. 26; d. of d. April 15, 1863.
Rose, W. A.; en. July 4, 1862; a. 23; d in prison.

Safrit, William; en. July 4, 1862; a. 34.
Shulebarger, J. L.; en. July 4, 1862; a. 18; c. November 6, 1863.
Sloop, Moses; en. July 4, 1862; a. 27; d. of d. November 19, 1862.
Waggoner, C. J.; en. July 4, 1862; a. 29.
Waggoner, D. M.; en. July 4, 1862; a. 27.
Wilhelm, J. B.; en. July 4, 1862; a. 26; d. of d. February 1, 1863.
Wilhelm, John; en. July 4, 1862; a. 30.
Wilhelm, L. A.; en. July 4, 1862; a. 32; w. at Winchester.
Winecoff, J. M.; en. July 4, 1862; a. 19; d. of d. November 16, 1862.

Company H

Officers

William H. Howerton, Capt.; en. July 4, 1862; a. 32; resigned.
Richard F. Hall, 2d. Lt.; en. July 4, 1862; a. 17; k. at Fredericksburg, December 13, 1862.
A. L. McCanless, 1st. Cor.; en. July 4, 1862; a. 22.
A. A. Scott, 2d. Cor.; en. July 4, 1862; a. 35; d. of w. received at Fredericksburg.
D. M. Barrier, 3d. Cor.; en. July 4, 1862; a. 31.
James M. Walker, 4th. Cor.; en. July 4, 1862; a. 32; d. of w. received at Gettysburg.

Privates

Casey, James; en. July 4, 1862; a. 33.
Conrey, Martin; en. July 4, 1862; a. 22.
Crider, John H.; en. July 4, 1862; a. 16.
Hackett, James; en. August 1, 1862; a. 33.
Hawkins, Wesley; en. July 4, 1862; a. 17.
Howerton, James H.; en. July 4, 1862; a. 24.
Kinerly, Robert C.; en. July 4, 1862; a. 27.
McCorkle, W. A.; en. July 4, 1862.
Russel, McKinzie; en. July 4, 1862; a. 24.
Smith, Joshua; en. July 4, 1862; a. 52.
Tonstall, William H.; en. July 4, 1862; a. 28.
Webb, J. P.; en. July 4, 1862; a. 17.

Company I

Officers

Albert W. Howarton, 1st. Lt.; en. July 4, 1862; a. 27.

Company K

Officers

A. A. Miller, Capt.; k. at Fredericksburg, 1862.
E. A. Propst, 1st. Lt.; pr. Capt. December 25, 1862; h. d. 1863; reënlisted in First Regiment Cavalry.
M. L. Brown, 2d. Lt.; k. at Fredericksburg, December 13, 1862.
J. R. Pinkston, 3d. Lt.; k. at Fredericksburg, December 13, 1862.
J. C. Lentz, 1st. Sgt.; w. at Fredericksburg, December 13, 1862, from which he died.
J. H. Trott, 2d. Sgt.; w. at Fredericksburg, December 13, 1862, from which he died.
G. A. J. Sechler, 3d. Sgt.; pr. to 3d. Lt. December 14, 1862; pr. to 1st. Lt. May 26, 1862; pr. Capt. 1863.
T. S. Rice, 1st. Cor.; pr. to 2d. Sgt. 1862.
W. A. Penninger, 2d. Cor.; d. of d.
W. H. Dean, 3d. Cor.; d. of d.
Caleb Barger, 4th. Cor.

Privates

Aaron, Henry.
Alsabrook, T. A.; k. at Fredericksburg, 1862.
Benson, J. B.
Black, J. A.
Black, M. B.; w. at Fredericksburg, 1862.
Bostian, A. A.
Canup, D. A.
Cheshier, J. W.; d. of d.
Cornell, J. L.
Correll,, J. W.; d. of d.
Correll, W. W.; d. of d.
Corriher, R. A.; arm amputated at Fredericksburg, 1862.
Corriher, R. A.; w. at Fredericksburg, 1862.
Craver, A. J.
Dickson, C. B.
Earnhardt, N.
Elliot, J. H.; d. of d.
Ennis, W. C.
Farris, C. D.
Gibbons, J. R.
Hare, J. M.
Hartsell, M. L.; d. of d.
Howard, B. W.; d. of d.

Howell, T. L.; w. at Fredericksburg, 1862.
Howell, W. R.; d. of d.
Jacobs, G. W.; d. of d.
Kennerly, D. C.; w. at Fredericksburg, 1862.
Kepley, J. A.
Kluttz, E. M.; d. of d.
Kluttz, G. C.; w. at Fredericksburg, 1862.
Kluttz, Henry.
Kluttz, Jesse.
Litaker, G. A.; k. at Fredericksburg, 1862.
Miller, D. M.; d. of d.
Morgan, L.
Morgan, Solomon; arm amputated at Fredericksburg.
Mowery, A. J.
Pinkston, J. F.; d. of d.
Rebles, J. T.; k.
Shaver, David.
Sides, John.
Swicegood, J. A.
Swink, Henry; d. of d.
Swink, G. B.; d. of d.
Swink, J. R.; d. of d.
Thomason, R. M.
Thompson, J. L.
Trott, Willis; d. of d.
Walton, A. L.; d. of d.
Windows, T. C.

SECOND REGIMENT (JUNIOR RESERVES)

Company B

Officers

W. H. Overman, Capt.
J. J. Trotter, 1st. Lt.; d. in camp.
N. D. Fetzer, 2d. Lt.
R. M. Furman, 3d. Lt.
H. C. Peeler, 1st. Sgt.
Henderson Fisher, 3d. Sgt.
Lee Heilig, Cor.
Calvin Kluttz, Colonel's Orderly.

Privates

Barringer, Paul.
Beaver, E.

Belk, W. R.
Bost, Henry.
Bostian, Amos.
Bostian, Moses.
Brown, J. F. E.
Brown, Joseph.
Brown, S. J. M.
Canup, John.
Corriher, Henry; d. in camp.
Cozort, Jesse.
Daniel, James.
Deal, John.
Earnhardt, Moses.
Goodman, Jackson; w. at Bentonville.
Goodman, Pink; w. at Weldon.
Hill, Frank.
Holhouser, Osborn.
Hollobough, John.
Holtshouser, Monroe.
Hunter, William; pr. to Lt. Company E.
Keifnie, M.
Kestler, J. C.
Kirk, Henry.
Laurence, J. W.
Lentz, Alfred.
Lyerly, Tobias.
May, Frank.
Miller, John W.; tr. to Eighth Regiment; w. at Bentonville.
Miller, Milas.
Mitchell, J. V.
Montgomery, C. A.
Morgan, Alexander.
Morgan, John C.; tr. to Eighth Regiment.
Olderson, J. B.
Pethel, Frank.
Redwine, Osborn.
Richie, Henry.
Shaver, John I.
Shoaf, R. A.
Shuping, Jacob.
Shuping, Lock.
Sloop, Abram.
Stirewalt, David.

Stirewalt, Jerry; d. in camp.
Thomason, Turner; tr.
Upright, Jerry.
Vanderburg, Osborn.
Waller, John.
Waller, Peter; d. in camp.
Weant, William.
Wilhelm, George.
Wyatt, John.
Yost, Jacob.

EIGHTH NORTH CAROLINA BATTALION JUNIOR RESERVES

Company A

Officers

William G. Watson, Capt.

Privates

Armfield, M. L.
Burke, A. L.
Repult, W. C.; d. of d.

SIXTH ALABAMA REGIMENT

Company I

Privates

Tait, Alexander I.; c. at Vicksburg, Miss.; July 4, 1863; c. at Columbus, Ga., 1865.

TENTH KENTUCKY CAVALRY

Officers

George M. Buis, Sergt.-Major; w.

FOURTH TEXAS REGIMENT

Company D

Privates

McNeely, Julius D.; tr. to General Hospital No. 10, Salisbury, N. C.

TENTH VIRGINIA CAVALRY

Company B

Officers

G. A. Bingham; en. 1861; elected 3d. Lt.; pr. 1st. Lt. acting Capt.
George Heinrich, 1st. Sgt.; en. 1861; c.
J. A. Clodfelter; en 1861; 2d. Sgt.; c. at Brandy Station; re-c. the same day; c. at Berksville.

Privates

Bingham, C. J.; en. December, 1862; w. at Ream's Station, August 25, 1864.
Hudson, J. A.; tr. from First North Carolina, 1862.
Leonard, Joe B.; en. 1861.
Lyerly, William; en. 1862.
Nooley, William; en. 1861.
Rice, Albert; en. 1861.
Rice, Davis; en. 1863.
Robinson, J. F.; en. 1861.
Woodson, H. N.; en. 1861.

TWELFTH VIRGINIA REGIMENT

Company H

Privates

Buis, John H.; c. at Richmond, 1865.

IRONCLAD RAM "ALBEMARLE"

Johnson, Thomas P.; Paymaster's Clerk; tr. to Fort Fisher, N. C.

INDEX

INDEX

INDEX

INDEX